SELECTED WRITINGS OF WILLIAM MORRIS

NEWS FROM NOWHERE, A DREAM OF JOHN BALL, HOPES AND FEARS FOR ART

WILLIAM MORRIS

This work is a product of its time and place and may include values, images, events, and language that are offensive to modern sensibilities. Reader discretion is advised.

News from Nowhere: Originally published in 1890, this work is in the public domain.

A Dream of John Ball: Originally published in 1888, this work is in the public domain.

Hopes & Fears For Art: Originally published in 1882, this work is in the public domain.

No copyright claim is made with respect to public domain works.

This work reflects minor editorial revisions to the original texts.

Cover art features the Tulip design, 1875, designed by William Morris (1834-1896), courtesy of the Art Institute of Chicago, CCO/Public Domain. Cover design created using Canva.com and reproduced pursuant to its free media license agreement.

CONTENTS

News from Nowhere   1
A Dream of John Ball   143
Hopes & Fears For Art   195

NEWS FROM NOWHERE

OR AN EPOCH OF REST, BEING SOME CHAPTERS FROM A UTOPIAN ROMANCE

1. DISCUSSION AND BED

Up at the League, says a friend, there had been one night a brisk conversational discussion, as to what would happen on the Morrow of the Revolution, finally shading off into a vigorous statement by various friends of their views on the future of the fully-developed new society.

Says our friend: Considering the subject, the discussion was good-tempered; for those present being used to public meetings and after-lecture debates, if they did not listen to each others' opinions (which could scarcely be expected of them), at all events did not always attempt to speak all together, as is the custom of people in ordinary polite society when conversing on a subject which interests them. For the rest, there were six persons present, and consequently six sections of the party were represented, four of which had strong but divergent Anarchist opinions. One of the sections, says our friend, a man whom he knows very well indeed, sat almost silent at the beginning of the discussion, but at last got drawn into it, and finished by roaring out very loud, and damning all the rest for fools; after which befel a period of noise, and then a lull, during which the aforesaid section, having said good-night very amicably, took his way home by himself to a western suburb, using the means of travelling which civilisation has forced upon us like a habit. As he sat in that vapour-bath of hurried and discontented humanity, a carriage of the underground railway, he, like others, stewed discontentedly, while in self-reproachful mood he turned over the many excellent and conclusive arguments which, though they lay at his fingers' ends, he had forgotten in the just past discussion. But this frame of mind he was so used to, that it didn't last him long, and after a brief discomfort, caused by disgust with himself for having lost his temper (which he was also well used to), he found himself musing on the subject-matter of discussion, but still discontentedly and unhappily. "If I could but see a day of it," he said to himself; "if I could but see it!"

As he formed the words, the train stopped at his station, five minutes' walk from his own house, which stood on the banks of the Thames, a little way above an ugly suspension bridge. He went out of the station, still discontented and unhappy, muttering "If I could but see it! if I could but see it!" but had not gone many steps towards the river before (says our friend who tells the story) all that discontent and trouble seemed to slip off him.

It was a beautiful night of early winter, the air just sharp enough to be refreshing after the hot room and the stinking railway carriage. The wind, which had lately turned a point or two north of west, had blown the sky clear of all cloud save a light fleck or two which went swiftly down the heavens. There was a young moon halfway up the sky, and as the home-farer caught sight of it, tangled in the branches of a tall old elm, he could scarce bring to his mind the shabby London suburb where he was, and he felt as if he were in a pleasant country place—pleasanter, indeed, than the deep country was as he had known it.

He came right down to the river-side, and lingered a little, looking over the low wall to note the moonlit river, near upon high water, go swirling and glittering up to Chiswick Eyot: as for the ugly bridge below, he did not notice it or think of it, except when for a moment (says our friend) it struck him that he missed the row of lights down stream. Then he turned to his house door and let himself in; and even as he shut the door to, disappeared all remembrance of that brilliant logic and foresight which had so illuminated the recent discussion; and of the discussion itself there remained no trace, save a vague hope, that was now become a pleasure, for days of peace and rest, and cleanness and smiling goodwill.

In this mood he tumbled into bed, and fell asleep after his wont, in two minutes' time; but (contrary to his wont) woke up again not long after in that curiously wide-awake condition which sometimes surprises even good sleepers; a condition under which we feel all our wits preternaturally sharpened, while all the miserable muddles we have ever got into, all the disgraces and losses of our lives, will insist on thrusting themselves forward for the consideration of those sharpened wits.

In this state he lay (says our friend) till he had almost begun to enjoy it: till the tale of his stupidities amused him, and the entanglements before him, which he saw so clearly, began to shape themselves into an amusing story for him.

He heard one o'clock strike, then two and then three; after which he fell asleep again. Our friend says that from that sleep he awoke once more, and afterwards went through such surprising adventures that he thinks that they should be told to our comrades, and indeed the public in general, and therefore proposes to tell them now. But, says he, I think it would be better if I told them in the first person, as if it were myself who had gone through them; which, indeed, will be the easier and more natural to me, since I understand the feelings and desires of the comrade of whom I am telling better than any one else in the world does.

2. A MORNING BATH

Well, I awoke, and found that I had kicked my bedclothes off; and no wonder, for it was hot and the sun shining brightly. I jumped up and washed and hurried on my clothes, but in a hazy and half-awake condition, as if I had slept for a long, long while, and could not shake off the weight of slumber. In fact, I rather took it for granted that I was at home in my own room than saw that it was so.

When I was dressed, I felt the place so hot that I made haste to get out of the room and out of the house; and my first feeling was a delicious relief caused by the fresh air and pleasant breeze; my second, as I began to gather my wits together, mere measureless wonder: for it was winter when I went to bed the last night, and now, by witness of the river-side trees, it was summer, a beautiful bright morning seemingly of early June. However, there was still the Thames sparkling under the sun, and near high water, as last night I had seen it gleaming under the moon.

I had by no means shaken off the feeling of oppression, and wherever I might have been should scarce have been quite conscious of the place; so it was no wonder that I felt rather puzzled in despite of the familiar face of the Thames. Withal I felt dizzy and queer; and remembering that people often got a boat and had a swim in mid-stream, I thought I would do no less. It seems very early, quoth I to myself, but I daresay I shall find someone at Biffin's to take me. However, I didn't get as far as Biffin's, or even turn to my left thitherward, because just then I began to see that there was a landing-stage right before me in front of my house: in fact, on the place where my next-door neighbour had rigged one up, though somehow it didn't look like that either. Down I went on to it, and sure enough among the empty boats moored to it lay a man on his sculls in a solid-looking tub of a boat clearly meant for bathers. He nodded to me, and bade me good-morning as if he expected me, so I jumped in without any words, and he paddled away quietly as I peeled for my swim. As we went, I looked down on the water, and couldn't help saying—

"How clear the water is this morning!"

"Is it?" said he; "I didn't notice it. You know the flood-tide always thickens it a bit."

"H'm," said I, "I have seen it pretty muddy even at half-ebb."

He said nothing in answer, but seemed rather astonished; and as he now lay just stemming the tide, and I had my clothes off, I jumped in without more ado.

Of course when I had my head above water again I turned towards the tide, and my eyes naturally sought for the bridge, and so utterly astonished was I by what I saw, that I forgot to strike out, and went spluttering under water again, and when I came up made straight for the boat; for I felt that I must ask some questions of my waterman, so bewildering had been the half-sight I had seen from the face of the river with the water hardly out of my eyes; though by this time I was quit of the slumbrous and dizzy feeling, and was wide-awake and clear-headed.

As I got in up the steps which he had lowered, and he held out his hand to help me, we went drifting speedily up towards Chiswick; but now he caught up the sculls and brought her head round again, and said—"A short swim, neighbour; but perhaps you find the water cold this morning, after your journey. Shall I put you ashore at once, or would you like to go down to Putney before breakfast?"

He spoke in a way so unlike what I should have expected from a Hammersmith waterman, that I stared at him, as I answered, "Please to hold her a little; I want to look about me a bit."

"All right," he said; "it's no less pretty in its way here than it is off Barn Elms; it's jolly everywhere this time in the morning. I'm glad you got up early; it's barely five o'clock yet."

If I was astonished with my sight of the river banks, I was no less astonished at my waterman, now that I had time to look at him and see him with my head and eyes clear.

He was a handsome young fellow, with a peculiarly pleasant and friendly look about his eyes,—an expression which was quite new to me then, though I soon became familiar with it. For the rest, he was dark-haired and berry-brown of skin, well-knit and strong, and obviously used to exercising his muscles, but with nothing rough or coarse about him, and clean as might be. His dress was not like any modern work-a-day clothes I had seen, but would have served very well as a costume for a picture of fourteenth century life: it was of dark blue cloth, simple enough, but of fine web, and without a stain on it. He had a brown leather belt round his waist, and I noticed that its clasp was of damascened steel beautifully wrought. In short, he seemed to be like some specially manly and refined young gentleman, playing waterman for a spree, and I concluded that this was the case.

I felt that I must make some conversation; so I pointed to the Surrey bank, where I noticed some light plank stages running down the foreshore, with windlasses at the landward end of them, and said, "What are they doing with those things here? If we were on the Tay, I should have said that they were for drawing the salmon nets; but here—"

"Well," said he, smiling, "of course that is what they *are* for. Where there are salmon, there are likely to be salmon-nets, Tay or Thames; but of course they are not always in use; we don't want salmon *every* day of the season."

I was going to say, "But is this the Thames?" but held my peace in my wonder, and turned my bewildered eyes eastward to look at the bridge again, and thence to the shores of the London river; and surely there was enough to astonish me. For though there was a bridge across the stream and houses on its banks, how all was changed from last night! The soap-works with their smoke-vomiting chimneys were gone; the engineer's works gone; the lead-works gone; and no sound of rivetting and hammering came down the west wind from Thorney-croft's. Then the bridge! I had perhaps dreamed of such a bridge, but never seen such an one out of an illuminated manuscript; for not even the Ponte Vecchio at Florence came anywhere near it. It was of stone arches, splendidly solid, and as graceful as they were strong; high enough also to let ordinary river traffic through easily. Over the parapet showed quaint and fanciful little buildings, which I supposed to be booths or shops, beset with painted and gilded vanes and spirelets. The stone was a little weathered, but showed no marks of the grimy sootiness which I was used to on every London building more than a year old. In short, to me a wonder of a bridge.

The sculler noted my eager astonished look, and said, as if in answer to my thoughts—

"Yes, it *is* a pretty bridge, isn't it? Even the up-stream bridges, which are so much smaller, are scarcely daintier, and the down-stream ones are scarcely more dignified and stately."

I found myself saying, almost against my will, "How old is it?"

"Oh, not very old," he said; "it was built or at least opened, in 2003. There used to be a rather plain timber bridge before then."

The date shut my mouth as if a key had been turned in a padlock fixed to my lips; for I saw that something inexplicable had happened, and that if I said much, I should be mixed up in a game of cross questions and crooked answers. So I tried to look unconcerned, and to glance in a matter-of-course way at the banks of the river, though this is what I saw up to the bridge and a little beyond; say as far as the site of the soap-works. Both shores had a line of very pretty houses, low and not large, standing back a little way from the river; they were mostly built of red brick and roofed with tiles, and looked, above all, comfortable, and as if they were, so to say, alive, and sympathetic with the life of the dwellers in them. There was a continuous garden in front of them, going down to the water's edge, in which the flowers were now blooming luxuriantly, and sending delicious waves of summer scent over the eddying stream. Behind the houses, I could see great trees rising, mostly planes, and looking down the water there were the reaches towards Putney almost as if they were a lake with a forest shore, so thick were the big trees; and I said aloud, but as if to myself—

"Well, I'm glad that they have not built over Barn Elms."

I blushed for my fatuity as the words slipped out of my mouth, and my companion looked at me with a half smile which I thought I understood; so to hide my confusion I said, "Please take me ashore now: I want to get my breakfast."

He nodded, and brought her head round with a sharp stroke, and in a trice we were at the landing-stage again. He jumped out and I followed him; and of course I was not surprised to see him wait, as if for the inevitable after-piece that follows the doing of a service to a fellow-citizen. So I put my hand into my waistcoat-pocket, and said, "How much?" though still with the uncomfortable feeling that perhaps I was offering money to a gentleman.

He looked puzzled, and said, "How much? I don't quite understand what you are asking about. Do you mean the tide? If so, it is close on the turn now."

I blushed, and said, stammering, "Please don't take it amiss if I ask you; I mean no offence: but what ought I to pay you? You see I am a stranger, and don't know your customs—or your coins."

And therewith I took a handful of money out of my pocket, as one does in a foreign country. And by the way, I saw that the silver had oxydised, and was like a blackleaded stove in colour.

He still seemed puzzled, but not at all offended; and he looked at the coins with some curiosity. I thought, Well after all, he *is* a waterman, and is considering what he may venture to take. He seems such a nice fellow that I'm sure I don't grudge him a little over-payment. I wonder, by the way, whether I couldn't hire him as a guide for a day or two, since he is so intelligent.

Therewith my new friend said thoughtfully:

"I think I know what you mean. You think that I have done you a service; so you feel yourself bound to give me something which I am not to give to a neighbour, unless he has done something special for me. I have heard of this kind of thing; but pardon me for saying, that it seems to us a troublesome and roundabout custom; and we don't know how to manage it. And you see this ferrying and giving people casts about the water is my *business*, which I would do for anybody; so to take gifts in connection with it would look very queer. Besides, if one person gave me something, then another might, and another, and so on; and I hope you won't think me rude if I say that I shouldn't know where to stow away so many mementos of friendship."

And he laughed loud and merrily, as if the idea of being paid for his work was a very funny joke. I confess I began to be afraid that the man was mad, though he looked sane enough; and I was rather glad to think that I was a good swimmer, since we were so close to a deep swift stream. However, he went on by no means like a madman:

"As to your coins, they are curious, but not very old; they seem to be all of the reign of Victoria; you might give them to some scantily-furnished museum. Ours has enough of such coins, besides a fair number of earlier ones, many of which are beautiful, whereas these nineteenth century ones are so beastly ugly, ain't they? We have a piece of Edward III., with the king in a ship, and little leopards and fleurs-de-lys all along the gunwale, so delicately worked. You see," he said, with something of a smirk, "I am fond of working in gold and fine metals; this buckle here is an early piece of mine."

No doubt I looked a little shy of him under the influence of that doubt as to his sanity. So he broke off short, and said in a kind voice:

"But I see that I am boring you, and I ask your pardon. For, not to mince matters, I can tell that you *are* a stranger, and must come from a place very unlike England. But also it is clear that it won't do to overdose you with information about this place, and that you had best suck it in little by little. Further, I should take it as very kind in you if you would allow me to be the showman of our new world to you, since you have stumbled on me first. Though indeed it will be a mere kindness on your part, for almost anybody would make as good a guide, and many much better."

There certainly seemed no flavour in him of Colney Hatch; and besides I thought I could easily shake him off if it turned out that he really was mad; so I said:

"It is a very kind offer, but it is difficult for me to accept it, unless—" I was going to say, Unless you will let me pay you properly; but fearing to stir up Colney Hatch again, I changed the sentence into, "I fear I shall be taking you away from your work—or your amusement."

"O," he said, "don't trouble about that, because it will give me an opportunity of doing a good turn to a friend of mine, who wants to take my work here. He is a weaver from Yorkshire, who has rather overdone himself between his weaving and his mathematics, both indoor work, you see; and being a great friend of mine, he naturally came to me to get him some outdoor work. If you think you can put up with me, pray take me as your guide."

He added presently: "It is true that I have promised to go up-stream to some special friends of mine, for the hay-harvest; but they won't be ready for us for more than a week: and besides, you might go with me, you know, and see some very nice people, besides making notes of our ways in Oxfordshire. You could hardly do better if you want to see the country."

I felt myself obliged to thank him, whatever might come of it; and he added eagerly:

"Well, then, that's settled. I will give my friend a call; he is living in the Guest House like you, and if he isn't up yet, he ought to be this fine summer morning."

Therewith he took a little silver bugle-horn from his girdle and blew two or three sharp but agreeable notes on it; and presently from the house which stood on the site of my old dwelling (of which more hereafter) another young man came sauntering towards us. He was not so well-looking or so strongly made as my sculler friend, being sandy-haired, rather pale, and not stout-built; but his face was not wanting in that happy and friendly expression which I had noticed in his friend. As he came up smiling towards us, I saw with pleasure that I must give up the Colney Hatch theory as to the waterman, for no two madmen ever behaved as they did before a sane man. His dress also was of the same cut as the first man's, though somewhat gayer, the surcoat being light green with a golden spray embroidered on the breast, and his belt being of filagree silver-work.

He gave me good-day very civilly, and greeting his friend joyously, said:

"Well, Dick, what is it this morning? Am I to have my work, or rather your work? I dreamed last night that we were off up the river fishing."

"All right, Bob," said my sculler; "you will drop into my place, and if you find it too much, there is George Brightling on the look out for a stroke of work, and he lives close handy to you. But see, here is a stranger who is willing to amuse me to-day by taking me as his guide about our country-side, and you may imagine I don't want to lose the opportunity; so you had better take to the boat at once. But in any case I shouldn't have kept you out of it for long, since I am due in the hay-fields in a few days."

The newcomer rubbed his hands with glee, but turning to me, said in a friendly voice:

"Neighbour, both you and friend Dick are lucky, and will have a good time to-day, as indeed I shall too. But you had better both come in with me at once and get something to eat, lest you should forget your dinner in your amusement. I suppose you came into the Guest House after I had gone to bed last night?"

I nodded, not caring to enter into a long explanation which would have led to nothing, and which in truth by this time I should have begun to doubt myself. And we all three turned toward the door of the Guest House.

3. THE GUEST HOUSE AND BREAKFAST THEREIN

I lingered a little behind the others to have a stare at this house, which, as I have told you, stood on the site of my old dwelling.

It was a longish building with its gable ends turned away from the road, and long traceried windows coming rather low down set in the wall that faced us. It was very handsomely built of red brick with a lead roof; and high up above the windows there ran a frieze of figure subjects in baked clay, very well executed, and designed with a force and directness which I had never noticed in modern work before. The subjects I recognised at once, and indeed was very particularly familiar with them.

However, all this I took in in a minute; for we were presently within doors, and standing in a hall with a floor of marble mosaic and an open timber roof. There were no windows on the side opposite to the river, but arches below leading into chambers, one of which showed a glimpse of a garden beyond, and above them a long space of wall gaily painted (in fresco, I thought) with similar subjects to those of the frieze outside; everything about the place was handsome and generously solid as to material; and though it was not very large (somewhat smaller than Crosby Hall perhaps), one felt in it that exhilarating sense of space and freedom which satisfactory architecture always gives to an unanxious man who is in the habit of using his eyes.

In this pleasant place, which of course I knew to be the hall of the Guest House, three young women were flitting to and fro. As they were the first of the sex I had seen on this eventful morning, I naturally looked at them very attentively, and found them at least as good as the gardens, the architecture, and the male men. As to their dress, which of course I took note of, I should say that they were decently veiled with drapery, and not bundled up with millinery; that they were clothed like women, not upholstered like armchairs, as most women of our time are. In short, their dress was somewhat between that of the ancient classical costume and the simpler forms of the fourteenth century garments, though it was clearly not an imitation of either: the materials were light and gay to suit the season. As to the women themselves, it was pleasant indeed to see them, they were so kind and happy-looking in expression of face, so shapely and well-knit of body, and thoroughly healthy-looking and strong. All were at least comely, and one of them very handsome and regular of feature. They came up to us at once merrily and without the least affectation of shyness, and all three shook hands with me as if I were a friend newly come back from a long journey: though I could not help noticing that they looked askance at my garments; for I had on my clothes of last night, and at the best was never a dressy person.

A word or two from Robert the weaver, and they bustled about on our behoof, and presently came and took us by the hands and led us to a table in the pleasantest corner of the hall, where our breakfast was spread for us; and, as we sat down, one of them hurried out by the chambers aforesaid, and came back again in a little while with a great bunch of roses, very different in size and quality to what Hammersmith had been wont to grow, but very like the produce of an old country garden. She hurried back thence into the buttery, and came back once more with a delicately made glass, into which she put the flowers and set them down in the midst of our table. One of the others, who had run off also, then came back with a big cabbage-leaf filled with strawberries, some of them barely ripe, and said as she set them on the table, "There, now; I thought of that before I got up this morning; but looking at the stranger here getting into your boat, Dick, put it out of my head; so that I was not before *all* the blackbirds: however, there are a few about as good as you will get them anywhere in Hammersmith this morning."

Robert patted her on the head in a friendly manner; and we fell to on our breakfast, which was simple enough, but most delicately cooked, and set on the table with much daintiness. The bread was particularly good, and was of several different kinds, from the big, rather close, dark-coloured, sweet-tasting farmhouse loaf, which was most to my liking, to the thin pipe-stems of wheaten crust, such as I have eaten in Turin.

As I was putting the first mouthfuls into my mouth my eye caught a carved and gilded inscription on the panelling, behind what we should have called the High Table in an Oxford college hall, and a familiar name in it forced me to read it through. Thus it ran:

"Guests and neighbours, on the site of this Guest-hall once stood the lecture-room of the Hammersmith Socialists. Drink a glass to the memory! May 1962."

It is difficult to tell you how I felt as I read these words, and I suppose my face showed how much I was moved, for both my friends looked curiously at me, and there was silence between us for a little while.

Presently the weaver, who was scarcely so well mannered a man as the ferryman, said to me rather awkwardly:

"Guest, we don't know what to call you: is there any indiscretion in asking you your name?"

"Well," said I, "I have some doubts about it myself; so suppose you call me Guest, which is a family name, you know, and add William to it if you please."

Dick nodded kindly to me; but a shade of anxiousness passed over the weaver's face, and he said—"I hope you don't mind my asking, but would you tell me where you come from? I am curious about such things for good reasons, literary reasons."

Dick was clearly kicking him underneath the table; but he was not much abashed, and awaited my answer somewhat eagerly. As for me, I was just going to blurt out "Hammersmith," when I bethought me what an entanglement of cross purposes that would lead us into; so I took time to invent a lie with circumstance, guarded by a little truth, and said:

"You see, I have been such a long time away from Europe that things seem strange to me now; but I was born and bred on the edge of Epping Forest; Walthamstow and Woodford, to wit."

"A pretty place, too," broke in Dick; "a very jolly place, now that the trees have had time to grow again since the great clearing of houses in 1955."

Quoth the irrepressible weaver: "Dear neighbour, since you knew the Forest some time ago, could you tell me what truth there is in the rumour that in the nineteenth century the trees were all pollards?"

This was catching me on my archæological natural-history side, and I fell into the trap without any thought of where and when I was; so I began on it, while one of the girls, the handsome one, who had been scattering little twigs of lavender and other sweet-smelling herbs about the floor, came near to listen, and stood behind me with her hand on my shoulder, in which she held some of the plant that I used to call balm: its strong sweet smell brought back to my mind my very early days in the kitchen-garden at Woodford, and the large blue plums which grew on the wall beyond the sweet-herb patch,—a connection of memories which all boys will see at once.

I started off: "When I was a boy, and for long after, except for a piece about Queen Elizabeth's Lodge, and for the part about High Beech, the Forest was almost wholly made up of pollard hornbeams mixed with holly thickets. But when the Corporation of London took it over about twenty-five years ago, the topping and lopping, which was a part of the old commoners' rights, came to an end, and the trees were let to grow. But I have not seen the place now for many years, except once, when we Leaguers went a pleasuring to High Beech. I was very much shocked then to see how it was built-over and altered; and the other day we heard that the philistines were going to landscape-garden it. But what you were saying about the building being stopped and the trees growing is only too good news;—only you know——"

At that point I suddenly remembered Dick's date, and stopped short rather confused. The eager weaver didn't notice my confusion, but said hastily, as if he were almost aware of his breach of good manners, "But, I say, how old are you?"

Dick and the pretty girl both burst out laughing, as if Robert's conduct were excusable on the grounds of eccentricity; and Dick said amidst his laughter:

"Hold hard, Bob; this questioning of guests won't do. Why, much learning is spoiling you. You remind me of the radical cobblers in the silly old novels, who, according to the authors, were prepared to trample down all good manners in the pursuit of utilitarian knowledge. The fact is, I begin to think that you have so muddled your head with mathematics, and with grubbing into those idiotic old books about political economy (he he!), that you scarcely know how to behave. Really, it is about time for you to take to some open-air work, so that you may clear away the cobwebs from your brain."

The weaver only laughed good-humouredly; and the girl went up to him and patted his cheek and said laughingly, "Poor fellow! he was born so."

As for me, I was a little puzzled, but I laughed also, partly for company's sake, and partly with pleasure at their unanxious happiness and good temper; and before Robert could make the excuse to me which he was getting ready, I said:

"But neighbours" (I had caught up that word), "I don't in the least mind answering questions, when I can do so: ask me as many as you please; it's fun for me. I will tell you all about Epping Forest when I was a boy, if you please; and as to my age, I'm not a fine lady, you know, so why shouldn't I tell you? I'm hard on fifty-six."

In spite of the recent lecture on good manners, the weaver could not help giving a long "whew" of astonishment, and the others were so amused by his *naïveté* that the merriment flitted all over their faces, though for courtesy's sake they forbore actual laughter; while I looked from one to the other in a puzzled manner, and at last said:

"Tell me, please, what is amiss: you know I want to learn from you. And please laugh; only tell me."

Well, they *did* laugh, and I joined them again, for the above-stated reasons. But at last the pretty woman said coaxingly—

"Well, well, he *is* rude, poor fellow! but you see I may as well tell you what he is thinking about: he means that you look rather old for your age. But surely there need be no wonder in that, since you have been travelling; and clearly from all you have been saying, in unsocial countries. It has often been said, and no doubt truly, that one ages very quickly if one lives amongst unhappy people. Also they say that southern England is a good place for keeping good looks." She blushed and said: "How old am I, do you think?"

"Well," quoth I, "I have always been told that a woman is as old as she looks, so without offence or flattery, I should say that you were twenty."

She laughed merrily, and said, "I am well served out for fishing for compliments, since I have to tell you the truth, to wit, that I am forty-two."

I stared at her, and drew musical laughter from her again; but I might well stare, for there was not a careful line on her face; her skin was as smooth as ivory, her cheeks full and round, her lips as red as the roses she had brought in; her beautiful arms, which she had bared for her work, firm and well-knit from shoulder to wrist. She blushed a little under my gaze, though it was clear that she had taken me for a man of eighty; so to pass it off I said—

"Well, you see, the old saw is proved right again, and I ought not to have let you tempt me into asking you a rude question."

She laughed again, and said: "Well, lads, old and young, I must get to my work now. We shall be rather busy here presently; and I want to clear it off soon, for I began to read a pretty old book yesterday, and I want to get on with it this morning: so good-bye for the present."

She waved a hand to us, and stepped lightly down the hall, taking (as Scott says) at least part of the sun from our table as she went.

When she was gone, Dick said "Now guest, won't you ask a question or two of our friend here? It is only fair that you should have your turn."

"I shall be very glad to answer them," said the weaver.

"If I ask you any questions, sir," said I, "they will not be very severe; but since I hear that you are a weaver, I should like to ask you something about that craft, as I am—or was—interested in it."

"Oh," said he, "I shall not be of much use to you there, I'm afraid. I only do the most mechanical kind of weaving, and am in fact but a poor craftsman, unlike Dick here. Then besides the weaving, I do a little with machine printing and composing, though I am little use at the finer kinds of printing; and moreover machine printing is beginning to die out, along with the waning of the plague of book-making, so I have had to turn to other things that I have a taste for, and have taken to mathematics; and also I am writing a sort of antiquarian book about the peaceable and private history, so to say, of the end of the nineteenth century,—more for the sake of giving a picture of the country before the fighting began than for anything else. That was why I asked you those questions about Epping Forest. You have rather puzzled me, I confess, though your information was so interesting. But later on, I hope, we may have some more talk together, when our friend Dick isn't here. I know he thinks me rather a grinder, and despises me for not being very deft with my hands: that's the way nowadays. From what I have read of the nineteenth century literature (and I have read a good deal), it is clear to me that this is a kind of revenge for the stupidity of that day, which despised everybody who *could* use his hands. But Dick, old fellow, *Ne quid nimis*! Don't overdo it!"

"Come now," said Dick, "am I likely to? Am I not the most tolerant man in the world? Am I not quite contented so long as you don't make me learn mathematics, or go into your new science of æsthetics, and let me do a little practical æsthetics with my gold and steel, and the blowpipe and the nice little hammer? But, hillo! here comes another questioner for you, my poor guest. I say, Bob, you must help me to defend him now."

"Here, Boffin," he cried out, after a pause; "here we are, if you must have it!"

I looked over my shoulder, and saw something flash and gleam in the sunlight that lay across the hall; so I turned round, and at my ease saw a splendid figure slowly sauntering over the pavement; a man whose surcoat was embroidered most copiously as well as elegantly, so that the sun flashed back from him as if he had been clad in golden armour. The man himself was tall, dark-haired, and exceedingly handsome, and though his face was no less kindly in expression than that of the others, he moved with that somewhat haughty mien which great beauty is apt to give to both men and women. He came and sat down at our table with a smiling face, stretching out his long legs and hanging his arm over the chair in the slowly graceful way which tall and well-built people may use without affectation. He was a man in the prime of life, but looked as happy as a child who has just got a new toy. He bowed gracefully to me and said—

"I see clearly that you are the guest, of whom Annie has just told me, who have come from some distant country that does not know of us, or our ways of life. So I daresay you would not mind answering me a few questions; for you see—"

Here Dick broke in: "No, please, Boffin! let it alone for the present. Of course you want the guest to be happy and comfortable; and how can that be if he has to trouble himself with answering all sorts of questions while he is still confused with the new customs and people about him? No, no: I am going to take him where he can ask questions himself, and have them answered; that is, to my great-grandfather in Bloomsbury: and I am sure you can't have anything to say against that. So instead of bothering, you had much better go out to James Allen's and get a carriage for me, as I shall drive him up myself; and please tell

Jim to let me have the old grey, for I can drive a wherry much better than a carriage. Jump up, old fellow, and don't be disappointed; our guest will keep himself for you and your stories."

I stared at Dick; for I wondered at his speaking to such a dignified-looking personage so familiarly, not to say curtly; for I thought that this Mr. Boffin, in spite of his well-known name out of Dickens, must be at the least a senator of these strange people. However, he got up and said, "All right, old oar-wearer, whatever you like; this is not one of my busy days; and though" (with a condescending bow to me) "my pleasure of a talk with this learned guest is put off, I admit that he ought to see your worthy kinsman as soon as possible. Besides, perhaps he will be the better able to answer *my* questions after his own have been answered."

And therewith he turned and swung himself out of the hall.

When he was well gone, I said: "Is it wrong to ask what Mr. Boffin is? whose name, by the way, reminds me of many pleasant hours passed in reading Dickens."

Dick laughed. "Yes, yes," said he, "as it does us. I see you take the allusion. Of course his real name is not Boffin, but Henry Johnson; we only call him Boffin as a joke, partly because he is a dustman, and partly because he will dress so showily, and get as much gold on him as a baron of the Middle Ages. As why should he not if he likes? only we are his special friends, you know, so of course we jest with him."

I held my tongue for some time after that; but Dick went on:

"He is a capital fellow, and you can't help liking him; but he has a weakness: he will spend his time in writing reactionary novels, and is very proud of getting the local colour right, as he calls it; and as he thinks you come from some forgotten corner of the earth, where people are unhappy, and consequently interesting to a story-teller, he thinks he might get some information out of you. O, he will be quite straightforward with you, for that matter. Only for your own comfort beware of him!"

"Well, Dick," said the weaver, doggedly, "I think his novels are very good."

"Of course you do," said Dick; "birds of a feather flock together; mathematics and antiquarian novels stand on much the same footing. But here he comes again."

And in effect the Golden Dustman hailed us from the hall-door; so we all got up and went into the porch, before which, with a strong grey horse in the shafts, stood a carriage ready for us which I could not help noticing. It was light and handy, but had none of that sickening vulgarity which I had known as inseparable from the carriages of our time, especially the "elegant" ones, but was as graceful and pleasant in line as a Wessex waggon. We got in, Dick and I. The girls, who had come into the porch to see us off, waved their hands to us; the weaver nodded kindly; the dustman bowed as gracefully as a troubadour; Dick shook the reins, and we were off.

4. A MARKET BY THE WAY

We turned away from the river at once, and were soon in the main road that runs through Hammersmith. But I should have had no guess as to where I was, if I had not started from the waterside; for King Street was gone, and the highway ran through wide sunny meadows and garden-like tillage. The Creek, which we crossed at once, had been rescued from its culvert, and as we went over its pretty bridge we saw its waters, yet swollen by the tide, covered with gay boats of different sizes. There were houses about, some on the road, some amongst the fields with pleasant lanes leading down to them, and each surrounded by a teeming garden. They were all pretty in design, and as solid as might be, but countryfied in appearance, like yeomen's dwellings; some of them of red brick like those by the river, but more of timber and plaster, which were by the necessity of their construction so like mediæval houses of the same materials that I fairly felt as if I were alive in the fourteenth century; a sensation helped out by the costume of the people that we met or passed, in whose dress there was nothing "modern." Almost everybody was gaily dressed, but especially the women, who were so well-looking, or even so handsome, that I could scarcely refrain my tongue from calling my companion's attention to the fact. Some faces I saw that were thoughtful, and in these I noticed great nobility of expression, but none that had a glimmer of unhappiness, and the greater part (we came upon a good many people) were frankly and openly joyous.

I thought I knew the Broadway by the lie of the roads that still met there. On the north side of the road was a range of buildings and courts, low, but very handsomely built and ornamented, and in that way forming a great contrast to the unpretentiousness of the houses round about; while above this lower building rose the steep lead-covered roof and the buttresses and higher part of the wall of a great hall, of a splendid and exuberant style of architecture, of which one can say little more than that it seemed to me to embrace the best qualities of the Gothic of northern Europe with those of the Saracenic and Byzantine, though there was no copying of any one of these styles. On the other, the south side, of the road was an octagonal building with a high roof, not unlike the Baptistry at Florence in outline, except that it was surrounded by a lean-to that clearly made an arcade or cloisters to it: it also was most delicately ornamented.

This whole mass of architecture which we had come upon so suddenly from amidst the pleasant fields was not only exquisitely beautiful in itself, but it bore upon it the expression of such generosity and abundance of life that I was exhilarated to a pitch that I had never yet reached. I fairly chuckled for pleasure. My friend seemed to understand it, and sat looking on me with a pleased and affectionate interest. We had pulled up amongst a crowd of carts, wherein sat handsome healthy-looking people, men, women, and children very gaily dressed, and which were clearly market carts, as they were full of very tempting-looking country produce.

I said, "I need not ask if this is a market, for I see clearly that it is; but what market is it that it is so splendid? And what is the glorious hall there, and what is the building on the south side?"

"O," said he, "it is just our Hammersmith market; and I am glad you like it so much, for we are really proud of it. Of course the hall inside is our winter Mote-House; for in summer we mostly meet in the fields down by the river opposite Barn Elms. The building on our right hand is our theatre: I hope you like it."

"I should be a fool if I didn't," said I.

He blushed a little as he said: "I am glad of that, too, because I had a hand in it; I made the great doors, which are of damascened bronze. We will look at them later in the day, perhaps: but we ought to be getting on now. As to the market, this is not one of our busy days; so we shall do better with it another time, because you will see more people."

I thanked him, and said: "Are these the regular country people? What very pretty girls there are amongst them."

As I spoke, my eye caught the face of a beautiful woman, tall, dark-haired, and white-skinned, dressed in a pretty light-green dress in honour of the season and the hot day, who smiled kindly on me, and more kindly still, I thought on Dick; so I stopped a minute, but presently went on:

"I ask because I do not see any of the country-looking people I should have expected to see at a market—I mean selling things there."

"I don't understand," said he, "what kind of people you would expect to see; nor quite what you mean by 'country' people. These are the neighbours, and that like they run in the Thames valley. There are parts of these islands which are rougher and rainier than we are here, and there people are rougher in their dress; and they themselves are tougher and more hard-bitten than we are to look at. But some people like their looks better than ours; they say they have more character in them—that's the word. Well, it's a matter of taste.—Anyhow, the cross between us and them generally turns out well," added he, thoughtfully.

I heard him, though my eyes were turned away from him, for that pretty girl was just disappearing through the gate with her big basket of early peas, and I felt that disappointed kind of feeling which overtakes one when one has seen an interesting or lovely face in the streets which one is never likely to see again; and I was silent a little. At last I said: "What I mean is, that I haven't seen any poor people about—not one."

He knit his brows, looked puzzled, and said: "No, naturally; if anybody is poorly, he is likely to be within doors, or at best crawling about the garden: but I don't know of any one sick at present. Why should you expect to see poorly people on the road?"

"No, no," I said; "I don't mean sick people. I mean poor people, you know; rough people."

"No," said he, smiling merrily, "I really do not know. The fact is, you must come along quick to my great-grandfather, who will understand you better than I do. Come on, Greylocks!" Therewith he shook the reins, and we jogged along merrily eastward.

5. CHILDREN ON THE ROAD

Past the Broadway there were fewer houses on either side. We presently crossed a pretty little brook that ran across a piece of land dotted over with trees, and awhile after came to another market and town-hall, as we should call it. Although there was nothing familiar to me in its surroundings, I knew pretty well where we were, and was not surprised when my guide said briefly, "Kensington Market."

Just after this we came into a short street of houses: or rather, one long house on either side of the way, built of timber and plaster, and with a pretty arcade over the footway before it.

Quoth Dick: "This is Kensington proper. People are apt to gather here rather thick, for they like the romance of the wood; and naturalists haunt it, too; for it is a wild spot even here, what there is of it; for it does not go far to the south: it goes from here northward and west right over Paddington and a little way down Notting Hill: thence it runs north-east to Primrose Hill, and so on; rather a narrow strip of it gets through Kingsland to Stoke-Newington and Clapton, where it spreads out along the heights above the Lea marshes; on the other side of which, as you know, is Epping Forest holding out a hand to it. This part we are just coming to is called Kensington Gardens; though why 'gardens' I don't know."

I rather longed to say, "Well, *I* know"; but there were so many things about me which I did *not* know, in spite of his assumptions, that I thought it better to hold my tongue.

The road plunged at once into a beautiful wood spreading out on either side, but obviously much further on the north side, where even the oaks and sweet chestnuts were of a good growth; while the quicker-growing trees (amongst which I thought the planes and sycamores too numerous) were very big and fine-grown.

It was exceedingly pleasant in the dappled shadow, for the day was growing as hot as need be, and the coolness and shade soothed my excited mind into a condition of dreamy pleasure, so that I felt as if I should like to go on for ever through that balmy freshness. My companion seemed to share in my feelings, and let the horse go slower and slower as he sat inhaling the green forest scents, chief amongst which was the smell of the trodden bracken near the wayside.

Romantic as this Kensington wood was, however, it was not lonely. We came on many groups both coming and going, or wandering in the edges of the wood. Amongst these were many children from six or eight years old up to sixteen or seventeen. They seemed to me to be especially fine specimens of their race, and enjoying themselves to the utmost; some of them were hanging about little tents pitched on the greensward, and by some of these fires were burning, with pots hanging over them gipsy fashion. Dick explained to me that there were scattered houses in the forest, and indeed we caught a glimpse of one or two. He said they were mostly quite small, such as used to be called cottages when there were slaves in the land, but they were pleasant enough and fitting for the wood.

"They must be pretty well stocked with children," said I, pointing to the many youngsters about the way.

"O," said he, "these children do not all come from the near houses, the woodland houses, but from the country-side generally. They often make up parties, and come to play in the woods for weeks together in summer-time, living in tents, as you see. We rather encourage them to it; they learn to do things for themselves, and get to notice the wild creatures; and, you see, the less they stew inside houses the better for them. Indeed, I must tell you that many grown people will go to live in the forests through the summer; though they for the most part go to the bigger ones, like Windsor, or the Forest of Dean, or the northern wastes. Apart from the other pleasures of it, it gives them a little rough work, which I am sorry to say is getting somewhat scarce for these last fifty years."

He broke off, and then said, "I tell you all this, because I see that if I talk I must be answering questions, which you are thinking, even if you are not speaking them out; but my kinsman will tell you more about it."

I saw that I was likely to get out of my depth again, and so merely for the sake of tiding over an awkwardness and to say something, I said—

"Well, the youngsters here will be all the fresher for school when the summer gets over and they have to go back again."

"School?" he said; "yes, what do you mean by that word? I don't see how it can have anything to do with children. We talk, indeed, of a school of herring, and a school of painting, and in the former sense we might talk of a school of children—but otherwise," said he, laughing, "I must own myself beaten."

Hang it! thought I, I can't open my mouth without digging up some new complexity. I wouldn't try to set my friend right in his etymology; and I thought I had best say nothing about the boy-farms which I had been used to call schools, as I saw pretty clearly that they had disappeared; so I said after a little fumbling, "I was using the word in the sense of a system of education."

"Education?" said he, meditatively, "I know enough Latin to know that the word must come from *educere*, to lead out; and I have heard it used; but I have never met anybody who could give me a clear explanation of what it means."

You may imagine how my new friends fell in my esteem when I heard this frank avowal; and I said, rather contemptuously, "Well, education means a system of teaching young people."

"Why not old people also?" said he with a twinkle in his eye. "But," he went on, "I can assure you our children learn, whether they go through a 'system of teaching' or not. Why, you will not find one of these children about here, boy or girl, who cannot swim; and every one of them has been used to tumbling about the little forest ponies—there's one of them now! They all of them know how to cook; the bigger lads can mow; many can thatch and do odd jobs at carpentering; or they know how to keep shop. I can tell you they know plenty of things."

"Yes, but their mental education, the teaching of their minds," said I, kindly translating my phrase.

"Guest," said he, "perhaps you have not learned to do these things I have been speaking about; and if that's the case, don't you run away with the idea that it doesn't take some skill to do them, and doesn't give plenty of work for one's mind: you would change your opinion if you saw a Dorsetshire lad thatching, for instance. But, however, I understand you to be speaking of book-learning; and as to that, it is a simple affair. Most children, seeing books lying about, manage to read by the time they are four years old; though I am told it has not always been so. As to writing, we do not encourage them to scrawl too early (though scrawl a little they will), because it gets them into a habit of ugly writing; and what's the use of a lot of ugly writing being done, when rough printing can be done so easily. You understand that handsome writing we like, and many people will write their books out when they make them, or get them written; I mean books of which only a few copies are needed—poems, and such like, you know. However, I am wandering from my lambs; but you must excuse me, for I am interested in this matter of writing, being myself a fair-writer."

"Well," said I, "about the children; when they know how to read and write, don't they learn something else—languages, for instance?"

"Of course," he said; "sometimes even before they can read, they can talk French, which is the nearest language talked on the other side of the water; and they soon get to know German also, which is talked by a huge number of communes and colleges on the mainland. These are the principal languages we speak in these islands, along with English or Welsh, or Irish, which is another form of Welsh; and children pick them up very quickly, because their elders all know them; and besides our guests from over sea often bring their children with them, and the little ones get together, and rub their speech into one another."

"And the older languages?" said I.

"O, yes," said he, "they mostly learn Latin and Greek along with the modern ones, when they do anything more than merely pick up the latter."

"And history?" said I; "how do you teach history?"

"Well," said he, "when a person can read, of course he reads what he likes to; and he can easily get someone to tell him what are the best books to read on such or such a subject, or to explain what he doesn't understand in the books when he is reading them."

"Well," said I, "what else do they learn? I suppose they don't all learn history?"

"No, no," said he; "some don't care about it; in fact, I don't think many do. I have heard my great-grandfather say that it is mostly in periods of turmoil and strife and confusion that people care much about history; and you know," said my friend, with an amiable smile, "we are not like that now. No; many people study facts about the make of things and the matters of cause and effect, so that knowledge increases on us, if that be good; and some, as you heard about friend Bob yonder, will spend time over mathematics. 'Tis no use forcing people's tastes."

Said I: "But you don't mean that children learn all these things?"

Said he: "That depends on what you mean by children; and also you must remember how much they differ. As a rule, they don't do much reading, except for a few story-books, till they are about fifteen years old; we don't encourage early bookishness: though you will find some children who *will* take to books very early; which perhaps is not good for them; but it's no use thwarting them; and very often it doesn't last long with them, and they find their level before they are twenty years old. You see, children are mostly given to imitating their elders, and when they see most people about them engaged in genuinely amusing work, like house-building and street-paving, and gardening, and the like, that is what they want to be doing; so I don't think we need fear having too many book-learned men."

What could I say? I sat and held my peace, for fear of fresh entanglements. Besides, I was using my eyes with all my might, wondering as the old horse jogged on, when I should come into London proper, and what it would be like now.

But my companion couldn't let his subject quite drop, and went on meditatively:

"After all, I don't know that it does them much harm, even if they do grow up book-students. Such people as that, 'tis a great pleasure seeing them so happy over work which is not much sought for. And besides, these students are generally such pleasant people; so kind and sweet tempered; so humble, and at the same time so anxious to teach everybody all that they know. Really, I like those that I have met prodigiously."

This seemed to me such very queer talk that I was on the point of asking him another question; when just as we came to the top of a rising ground, down a long glade of the wood on my right I caught sight of a stately building whose outline was familiar to me, and I cried out, "Westminster Abbey!"

"Yes," said Dick, "Westminster Abbey—what there is left of it."

"Why, what have you done with it?" quoth I in terror.

"What have *we* done with it?" said he; "nothing much, save clean it. But you know the whole outside was spoiled centuries ago: as to the inside, that remains in its beauty after the great clearance, which took place over a hundred years ago, of the beastly monuments to fools and knaves, which once blocked it up, as great-grandfather says."

We went on a little further, and I looked to the right again, and said, in rather a doubtful tone of voice, "Why, there are the Houses of Parliament! Do you still use them?"

He burst out laughing, and was some time before he could control himself; then he clapped me on the back and said:

"I take you, neighbour; you may well wonder at our keeping them standing, and I know something about that, and my old kinsman has given me books to read about the strange game that they played there. Use them! Well, yes, they are used for a sort of subsidiary market, and a storage place for manure, and they are handy for that, being on the waterside. I believe it was intended to pull them down quite at the beginning of our days; but there was, I am told, a queer antiquarian society, which had done some service in past times, and which straightway set up its pipe against their destruction, as it has done with many other buildings, which most people looked upon as worthless, and public nuisances; and it was so energetic, and had such good reasons to give, that it generally gained its point; and I must say that when all is said I am glad of it: because you know at the worst these silly old buildings serve as a kind of foil to the beautiful ones which we build now. You will see several others in these parts; the place my great-grandfather lives in, for instance, and a big building called St. Paul's. And you see, in this matter we need not grudge a few poorish buildings standing, because we can always build elsewhere; nor need we be anxious as to the breeding of pleasant work in such matters, for there is always room for more and more work in a new building, even without making it pretentious. For instance, elbow-room *within* doors is to me so delightful that if I were driven to it I would most sacrifice outdoor space to it. Then, of course, there is the ornament, which, as we must all allow, may easily be overdone in mere living houses, but can hardly be in mote-halls and markets, and so forth. I must tell you, though, that my great-grandfather sometimes tells me I am a little cracked on this subject of fine building; and indeed I *do* think that the energies of mankind are chiefly of use to them for such work; for in that direction I can see no end to the work, while in many others a limit does seem possible."

6. A LITTLE SHOPPING

As he spoke, we came suddenly out of the woodland into a short street of handsomely built houses, which my companion named to me at once as Piccadilly: the lower part of these I should have called shops, if it had not been that, as far as I could see, the people were ignorant of the arts of buying and selling. Wares were displayed in their finely designed fronts, as if to tempt people in, and people stood and looked at them, or went in and came out with parcels under their arms, just like the real thing. On each side of the street ran an elegant arcade to protect foot-passengers, as in some of the old Italian cities. About halfway down, a huge building of the kind I was now prepared to expect told me that this also was a centre of some kind, and had its special public buildings.

Said Dick: "Here, you see, is another market on a different plan from most others: the upper stories of these houses are used for guest-houses; for people from all about the country are apt to drift up hither from time to time, as folk are very thick upon the ground, which you will see evidence of presently, and there are people who are fond of crowds, though I can't say that I am."

I couldn't help smiling to see how long a tradition would last. Here was the ghost of London still asserting itself as a centre,—an intellectual centre, for aught I knew. However, I said nothing, except that I asked him to drive very slowly, as the things in the booths looked exceedingly pretty.

"Yes," said he, "this is a very good market for pretty things, and is mostly kept for the handsomer goods, as the Houses-of-Parliament market, where they set out cabbages and turnips and such like things, along with beer and the rougher kind of wine, is so near."

Then he looked at me curiously, and said, "Perhaps you would like to do a little shopping, as 'tis called."

I looked at what I could see of my rough blue duds, which I had plenty of opportunity of contrasting with the gay attire of the citizens we had come across; and I thought that if, as seemed likely, I should presently be shown about as a curiosity for the amusement of this most unbusinesslike people, I should like to look a little less like a discharged ship's purser. But in spite of all that had happened, my hand went down into my pocket again, where to my dismay it met nothing metallic except two rusty old keys, and I remembered that amidst our talk in the guest-hall at Hammersmith I had taken the cash out of my pocket to show to the pretty Annie, and had left it lying there. My face fell fifty per cent., and Dick, beholding me, said rather sharply—

"Hilloa, Guest! what's the matter now? Is it a wasp?"

"No," said I, "but I've left it behind."

"Well," said he, "whatever you have left behind, you can get in this market again, so don't trouble yourself about it."

I had come to my senses by this time, and remembering the astounding customs of this country, had no mind for another lecture on social economy and the Edwardian coinage; so I said only—

"My clothes—Couldn't I? You see—What do think could be done about them?"

He didn't seem in the least inclined to laugh, but said quite gravely:

"O don't get new clothes yet. You see, my great-grandfather is an antiquarian, and he will want to see you just as you are. And, you know, I mustn't preach to you, but surely it wouldn't be right for you to take away people's pleasure of studying your attire, by just going and making yourself like everybody else. You feel that, don't you?" said he, earnestly.

I did *not* feel it my duty to set myself up for a scarecrow amidst this beauty-loving people, but I saw I had got across some ineradicable prejudice, and that it wouldn't do to quarrel with my new friend. So I merely said, "O certainly, certainly."

"Well," said he, pleasantly, "you may as well see what the inside of these booths is like: think of something you want."

Said I: "Could I get some tobacco and a pipe?"

"Of course," said he; "what was I thinking of, not asking you before? Well, Bob is always telling me that we non-smokers are a selfish lot, and I'm afraid he is right. But come along; here is a place just handy."

Therewith he drew rein and jumped down, and I followed. A very handsome woman, splendidly clad in figured silk, was slowly passing by, looking into the windows as she went. To her quoth Dick: "Maiden, would you kindly hold our horse while we go in for a little?" She nodded to us with a kind smile, and fell to patting the horse with her pretty hand.

"What a beautiful creature!" said I to Dick as we entered.

"What, old Greylocks?" said he, with a sly grin.

"No, no," said I; "Goldylocks,—the lady."

"Well, so she is," said he. "'Tis a good job there are so many of them that every Jack may have his Jill: else I fear that we should get fighting for them. Indeed," said he, becoming very grave, "I don't say that it does not happen even now, sometimes. For you know love is not a very reasonable thing, and perversity and self-will are commoner than some of our moralists think." He added, in a still more sombre tone: "Yes, only a month ago there was a mishap down by us, that in the end cost the lives of two men and a woman, and, as it were, put out the sunlight for us for a while. Don't ask me about it just now; I may tell you about it later on."

By this time we were within the shop or booth, which had a counter, and shelves on the walls, all very neat, though without any pretence of showiness, but otherwise not very different to what I had been used to. Within were a couple of children—a brown-skinned boy of about twelve, who sat reading a book, and a pretty little girl of about a year older, who was sitting also reading behind the counter; they were obviously brother and sister.

"Good morning, little neighbours," said Dick. "My friend here wants tobacco and a pipe; can you help him?"

"O yes, certainly," said the girl with a sort of demure alertness which was somewhat amusing. The boy looked up, and fell to staring at my outlandish attire, but presently reddened and turned his head, as if he knew that he was not behaving prettily.

"Dear neighbour," said the girl, with the most solemn countenance of a child playing at keeping shop, "what tobacco is it you would like?"

"Latakia," quoth I, feeling as if I were assisting at a child's game, and wondering whether I should get anything but make-believe.

But the girl took a dainty little basket from a shelf beside her, went to a jar, and took out a lot of tobacco and put the filled basket down on the counter before me, where I could both smell and see that it was excellent Latakia.

"But you haven't weighed it," said I, "and—and how much am I to take?"

"Why," she said, "I advise you to cram your bag, because you may be going where you can't get Latakia. Where is your bag?"

I fumbled about, and at last pulled out my piece of cotton print which does duty with me for a tobacco pouch. But the girl looked at it with some disdain, and said—

"Dear neighbour, I can give you something much better than that cotton rag." And she tripped up the shop and came back presently, and as she passed the boy whispered something in his ear, and he nodded and got up and went out. The girl held up in her finger and thumb a red morocco bag, gaily embroidered, and said, "There, I have chosen one for you, and you are to have it: it is pretty, and will hold a lot."

Therewith she fell to cramming it with the tobacco, and laid it down by me and said, "Now for the pipe: that also you must let me choose for you; there are three pretty ones just come in."

She disappeared again, and came back with a big-bowled pipe in her hand, carved out of some hard wood very elaborately, and mounted in gold sprinkled with little gems. It was, in short, as pretty and gay a toy as I had ever seen; something like the best kind of Japanese work, but better.

"Dear me!" said I, when I set eyes on it, "this is altogether too grand for me, or for anybody but the Emperor of the World. Besides, I shall lose it: I always lose my pipes."

The child seemed rather dashed, and said, "Don't you like it, neighbour?"

"O yes," I said, "of course I like it."

"Well, then, take it," said she, "and don't trouble about losing it. What will it matter if you do? Somebody is sure to find it, and he will use it, and you can get another."

I took it out of her hand to look at it, and while I did so, forgot my caution, and said, "But however am I to pay for such a thing as this?"

Dick laid his hand on my shoulder as I spoke, and turning I met his eyes with a comical expression in them, which warned me against another exhibition of extinct commercial morality; so I reddened and held my tongue, while the girl simply looked at me with the deepest gravity, as if I were a foreigner blundering in my speech, for she clearly didn't understand me a bit.

"Thank you so very much," I said at last, effusively, as I put the pipe in my pocket, not without a qualm of doubt as to whether I shouldn't find myself before a magistrate presently.

"O, you are so very welcome," said the little lass, with an affectation of grown-up manners at their best which was very quaint. "It is such a pleasure to serve dear old gentlemen like you; especially when one can see at once that you have come from far over sea."

"Yes, my dear," quoth I, "I have been a great traveller."

As I told this lie from pure politeness, in came the lad again, with a tray in his hands, on which I saw a long flask and two beautiful glasses. "Neighbours," said the girl (who did all the talking, her brother being very shy, clearly) "please to drink a glass to us before you go, since we do not have guests like this every day."

Therewith the boy put the tray on the counter and solemnly poured out a straw-coloured wine into the long bowls. Nothing loth, I drank, for I was thirsty with the hot day; and thinks I, I am yet in the world, and the grapes of the Rhine have not yet lost their flavour; for if ever I drank good Steinberg, I drank it that morning; and I made a mental note to ask Dick how they managed to make fine wine when there were no longer labourers compelled to drink rot-gut instead of the fine wine which they themselves made.

"Don't you drink a glass to us, dear little neighbours?" said I.

"I don't drink wine," said the lass; "I like lemonade better: but I wish your health!"

"And I like ginger-beer better," said the little lad.

Well, well, thought I, neither have children's tastes changed much. And therewith we gave them good day and went out of the booth.

To my disappointment, like a change in a dream, a tall old man was holding our horse instead of the beautiful woman. He explained to us that the maiden could not wait, and that he had taken her place; and he winked at us and laughed when he saw how our faces fell, so that we had nothing for it but to laugh also—

"Where are you going?" said he to Dick.

"To Bloomsbury," said Dick.

"If you two don't want to be alone, I'll come with you," said the old man.

"All right," said Dick, "tell me when you want to get down and I'll stop for you. Let's get on."

So we got under way again; and I asked if children generally waited on people in the markets. "Often enough," said he, "when it isn't a matter of dealing with heavy weights, but by no means always. The children like to amuse themselves with it, and it is good for them, because they handle a lot of diverse wares and get to learn about them, how they are made, and where they come from, and so on. Besides, it is such very easy work that anybody can do it. It is said that in the early days of our epoch there were a good many people who were hereditarily afflicted with a disease called Idleness, because they were the direct descendants of those who in the bad times used to force other people to work for them—the people, you know, who are called slave-holders or employers of labour in the history books. Well, these Idleness-stricken people used to serve booths *all* their time, because they were fit for so little. Indeed, I believe that at one time they were actually *compelled* to do some such work, because they, especially the women, got so ugly and produced such ugly children if their disease was not treated sharply, that the neighbours couldn't stand it. However, I'm happy to say that all that is gone by now; the disease is either extinct, or exists in such a mild form that a short course of aperient medicine carries it off. It is sometimes called the Blue-devils now, or the Mulleygrubs. Queer names, ain't they?"

"Yes," said I, pondering much. But the old man broke in:

"Yes, all that is true, neighbour; and I have seen some of those poor women grown old. But my father used to know some of them when they were young; and he said that they were as little like young women as might be: they had hands like bunches of skewers, and wretched little arms like sticks; and waists like hour-glasses, and thin lips and peaked noses and pale cheeks; and they were always pretending to be offended at anything you said or did to them. No wonder they bore ugly children, for no one except men like them could be in love with them—poor things!"

He stopped, and seemed to be musing on his past life, and then said:

"And do you know, neighbours, that once on a time people were still anxious about that disease of Idleness: at one time we gave ourselves a great deal of trouble in trying to cure people of it. Have you not read any of the medical books on the subject?"

"No," said I; for the old man was speaking to me.

"Well," said he, "it was thought at the time that it was the survival of the old mediæval disease of leprosy: it seems it was very catching, for many of the people afflicted by it were much secluded, and were waited upon by a special class of diseased persons queerly dressed up, so that they might be known. They wore amongst other garments, breeches made of worsted velvet, that stuff which used to be called plush some years ago."

All this seemed very interesting to me, and I should like to have made the old man talk more. But Dick got rather restive under so much ancient history: besides, I suspect he wanted to keep me as fresh as he could for his great-grandfather. So he burst out laughing at last, and said: "Excuse me, neighbours, but I can't help it. Fancy people not liking to work!—it's too ridiculous. Why, even you like to work, old fellow—sometimes," said he, affectionately patting the old horse with the whip. "What a queer disease! it may well be called Mulleygrubs!"

And he laughed out again most boisterously; rather too much so, I thought, for his usual good manners; and I laughed with him for company's sake, but from the teeth outward only; for *I* saw nothing funny in people not liking to work, as you may well imagine.

7. TRAFALGAR SQUARE

And now again I was busy looking about me, for we were quite clear of Piccadilly Market, and were in a region of elegantly-built much ornamented houses, which I should have called villas if they had been ugly and pretentious, which was very far from being the case. Each house stood in a garden carefully cultivated, and running over with flowers. The blackbirds were singing their best amidst the garden-trees, which, except for a bay here and there, and occasional groups of limes, seemed to be all fruit-trees: there were a great many cherry-trees, now all laden with fruit; and several times as we passed by a garden we were offered baskets of fine fruit by children and young girls. Amidst all these gardens and houses it was of course impossible to trace the sites of the old streets: but it seemed to me that the main roadways were the same as of old.

We came presently into a large open space, sloping somewhat toward the south, the sunny site of which had been taken advantage of for planting an orchard, mainly, as I could see, of apricot-trees, in the midst of which was a pretty gay little structure of wood, painted and gilded, that looked like a refreshment-stall. From the southern side of the said orchard ran a long road, chequered over with the shadow of tall old pear trees, at the end of which showed the high tower of the Parliament House, or Dung Market.

A strange sensation came over me; I shut my eyes to keep out the sight of the sun glittering on this fair abode of gardens, and for a moment there passed before them a phantasmagoria of another day. A great space surrounded by tall ugly houses, with an ugly church at the corner and a nondescript ugly cupolaed building at my back; the roadway thronged with a sweltering and excited crowd, dominated by omnibuses crowded with spectators. In the midst a paved be-fountained square, populated only by a few men dressed in blue, and a good many singularly ugly bronze images (one on the top of a tall column). The said square guarded up to the edge of the roadway by a four-fold line of big men clad in blue, and across the southern roadway the helmets of a band of horse-soldiers, dead white in the greyness of the chilly November afternoon—I opened my eyes to the sunlight again and looked round me, and cried out among the whispering trees and odorous blossoms, "Trafalgar Square!"

"Yes," said Dick, who had drawn rein again, "so it is. I don't wonder at your finding the name ridiculous: but after all, it was nobody's business to alter it, since the name of a dead folly doesn't bite. Yet sometimes I think we might have given it a name which would have commemorated the great battle which was fought on the spot itself in 1952,—that was important enough, if the historians don't lie."

"Which they generally do, or at least did," said the old man. "For instance, what can you make of this, neighbours? I have read a muddled account in a book—O a stupid book—called James' Social Democratic History, of a fight which took place here in or about the year 1887 (I am bad at dates). Some people, says this story, were going to hold a ward-mote here, or some such thing, and the Government of London, or the Council, or the Commission, or what not other barbarous half-hatched body of fools, fell upon these citizens (as they were then called) with the armed hand. That seems too ridiculous to be true; but according to this version of the story, nothing much came of it, which certainly *is* too ridiculous to be true."

"Well," quoth I, "but after all your Mr. James is right so far, and it *is* true; except that there was no fighting, merely unarmed and peaceable people attacked by ruffians armed with bludgeons."

"And they put up with that?" said Dick, with the first unpleasant expression I had seen on his good-tempered face.

Said I, reddening: "We *had* to put up with it; we couldn't help it."

The old man looked at me keenly, and said: "You seem to know a great deal about it, neighbour! And is it really true that nothing came of it?"

"This came of it," said I, "that a good many people were sent to prison because of it."

"What, of the bludgeoners?" said the old man. "Poor devils!"

"No, no," said I, "of the bludgeoned."

Said the old man rather severely: "Friend, I expect that you have been reading some rotten collection of lies, and have been taken in by it too easily."

"I assure you," said I, "what I have been saying is true."

"Well, well, I am sure you think so, neighbour," said the old man, "but I don't see why you should be so cocksure."

As I couldn't explain why, I held my tongue. Meanwhile Dick, who had been sitting with knit brows, cogitating, spoke at last, and said gently and rather sadly:

"How strange to think that there have been men like ourselves, and living in this beautiful and happy country, who I suppose had feelings and affections like ourselves, who could yet do such dreadful things."

"Yes," said I, in a didactic tone; "yet after all, even those days were a great improvement on the days that had gone before them. Have you not read of the Mediæval period, and the ferocity of its criminal laws; and how in those days men fairly seemed to have enjoyed tormenting their fellow men?—nay, for the matter of that, they made their God a tormentor and a jailer rather than anything else."

"Yes," said Dick, "there are good books on that period also, some of which I have read. But as to the great improvement of the nineteenth century, I don't see it. After all, the Mediæval folk acted after their conscience, as your remark about their God (which is true) shows, and they were ready to bear what they inflicted on others; whereas the nineteenth century ones were hypocrites, and pretended to be humane, and yet went on tormenting those whom they dared to treat so by shutting them up in prison, for no reason at all, except that they were what they themselves, the prison-masters, had forced them to be. O, it's horrible to think of!"

"But perhaps," said I, "they did not know what the prisons were like."

Dick seemed roused, and even angry. "More shame for them," said he, "when you and I know it all these years afterwards. Look you, neighbour, they couldn't fail to know what a disgrace a prison is to the Commonwealth at the best, and that their prisons were a good step on towards being at the worst."

Quoth I: "But have you no prisons at all now?"

As soon as the words were out of my mouth, I felt that I had made a mistake, for Dick flushed red and frowned, and the old man looked surprised and pained; and presently Dick said angrily, yet as if restraining himself somewhat—

"Man alive! how can you ask such a question? Have I not told you that we know what a prison means by the undoubted evidence of really trustworthy books, helped out by our own imaginations? And haven't you specially called me to notice that the people about the roads and streets look happy? and how could they look happy if they knew that their neighbours were shut up in prison, while they bore such things quietly? And if there were people in prison, you couldn't hide it from folk, like you may an occasional man-slaying; because that isn't done of set purpose, with a lot of people backing up the slayer in cold blood, as this prison business is. Prisons, indeed! O no, no, no!"

He stopped, and began to cool down, and said in a kind voice: "But forgive me! I needn't be so hot about it, since there are *not* any prisons: I'm afraid you will think the worse of me for losing my temper. Of course, you, coming from the outlands, cannot be expected to know about these things. And now I'm afraid I have made you feel uncomfortable."

In a way he had; but he was so generous in his heat, that I liked him the better for it, and I said:

"No, really 'tis all my fault for being so stupid. Let me change the subject, and ask you what the stately building is on our left just showing at the end of that grove of plane-trees?"

"Ah," he said, "that is an old building built before the middle of the twentieth century, and as you see, in a queer fantastic style not over beautiful; but there are some fine things inside it, too, mostly pictures, some very old. It is called the National Gallery; I have sometimes puzzled as to what the name means: anyhow, nowadays wherever there is a place where pictures are kept as curiosities permanently it is called a National Gallery, perhaps after this one. Of course there are a good many of them up and down the country."

I didn't try to enlighten him, feeling the task too heavy; but I pulled out my magnificent pipe and fell a-smoking, and the old horse jogged on again. As we went, I said:

"This pipe is a very elaborate toy, and you seem so reasonable in this country, and your architecture is so good, that I rather wonder at your turning out such trivialities."

It struck me as I spoke that this was rather ungrateful of me, after having received such a fine present; but Dick didn't seem to notice my bad manners, but said:

"Well, I don't know; it is a pretty thing, and since nobody need make such things unless they like, I don't see why they shouldn't make them, if they like. Of course, if carvers were scarce they would all be busy on the architecture, as you call it, and then these 'toys' (a good word) would not be made; but since there are plenty of people who can carve—in fact, almost everybody, and as work is somewhat scarce, or we are afraid it may be, folk do not discourage this kind of petty work."

He mused a little, and seemed somewhat perturbed; but presently his face cleared, and he said: "After all, you must admit that the pipe is a very pretty thing, with the little people under the trees all cut so clean and sweet;—too elaborate for a pipe, perhaps, but—well, it is very pretty."

"Too valuable for its use, perhaps," said I.

"What's that?" said he; "I don't understand."

I was just going in a helpless way to try to make him understand, when we came by the gates of a big rambling building, in which work of some sort seemed going on. "What building is that?" said I, eagerly; for it was a pleasure amidst all these strange things to see something a little like what I was used to: "it seems to be a factory."

"Yes," he said, "I think I know what you mean, and that's what it is; but we don't call them factories now, but Banded-workshops: that is, places where people collect who want to work together."

"I suppose," said I, "power of some sort is used there?"

"No, no," said he. "Why should people collect together to use power, when they can have it at the places where they live, or hard by, any two or three of them; or any one, for the matter of that? No; folk collect in these Banded-workshops to do hand-work in which working together is necessary or convenient; such work is often very pleasant. In there, for instance, they make pottery and glass,—there, you can see the tops of the furnaces. Well, of course it's handy to have fair-sized ovens and kilns and glass-pots, and a good lot of things to use them for: though of course there are a good many such places, as it would be ridiculous if a man had a liking for pot-making or glass-blowing that he should have to live in one place or be obliged to forego the work he liked."

"I see no smoke coming from the furnaces," said I.

"Smoke?" said Dick; "why should you see smoke?"

I held my tongue, and he went on: "It's a nice place inside, though as plain as you see outside. As to the crafts, throwing the clay must be jolly work: the glass-blowing is rather a sweltering job; but some folk like it very much indeed; and I don't much wonder: there is such a sense of power, when you have got deft in it, in dealing with the hot metal. It makes a lot of pleasant work," said he, smiling, "for however much care you take of such goods, break they will, one day or another, so there is always plenty to do."

I held my tongue and pondered.

We came just here on a gang of men road-mending which delayed us a little; but I was not sorry for it; for all I had seen hitherto seemed a mere part of a summer holiday; and I wanted to see how this folk would set to on a piece of real necessary work. They had been resting, and had only just begun work again as we came up; so that the rattle of the picks was what woke me from my musing. There were about a dozen of them, strong young men, looking much like a boating party at Oxford would have looked in the days I remembered, and not more troubled with their work: their outer raiment lay on the road-side in an orderly pile under the guardianship of a six-year-old boy, who had his arm thrown over the neck of a big mastiff, who was as happily lazy as if the summer-day had been made for him alone. As I eyed the pile of clothes, I could see the gleam of gold and silk embroidery on it, and judged that some of these workmen had tastes akin to those of the Golden Dustman of Hammersmith. Beside them lay a good big basket that had hints about it of cold pie and wine: a half dozen of young women stood by watching the work or the workers, both of which were worth watching, for the latter smote great strokes and were very deft in their labour, and as handsome clean-built fellows as you might find a dozen of in a summer day. They were laughing and talking merrily with each other and the women, but presently their foreman looked up and saw our way stopped. So he stayed his pick and sang out, "Spell ho, mates! here are neighbours want to get past." Whereon the others stopped also, and, drawing around us, helped the old horse by easing our wheels over the half undone road, and then, like men with a pleasant task on hand, hurried back to their work, only stopping to give us a smiling good-day; so that the sound of the picks broke out again before Greylocks had taken to his jog-trot. Dick looked back over his shoulder at them and said:

"They are in luck to-day: it's right down good sport trying how much pick-work one can get into an hour; and I can see those neighbours know their business well. It is not a mere matter of strength getting on quickly with such work; is it, guest?"

"I should think not," said I, "but to tell you the truth, I have never tried my hand at it."

"Really?" said he gravely, "that seems a pity; it is good work for hardening the muscles, and I like it; though I admit it is pleasanter the second week than the first. Not that I am a good hand at it: the fellows used to chaff me at one job where I was working, I remember, and sing out to me, 'Well rowed, stroke!' 'Put your back into it, bow!'"

"Not much of a joke," quoth I.

"Well," said Dick, "everything seems like a joke when we have a pleasant spell of work on, and good fellows merry about us; we feels so happy, you know." Again I pondered silently.

8. AN OLD FRIEND

We now turned into a pleasant lane where the branches of great plane-trees nearly met overhead, but behind them lay low houses standing rather close together.

"This is Long Acre," quoth Dick; "so there must once have been a cornfield here. How curious it is that places change so, and yet keep their old names! Just look how thick the houses stand! and they are still going on building, look you!"

"Yes," said the old man, "but I think the cornfields must have been built over before the middle of the nineteenth century. I have heard that about here was one of the thickest parts of the town. But I must get down here, neighbours; I have got to call on a friend who lives in the gardens behind this Long Acre. Good-bye and good luck, Guest!"

And he jumped down and strode away vigorously, like a young man.

"How old should you say that neighbour will be?" said I to Dick as we lost sight of him; for I saw that he was old, and yet he looked dry and sturdy like a piece of old oak; a type of old man I was not used to seeing.

"O, about ninety, I should say," said Dick.

"How long-lived your people must be!" said I.

"Yes," said Dick, "certainly we have beaten the threescore-and-ten of the old Jewish proverb-book. But then you see that was written of Syria, a hot dry country, where people live faster than in our temperate climate. However, I don't think it matters much, so long as a man is healthy and happy while he *is* alive. But now, Guest, we are so near to my old kinsman's dwelling-place that I think you had better keep all future questions for him."

I nodded a yes; and therewith we turned to the left, and went down a gentle slope through some beautiful rose-gardens, laid out on what I took to be the site of Endell Street. We passed on, and Dick drew rein an instant as we came across a long straightish road with houses scantily scattered up and down it. He waved his hand right and left, and said, "Holborn that side, Oxford Road that. This was once a very important part of the crowded city outside the ancient walls of the Roman and Mediæval burg: many of the feudal nobles of the Middle Ages, we are told, had big houses on either side of Holborn. I daresay you remember that the Bishop of Ely's house is mentioned in Shakespeare's play of King Richard III.; and there are some remains of that still left. However, this road is not of the same importance, now that the ancient city is gone, walls and all."

He drove on again, while I smiled faintly to think how the nineteenth century, of which such big words have been said, counted for nothing in the memory of this man, who read Shakespeare and had not forgotten the Middle Ages.

We crossed the road into a short narrow lane between the gardens, and came out again into a wide road, on one side of which was a great and long building, turning its gables away from the highway, which I saw at once was another public group. Opposite to it was a wide space of greenery, without any wall or fence of any kind. I looked through the trees and saw beyond them a pillared portico quite familiar to me—no less old a friend, in fact, than the British Museum. It rather took my breath away, amidst all the strange things I had seen; but I held my tongue and let Dick speak. Said he:

"Yonder is the British Museum, where my great-grandfather mostly lives; so I won't say much about it. The building on the left is the Museum Market, and I think we had better turn in there for a minute or two; for Greylocks will be wanting his rest and his oats; and I suppose you will stay with my kinsman the greater part of the day; and to say the truth, there may be some one there whom I particularly want to see, and perhaps have a long talk with."

He blushed and sighed, not altogether with pleasure, I thought; so of course I said nothing, and he turned the horse under an archway which brought us into a very large paved quadrangle, with a big sycamore tree in each corner and a plashing fountain in the midst. Near the fountain were a few market stalls, with awnings over them of gay striped linen cloth, about which some people, mostly women and children, were moving quietly, looking at the goods exposed there. The ground floor of the building round the quadrangle was occupied by a wide arcade or cloister, whose fanciful but strong architecture I could not enough admire. Here also a few people were sauntering or sitting reading on the benches.

Dick said to me apologetically: "Here as elsewhere there is little doing to-day; on a Friday you would see it thronged, and gay with people, and in the afternoon there is generally music about the fountain. However, I daresay we shall have a pretty good gathering at our mid-day meal."

We drove through the quadrangle and by an archway, into a large handsome stable on the other side, where we speedily stalled the old nag and made him happy with horse-meat, and then turned and walked back again through the market, Dick looking rather thoughtful, as it seemed to me.

I noticed that people couldn't help looking at me rather hard, and considering my clothes and theirs, I didn't wonder; but whenever they caught my eye they made me a very friendly sign of greeting.

We walked straight into the forecourt of the Museum, where, except that the railings were gone, and the whispering boughs of the trees were all about, nothing seemed changed; the very pigeons were wheeling about the building and clinging to the ornaments of the pediment as I had seen them of old.

Dick seemed grown a little absent, but he could not forbear giving me an architectural note, and said:

"It is rather an ugly old building, isn't it? Many people have wanted to pull it down and rebuild it: and perhaps if work does really get scarce we may yet do so. But, as my great grandfather will tell you, it would not be quite a straightforward job; for there are wonderful collections in there of all kinds of antiquities, besides an enormous library with many exceedingly beautiful books in it, and many most useful ones as genuine records, texts of ancient works and the like; and the worry and anxiety, and even risk, there would be in moving all this has saved the buildings themselves. Besides, as we said before, it is not a bad thing to have some record of what our forefathers thought a handsome building. For there is plenty of labour and material in it."

"I see there is," said I, "and I quite agree with you. But now hadn't we better make haste to see your great-grandfather?"

In fact, I could not help seeing that he was rather dallying with the time. He said, "Yes, we will go into the house in a minute. My kinsman is too old to do much work in the Museum, where he was a custodian of the books for many years; but he still lives here a good deal; indeed I think," said he, smiling, "that he looks upon himself as a part of the books, or the books a part of him, I don't know which."

He hesitated a little longer, then flushing up, took my hand, and saying, "Come along, then!" led me toward the door of one of the old official dwellings.

9. CONCERNING LOVE

"Your kinsman doesn't much care for beautiful building, then," said I, as we entered the rather dreary classical house; which indeed was as bare as need be, except for some big pots of the June flowers which stood about here and there; though it was very clean and nicely whitewashed.

"O I don't know," said Dick, rather absently. "He is getting old, certainly, for he is over a hundred and five, and no doubt he doesn't care about moving. But of course he could live in a prettier house if he liked: he is not obliged to live in one place any more than any one else. This way, Guest."

And he led the way upstairs, and opening a door we went into a fair-sized room of the old type, as plain as the rest of the house, with a few necessary pieces of furniture, and those very simple and even rude, but solid and with a good deal of carving about them, well designed but rather crudely executed. At the furthest corner of the room, at a desk near the window, sat a little old man in a roomy oak chair, well becushioned. He was dressed in a sort of Norfolk jacket of blue serge worn threadbare, with breeches of the same, and grey worsted stockings. He jumped up from his chair, and cried out in a voice of considerable volume for such an old man, "Welcome, Dick, my lad; Clara is here, and will be more than glad to see you; so keep your heart up."

"Clara here?" quoth Dick; "if I had known, I would not have brought—At least, I mean I would—"

He was stuttering and confused, clearly because he was anxious to say nothing to make me feel one too many. But the old man, who had not seen me at first, helped him out by coming forward and saying to me in a kind tone:

"Pray pardon me, for I did not notice that Dick, who is big enough to hide anybody, you know, had brought a friend with him. A most hearty welcome to you! All the more, as I almost hope that you are going to amuse an old man by giving him news from over sea, for I can see that you are come from over the water and far off countries."

He looked at me thoughtfully, almost anxiously, as he said in a changed voice, "Might I ask you where you come from, as you are so clearly a stranger?"

I said in an absent way: "I used to live in England, and now I am come back again; and I slept last night at the Hammersmith Guest House."

He bowed gravely, but seemed, I thought, a little disappointed with my answer. As for me, I was now looking at him harder than good manners allowed of; perhaps; for in truth his face, dried-apple-like as it was, seemed strangely familiar to me; as if I had seen it before—in a looking-glass it might be, said I to myself.

"Well," said the old man, "wherever you come from, you are come among friends. And I see my kinsman Richard Hammond has an air about him as if he had brought you here for me to do something for you. Is that so, Dick?"

Dick, who was getting still more absent-minded and kept looking uneasily at the door, managed to say, "Well, yes, kinsman: our guest finds things much altered, and cannot understand it; nor can I; so I thought I would bring him to you, since you know more of all that has happened within the last two hundred years than any body else does.—What's that?"

And he turned toward the door again. We heard footsteps outside; the door opened, and in came a very beautiful young woman, who stopped short on seeing Dick, and flushed as red as a rose, but faced him nevertheless. Dick looked at her hard, and half reached out his hand toward her, and his whole face quivered with emotion.

The old man did not leave them long in this shy discomfort, but said, smiling with an old man's mirth:

"Dick, my lad, and you, my dear Clara, I rather think that we two oldsters are in your way; for I think you will have plenty to say to each other. You had better go into Nelson's room up above; I know he has gone out; and he has just been covering the walls all over with mediæval books, so it will be pretty enough even for you two and your renewed pleasure."

The girl reached out her hand to Dick, and taking his led him out of the room, looking straight before her; but it was easy to see that her blushes came from happiness, not anger; as, indeed, love is far more self-conscious than wrath.

When the door had shut on them the old man turned to me, still smiling, and said:

"Frankly, my dear guest, you will do me a great service if you are come to set my old tongue wagging. My love of talk still abides with me, or rather grows on me; and though it is pleasant enough to see these youngsters moving about and playing together so seriously, as if the whole world depended on their kisses (as indeed it does somewhat), yet I don't think my tales of the past interest them much. The last harvest, the last baby, the last knot of carving in the market-place, is history enough for them. It was different, I think, when I was a lad, when we were not so assured of peace and continuous plenty as we are now— Well, well! Without putting you to the question, let me ask you this: Am I to consider you as an enquirer who knows a little of our modern ways of life, or as one who comes from some place where the very foundations of life are different from ours,—do you know anything or nothing about us?"

He looked at me keenly and with growing wonder in his eyes as he spoke; and I answered in a low voice:

"I know only so much of your modern life as I could gather from using my eyes on the way here from Hammersmith, and from asking some questions of Richard Hammond, most of which he could hardly understand."

The old man smiled at this. "Then," said he, "I am to speak to you as—"

"As if I were a being from another planet," said I.

The old man, whose name, by the bye, like his kinsman's, was Hammond, smiled and nodded, and wheeling his seat round to me, bade me sit in a heavy oak chair, and said, as he saw my eyes fix on its curious carving:

"Yes, I am much tied to the past, my past, you understand. These very pieces of furniture belong to a time before my early days; it was my father who got them made; if they had been done within the last fifty years they would have been much cleverer in execution; but I don't think I should have liked them the better. We were almost beginning again in those days: and they were brisk, hot-headed times. But you hear how garrulous I am: ask me questions, ask me questions about anything, dear guest; since I must talk, make my talk profitable to you."

I was silent for a minute, and then I said, somewhat nervously: "Excuse me if I am rude; but I am so much interested in Richard, since he has been so kind to me, a perfect stranger, that I should like to ask a question about him."

"Well," said old Hammond, "if he were not 'kind', as you call it, to a perfect stranger he would be thought a strange person, and people would be apt to shun him. But ask on, ask on! don't be shy of asking."

Said I: "That beautiful girl, is he going to be married to her?"

"Well," said he, "yes, he is. He has been married to her once already, and now I should say it is pretty clear that he will be married to her again."

"Indeed," quoth I, wondering what that meant.

"Here is the whole tale," said old Hammond; "a short one enough; and now I hope a happy one: they lived together two years the first time; were both very young; and then she got it into her head that she was in love with somebody else. So she left poor Dick; I say *poor* Dick, because he had not found any one else. But it did not last long, only about a year. Then she came to me, as she was in the habit of bringing her troubles to the old carle, and asked me how Dick was, and whether he was happy, and all the rest of it. So I saw how the land lay, and said that he was very unhappy, and not at all well; which last at any rate was a lie. There, you can guess the rest. Clara came to have a long talk with me to-day, but Dick will serve her turn much better. Indeed, if he hadn't chanced in upon me to-day I should have had to have sent for him to-morrow."

"Dear me," said I. "Have they any children?"

"Yes," said he, "two; they are staying with one of my daughters at present, where, indeed, Clara has mostly been. I wouldn't lose sight of her, as I felt sure they would come together again: and Dick, who is the best of good fellows, really took the matter to heart. You see, he had no other love to run to, as she had. So I managed it all; as I have done with such-like matters before."

"Ah," said I, "no doubt you wanted to keep them out of the Divorce Court: but I suppose it often has to settle such matters."

"Then you suppose nonsense," said he. "I know that there used to be such lunatic affairs as divorce-courts: but just consider; all the cases that came into them were matters of property quarrels: and I think, dear guest," said he, smiling, "that though you do come from another planet, you can see from the mere outside look of our world that quarrels about private property could not go on amongst us in our days."

Indeed, my drive from Hammersmith to Bloomsbury, and all the quiet happy life I had seen so many hints of, even apart from my shopping, would have been enough to tell me that "the sacred rights of property," as we used to think of them, were now no more. So I sat silent while the old man took up the thread of the discourse again, and said:

"Well, then, property quarrels being no longer possible, what remains in these matters that a court of law could deal with? Fancy a court for enforcing a contract of passion or sentiment! If such a thing were needed as a *reductio ad absurdum* of the enforcement of contract, such a folly would do that for us."

He was silent again a little, and then said: "You must understand once for all that we have changed these matters; or rather, that our way of looking at them has changed, as we have changed within the last two hundred years. We do not deceive ourselves, indeed, or believe that we can get rid of all the trouble that besets the dealings between the sexes. We know that we must face the unhappiness that comes of man and woman confusing the relations between natural passion, and sentiment, and the friendship which, when things go well, softens the awakening from passing illusions: but we are not so mad as to pile up degradation on that unhappiness by engaging in sordid squabbles about livelihood and position, and the power of tyrannising over the children who have been the results of love or lust."

Again he paused awhile, and again went on: "Calf love, mistaken for a heroism that shall be lifelong, yet early waning into disappointment; the inexplicable desire that comes on a man of riper years to be the all-in-all to some one woman, whose ordinary human kindness and human beauty he has idealised into superhuman perfection, and made the one object of his desire; or lastly the reasonable longing of a strong and thoughtful man to become the most intimate friend of some beautiful and wise woman, the very type of the beauty and glory of the world which we love so well,—as we exult in all the pleasure and exaltation of spirit which goes with these things, so we set ourselves to bear the sorrow which not unseldom goes with them also; remembering those lines of the ancient poet (I quote roughly from memory one of the many translations of the nineteenth century):

'For this the Gods have fashioned man's grief and evil day
That still for man hereafter might be the tale and the lay.'

Well, well, 'tis little likely anyhow that all tales shall be lacking, or all sorrow cured."

He was silent for some time, and I would not interrupt him. At last he began again: "But you must know that we of these generations are strong and healthy of body, and live easily; we pass our lives in reasonable strife with nature, exercising not one side of ourselves only, but all sides, taking the keenest pleasure in all the life of the world. So it is a point of honour with us not to be self-centred; not to suppose that the world must cease because one man is sorry; therefore we should think it foolish, or if you will, criminal, to exaggerate these matters of sentiment and sensibility: we are no more inclined to eke out our sentimental sorrows than to cherish our bodily pains; and we recognise that there are other pleasures besides love-making. You must remember, also, that we are long-lived, and that therefore beauty both in man and woman is not so fleeting as it was in the days when we were burdened so heavily by self-inflicted diseases. So we shake off these griefs in a way which perhaps the sentimentalists of other times would think contemptible and unheroic, but which we think necessary and manlike. As on the other hand, therefore, we have ceased to be commercial in our love-matters, so also we have ceased to be *artificially* foolish. The folly which comes by nature, the unwisdom of the immature man, or the older man caught in a trap, we must put up with that, nor are we much ashamed of it; but to be conventionally sensitive or sentimental—my friend, I am old and perhaps disappointed, but at least I think we have cast off *some* of the follies of the older world."

He paused, as if for some words of mine; but I held my peace: then he went on: "At least, if we suffer from the tyranny and fickleness of nature or our own want of experience, we neither grimace about it, nor lie. If there must be sundering betwixt those who meant never to sunder, so it must be: but there need be no pretext of unity when the reality of it is gone: nor do we drive those who well know that they are incapable of it to profess an undying sentiment which they cannot really feel: thus it is that as that monstrosity of venal lust is no longer possible, so also it is no longer needed. Don't misunderstand me. You did not seemed shocked when I told you that there were no law-courts to enforce contracts of sentiment or passion; but so curiously are men made, that perhaps you will be shocked when I tell you that there is no code of public opinion which takes the place of such courts, and which might be as tyrannical and unreasonable as they were. I do not say that people don't judge their neighbours' conduct, sometimes, doubtless, unfairly. But I do say that there is no unvarying conventional set of rules by which people are judged; no bed of Procrustes to stretch or cramp their minds and lives; no hypocritical excommunication which people are *forced* to pronounce, either by unconsidered habit, or by the unexpressed threat of the lesser interdict if they are lax in their hypocrisy. Are you shocked now?"

"N-o—no," said I, with some hesitation. "It is all so different."

"At any rate," said he, "one thing I think I can answer for: whatever sentiment there is, it is real—and general; it is not confined to people very specially refined. I am also pretty sure, as I hinted to you just now, that there is not by a great way as much suffering involved in these matters either to men or to women as there used to be. But excuse me for being so prolix on this question! You know you asked to be treated like a being from another planet."

"Indeed I thank you very much," said I. "Now may I ask you about the position of women in your society?"

He laughed very heartily for a man of his years, and said: "It is not without reason that I have got a reputation as a careful student of history. I believe I really do understand 'the Emancipation of Women movement' of the nineteenth century. I doubt if any other man now alive does."

"Well?" said I, a little bit nettled by his merriment.

"Well," said he, "of course you will see that all that is a dead controversy now. The men have no longer any opportunity of tyrannising over the women, or the women over the men; both of which things took place in those old times. The women do what they can do best, and what they like best, and the men are neither jealous of it or injured by it. This is such a commonplace that I am almost ashamed to state it."

I said, "O; and legislation? do they take any part in that?"

Hammond smiled and said: "I think you may wait for an answer to that question till we get on to the subject of legislation. There may be novelties to you in that subject also."

"Very well," I said; "but about this woman question? I saw at the Guest House that the women were waiting on the men: that seems a little like reaction doesn't it?"

"Does it?" said the old man; "perhaps you think housekeeping an unimportant occupation, not deserving of respect. I believe that was the opinion of the 'advanced' women of the nineteenth century, and their male backers. If it is yours, I recommend to your notice an old Norwegian folk-lore tale called How the Man minded the House, or some such title; the result of which minding was that, after various tribulations, the man and the family cow balanced each other at the end of a rope, the man hanging halfway up the chimney, the cow dangling from the roof, which, after the fashion of the country, was of turf and sloping down low to the ground. Hard on the cow, *I* think. Of course no such mishap could happen to such a superior person as yourself," he added, chuckling.

I sat somewhat uneasy under this dry gibe. Indeed, his manner of treating this latter part of the question seemed to me a little disrespectful.

"Come, now, my friend," quoth he, "don't you know that it is a great pleasure to a clever woman to manage a house skilfully, and to do it so that all the housemates about her look pleased, and are grateful to her? And then, you know, everybody likes to be ordered about by a pretty woman: why, it is one of the pleasantest forms of flirtation. You are not so old that you cannot remember that. Why, I remember it well."

And the old fellow chuckled again, and at last fairly burst out laughing.

"Excuse me," said he, after a while; "I am not laughing at anything you could be thinking of; but at that silly nineteenth-century fashion, current amongst rich so-called cultivated people, of ignoring all the steps by which their daily dinner was reached, as matters too low for their lofty intelligence. Useless idiots! Come, now, I am a 'literary man,' as we queer animals used to be called, yet I am a pretty good cook myself."

"So am I," said I.

"Well, then," said he, "I really think you can understand me better than you would seem to do, judging by your words and your silence."

Said I: "Perhaps that is so; but people putting in practice commonly this sense of interest in the ordinary occupations of life rather startles me. I will ask you a question or two presently about that. But I want to return to the position of women amongst you. You have studied the 'emancipation of women' business of the nineteenth century: don't you remember that some of the 'superior' women wanted to emancipate the more intelligent part of their sex from the bearing of children?"

The old man grew quite serious again. Said he: "I *do* remember about that strange piece of baseless folly, the result, like all other follies of the period, of the hideous class tyranny which then obtained. What do we think of it now? you would say. My friend, that is a question easy to answer. How could it possibly be but that maternity should be highly honoured amongst us? Surely it is a matter of course that the natural and necessary pains which the mother must go through form a bond of union between man and woman, an extra stimulus to love and affection between them, and that this is universally recognised. For the rest, remember that all the *artificial* burdens of motherhood are now done away with. A mother has no longer any mere sordid anxieties for the future of her children. They may indeed turn out better or worse; they may disappoint her highest hopes; such anxieties as these are a part of the mingled pleasure and pain which goes to make up the life of mankind. But at least she is spared the fear (it was most commonly the certainty) that artificial disabilities would make her children something less than men and women: she knows that they will live and act according to the measure of their own faculties. In times past, it is clear that the 'Society' of the day helped its Judaic god, and the 'Man of Science' of the time, in visiting the sins of the fathers upon the children. How to reverse this process, how to take the sting out of heredity, has for long been one of the most constant cares of the thoughtful men amongst us. So that, you see, the ordinarily healthy woman (and almost all our women are both healthy and at least comely), respected as a child-bearer and rearer of children, desired as a woman, loved as a companion, unanxious for the future of her children, has far more instinct for maternity than the poor drudge and mother of drudges of past days could ever have had; or than her sister of the upper classes, brought up in affected ignorance of natural facts, reared in an atmosphere of mingled prudery and prurience."

"You speak warmly," I said, "but I can see that you are right."

"Yes," he said, "and I will point out to you a token of all the benefits which we have gained by our freedom. What did you think of the looks of the people whom you have come across to-day?"

Said I: "I could hardly have believed that there could be so many good-looking people in any civilised country."

He crowed a little, like the old bird he was. "What! are we still civilised?" said he. "Well, as to our looks, the English and Jutish blood, which on the whole is predominant here, used not to produce much beauty. But I think we have improved it. I know a man who has a large collection of portraits printed from photographs of the nineteenth century, and going over those and comparing them with the everyday faces in these times, puts the improvement in our good looks beyond a doubt. Now, there are some people who think it not too fantastic to connect this increase of beauty directly with our freedom and good sense in the matters we have been speaking of: they believe that a child born from the natural and healthy love between a man and a woman, even if that be transient, is likely to turn out better in all ways, and especially in bodily beauty, than the birth of the respectable commercial marriage bed, or of the dull despair of the drudge of that system. They say, Pleasure begets pleasure. What do you think?"

"I am much of that mind," said I.

10. QUESTIONS AND ANSWERS

"Well," said the old man, shifting in his chair, "you must get on with your questions, Guest; I have been some time answering this first one."

Said I: "I want an extra word or two about your ideas of education; although I gathered from Dick that you let your children run wild and didn't teach them anything; and in short, that you have so refined your education, that now you have none."

"Then you gathered left-handed," quoth he. "But of course I understand your point of view about education, which is that of times past, when 'the struggle for life,' as men used to phrase it (*i.e.*, the struggle for a slave's rations on one side, and for a bouncing share of the slave-holders' privilege on the other), pinched 'education' for most people into a niggardly dole of not very accurate information; something to be swallowed by the beginner in the art of living whether he liked it or not, and was hungry for it or not: and which had been chewed and digested over and over again by people who didn't care about it in order to serve it out to other people who didn't care about it."

I stopped the old man's rising wrath by a laugh, and said: "Well, *you* were not taught that way, at any rate, so you may let your anger run off you a little."

"True, true," said he, smiling. "I thank you for correcting my ill-temper: I always fancy myself as living in any period of which we may be speaking. But, however, to put it in a cooler way: you expected to see children thrust into schools when they had reached an age conventionally supposed to be the due age, whatever their varying faculties and dispositions might be, and when there, with like disregard to facts to be subjected to a certain conventional course of 'learning.' My friend, can't you see that such a proceeding means ignoring the fact of *growth*, bodily and mental? No one could come out of such a mill uninjured; and those only would avoid being crushed by it who would have the spirit of rebellion strong in them. Fortunately most children have had that at all times, or I do not know that we should ever have reached our present position. Now you see what it all comes to. In the old times all this was the result of *poverty*. In the nineteenth century, society was so miserably poor, owing to the systematised robbery on which it was founded, that real education was impossible for anybody. The whole theory of their so-called education was that it was necessary to shove a little information into a child, even if it were by means of torture, and accompanied by twaddle which it was well known was of no use, or else he would lack information lifelong: the hurry of poverty forbade anything else. All that is past; we are no longer hurried, and the information lies ready to each one's hand when his own inclinations impel him to seek it. In this as in other matters we have become wealthy: we can afford to give ourselves time to grow."

"Yes," said I, "but suppose the child, youth, man, never wants the information, never grows in the direction you might hope him to do: suppose, for instance, he objects to learning arithmetic or mathematics; you can't force him when he *is* grown; can't you force him while he is growing, and oughtn't you to do so?"

"Well," said he, "were you forced to learn arithmetic and mathematics?"

"A little," said I.

"And how old are you now?"

"Say fifty-six," said I.

"And how much arithmetic and mathematics do you know now?" quoth the old man, smiling rather mockingly.

Said I: "None whatever, I am sorry to say."

Hammond laughed quietly, but made no other comment on my admission, and I dropped the subject of education, perceiving him to be hopeless on that side.

I thought a little, and said: "You were speaking just now of households: that sounded to me a little like the customs of past times; I should have thought you would have lived more in public."

"Phalangsteries, eh?" said he. "Well, we live as we like, and we like to live as a rule with certain house-mates that we have got used to. Remember, again, that poverty is extinct, and that the Fourierist phalangsteries and all their kind, as was but natural at the time, implied nothing but a refuge from mere destitution. Such a way of life as that, could only have been conceived of by people surrounded by the worst form of poverty. But you must understand therewith, that though separate households are the rule amongst us, and though they differ in their habits more or less, yet no door is shut to any good-tempered person who is content to live as the other house-mates do: only of course it would be unreasonable for one man to drop into a household and bid the folk of it to alter their habits to please him, since he can go elsewhere and live as he pleases. However, I need not say much about all this, as you are going up the river with Dick, and will find out for yourself by experience how these matters are managed."

After a pause, I said: "Your big towns, now; how about them? London, which —which I have read about as the modern Babylon of civilization, seems to have disappeared."

"Well, well," said old Hammond, "perhaps after all it is more like ancient Babylon now than the 'modern Babylon' of the nineteenth century was. But let that pass. After all, there is a good deal of population in places between here and Hammersmith; nor have you seen the most populous part of the town yet."

"Tell me, then," said I, "how is it towards the east?"

Said he: "Time was when if you mounted a good horse and rode straight away from my door here at a round trot for an hour and a half; you would still be in the thick of London, and the greater part of that would be 'slums,' as they were called; that is to say, places of torture for innocent men and women; or worse, stews for rearing and breeding men and women in such degradation that that torture should seem to them mere ordinary and natural life."

"I know, I know," I said, rather impatiently. "That was what was; tell me something of what is. Is any of that left?"

"Not an inch," said he; "but some memory of it abides with us, and I am glad of it. Once a year, on May-day, we hold a solemn feast in those easterly communes of London to commemorate The Clearing of Misery, as it is called. On that day we have music and dancing, and merry games and happy feasting on the site of some of the worst of the old slums, the traditional memory of which we have kept. On that occasion the custom is for the prettiest girls to sing some of the old revolutionary songs, and those which were the groans of the discontent, once so hopeless, on the very spots where those terrible crimes of class-murder were committed day by day for so many years. To a man like me, who have studied the past so diligently, it is a curious and touching sight to see some beautiful girl, daintily clad, and crowned with flowers from the neighbouring meadows, standing amongst the happy people, on some mound where of old time stood the wretched apology for a house, a den in which men and women lived packed amongst the filth like pilchards in a cask; lived in such a way that they could only have endured it, as I said just now, by being degraded out of humanity—to hear the terrible words of threatening and lamentation coming from her sweet and beautiful lips, and she unconscious of their real meaning: to hear her, for instance, singing Hood's Song of the Shirt, and to think that all the time she does not understand what it is all about—a tragedy grown inconceivable to her and her listeners. Think of that, if you can, and of how glorious life is grown!"

"Indeed," said I, "it is difficult for me to think of it."

And I sat watching how his eyes glittered, and how the fresh life seemed to glow in his face, and I wondered how at his age he should think of the happiness of the world, or indeed anything but his coming dinner.

"Tell me in detail," said I, "what lies east of Bloomsbury now?"

Said he: "There are but few houses between this and the outer part of the old city; but in the city we have a thickly-dwelling population. Our forefathers, in the first clearing of the slums, were not in a hurry to pull down the houses in what was called at the end of the nineteenth century the business quarter of the town, and what later got to be known as the Swindling Kens. You see, these houses, though they stood hideously thick on the ground, were roomy and fairly solid in building, and clean, because they were not used for living in, but as mere gambling booths; so the poor people from the cleared slums took them for lodgings and dwelt there, till the folk of those days had time to think of something better for them; so the buildings were pulled down so gradually that people got used to living thicker on the ground there than in most places; therefore it remains the most populous part of London, or perhaps of all these islands. But it is very pleasant there, partly because of the splendour of the architecture, which goes further than what you will see elsewhere. However, this crowding, if it may be called so, does not go further than a street called Aldgate, a name which perhaps you may have heard of. Beyond that the houses are scattered wide about the meadows there, which are very beautiful, especially when you get on to the lovely river Lea (where old Isaak Walton used to fish, you know) about the places called Stratford and Old Ford, names which of course you will not have heard of, though the Romans were busy there once upon a time."

Not heard of them! thought I to myself. How strange! that I who had seen the very last remnant of the pleasantness of the meadows by the Lea destroyed, should have heard them spoken of with pleasantness come back to them in full measure.

Hammond went on: "When you get down to the Thames side you come on the Docks, which are works of the nineteenth century, and are still in use, although not so thronged as they once were, since we discourage centralisation all we can, and we have long ago dropped the pretension to be the market of the world. About these Docks are a good few houses, which, however, are not inhabited by many people permanently; I mean, those who use them come and go a good deal, the place being too low and marshy for pleasant dwelling. Past the Docks eastward and landward it is all flat pasture, once marsh, except for a few gardens, and there are very few permanent dwellings there: scarcely anything but a few sheds, and cots for the men who come to look after the great herds of cattle pasturing there. But however, what with the beasts and the men, and the scattered red-tiled roofs and the big hayricks, it does not make a bad holiday to get a quiet pony and ride about there on a sunny afternoon of autumn, and look over the river and the craft passing up and down, and on to Shooters' Hill and the Kentish uplands, and then turn round to the wide green sea of the Essex marshland, with the great domed line of the sky, and the sun shining down in one flood of peaceful light over the long distance. There is a place called Canning's Town, and further out, Silvertown, where the pleasant meadows are at their pleasantest: doubtless they were once slums, and wretched enough."

The names grated on my ear, but I could not explain why to him. So I said: "And south of the river, what is it like?"

He said: "You would find it much the same as the land about Hammersmith. North, again, the land runs up high, and there is an agreeable and well-built town called Hampstead, which fitly ends London on that side. It looks down on the north-western end of the forest you passed through."

I smiled. "So much for what was once London," said I. "Now tell me about the other towns of the country."

He said: "As to the big murky places which were once, as we know, the centres of manufacture, they have, like the brick and mortar desert of London, disappeared; only, since they were centres of nothing but 'manufacture,' and served no purpose but that of the gambling market, they have left less signs of their existence than London. Of course, the great change in the use of mechanical force made this an easy matter, and some approach to their break-up as centres would probably have taken place, even if we had not changed our habits so much: but they being such as they were, no sacrifice would have seemed too great a price to pay for getting rid of the 'manufacturing districts,' as they used to be called. For the rest, whatever coal or mineral we need is brought to grass and sent whither it is needed with as little as possible of dirt, confusion, and the distressing of quiet people's lives. One is tempted to believe from what one has read of the condition of those districts in the nineteenth century, that those who had them under their power worried, befouled, and degraded men out of malice prepense: but it was not so; like the mis-education of which we were talking just now, it came of their dreadful poverty. They were obliged to put up with everything, and even pretend that they liked it; whereas we can now deal with things reasonably, and refuse to be saddled with what we do not want."

I confess I was not sorry to cut short with a question his glorifications of the age he lived in. Said I: "How about the smaller towns? I suppose you have swept those away entirely?"

"No, no," said he, "it hasn't gone that way. On the contrary, there has been but little clearance, though much rebuilding, in the smaller towns. Their suburbs, indeed, when they had any, have melted away into the general country, and space and elbow-room has been got in their centres: but there are the towns still with their streets and squares and market-places; so that it is by means of these smaller towns that we of to-day can get some kind of idea of what the towns of the older world were like;—I mean to say at their best."

"Take Oxford, for instance," said I.

"Yes," said he, "I suppose Oxford was beautiful even in the nineteenth century. At present it has the great interest of still preserving a great mass of pre-commercial building, and is a very beautiful place, yet there are many towns which have become scarcely less beautiful."

Said I: "In passing, may I ask if it is still a place of learning?"

"Still?" said he, smiling. "Well, it has reverted to some of its best traditions; so you may imagine how far it is from its nineteenth-century position. It is real learning, knowledge cultivated for its own sake—the Art of Knowledge, in short —which is followed there, not the Commercial learning of the past. Though perhaps you do not know that in the nineteenth century Oxford and its less interesting sister Cambridge became definitely commercial. They (and especially Oxford) were the breeding places of a peculiar class of parasites, who called themselves cultivated people; they were indeed cynical enough, as the so-called educated classes of the day generally were; but they affected an exaggeration of cynicism in order that they might be thought knowing and worldly-wise. The rich middle classes (they had no relation with the working classes) treated them with the kind of contemptuous toleration with which a mediæval baron treated his jester; though it must be said that they were by no means so pleasant as the old jesters were, being, in fact, *the* bores of society. They were laughed at, despised—and paid. Which last was what they aimed at."

Dear me! thought I, how apt history is to reverse contemporary judgments. Surely only the worst of them were as bad as that. But I must admit that they were mostly prigs, and that they *were* commercial. I said aloud, though more to myself than to Hammond, "Well, how could they be better than the age that made them?"

"True," he said, "but their pretensions were higher."

"Were they?" said I, smiling.

"You drive me from corner to corner," said he, smiling in turn. "Let me say at least that they were a poor sequence to the aspirations of Oxford of 'the barbarous Middle Ages.'"

"Yes, that will do," said I.

"Also," said Hammond, "what I have been saying of them is true in the main. But ask on!"

I said: "We have heard about London and the manufacturing districts and the ordinary towns: how about the villages?"

Said Hammond: "You must know that toward the end of the nineteenth century the villages were almost destroyed, unless where they became mere adjuncts to the manufacturing districts, or formed a sort of minor manufacturing districts themselves. Houses were allowed to fall into decay and actual ruin; trees were cut down for the sake of the few shillings which the poor sticks would fetch; the building became inexpressibly mean and hideous. Labour was scarce; but wages fell nevertheless. All the small country arts of life which once added to the little pleasures of country people were lost. The country produce which passed through the hands of the husbandmen never got so far as their mouths. Incredible shabbiness and niggardly pinching reigned over the fields and acres which, in spite of the rude and careless husbandry of the times, were so kind and bountiful. Had you any inkling of all this?"

"I have heard that it was so," said I "but what followed?"

"The change," said Hammond, "which in these matters took place very early in our epoch, was most strangely rapid. People flocked into the country villages, and, so to say, flung themselves upon the freed land like a wild beast upon his prey; and in a very little time the villages of England were more populous than they had been since the fourteenth century, and were still growing fast. Of course, this invasion of the country was awkward to deal with, and would have created much misery, if the folk had still been under the bondage of class monopoly. But as it was, things soon righted themselves. People found out what they were fit for, and gave up attempting to push themselves into occupations in which they must needs fail. The town invaded the country; but the invaders, like the warlike invaders of early days, yielded to the influence of their surroundings, and became country people; and in their turn, as they became more numerous than the townsmen, influenced them also; so that the difference between town and country grew less and less; and it was indeed this world of the country vivified by the thought and briskness of town-bred folk which has produced that happy and leisurely but eager life of which you have had a first taste. Again I say, many blunders were made, but we have had time to set them right. Much was left for the men of my earlier life to deal with. The crude ideas of the first half of the twentieth century, when men were still oppressed by the fear of poverty, and did not look enough to the present pleasure of ordinary daily life, spoilt a great deal of what the commercial age had left us of external beauty: and I admit that it was but slowly that men recovered from the injuries that they inflicted on themselves even after they became free. But slowly as the recovery came, it *did* come; and the more you see of us, the clearer it will be to you that we are happy. That we live amidst beauty without any fear of becoming effeminate; that we have plenty to do, and on the whole enjoy doing it. What more can we ask of life?"

He paused, as if he were seeking for words with which to express his thought. Then he said:

"This is how we stand. England was once a country of clearings amongst the woods and wastes, with a few towns interspersed, which were fortresses for the feudal army, markets for the folk, gathering places for the craftsmen. It then became a country of huge and foul workshops and fouler gambling-dens, surrounded by an ill-kept, poverty-stricken farm, pillaged by the masters of the workshops. It is now a garden, where nothing is wasted and nothing is spoilt, with the necessary dwellings, sheds, and workshops scattered up and down the country, all trim and neat and pretty. For, indeed, we should be too much ashamed of ourselves if we allowed the making of goods, even on a large scale, to carry with it the appearance, even, of desolation and misery. Why, my friend, those housewives we were talking of just now would teach us better than that."

Said I: "This side of your change is certainly for the better. But though I shall soon see some of these villages, tell me in a word or two what they are like, just to prepare me."

"Perhaps," said he, "you have seen a tolerable picture of these villages as they were before the end of the nineteenth century. Such things exist."

"I have seen several of such pictures," said I.

"Well," said Hammond, "our villages are something like the best of such places, with the church or mote-house of the neighbours for their chief building. Only note that there are no tokens of poverty about them: no tumble-down picturesque; which, to tell you the truth, the artist usually availed himself of to veil his incapacity for drawing architecture. Such things do not please us, even when they indicate no misery. Like the mediævals, we like everything trim and clean, and orderly and bright; as people always do when they have any sense of architectural power; because then they know that they can have what they want, and they won't stand any nonsense from Nature in their dealings with her."

"Besides the villages, are there any scattered country houses?" said I.

"Yes, plenty," said Hammond; "in fact, except in the wastes and forests and amongst the sand-hills (like Hindhead in Surrey), it is not easy to be out of sight of a house; and where the houses are thinly scattered they run large, and are more like the old colleges than ordinary houses as they used to be. That is done for the sake of society, for a good many people can dwell in such houses, as the country dwellers are not necessarily husbandmen; though they almost all help in such work at times. The life that goes on in these big dwellings in the country is very pleasant, especially as some of the most studious men of our time live in them, and altogether there is a great variety of mind and mood to be found in them which brightens and quickens the society there."

"I am rather surprised," said I, "by all this, for it seems to me that after all the country must be tolerably populous."

"Certainly," said he; "the population is pretty much the same as it was at the end of the nineteenth century; we have spread it, that is all. Of course, also, we have helped to populate other countries—where we were wanted and were called for."

Said I: "One thing, it seems to me, does not go with your word of 'garden' for the country. You have spoken of wastes and forests, and I myself have seen the beginning of your Middlesex and Essex forest. Why do you keep such things in a garden? and isn't it very wasteful to do so?"

"My friend," he said, "we like these pieces of wild nature, and can afford them, so we have them; let alone that as to the forests, we need a great deal of timber, and suppose that our sons and sons' sons will do the like. As to the land being a garden, I have heard that they used to have shrubberies and rockeries in gardens once; and though I might not like the artificial ones, I assure you that some of the natural rockeries of our garden are worth seeing. Go north this summer and look at the Cumberland and Westmoreland ones,—where, by the way, you will see some sheep-feeding, so that they are not so wasteful as you think; not so wasteful as forcing-grounds for fruit out of season, *I* think. Go and have a look at the sheep-walks high up the slopes between Ingleborough and Pen-y-gwent, and tell me if you think we *waste* the land there by not covering it with factories for making things that nobody wants, which was the chief business of the nineteenth century."

"I will try to go there," said I.

"It won't take much trying," said he.

11. CONCERNING GOVERNMENT

"Now," said I, "I have come to the point of asking questions which I suppose will be dry for you to answer and difficult for you to explain; but I have foreseen for some time past that I must ask them, will I 'nill I. What kind of a government have you? Has republicanism finally triumphed? or have you come to a mere dictatorship, which some persons in the nineteenth century used to prophesy as the ultimate outcome of democracy? Indeed, this last question does not seem so very unreasonable, since you have turned your Parliament House into a dung-market. Or where do you house your present Parliament?"

The old man answered my smile with a hearty laugh, and said: "Well, well, dung is not the worst kind of corruption; fertility may come of that, whereas mere dearth came from the other kind, of which those walls once held the great supporters. Now, dear guest, let me tell you that our present parliament would be hard to house in one place, because the whole people is our parliament."

"I don't understand," said I.

"No, I suppose not," said he. "I must now shock you by telling you that we have no longer anything which you, a native of another planet, would call a government."

"I am not so much shocked as you might think," said I, "as I know something about governments. But tell me, how do you manage, and how have you come to this state of things?"

Said he: "It is true that we have to make some arrangements about our affairs, concerning which you can ask presently; and it is also true that everybody does not always agree with the details of these arrangements; but, further, it is true that a man no more needs an elaborate system of government, with its army, navy, and police, to force him to give way to the will of the majority of his *equals*, than he wants a similar machinery to make him understand that his head and a stone wall cannot occupy the same space at the same moment. Do you want further explanation?"

"Well, yes, I do," quoth I.

Old Hammond settled himself in his chair with a look of enjoyment which rather alarmed me, and made me dread a scientific disquisition: so I sighed and abided. He said:

"I suppose you know pretty well what the process of government was in the bad old times?"

"I am supposed to know," said I.

(Hammond) What was the government of those days? Was it really the Parliament or any part of it?

(I) No.

(H.) Was not the Parliament on the one side a kind of watch-committee sitting to see that the interests of the Upper Classes took no hurt; and on the other side a sort of blind to delude the people into supposing that they had some share in the management of their own affairs?

(I) History seems to show us this.

(H.) To what extent did the people manage their own affairs?

(I) I judge from what I have heard that sometimes they forced the Parliament to make a law to legalise some alteration which had already taken place.

(H.) Anything else?

(I) I think not. As I am informed, if the people made any attempt to deal with the *cause* of their grievances, the law stepped in and said, this is sedition, revolt, or what not, and slew or tortured the ringleaders of such attempts.

(H.) If Parliament was not the government then, nor the people either, what was the government?

(I) Can you tell me?

(H.) I think we shall not be far wrong if we say that government was the Law-Courts, backed up by the executive, which handled the brute force that the deluded people allowed them to use for their own purposes; I mean the army, navy, and police.

(I) Reasonable men must needs think you are right.

(H.) Now as to those Law-Courts. Were they places of fair dealing according to the ideas of the day? Had a poor man a good chance of defending his property and person in them?

(I) It is a commonplace that even rich men looked upon a law-suit as a dire misfortune, even if they gained the case; and as for a poor one—why, it was considered a miracle of justice and beneficence if a poor man who had once got into the clutches of the law escaped prison or utter ruin.

(H.) It seems, then, my son, that the government by law-courts and police, which was the real government of the nineteenth century, was not a great success even to the people of that day, living under a class system which proclaimed inequality and poverty as the law of God and the bond which held the world together.

(I) So it seems, indeed.

(H.) And now that all this is changed, and the "rights of property," which mean the clenching the fist on a piece of goods and crying out to the neighbours, You shan't have this!—now that all this has disappeared so utterly that it is no longer possible even to jest upon its absurdity, is such a Government possible?

(I) It is impossible.

(H.) Yes, happily. But for what other purpose than the protection of the rich from the poor, the strong from the weak, did this Government exist?

(I.) I have heard that it was said that their office was to defend their own citizens against attack from other countries.

(H.) It was said; but was anyone expected to believe this? For instance, did the English Government defend the English citizen against the French?

(I) So it was said.

(H.) Then if the French had invaded England and conquered it, they would not have allowed the English workmen to live well?

(I, laughing) As far as I can make out, the English masters of the English workmen saw to that: they took from their workmen as much of their livelihood as they dared, because they wanted it for themselves.

(H.) But if the French had conquered, would they not have taken more still from the English workmen?

(I) I do not think so; for in that case the English workmen would have died of starvation; and then the French conquest would have ruined the French, just as if the English horses and cattle had died of under-feeding. So that after all, the English *workmen* would have been no worse off for the conquest: their French Masters could have got no more from them than their English masters did.

(H.) This is true; and we may admit that the pretensions of the government to defend the poor (*i.e.*, the useful) people against other countries come to nothing. But that is but natural; for we have seen already that it was the function of government to protect the rich against the poor. But did not the government defend its rich men against other nations?

(I) I do not remember to have heard that the rich needed defence; because it is said that even when two nations were at war, the rich men of each nation gambled with each other pretty much as usual, and even sold each other weapons wherewith to kill their own countrymen.

(H.) In short, it comes to this, that whereas the so-called government of protection of property by means of the law-courts meant destruction of wealth, this defence of the citizens of one country against those of another country by means of war or the threat of war meant pretty much the same thing.

(I) I cannot deny it.

(H.) Therefore the government really existed for the destruction of wealth?

(I) So it seems. And yet——

(H.) Yet what?

(I) There were many rich people in those times.

(H.) You see the consequences of that fact?

(I) I think I do. But tell me out what they were.

(H.) If the government habitually destroyed wealth, the country must have been poor?

(I) Yes, certainly.

(H.) Yet amidst this poverty the persons for the sake of whom the government existed insisted on being rich whatever might happen?

(I) So it was.

(H.) What must happen if in a poor country some people insist on being rich at the expense of the others?

(I) Unutterable poverty for the others. All this misery, then, was caused by the destructive government of which we have been speaking?

(H.) Nay, it would be incorrect to say so. The government itself was but the necessary result of the careless, aimless tyranny of the times; it was but the machinery of tyranny. Now tyranny has come to an end, and we no longer need such machinery; we could not possibly use it since we are free. Therefore in your sense of the word we have no government. Do you understand this now?

(I) Yes, I do. But I will ask you some more questions as to how you as free men manage your affairs.

(H.) With all my heart. Ask away.

12. CONCERNING THE ARRANGEMENT OF LIFE

"Well," I said, "about those 'arrangements' which you spoke of as taking the place of government, could you give me any account of them?"

"Neighbour," he said, "although we have simplified our lives a great deal from what they were, and have got rid of many conventionalities and many sham wants, which used to give our forefathers much trouble, yet our life is too complex for me to tell you in detail by means of words how it is arranged; you must find that out by living amongst us. It is true that I can better tell you what we don't do, than what we do do."

"Well?" said I.

"This is the way to put it," said he: "We have been living for a hundred and fifty years, at least, more or less in our present manner, and a tradition or habit of life has been growing on us; and that habit has become a habit of acting on the whole for the best. It is easy for us to live without robbing each other. It would be possible for us to contend with and rob each other, but it would be harder for us than refraining from strife and robbery. That is in short the foundation of our life and our happiness."

"Whereas in the old days," said I, "it was very hard to live without strife and robbery. That's what you mean, isn't it, by giving me the negative side of your good conditions?"

"Yes," he said, "it was so hard, that those who habitually acted fairly to their neighbours were celebrated as saints and heroes, and were looked up to with the greatest reverence."

"While they were alive?" said I.

"No," said he, "after they were dead."

"But as to these days," I said; "you don't mean to tell me that no one ever transgresses this habit of good fellowship?"

"Certainly not," said Hammond, "but when the transgressions occur, everybody, transgressors and all, know them for what they are; the errors of friends, not the habitual actions of persons driven into enmity against society."

"I see," said I; "you mean that you have no 'criminal' classes."

"How could we have them," said he, "since there is no rich class to breed enemies against the state by means of the injustice of the state?"

Said I: "I thought that I understood from something that fell from you a little while ago that you had abolished civil law. Is that so, literally?"

"It abolished itself, my friend," said he. "As I said before, the civil law-courts were upheld for the defence of private property; for nobody ever pretended that it was possible to make people act fairly to each other by means of brute force. Well, private property being abolished, all the laws and all the legal 'crimes' which it had manufactured of course came to an end. Thou shalt not steal, had to be translated into, Thou shalt work in order to live happily. Is there any need to enforce that commandment by violence?"

"Well," said I, "that is understood, and I agree with it; but how about crimes of violence? would not their occurrence (and you admit that they occur) make criminal law necessary?"

Said he: "In your sense of the word, we have no criminal law either. Let us look at the matter closer, and see whence crimes of violence spring. By far the greater part of these in past days were the result of the laws of private property, which forbade the satisfaction of their natural desires to all but a privileged few, and of the general visible coercion which came of those laws. All that cause of violent crime is gone. Again, many violent acts came from the artificial perversion of the sexual passions, which caused overweening jealousy and the like miseries. Now, when you look carefully into these, you will find that what lay at the bottom of them was mostly the idea (a law-made idea) of the woman being the property of the man, whether he were husband, father, brother, or what not. That idea has of course vanished with private property, as well as certain follies about the 'ruin' of women for following their natural desires in an illegal way, which of course was a convention caused by the laws of private property.

"Another cognate cause of crimes of violence was the family tyranny, which was the subject of so many novels and stories of the past, and which once more was the result of private property. Of course that is all ended, since families are held together by no bond of coercion, legal or social, but by mutual liking and affection, and everybody is free to come or go as he or she pleases. Furthermore, our standards of honour and public estimation are very different from the old ones; success in besting our neighbours is a road to renown now closed, let us hope for ever. Each man is free to exercise his special faculty to the utmost, and every one encourages him in so doing. So that we have got rid of the scowling envy, coupled by the poets with hatred, and surely with good reason; heaps of unhappiness and ill-blood were caused by it, which with irritable and passionate men—*i.e.*, energetic and active men—often led to violence."

I laughed, and said: "So that you now withdraw your admission, and say that there is no violence amongst you?"

"No," said he, "I withdraw nothing; as I told you, such things will happen. Hot blood will err sometimes. A man may strike another, and the stricken strike back again, and the result be a homicide, to put it at the worst. But what then? Shall we the neighbours make it worse still? Shall we think so poorly of each other as to suppose that the slain man calls on us to revenge him, when we know that if he had been maimed, he would, when in cold blood and able to weigh all the circumstances, have forgiven his manner? Or will the death of the slayer bring the slain man to life again and cure the unhappiness his loss has caused?"

"Yes," I said, "but consider, must not the safety of society be safeguarded by some punishment?"

"There, neighbour!" said the old man, with some exultation "You have hit the mark. That *punishment* of which men used to talk so wisely and act so foolishly, what was it but the expression of their fear? And they had need to fear, since they—*i.e.*, the rulers of society—were dwelling like an armed band in a hostile country. But we who live amongst our friends need neither fear nor punish. Surely if we, in dread of an occasional rare homicide, an occasional rough blow, were solemnly and legally to commit homicide and violence, we could only be a society of ferocious cowards. Don't you think so, neighbour?"

"Yes, I do, when I come to think of it from that side," said I.

"Yet you must understand," said the old man, "that when any violence is committed, we expect the transgressor to make any atonement possible to him, and he himself expects it. But again, think if the destruction or serious injury of a man momentarily overcome by wrath or folly can be any atonement to the commonwealth? Surely it can only be an additional injury to it."

Said I: "But suppose the man has a habit of violence,—kills a man a year, for instance?"

"Such a thing is unknown," said he. "In a society where there is no punishment to evade, no law to triumph over, remorse will certainly follow transgression."

"And lesser outbreaks of violence," said I, "how do you deal with them? for hitherto we have been talking of great tragedies, I suppose?"

Said Hammond: "If the ill-doer is not sick or mad (in which case he must be restrained till his sickness or madness is cured) it is clear that grief and humiliation must follow the ill-deed; and society in general will make that pretty clear to the ill-doer if he should chance to be dull to it; and again, some kind of atonement will follow,—at the least, an open acknowledgement of the grief and humiliation. Is it so hard to say, I ask your pardon, neighbour?—Well, sometimes it is hard—and let it be."

"You think that enough?" said I.

"Yes," said he, "and moreover it is all that we *can* do. If in addition we torture the man, we turn his grief into anger, and the humiliation he would otherwise feel for *his* wrong-doing is swallowed up by a hope of revenge for *our* wrong-doing to him. He has paid the legal penalty, and can 'go and sin again' with comfort. Shall we commit such a folly, then? Remember Jesus had got the legal penalty remitted before he said 'Go and sin no more.' Let alone that in a society of equals you will not find any one to play the part of torturer or jailer, though many to act as nurse or doctor."

"So," said I, "you consider crime a mere spasmodic disease, which requires no body of criminal law to deal with it?"

"Pretty much so," said he; "and since, as I have told you, we are a healthy people generally, so we are not likely to be much troubled with *this* disease."

"Well, you have no civil law, and no criminal law. But have you no laws of the market, so to say—no regulation for the exchange of wares? for you must exchange, even if you have no property."

Said he: "We have no obvious individual exchange, as you saw this morning when you went a-shopping; but of course there are regulations of the markets, varying according to the circumstances and guided by general custom. But as these are matters of general assent, which nobody dreams of objecting to, so also we have made no provision for enforcing them: therefore I don't call them laws. In law, whether it be criminal or civil, execution always follows judgment, and someone must suffer. When you see the judge on his bench, you see through him, as clearly as if he were made of glass, the policeman to emprison, and the soldier to slay some actual living person. Such follies would make an agreeable market, wouldn't they?"

"Certainly," said I, "that means turning the market into a mere battle-field, in which many people must suffer as much as in the battle-field of bullet and bayonet. And from what I have seen I should suppose that your marketing, great and little, is carried on in a way that makes it a pleasant occupation."

"You are right, neighbour," said he. "Although there are so many, indeed by far the greater number amongst us, who would be unhappy if they were not engaged in actually making things, and things which turn out beautiful under their hands,—there are many, like the housekeepers I was speaking of, whose delight is in administration and organisation, to use long-tailed words; I mean people who like keeping things together, avoiding waste, seeing that nothing sticks fast uselessly. Such people are thoroughly happy in their business, all the more as they are dealing with actual facts, and not merely passing counters round to see what share they shall have in the privileged taxation of useful people, which was the business of the commercial folk in past days. Well, what are you going to ask me next?"

13. CONCERNING POLITICS

Said I: "How do you manage with politics?"

Said Hammond, smiling: "I am glad that it is of *me* that you ask that question;

I do believe that anybody else would make you explain yourself, or try to do so, till you were sickened of asking questions. Indeed, I believe I am the only man in England who would know what you mean; and since I know, I will answer your question briefly by saying that we are very well off as to politics,—because we have none. If ever you make a book out of this conversation, put this in a chapter by itself, after the model of old Horrebow's Snakes in Iceland."

"I will," said I.

14. HOW MATTERS ARE MANAGED

Said I: "How about your relations with foreign nations?"

"I will not affect not to know what you mean," said he, "but I will tell you at once that the whole system of rival and contending nations which played so great a part in the 'government' of the world of civilisation has disappeared along with the inequality betwixt man and man in society."

"Does not that make the world duller?" said I.

"Why?" said the old man.

"The obliteration of national variety," said I.

"Nonsense," he said, somewhat snappishly. "Cross the water and see. You will find plenty of variety: the landscape, the building, the diet, the amusements, all various. The men and women varying in looks as well as in habits of thought; the costume far more various than in the commercial period. How should it add to the variety or dispel the dulness, to coerce certain families or tribes, often heterogeneous and jarring with one another, into certain artificial and mechanical groups, and call them nations, and stimulate their patriotism—*i.e.*, their foolish and envious prejudices?"

"Well—I don't know how," said I.

"That's right," said Hammond cheerily; "you can easily understand that now we are freed from this folly it is obvious to us that by means of this very diversity the different strains of blood in the world can be serviceable and pleasant to each other, without in the least wanting to rob each other: we are all bent on the same enterprise, making the most of our lives. And I must tell you whatever quarrels or misunderstandings arise, they very seldom take place between people of different race; and consequently since there is less unreason in them, they are the more readily appeased."

"Good," said I, "but as to those matters of politics; as to general differences of opinion in one and the same community. Do you assert that there are none?"

"No, not at all," said he, somewhat snappishly; "but I do say that differences of opinion about real solid things need not, and with us do not, crystallise people into parties permanently hostile to one another, with different theories as to the build of the universe and the progress of time. Isn't that what politics used to mean?"

"H'm, well," said I, "I am not so sure of that."

Said he: "I take, you, neighbour; they only *pretended* to this serious difference of opinion; for if it had existed they could not have dealt together in the ordinary business of life; couldn't have eaten together, bought and sold together, gambled together, cheated other people together, but must have fought whenever they met: which would not have suited them at all. The game of the masters of politics was to cajole or force the public to pay the expense of a luxurious life and exciting amusement for a few cliques of ambitious persons: and the *pretence* of serious difference of opinion, belied by every action of their lives, was quite good enough for that. What has all that got to do with us?"

Said I: "Why, nothing, I should hope. But I fear—In short, I have been told that political strife was a necessary result of human nature."

"Human nature!" cried the old boy, impetuously; "what human nature? The human nature of paupers, of slaves, of slave-holders, or the human nature of wealthy freemen? Which? Come, tell me that!"

"Well," said I, "I suppose there would be a difference according to circumstances in people's action about these matters."

"I should think so, indeed," said he. "At all events, experience shows that it is so. Amongst us, our differences concern matters of business, and passing events as to them, and could not divide men permanently. As a rule, the immediate outcome shows which opinion on a given subject is the right one; it is a matter of fact, not of speculation. For instance, it is clearly not easy to knock up a political party on the question as to whether haymaking in such and such a country-side shall begin this week or next, when all men agree that it must at latest begin the week after next, and when any man can go down into the fields himself and see whether the seeds are ripe enough for the cutting."

Said I: "And you settle these differences, great and small, by the will of the majority, I suppose?"

"Certainly," said he; "how else could we settle them? You see in matters which are merely personal which do not affect the welfare of the community—how a man shall dress, what he shall eat and drink, what he shall write and read, and so forth—there can be no difference of opinion, and everybody does as he pleases. But when the matter is of common interest to the whole community, and the doing or not doing something affects everybody, the majority must have their way; unless the minority were to take up arms and show by force that they were the effective or real majority; which, however, in a society of men who are free and equal is little likely to happen; because in such a community the apparent majority *is* the real majority, and the others, as I have hinted before, know that too well to obstruct from mere pigheadedness; especially as they have had plenty of opportunity of putting forward their side of the question."

"How is that managed?" said I.

"Well," said he, "let us take one of our units of management, a commune, or a ward, or a parish (for we have all three names, indicating little real distinction between them now, though time was there was a good deal). In such a district, as you would call it, some neighbours think that something ought to be done or undone: a new town-hall built; a clearance of inconvenient houses; or say a stone bridge substituted for some ugly old iron one,—there you have undoing and doing in one. Well, at the next ordinary meeting of the neighbours, or Mote, as we call it, according to the ancient tongue of the times before bureaucracy, a neighbour proposes the change, and of course, if everybody agrees, there is an end of discussion, except about details. Equally, if no one backs the proposer,— 'seconds him,' it used to be called—the matter drops for the time being; a thing not likely to happen amongst reasonable men, however, as the proposer is sure to have talked it over with others before the Mote. But supposing the affair proposed and seconded, if a few of the neighbours disagree to it, if they think that the beastly iron bridge will serve a little longer and they don't want to be bothered with building a new one just then, they don't count heads that time, but put off the formal discussion to the next Mote; and meantime arguments *pro* and *con* are flying about, and some get printed, so that everybody knows what is going on; and when the Mote comes together again there is a regular discussion and at last a vote by show of hands. If the division is a close one, the question is again put off for further discussion; if the division is a wide one, the minority are asked if they will yield to the more general opinion, which they often, nay, most commonly do. If they refuse, the question is debated a third time, when, if the minority has not perceptibly grown, they always give way; though I believe there is some half-forgotten rule by which they might still carry it on further; but I say, what always happens is that they are convinced, not perhaps that their view is the wrong one, but they cannot persuade or force the community to adopt it."

"Very good," said I; "but what happens if the divisions are still narrow?"

Said he: "As a matter of principle and according to the rule of such cases, the question must then lapse, and the majority, if so narrow, has to submit to sitting down under the *status quo*. But I must tell you that in point of fact the minority very seldom enforces this rule, but generally yields in a friendly manner."

"But do you know," said I, "that there is something in all this very like democracy; and I thought that democracy was considered to be in a moribund condition many, many years ago."

The old boy's eyes twinkled. "I grant you that our methods have that drawback. But what is to be done? We can't get *anyone* amongst us to complain of his not always having his own way in the teeth of the community, when it is clear that *everybody* cannot have that indulgence. What is to be done?"

"Well," said I, "I don't know."

Said he: "The only alternatives to our method that I can conceive of are these. First, that we should choose out, or breed, a class of superior persons capable of judging on all matters without consulting the neighbours; that, in short, we should get for ourselves what used to be called an aristocracy of intellect; or, secondly, that for the purpose of safe-guarding the freedom of the individual will, we should revert to a system of private property again, and have slaves and slave-holders once more. What do you think of those two expedients?"

"Well," said I, "there is a third possibility—to wit, that every man should be quite independent of every other, and that thus the tyranny of society should be abolished."

He looked hard at me for a second or two, and then burst out laughing very heartily; and I confess that I joined him. When he recovered himself he nodded at me, and said: "Yes, yes, I quite agree with you—and so we all do."

"Yes," I said, "and besides, it does not press hardly on the minority: for, take this matter of the bridge, no man is obliged to work on it if he doesn't agree to its building. At least, I suppose not."

He smiled, and said: "Shrewdly put; and yet from the point of view of the native of another planet. If the man of the minority does find his feelings hurt, doubtless he may relieve them by refusing to help in building the bridge. But, dear neighbour, that is not a very effective salve for the wound caused by the 'tyranny of a majority' in our society; because all work that is done is either beneficial or hurtful to every member of society. The man is benefited by the bridge-building if it turns out a good thing, and hurt by it if it turns out a bad one, whether he puts a hand to it or not; and meanwhile he is benefiting the bridge-builders by his work, whatever that may be. In fact, I see no help for him except the pleasure of saying 'I told you so' if the bridge-building turns out to be a mistake and hurts him; if it benefits him he must suffer in silence. A terrible tyranny our Communism, is it not? Folk used often to be warned against this very unhappiness in times past, when for every well-fed, contented person you saw a thousand miserable starvelings. Whereas for us, we grow fat and well-liking on the tyranny; a tyranny, to say the truth, not to be made visible by any microscope I know. Don't be afraid, my friend; we are not going to seek for troubles by calling our peace and plenty and happiness by ill names whose very meaning we have forgotten!"

He sat musing for a little, and then started and said: "Are there any more questions, dear guest? The morning is waning fast amidst my garrulity?"

15. ON THE LACK OF INCENTIVE TO LABOUR IN A COMMUNIST SOCIETY

"Yes," said I. "I was expecting Dick and Clara to make their appearance any moment: but is there time to ask just one or two questions before they come?"

"Try it, dear neighbour—try it," said old Hammond. "For the more you ask me the better I am pleased; and at any rate if they do come and find me in the middle of an answer, they must sit quiet and pretend to listen till I come to an end. It won't hurt them; they will find it quite amusing enough to sit side by side, conscious of their proximity to each other."

I smiled, as I was bound to, and said: "Good; I will go on talking without noticing them when they come in. Now, this is what I want to ask you about—to wit, how you get people to work when there is no reward of labour, and especially how you get them to work strenuously?"

"No reward of labour?" said Hammond, gravely. "The reward of labour is *life*. Is that not enough?"

"But no reward for especially good work," quoth I.

"Plenty of reward," said he—"the reward of creation. The wages which God gets, as people might have said time agone. If you are going to ask to be paid for the pleasure of creation, which is what excellence in work means, the next thing we shall hear of will be a bill sent in for the begetting of children."

"Well, but," said I, "the man of the nineteenth century would say there is a natural desire towards the procreation of children, and a natural desire not to work."

"Yes, yes," said he, "I know the ancient platitude,—wholly untrue; indeed, to us quite meaningless. Fourier, whom all men laughed at, understood the matter better."

"Why is it meaningless to you?" said I.

He said: "Because it implies that all work is suffering, and we are so far from thinking that, that, as you may have noticed, whereas we are not short of wealth, there is a kind of fear growing up amongst us that we shall one day be short of work. It is a pleasure which we are afraid of losing, not a pain."

"Yes," said I, "I have noticed that, and I was going to ask you about that also. But in the meantime, what do you positively mean to assert about the pleasurableness of work amongst you?"

"This, that *all* work is now pleasurable; either because of the hope of gain in honour and wealth with which the work is done, which causes pleasurable excitement, even when the actual work is not pleasant; or else because it has grown into a pleasurable *habit*, as in the case with what you may call mechanical work; and lastly (and most of our work is of this kind) because there is conscious sensuous pleasure in the work itself; it is done, that is, by artists."

"I see," said I. "Can you now tell me how you have come to this happy condition? For, to speak plainly, this change from the conditions of the older world seems to me far greater and more important than all the other changes you have told me about as to crime, politics, property, marriage."

"You are right there," said he. "Indeed, you may say rather that it is this change which makes all the others possible. What is the object of Revolution? Surely to make people happy. Revolution having brought its foredoomed change about, how can you prevent the counter-revolution from setting in except by making people happy? What! shall we expect peace and stability from unhappiness? The gathering of grapes from thorns and figs from thistles is a reasonable expectation compared with that! And happiness without happy daily work is impossible."

"Most obviously true," said I: for I thought the old boy was preaching a little. "But answer my question, as to how you gained this happiness."

"Briefly," said he, "by the absence of artificial coercion, and the freedom for every man to do what he can do best, joined to the knowledge of what productions of labour we really wanted. I must admit that this knowledge we reached slowly and painfully."

"Go on," said I, "give me more detail; explain more fully. For this subject interests me intensely."

"Yes, I will," said he; "but in order to do so I must weary you by talking a little about the past. Contrast is necessary for this explanation. Do you mind?"

"No, no," said I.

Said he, settling himself in his chair again for a long talk: "It is clear from all that we hear and read, that in the last age of civilisation men had got into a vicious circle in the matter of production of wares. They had reached a wonderful facility of production, and in order to make the most of that facility they had gradually created (or allowed to grow, rather) a most elaborate system of buying and selling, which has been called the World-Market; and that World-Market, once set a-going, forced them to go on making more and more of these wares, whether they needed them or not. So that while (of course) they could not free themselves from the toil of making real necessaries, they created in a never-ending series sham or artificial necessaries, which became, under the iron rule of the aforesaid World-Market, of equal importance to them with the real necessaries which supported life. By all this they burdened themselves with a prodigious mass of work merely for the sake of keeping their wretched system going."

"Yes—and then?" said I.

"Why, then, since they had forced themselves to stagger along under this horrible burden of unnecessary production, it became impossible for them to look upon labour and its results from any other point of view than one—to wit, the ceaseless endeavour to expend the least possible amount of labour on any article made, and yet at the same time to make as many articles as possible. To this 'cheapening of production', as it was called, everything was sacrificed: the happiness of the workman at his work, nay, his most elementary comfort and bare health, his food, his clothes, his dwelling, his leisure, his amusement, his education—his life, in short—did not weigh a grain of sand in the balance against this dire necessity of 'cheap production' of things, a great part of which were not worth producing at all. Nay, we are told, and we must believe it, so overwhelming is the evidence, though many of our people scarcely *can* believe it, that even rich and powerful men, the masters of the poor devils aforesaid, submitted to live amidst sights and sounds and smells which it is in the very nature of man to abhor and flee from, in order that their riches might bolster up this supreme folly. The whole community, in fact, was cast into the jaws of this ravening monster, 'the cheap production' forced upon it by the World-Market."

"Dear me!" said I. "But what happened? Did not their cleverness and facility in production master this chaos of misery at last? Couldn't they catch up with the World-Market, and then set to work to devise means for relieving themselves from this fearful task of extra labour?"

He smiled bitterly. "Did they even try to?" said he. "I am not sure. You know that according to the old saw the beetle gets used to living in dung; and these people, whether they found the dung sweet or not, certainly lived in it."

His estimate of the life of the nineteenth century made me catch my breath a little; and I said feebly, "But the labour-saving machines?"

"Heyday!" quoth he. "What's that you are saying? the labour-saving machines? Yes, they were made to 'save labour' (or, to speak more plainly, the lives of men) on one piece of work in order that it might be expended—I will say wasted—on another, probably useless, piece of work. Friend, all their devices for cheapening labour simply resulted in increasing the burden of labour. The appetite of the World-Market grew with what it fed on: the countries within the ring of 'civilisation' (that is, organised misery) were glutted with the abortions of the market, and force and fraud were used unsparingly to 'open up' countries *outside* that pale. This process of 'opening up' is a strange one to those who have read the professions of the men of that period and do not understand their practice; and perhaps shows us at its worst the great vice of the nineteenth century, the use of hypocrisy and cant to evade the responsibility of vicarious ferocity. When the civilised World-Market coveted a country not yet in its clutches, some transparent pretext was found—the suppression of a slavery different from and not so cruel as that of commerce; the pushing of a religion no longer believed in by its promoters; the 'rescue' of some desperado or homicidal madman whose misdeeds had got him into trouble amongst the natives of the 'barbarous' country—any stick, in short, which would beat the dog at all. Then some bold, unprincipled, ignorant adventurer was found (no difficult task in the days of competition), and he was bribed to 'create a market' by breaking up whatever traditional society there might be in the doomed country, and by destroying whatever leisure or pleasure he found there. He forced wares on the natives which they did not want, and took their natural products in 'exchange,' as this form of robbery was called, and thereby he 'created new wants,' to supply which (that is, to be allowed to live by their new masters) the hapless, helpless people had to sell themselves into the slavery of hopeless toil so that they might have something wherewith to purchase the nullities of 'civilisation.' "Ah," said the old man, pointing to the Museum, "I have read books and papers in there, telling strange stories indeed of the dealings of civilisation (or organised misery) with 'non-civilisation'; from the time when the British Government deliberately sent blankets infected with small-pox as choice gifts to inconvenient tribes of Redskins, to the time when Africa was infested by a man named Stanley, who—"

"Excuse me," said I, "but as you know, time presses; and I want to keep our question on the straightest line possible; and I want at once to ask this about these wares made for the World-Market—how about their quality; these people who were so clever about making goods, I suppose they made them well?"

"Quality!" said the old man crustily, for he was rather peevish at being cut short in his story; "how could they possibly attend to such trifles as the quality of the wares they sold? The best of them were of a lowish average, the worst were transparent make-shifts for the things asked for, which nobody would have put up with if they could have got anything else. It was a current jest of the time that the wares were made to sell and not to use; a jest which you, as coming from another planet, may understand, but which our folk could not."

Said I: "What! did they make nothing well?"

"Why, yes," said he, "there was one class of goods which they did make thoroughly well, and that was the class of machines which were used for making things. These were usually quite perfect pieces of workmanship, admirably adapted to the end in view. So that it may be fairly said that the great achievement of the nineteenth century was the making of machines which were wonders of invention, skill, and patience, and which were used for the production of measureless quantities of worthless make-shifts. In truth, the owners of the machines did not consider anything which they made as wares, but simply as means for the enrichment of themselves. Of course the only admitted test of utility in wares was the finding of buyers for them—wise men or fools, as it might chance."

"And people put up with this?" said I.

"For a time," said he.

"And then?"

"And then the overturn," said the old man, smiling, "and the nineteenth century saw itself as a man who has lost his clothes whilst bathing, and has to walk naked through the town."

"You are very bitter about that unlucky nineteenth century," said I.

"Naturally," said he, "since I know so much about it."

He was silent a little, and then said: "There are traditions—nay, real histories—in our family about it: my grandfather was one of its victims. If you know something about it, you will understand what he suffered when I tell you that he was in those days a genuine artist, a man of genius, and a revolutionist."

"I think I do understand," said I: "but now, as it seems, you have reversed all this?"

"Pretty much so," said he. "The wares which we make are made because they are needed: men make for their neighbours' use as if they were making for themselves, not for a vague market of which they know nothing, and over which they have no control: as there is no buying and selling, it would be mere insanity to make goods on the chance of their being wanted; for there is no longer anyone who can be compelled to buy them. So that whatever is made is good, and thoroughly fit for its purpose. Nothing can be made except for genuine use; therefore no inferior goods are made. Moreover, as aforesaid, we have now found out what we want, so we make no more than we want; and as we are not driven to make a vast quantity of useless things we have time and resources enough to consider our pleasure in making them. All work which would be irksome to do by hand is done by immensely improved machinery; and in all work which it is a pleasure to do by hand machinery is done without. There is no difficulty in finding work which suits the special turn of mind of everybody; so that no man is sacrificed to the wants of another. From time to time, when we have found out that some piece of work was too disagreeable or troublesome, we have given it up and done altogether without the thing produced by it. Now, surely you can see that under these circumstances all the work that we do is an exercise of the mind and body more or less pleasant to be done: so that instead of avoiding work everybody seeks it: and, since people have got defter in doing the work generation after generation, it has become so easy to do, that it seems as if there were less done, though probably more is produced. I suppose this explains that fear, which I hinted at just now, of a possible scarcity in work, which perhaps you have already noticed, and which is a feeling on the increase, and has been for a score of years."

"But do you think," said I, "that there is any fear of a work-famine amongst you?"

"No, I do not," said he, "and I will tell why; it is each man's business to make his own work pleasanter and pleasanter, which of course tends towards raising the standard of excellence, as no man enjoys turning out work which is not a credit to him, and also to greater deliberation in turning it out; and there is such a vast number of things which can be treated as works of art, that this alone gives employment to a host of deft people. Again, if art be inexhaustible, so is science also; and though it is no longer the only innocent occupation which is thought worth an intelligent man spending his time upon, as it once was, yet there are, and I suppose will be, many people who are excited by its conquest of difficulties, and care for it more than for anything else. Again, as more and more of pleasure is imported into work, I think we shall take up kinds of work which produce desirable wares, but which we gave up because we could not carry them on pleasantly. Moreover, I think that it is only in parts of Europe which are more advanced than the rest of the world that you will hear this talk of the fear of a work-famine. Those lands which were once the colonies of Great Britain, for instance, and especially America—that part of it, above all, which was once the United states— are now and will be for a long while a great resource to us. For these lands, and, I say, especially the northern parts of America, suffered so terribly from the full force of the last days of civilisation, and became such horrible places to live in, that they are now very backward in all that makes life pleasant. Indeed, one may say that for nearly a hundred years the people of the northern parts of America have been engaged in gradually making a dwelling-place out of a stinking dust-heap; and there is still a great deal to do, especially as the country is so big."

"Well," said I, "I am exceedingly glad to think that you have such a prospect of happiness before you. But I should like to ask a few more questions, and then I have done for to-day."

16. DINNER IN THE HALL OF THE BLOOMSBURY MARKET

As I spoke, I heard footsteps near the door; the latch yielded, and in came our two lovers, looking so handsome that one had no feeling of shame in looking on at their little-concealed love-making; for indeed it seemed as if all the world must be in love with them. As for old Hammond, he looked on them like an artist who has just painted a picture nearly as well as he thought he could when he began it, and was perfectly happy. He said:

"Sit down, sit down, young folk, and don't make a noise. Our guest here has still some questions to ask me."

"Well, I should suppose so," said Dick; "you have only been three hours and a half together; and it isn't to be hoped that the history of two centuries could be told in three hours and a half: let alone that, for all I know, you may have been wandering into the realms of geography and craftsmanship."

"As to noise, my dear kinsman," said Clara, "you will very soon be disturbed by the noise of the dinner-bell, which I should think will be very pleasant music to our guest, who breakfasted early, it seems, and probably had a tiring day yesterday."

I said: "Well, since you have spoken the word, I begin to feel that it is so; but I have been feeding myself with wonder this long time past: really, it's quite true," quoth I, as I saw her smile, O so prettily! But just then from some tower high up in the air came the sound of silvery chimes playing a sweet clear tune, that sounded to my unaccustomed ears like the song of the first blackbird in the spring, and called a rush of memories to my mind, some of bad times, some of good, but all sweetened now into mere pleasure.

"No more questions now before dinner," said Clara; and she took my hand as an affectionate child would, and led me out of the room and down stairs into the forecourt of the Museum, leaving the two Hammonds to follow as they pleased.

We went into the market-place which I had been in before, a thinnish stream of elegantly[1] dressed people going in along with us. We turned into the cloister and came to a richly moulded and carved doorway, where a very pretty dark-haired young girl gave us each a beautiful bunch of summer flowers, and we entered a hall much bigger than that of the Hammersmith Guest House, more elaborate in its architecture and perhaps more beautiful. I found it difficult to keep my eyes off the wall-pictures (for I thought it bad manners to stare at Clara all the time, though she was quite worth it). I saw at a glance that their subjects were taken from queer old-world myths and imaginations which in yesterday's world only about half a dozen people in the country knew anything about; and when the two Hammonds sat down opposite to us, I said to the old man, pointing to the frieze:

"How strange to see such subjects here!"

"Why?" said he. "I don't see why you should be surprised; everybody knows the tales; and they are graceful and pleasant subjects, not too tragic for a place where people mostly eat and drink and amuse themselves, and yet full of incident."

I smiled, and said: "Well, I scarcely expected to find record of the Seven Swans and the King of the Golden Mountain and Faithful Henry, and such curious pleasant imaginations as Jacob Grimm got together from the childhood of the world, barely lingering even in his time: I should have thought you would have forgotten such childishness by this time."

The old man smiled, and said nothing; but Dick turned rather red, and broke out:

"What *do* you mean, guest? I think them very beautiful, I mean not only the pictures, but the stories; and when we were children we used to imagine them going on in every wood-end, by the bight of every stream: every house in the fields was the Fairyland King's House to us. Don't you remember, Clara?"

"Yes," she said; and it seemed to me as if a slight cloud came over her fair face. I was going to speak to her on the subject, when the pretty waitresses came to us smiling, and chattering sweetly like reed warblers by the river side, and fell to giving us our dinner. As to this, as at our breakfast, everything was cooked and served with a daintiness which showed that those who had prepared it were interested in it; but there was no excess either of quantity or of gourmandise; everything was simple, though so excellent of its kind; and it was made clear to us that this was no feast, only an ordinary meal. The glass, crockery, and plate were very beautiful to my eyes, used to the study of mediæval art; but a nineteenth-century club-haunter would, I daresay, have found them rough and lacking in finish; the crockery being lead-glazed pot-ware, though beautifully ornamented; the only porcelain being here and there a piece of old oriental ware. The glass, again, though elegant and quaint, and very varied in form, was somewhat bubbled and hornier in texture than the commercial articles of the nineteenth century. The furniture and general fittings of the hall were much of a piece with the table-gear, beautiful in form and highly ornamented, but without the commercial "finish" of the joiners and cabinet-makers of our time. Withal, there was a total absence of what the nineteenth century calls "comfort"—that is, stuffy inconvenience; so that, even apart from the delightful excitement of the day, I had never eaten my dinner so pleasantly before.

When we had done eating, and were sitting a little while, with a bottle of very good Bordeaux wine before us, Clara came back to the question of the subject-matter of the pictures, as though it had troubled her.

She looked up at them, and said: "How is it that though we are so interested with our life for the most part, yet when people take to writing poems or painting pictures they seldom deal with our modern life, or if they do, take good care to make their poems or pictures unlike that life? Are we not good enough to paint ourselves? How is it that we find the dreadful times of the past so interesting to us—in pictures and poetry?"

Old Hammond smiled. "It always was so, and I suppose always will be," said he, "however it may be explained. It is true that in the nineteenth century, when there was so little art and so much talk about it, there was a theory that art and imaginative literature ought to deal with contemporary life; but they never did so; for, if there was any pretence of it, the author always took care (as Clara hinted just now) to disguise, or exaggerate, or idealise, and in some way or another make it strange; so that, for all the verisimilitude there was, he might just as well have dealt with the times of the Pharaohs."

"Well," said Dick, "surely it is but natural to like these things strange; just as when we were children, as I said just now, we used to pretend to be so-and-so in such-and-such a place. That's what these pictures and poems do; and why shouldn't they?"

"Thou hast hit it, Dick," quoth old Hammond; "it is the child-like part of us that produces works of imagination. When we are children time passes so slow with us that we seem to have time for everything."

He sighed, and then smiled and said: "At least let us rejoice that we have got back our childhood again. I drink to the days that are!"

"Second childhood," said I in a low voice, and then blushed at my double rudeness, and hoped that he hadn't heard. But he had, and turned to me smiling, and said: "Yes, why not? And for my part, I hope it may last long; and that the world's next period of wise and unhappy manhood, if that should happen, will speedily lead us to a third childhood: if indeed this age be not our third. Meantime, my friend, you must know that we are too happy, both individually and collectively, to trouble ourselves about what is to come hereafter."

"Well, for my part," said Clara, "I wish we were interesting enough to be written or painted about."

Dick answered her with some lover's speech, impossible to be written down, and then we sat quiet a little.

17. HOW THE CHANGE CAME

Dick broke the silence at last, saying: "Guest, forgive us for a little after-dinner dulness. What would you like to do? Shall we have out Greylocks and trot back to Hammersmith? or will you come with us and hear some Welsh folk sing in a hall close by here? or would you like presently to come with me into the City and see some really fine building? or—what shall it be?"

"Well," said I, "as I am a stranger, I must let you choose for me."

In point of fact, I did not by any means want to be 'amused' just then; and also I rather felt as if the old man, with his knowledge of past times, and even a kind of inverted sympathy for them caused by his active hatred of them, was as it were a blanket for me against the cold of this very new world, where I was, so to say, stripped bare of every habitual thought and way of acting; and I did not want to leave him too soon. He came to my rescue at once, and said—

"Wait a bit, Dick; there is someone else to be consulted besides you and the guest here, and that is I. I am not going to lose the pleasure of his company just now, especially as I know he has something else to ask me. So go to your Welshmen, by all means; but first of all bring us another bottle of wine to this nook, and then be off as soon as you like; and come again and fetch our friend to go westward, but not too soon."

Dick nodded smilingly, and the old man and I were soon alone in the great hall, the afternoon sun gleaming on the red wine in our tall quaint-shaped glasses. Then said Hammond:

"Does anything especially puzzle you about our way of living, now you have heard a good deal and seen a little of it?"

Said I: "I think what puzzles me most is how it all came about."

"It well may," said he, "so great as the change is. It would be difficult indeed to tell you the whole story, perhaps impossible: knowledge, discontent, treachery, disappointment, ruin, misery, despair—those who worked for the change because they could see further than other people went through all these phases of suffering; and doubtless all the time the most of men looked on, not knowing what was doing, thinking it all a matter of course, like the rising and setting of the sun—and indeed it was so."

"Tell me one thing, if you can," said I. "Did the change, the 'revolution' it used to be called, come peacefully?"

"Peacefully?" said he; "what peace was there amongst those poor confused wretches of the nineteenth century? It was war from beginning to end: bitter war, till hope and pleasure put an end to it."

"Do you mean actual fighting with weapons?" said I, "or the strikes and lockouts and starvation of which we have heard?"

"Both, both," he said. "As a matter of fact, the history of the terrible period of transition from commercial slavery to freedom may thus be summarised.

When the hope of realising a communal condition of life for all men arose, quite late in the nineteenth century, the power of the middle classes, the then tyrants of society, was so enormous and crushing, that to almost all men, even those who had, you may say despite themselves, despite their reason and judgment, conceived such hopes, it seemed a dream. So much was this the case that some of those more enlightened men who were then called Socialists, although they well knew, and even stated in public, that the only reasonable condition of Society was that of pure Communism (such as you now see around you), yet shrunk from what seemed to them the barren task of preaching the realisation of a happy dream. Looking back now, we can see that the great motive-power of the change was a longing for freedom and equality, akin if you please to the unreasonable passion of the lover; a sickness of heart that rejected with loathing the aimless solitary life of the well-to-do educated man of that time: phrases, my dear friend, which have lost their meaning to us of the present day; so far removed we are from the dreadful facts which they represent.

"Well, these men, though conscious of this feeling, had no faith in it, as a means of bringing about the change. Nor was that wonderful: for looking around them they saw the huge mass of the oppressed classes too much burdened with the misery of their lives, and too much overwhelmed by the selfishness of misery, to be able to form a conception of any escape from it except by the ordinary way prescribed by the system of slavery under which they lived; which was nothing more than a remote chance of climbing out of the oppressed into the oppressing class.

"Therefore, though they knew that the only reasonable aim for those who would better the world was a condition of equality; in their impatience and despair they managed to convince themselves that if they could by hook or by crook get the machinery of production and the management of property so altered that the 'lower classes' (so the horrible word ran) might have their slavery somewhat ameliorated, they would be ready to fit into this machinery, and would use it for bettering their condition still more and still more, until at last the result would be a practical equality (they were very fond of using the word 'practical'), because 'the rich' would be forced to pay so much for keeping 'the poor' in a tolerable condition that the condition of riches would become no longer valuable and would gradually die out. Do you follow me?"

"Partly," said I. "Go on."

Said old Hammond: "Well, since you follow me, you will see that as a theory this was not altogether unreasonable; but 'practically,' it turned out a failure."

"How so?" said I.

"Well, don't you see," said he, "because it involved the making of a machinery by those who didn't know what they wanted the machines to do. So far as the masses of the oppressed class furthered this scheme of improvement, they did it to get themselves improved slave-rations—as many of them as could.

And if those classes had really been incapable of being touched by that instinct which produced the passion for freedom and equality aforesaid, what would have happened, I think, would have been this: that a certain part of the working classes would have been so far improved in condition that they would have approached the condition of the middling rich men; but below them would have been a great class of most miserable slaves, whose slavery would have been far more hopeless than the older class-slavery had been."

"What stood in the way of this?" said I.

"Why, of course," said he, "just that instinct for freedom aforesaid. It is true that the slave-class could not conceive the happiness of a free life. Yet they grew to understand (and very speedily too) that they were oppressed by their masters, and they assumed, you see how justly, that they could do without them, though perhaps they scarce knew how; so that it came to this, that though they could not look forward to the happiness or peace of the freeman, they did at least look forward to the war which a vague hope told them would bring that peace about."

"Could you tell me rather more closely what actually took place?" said I; for I thought *him* rather vague here.

"Yes," he said, "I can. That machinery of life for the use of people who didn't know what they wanted of it, and which was known at the time as State Socialism, was partly put in motion, though in a very piecemeal way. But it did not work smoothly; it was, of course, resisted at every turn by the capitalists; and no wonder, for it tended more and more to upset the commercial system I have told you of; without providing anything really effective in its place. The result was growing confusion, great suffering amongst the working classes, and, as a consequence, great discontent. For a long time matters went on like this. The power of the upper classes had lessened, as their command over wealth lessened, and they could not carry things wholly by the high hand as they had been used to in earlier days. So far the State Socialists were justified by the result. On the other hand, the working classes were ill-organised, and growing poorer in reality, in spite of the gains (also real in the long run) which they had forced from the masters. Thus matters hung in the balance; the masters could not reduce their slaves to complete subjection, though they put down some feeble and partial riots easily enough. The workers forced their masters to grant them ameliorations, real or imaginary, of their condition, but could not force freedom from them. At last came a great crash. To explain this you must understand that very great progress had been made amongst the workers, though as before said but little in the direction of improved livelihood."

I played the innocent and said: "In what direction could they improve, if not in livelihood?"

Said he: "In the power to bring about a state of things in which livelihood would be full, and easy to gain. They had at last learned how to combine after a long period of mistakes and disasters. The workmen had now a regular organization in the struggle against their masters, a struggle which for more than half a century had been accepted as an inevitable part of the conditions of the modern system of labour and production. This combination had now taken the form of a federation of all or almost all the recognised wage-paid employments, and it was by its means that those betterments of the conditions of the workmen had been forced from the masters: and though they were not seldom mixed up with the rioting that happened, especially in the earlier days of their organization, it by no means formed an essential part of their tactics; indeed at the time I am now speaking of they had got to be so strong that most commonly the mere threat of a 'strike' was enough to gain any minor point: because they had given up the foolish tactics of the ancient trades unions of calling out of work a part only of the workers of such and such an industry, and supporting them while out of work on the labour of those that remained in. By this time they had a biggish fund of money for the support of strikes, and could stop a certain industry altogether for a time if they so determined."

Said I: "Was there not a serious danger of such moneys being misused—of jobbery, in fact?"

Old Hammond wriggled uneasily on his seat, and said:

"Though all this happened so long ago, I still feel the pain of mere shame when I have to tell you that it was more than a danger: that such rascality often happened; indeed more than once the whole combination seemed dropping to pieces because of it: but at the time of which I am telling, things looked so threatening, and to the workmen at least the necessity of their dealing with the fast-gathering trouble which the labour-struggle had brought about, was so clear, that the conditions of the times had begot a deep seriousness amongst all reasonable people; a determination which put aside all non-essentials, and which to thinking men was ominous of the swiftly-approaching change: such an element was too dangerous for mere traitors and self-seekers, and one by one they were thrust out and mostly joined the declared reactionaries."

"How about those ameliorations," said I; "what were they? or rather of what nature?"

Said he: "Some of them, and these of the most practical importance to the mens' livelihood, were yielded by the masters by direct compulsion on the part of the men; the new conditions of labour so gained were indeed only customary, enforced by no law: but, once established, the masters durst not attempt to withdraw them in face of the growing power of the combined workers. Some again were steps on the path of 'State Socialism'; the most important of which can be speedily summed up. At the end of the nineteenth century the cry arose for compelling the masters to employ their men a less number of hours in the day: this cry gathered volume quickly, and the masters had to yield to it. But it was, of course, clear that unless this meant a higher price for work per hour, it would be a mere nullity, and that the masters, unless forced, would reduce it to that. Therefore after a long struggle another law was passed fixing a minimum price for labour in the most important industries; which again had to be supplemented by a law fixing the maximum price on the chief wares then considered necessary for a workman's life."

"You were getting perilously near to the late Roman poor-rates," said I, smiling, "and the doling out of bread to the proletariat."

"So many said at the time," said the old man drily; "and it has long been a commonplace that that slough awaits State Socialism in the end, if it gets to the end, which as you know it did not with us. However it went further than this minimum and maximum business, which by the by we can now see was necessary. The government now found it imperative on them to meet the outcry of the master class at the approaching destruction of Commerce (as desirable, had they known it, as the extinction of the cholera, which has since happily taken place). And they were forced to meet it by a measure hostile to the masters, the establishment of government factories for the production of necessary wares, and markets for their sale. These measures taken altogether did do something: they were in fact of the nature of regulations made by the commander of a beleaguered city. But of course to the privileged classes it seemed as if the end of the world were come when such laws were enacted.

"Nor was that altogether without a warrant: the spread of communistic theories, and the partial practice of State Socialism had at first disturbed, and at last almost paralysed the marvellous system of commerce under which the old world had lived so feverishly, and had produced for some few a life of gambler's pleasure, and for many, or most, a life of mere misery: over and over again came 'bad times' as they were called, and indeed they were bad enough for the wage-slaves. The year 1952 was one of the worst of these times; the workmen suffered dreadfully: the partial, inefficient government factories, which were terribly jobbed, all but broke down, and a vast part of the population had for the time being to be fed on undisguised "charity" as it was called.

"The Combined Workers watched the situation with mingled hope and anxiety. They had already formulated their general demands; but now by a solemn and universal vote of the whole of their federated societies, they insisted on the first step being taken toward carrying out their demands: this step would have led directly to handing over the management of the whole natural resources of the country, together with the machinery for using them into the power of the Combined Workers, and the reduction of the privileged classes into the position of pensioners obviously dependent on the pleasure of the workers. The 'Resolution,' as it was called, which was widely published in the newspapers of the day, was in fact a declaration of war, and was so accepted by the master class. They began henceforward to prepare for a firm stand against the 'brutal and ferocious communism of the day,' as they phrased it. And as they were in many ways still very powerful, or seemed so to be; they still hoped by means of brute force to regain some of what they had lost, and perhaps in the end the whole of it. It was said amongst them on all hands that it had been a great mistake of the various governments not to have resisted sooner; and the liberals and radicals (the name as perhaps you may know of the more democratically inclined part of the ruling classes) were much blamed for having led the world to this pass by their mis-timed pedantry and foolish sentimentality: and one Gladstone, or Gledstein (probably, judging by this name, of Scandinavian descent), a notable politician of the nineteenth century, was especially singled out for reprobation in this respect. I need scarcely point out to you the absurdity of all this. But terrible tragedy lay hidden behind this grinning through a horse-collar of the reactionary party. 'The insatiable greed of the lower classes must be repressed'—'The people must be taught a lesson'—these were the sacramental phrases current amongst the reactionists, and ominous enough they were."

The old man stopped to look keenly at my attentive and wondering face; and then said:

"I know, dear guest, that I have been using words and phrases which few people amongst us could understand without long and laborious explanation; and not even then perhaps. But since you have not yet gone to sleep, and since I am speaking to you as to a being from another planet, I may venture to ask you if you have followed me thus far?"

"O yes," said I, "I quite understand: pray go on; a great deal of what you have been saying was common place with us—when—when—"

"Yes," said he gravely, "when you were dwelling in the other planet. Well, now for the crash aforesaid.

"On some comparatively trifling occasion a great meeting was summoned by the workmen leaders to meet in Trafalgar Square (about the right to meet in which place there had for years and years been bickering). The civic bourgeois guard (called the police) attacked the said meeting with bludgeons, according to their custom; many people were hurt in the *mêlée*, of whom five in all died, either trampled to death on the spot, or from the effects of their cudgelling; the meeting was scattered, and some hundred of prisoners cast into gaol. A similar meeting had been treated in the same way a few days before at a place called Manchester, which has now disappeared. Thus the 'lesson' began. The whole country was thrown into a ferment by this; meetings were held which attempted some rough organisation for the holding of another meeting to retort on the authorities. A huge crowd assembled in Trafalgar Square and the neighbourhood (then a place of crowded streets), and was too big for the bludgeon-armed police to cope with; there was a good deal of dry-blow fighting; three or four of the people were killed, and half a score of policemen were crushed to death in the throng, and the rest got away as they could. This was a victory for the people as far as it went. The next day all London (remember what it was in those days) was in a state of turmoil. Many of the rich fled into the country; the executive got together soldiery, but did not dare to use them; and the police could not be massed in any one place, because riots or threats of riots were everywhere. But in Manchester, where the people were not so courageous or not so desperate as in London, several of the popular leaders were arrested. In London a convention of leaders was got together from the Federation of Combined Workmen, and sat under the old revolutionary name of the Committee of Public Safety; but as they had no drilled and armed body of men to direct, they attempted no aggressive measures, but only placarded the walls with somewhat vague appeals to the workmen not to allow themselves to be trampled upon. However, they called a meeting in Trafalgar Square for the day fortnight of the last-mentioned skirmish.

"Meantime the town grew no quieter, and business came pretty much to an end. The newspapers—then, as always hitherto, almost entirely in the hands of the masters—clamoured to the Government for repressive measures; the rich citizens were enrolled as an extra body of police, and armed with bludgeons like them; many of these were strong, well-fed, full-blooded young men, and had plenty of stomach for fighting; but the Government did not dare to use them, and contented itself with getting full powers voted to it by the Parliament for suppressing any revolt, and bringing up more and more soldiers to London. Thus passed the week after the great meeting; almost as large a one was held on the Sunday, which went off peaceably on the whole, as no opposition to it was offered, and again the people cried 'victory.' But on the Monday the people woke up to find that they were hungry. During the last few days there had been groups of men parading the streets asking (or, if you please, demanding) money to buy food; and what for goodwill, what for fear, the richer people gave them a good deal. The authorities of the parishes also (I haven't time to explain that phrase at present) gave willy-nilly what provisions they could to wandering people; and the Government, by means of its feeble national workshops, also fed a good number of half-starved folk. But in addition to this, several bakers' shops and other provision stores had been emptied without a great deal of disturbance. So far, so good. But on the Monday in question the Committee of Public Safety, on the one hand afraid of general unorganised pillage, and on the other emboldened by the wavering conduct of the authorities, sent a deputation provided with carts and all necessary gear to clear out two or three big provision stores in the centre of the town, leaving papers with the shop managers promising to pay the price of them: and also in the part of the town where they were strongest they took possession of several bakers' shops and set men at work in them for the benefit of the people;—all of which was done with little or no disturbance, the police assisting in keeping order at the sack of the stores, as they would have done at a big fire.

"But at this last stroke the reactionaries were so alarmed, that they were, determined to force the executive into action. The newspapers next day all blazed into the fury of frightened people, and threatened the people, the Government, and everybody they could think of, unless 'order were at once restored.' A deputation of leading commercial people waited on the Government and told them that if they did not at once arrest the Committee of Public Safety, they themselves would gather a body of men, arm them, and fall on 'the incendiaries,' as they called them.

"They, together with a number of the newspaper editors, had a long interview with the heads of the Government and two or three military men, the deftest in their art that the country could furnish. The deputation came away from that interview, says a contemporary eye-witness, smiling and satisfied, and said no more about raising an anti-popular army, but that afternoon left London with their families for their country seats or elsewhere.

"The next morning the Government proclaimed a state of siege in London, —a thing common enough amongst the absolutist governments on the Continent, but unheard-of in England in those days. They appointed the youngest and cleverest of their generals to command the proclaimed district; a man who had won a certain sort of reputation in the disgraceful wars in which the country had been long engaged from time to time. The newspapers were in ecstacies, and all the most fervent of the reactionaries now came to the front; men who in ordinary times were forced to keep their opinions to themselves or their immediate circle, but who began to look forward to crushing once for all the Socialist, and even democratic tendencies, which, said they, had been treated with such foolish indulgence for the last sixty years.

"But the clever general took no visible action; and yet only a few of the minor newspapers abused him; thoughtful men gathered from this that a plot was hatching. As for the Committee of Public Safety, whatever they thought of their position, they had now gone too far to draw back; and many of them, it seems, thought that the government would not act. They went on quietly organising their food supply, which was a miserable driblet when all is said; and also as a retort to the state of siege, they armed as many men as they could in the quarter where they were strongest, but did not attempt to drill or organise them, thinking, perhaps, that they could not at the best turn them into trained soldiers till they had some breathing space. The clever general, his soldiers, and the police did not meddle with all this in the least in the world; and things were quieter in London that week-end; though there were riots in many places of the provinces, which were quelled by the authorities without much trouble. The most serious of these were at Glasgow and Bristol.

"Well, the Sunday of the meeting came, and great crowds came to Trafalgar Square in procession, the greater part of the Committee amongst them, surrounded by their band of men armed somehow or other. The streets were quite peaceful and quiet, though there were many spectators to see the procession pass. Trafalgar Square had no body of police in it; the people took quiet possession of it, and the meeting began. The armed men stood round the principal platform, and there were a few others armed amidst the general crowd; but by far the greater part were unarmed.

"Most people thought the meeting would go off peaceably; but the members of the Committee had heard from various quarters that something would be attempted against them; but these rumours were vague, and they had no idea of what threatened. They soon found out.

"For before the streets about the Square were filled, a body of soldiers poured into it from the north-west corner and took up their places by the houses that stood on the west side. The people growled at the sight of the red-coats; the armed men of the Committee stood undecided, not knowing what to do; and indeed this new influx so jammed the crowd together that, unorganised as they were, they had little chance of working through it. They had scarcely grasped the fact of their enemies being there, when another column of soldiers, pouring out of the streets which led into the great southern road going down to the Parliament House (still existing, and called the Dung Market), and also from the embankment by the side of the Thames, marched up, pushing the crowd into a denser and denser mass, and formed along the south side of the Square. Then any of those who could see what was going on, knew at once that they were in a trap, and could only wonder what would be done with them.

"The closely-packed crowd would not or could not budge, except under the influence of the height of terror, which was soon to be supplied to them. A few of the armed men struggled to the front, or climbed up to the base of the monument which then stood there, that they might face the wall of hidden fire before them; and to most men (there were many women amongst them) it seemed as if the end of the world had come, and to-day seemed strangely different from yesterday. No sooner were the soldiers drawn up aforesaid than, says an eye-witness, 'a glittering officer on horseback came prancing out from the ranks on the south, and read something from a paper which he held in his hand; which something, very few heard; but I was told afterwards that it was an order for us to disperse, and a warning that he had legal right to fire on the crowd else, and that he would do so. The crowd took it as a challenge of some sort, and a hoarse threatening roar went up from them; and after that there was comparative silence for a little, till the officer had got back into the ranks. I was near the edge of the crowd, towards the soldiers,' says this eye-witness, 'and I saw three little machines being wheeled out in front of the ranks, which I knew for mechanical guns. I cried out, "Throw yourselves down! they are going to fire!" But no one scarcely could throw himself down, so tight as the crowd were packed. I heard a sharp order given, and wondered where I should be the next minute; and then—It was as if the earth had opened, and hell had come up bodily amidst us. It is no use trying to describe the scene that followed. Deep lanes were mowed amidst the thick crowd; the dead and dying covered the ground, and the shrieks and wails and cries of horror filled all the air, till it seemed as if there were nothing else in the world but murder and death. Those of our armed men who were still unhurt cheered wildly and opened a scattering fire on the soldiers. One or two soldiers fell; and I saw the officers going up and down the ranks urging the men to fire again; but they received the orders in sullen silence, and let the butts of their guns fall. Only one sergeant ran to a machine-gun and began to set it going; but a tall young man, an officer too, ran out of the ranks and dragged him back by the collar; and the soldiers stood there motionless while the horror-stricken crowd, nearly wholly unarmed (for most of the armed men had fallen in that first discharge), drifted out of the Square. I was told afterwards that the soldiers on the west side had fired also, and done their part of the slaughter. How I got out of the Square I scarcely know: I went, not feeling the ground under me, what with rage and terror and despair.'

"So says our eye-witness. The number of the slain on the side of the people in that shooting during a minute was prodigious; but it was not easy to come at the truth about it; it was probably between one and two thousand. Of the soldiers, six were killed outright, and a dozen wounded."

I listened, trembling with excitement. The old man's eyes glittered and his face flushed as he spoke, and told the tale of what I had often thought might happen. Yet I wondered that he should have got so elated about a mere massacre, and I said:

"How fearful! And I suppose that this massacre put an end to the whole revolution for that time?"

"No, no," cried old Hammond; "it began it!"

He filled his glass and mine, and stood up and cried out, "Drink this glass to the memory of those who died there, for indeed it would be a long tale to tell how much we owe them."

I drank, and he sat down again and went on.

"That massacre of Trafalgar Square began the civil war, though, like all such events, it gathered head slowly, and people scarcely knew what a crisis they were acting in.

"Terrible as the massacre was, and hideous and overpowering as the first terror had been, when the people had time to think about it, their feeling was one of anger rather than fear; although the military organisation of the state of siege was now carried out without shrinking by the clever young general. For though the ruling-classes when the news spread next morning felt one gasp of horror and even dread, yet the Government and their immediate backers felt that now the wine was drawn and must be drunk. However, even the most reactionary of the capitalist papers, with two exceptions, stunned by the tremendous news, simply gave an account of what had taken place, without making any comment upon it. The exceptions were one, a so-called 'liberal' paper (the Government of the day was of that complexion), which, after a preamble in which it declared its undeviating sympathy with the cause of labour, proceeded to point out that in times of revolutionary disturbance it behoved the Government to be just but firm, and that by far the most merciful way of dealing with the poor madmen who were attacking the very foundations of society (which had made them mad and poor) was to shoot them at once, so as to stop others from drifting into a position in which they would run a chance of being shot. In short, it praised the determined action of the Government as the acme of human wisdom and mercy, and exulted in the inauguration of an epoch of reasonable democracy free from the tyrannical fads of Socialism.

"The other exception was a paper thought to be one of the most violent opponents of democracy, and so it was; but the editor of it found his manhood, and spoke for himself and not for his paper. In a few simple, indignant words he asked people to consider what a society was worth which had to be defended by the massacre of unarmed citizens, and called on the Government to withdraw their state of siege and put the general and his officers who fired on the people on their trial for murder. He went further, and declared that whatever his opinion might be as to the doctrines of the Socialists, he for one should throw in his lot with the people, until the Government atoned for their atrocity by showing that they were prepared to listen to the demands of men who knew what they wanted, and whom the decrepitude of society forced into pushing their demands in some way or other.

"Of course, this editor was immediately arrested by the military power; but his bold words were already in the hands of the public, and produced a great effect: so great an effect that the Government, after some vacillation, withdrew the state of siege; though at the same time it strengthened the military organisation and made it more stringent. Three of the Committee of Public Safety had been slain in Trafalgar Square: of the rest the greater part went back to their old place of meeting, and there awaited the event calmly. They were arrested there on the Monday morning, and would have been shot at once by the general, who was a mere military machine, if the Government had not shrunk before the responsibility of killing men without any trial. There was at first a talk of trying them by a special commission of judges, as it was called—*i.e.*, before a set of men bound to find them guilty, and whose business it was to do so. But with the Government the cold fit had succeeded to the hot one; and the prisoners were brought before a jury at the assizes. There a fresh blow awaited the Government; for in spite of the judge's charge, which distinctly instructed the jury to find the prisoners guilty, they were acquitted, and the jury added to their verdict a presentment, in which they condemned the action of the soldiery, in the queer phraseology of the day, as 'rash, unfortunate, and unnecessary.' The Committee of Public Safety renewed its sittings, and from thenceforth was a popular rallying-point in opposition to the Parliament. The Government now gave way on all sides, and made a show of yielding to the demands of the people, though there was a widespread plot for effecting a coup d'état set on foot between the leaders of the two so-called opposing parties in the parliamentary faction fight. The well-meaning part of the public was overjoyed, and thought that all danger of a civil war was over. The victory of the people was celebrated by huge meetings held in the parks and elsewhere, in memory of the victims of the great massacre.

"But the measures passed for the relief of the workers, though to the upper classes they seemed ruinously revolutionary, were not thorough enough to give the people food and a decent life, and they had to be supplemented by unwritten enactments without legality to back them. Although the Government and Parliament had the law-courts, the army, and 'society' at their backs, the Committee of Public Safety began to be a force in the country, and really represented the producing classes. It began to improve immensely in the days which followed on the acquittal of its members. Its old members had little administrative capacity, though with the exception of a few self-seekers and traitors, they were honest, courageous men, and many of them were endowed with considerable talent of other kinds. But now that the times called for immediate action, came forward the men capable of setting it on foot; and a new network of workmen's associations grew up very speedily, whose avowed single object was the tiding over of the ship of the community into a simple condition of Communism; and as they practically undertook also the management of the ordinary labour-war, they soon became the mouthpiece and intermediary of the whole of the working classes; and the manufacturing profit-grinders now found themselves powerless before this combination; unless *their* committee, Parliament, plucked up courage to begin the civil war again, and to shoot right and left, they were bound to yield to the demands of the men whom they employed, and pay higher and higher wages for shorter and shorter day's work. Yet one ally they had, and that was the rapidly approaching breakdown of the whole system founded on the World-Market and its supply; which now became so clear to all people, that the middle classes, shocked for the moment into condemnation of the Government for the great massacre, turned round nearly in a mass, and called on the Government to look to matters, and put an end to the tyranny of the Socialist leaders.

"Thus stimulated, the reactionist plot exploded probably before it was ripe; but this time the people and their leaders were forewarned, and, before the reactionaries could get under way, had taken the steps they thought necessary.

"The Liberal Government (clearly by collusion) was beaten by the Conservatives, though the latter were nominally much in the minority. The popular representatives in the House understood pretty well what this meant, and after an attempt to fight the matter out by divisions in the House of Commons, they made a protest, left the House, and came in a body to the Committee of Public Safety: and the civil war began again in good earnest.

"Yet its first act was not one of mere fighting. The new Tory Government determined to act, yet durst not re-enact the state of siege, but it sent a body of soldiers and police to arrest the Committee of Public Safety in the lump. They made no resistance, though they might have done so, as they had now a considerable body of men who were quite prepared for extremities. But they were determined to try first a weapon which they thought stronger than street fighting.

"The members of the Committee went off quietly to prison; but they had left their soul and their organisation behind them. For they depended not on a carefully arranged centre with all kinds of checks and counter-checks about it, but on a huge mass of people in thorough sympathy with the movement, bound together by a great number of links of small centres with very simple instructions. These instructions were now carried out.

"The next morning, when the leaders of the reaction were chuckling at the effect which the report in the newspapers of their stroke would have upon the public—no newspapers appeared; and it was only towards noon that a few straggling sheets, about the size of the gazettes of the seventeenth century, worked by policemen, soldiers, managers, and press-writers, were dribbled through the streets. They were greedily seized on and read; but by this time the serious part of their news was stale, and people did not need to be told that the GENERAL STRIKE had begun. The railways did not run, the telegraph-wires were unserved; flesh, fish, and green stuff brought to market was allowed to lie there still packed and perishing; the thousands of middle-class families, who were utterly dependant for the next meal on the workers, made frantic efforts through their more energetic members to cater for the needs of the day, and amongst those of them who could throw off the fear of what was to follow, there was, I am told, a certain enjoyment of this unexpected picnic—a forecast of the days to come, in which all labour grew pleasant.

"So passed the first day, and towards evening the Government grew quite distracted. They had but one resource for putting down any popular movement—to wit, mere brute-force; but there was nothing for them against which to use their army and police: no armed bodies appeared in the streets; the offices of the Federated Workmen were now, in appearance, at least, turned into places for the relief of people thrown out of work, and under the circumstances, they durst not arrest the men engaged in such business, all the more, as even that night many quite respectable people applied at these offices for relief, and swallowed down the charity of the revolutionists along with their supper. So the Government massed soldiers and police here and there—and sat still for that night, fully expecting on the morrow some manifesto from 'the rebels,' as they now began to be called, which would give them an opportunity of acting in some way or another. They were disappointed. The ordinary newspapers gave up the struggle that morning, and only one very violent reactionary paper (called the *Daily Telegraph*) attempted an appearance, and rated 'the rebels' in good set terms for their folly and ingratitude in tearing out the bowels of their 'common mother,' the English Nation, for the benefit of a few greedy paid agitators, and the fools whom they were deluding. On the other hand, the Socialist papers (of which three only, representing somewhat different schools, were published in London) came out full to the throat of well-printed matter. They were greedily bought by the whole public, who, of course, like the Government, expected a manifesto in them. But they found no word of reference to the great subject. It seemed as if their editors had ransacked their drawers for articles which would have been in place forty years before, under the technical name of educational articles. Most of these were admirable and straightforward expositions of the doctrines and practice of Socialism, free from haste and spite and hard words, and came upon the public with a kind of May-day freshness, amidst the worry and terror of the moment; and though the knowing well understood that the meaning of this move in the game was mere defiance, and a token of irreconcilable hostility to the then rulers of society, and though, also, they were meant for nothing else by 'the rebels,' yet they really had their effect as 'educational articles.' However, 'education' of another kind was acting upon the public with irresistible power, and probably cleared their heads a little.

"As to the Government, they were absolutely terrified by this act of 'boycotting' (the slang word then current for such acts of abstention). Their counsels became wild and vacillating to the last degree: one hour they were for giving way for the present till they could hatch another plot; the next they all but sent an order for the arrest in the lump of all the workmen's committees; the next they were on the point of ordering their brisk young general to take any excuse that offered for another massacre. But when they called to mind that the soldiery in that 'Battle' of Trafalgar Square were so daunted by the slaughter which they had made, that they could not be got to fire a second volley, they shrank back again from the dreadful courage necessary for carrying out another massacre. Meantime the prisoners, brought the second time before the magistrates under a strong escort of soldiers, were the second time remanded.

"The strike went on this day also. The workmen's committees were extended, and gave relief to great numbers of people, for they had organised a considerable amount of production of food by men whom they could depend upon. Quite a number of well-to-do people were now compelled to seek relief of them. But another curious thing happened: a band of young men of the upper classes armed themselves, and coolly went marauding in the streets, taking what suited them of such eatables and portables that they came across in the shops which had ventured to open. This operation they carried out in Oxford Street, then a great street of shops of all kinds. The Government, being at that hour in one of their yielding moods, thought this a fine opportunity for showing their impartiality in the maintenance of 'order,' and sent to arrest these hungry rich youths; who, however, surprised the police by a valiant resistance, so that all but three escaped. The Government did not gain the reputation for impartiality which they expected from this move; for they forgot that there were no evening papers; and the account of the skirmish spread wide indeed, but in a distorted form for it was mostly told simply as an exploit of the starving people from the East-end; and everybody thought it was but natural for the Government to put them down when and where they could.

"That evening the rebel prisoners were visited in their cells by *very* polite and sympathetic persons, who pointed out to them what a suicidal course they were following, and how dangerous these extreme courses were for the popular cause. Says one of the prisoners: 'It was great sport comparing notes when we came out anent the attempt of the Government to "get at" us separately in prison, and how we answered the blandishments of the highly "intelligent and refined" persons set on to pump us. One laughed; another told extravagant long-bow stories to the envoy; a third held a sulky silence; a fourth damned the polite spy and bade him hold his jaw—and that was all they got out of us.'

"So passed the second day of the great strike. It was clear to all thinking people that the third day would bring on the crisis; for the present suspense and ill-concealed terror was unendurable. The ruling classes, and the middle-class non-politicians who had been their real strength and support, were as sheep lacking a shepherd; they literally did not know what to do.

"One thing they found they had to do: try to get the 'rebels' to do something. So the next morning, the morning of the third day of the strike, when the members of the Committee of Public Safety appeared again before the magistrate, they found themselves treated with the greatest possible courtesy—in fact, rather as envoys and ambassadors than prisoners. In short, the magistrate had received his orders; and with no more to do than might come of a long stupid speech, which might have been written by Dickens in mockery, he discharged the prisoners, who went back to their meeting-place and at once began a due sitting. It was high time. For this third day the mass was fermenting indeed. There was, of course, a vast number of working people who were not organised in the least in the world; men who had been used to act as their masters drove them, or rather as the system drove, of which their masters were a part. That system was now falling to pieces, and the old pressure of the master having been taken off these poor men, it seemed likely that nothing but the mere animal necessities and passions of men would have any hold on them, and that mere general overturn would be the result. Doubtless this would have happened if it had not been that the huge mass had been leavened by Socialist opinion in the first place, and in the second by actual contact with declared Socialists, many or indeed most of whom were members of those bodies of workmen above said.

If anything of this kind had happened some years before, when the masters of labour were still looked upon as the natural rulers of the people, and even the poorest and most ignorant man leaned upon them for support, while they submitted to their fleecing, the entire break-up of all society would have followed. But the long series of years during which the workmen had learned to despise their rulers, had done away with their dependence upon them, and they were now beginning to trust (somewhat dangerously, as events proved) in the non-legal leaders whom events had thrust forward; and though most of these were now become mere figure-heads, their names and reputations were useful in this crisis as a stop-gap.

"The effect of the news, therefore, of the release of the Committee gave the Government some breathing time: for it was received with the greatest joy by the workers, and even the well-to-do saw in it a respite from the mere destruction which they had begun to dread, and the fear of which most of them attributed to the weakness of the Government. As far as the passing hour went, perhaps they were right in this."

"How do you mean?" said I. "What could the Government have done? I often used to think that they would be helpless in such a crisis."

Said old Hammond: "Of course I don't doubt that in the long run matters would have come about as they did. But if the Government could have treated their army as a real army, and used them strategically as a general would have done, looking on the people as a mere open enemy to be shot at and dispersed wherever they turned up, they would probably have gained the victory at the time."

"But would the soldiers have acted against the people in this way?" said I.

Said he: "I think from all I have heard that they would have done so if they had met bodies of men armed however badly, and however badly they had been organised. It seems also as if before the Trafalgar Square massacre they might as a whole have been depended upon to fire upon an unarmed crowd, though they were much honeycombed by Socialism. The reason for this was that they dreaded the use by apparently unarmed men of an explosive called dynamite, of which many loud boasts were made by the workers on the eve of these events; although it turned out to be of little use as a material for war in the way that was expected. Of course the officers of the soldiery fanned this fear to the utmost, so that the rank and file probably thought on that occasion that they were being led into a desperate battle with men who were really armed, and whose weapon was the more dreadful, because it was concealed. After that massacre, however, it was at all times doubtful if the regular soldiers would fire upon an unarmed or half-armed crowd."

Said I: "The regular soldiers? Then there were other combatants against the people?"

"Yes," said he, "we shall come to that presently."

"Certainly," I said, "you had better go on straight with your story. I see that time is wearing."

Said Hammond: "The Government lost no time in coming to terms with the Committee of Public Safety; for indeed they could think of nothing else than the danger of the moment. They sent a duly accredited envoy to treat with these men, who somehow had obtained dominion over people's minds, while the formal rulers had no hold except over their bodies. There is no need at present to go into the details of the truce (for such it was) between these high contracting parties, the Government of the empire of Great Britain and a handful of working-men (as they were called in scorn in those days), amongst whom, indeed, were some very capable and 'square-headed' persons, though, as aforesaid, the abler men were not then the recognised leaders. The upshot of it was that all the definite claims of the people had to be granted. We can now see that most of these claims were of themselves not worth either demanding or resisting; but they were looked on at that time as most important, and they were at least tokens of revolt against the miserable system of life which was then beginning to tumble to pieces. One claim, however, was of the utmost immediate importance, and this the Government tried hard to evade; but as they were not dealing with fools, they had to yield at last. This was the claim of recognition and formal status for the Committee of Public Safety, and all the associations which it fostered under its wing. This it is clear meant two things: first, amnesty for 'the rebels,' great and small, who, without a distinct act of civil war, could no longer be attacked; and next, a continuance of the organised revolution. Only one point the Government could gain, and that was a name. The dreadful revolutionary title was dropped, and the body, with its branches, acted under the respectable name of the 'Board of Conciliation and its local offices.' Carrying this name, it became the leader of the people in the civil war which soon followed."

"O," said I, somewhat startled, "so the civil war went on, in spite of all that had happened?"

"So it was," said he. "In fact, it was this very legal recognition which made the civil war possible in the ordinary sense of war; it took the struggle out of the element of mere massacres on one side, and endurance plus strikes on the other."

"And can you tell me in what kind of way the war was carried on?" said I.

"Yes" he said; "we have records and to spare of all that; and the essence of them I can give you in a few words. As I told you, the rank and file of the army was not to be trusted by the reactionists; but the officers generally were prepared for anything, for they were mostly the very stupidest men in the country. Whatever the Government might do, a great part of the upper and middle classes were determined to set on foot a counter revolution; for the Communism which now loomed ahead seemed quite unendurable to them. Bands of young men, like the marauders in the great strike of whom I told you just now, armed themselves and drilled, and began on any opportunity or pretence to skirmish with the people in the streets. The Government neither helped them nor put them down, but stood by, hoping that something might come of it. These 'Friends of Order,' as they were called, had some successes at first, and grew bolder; they got many officers of the regular army to help them, and by their means laid hold of munitions of war of all kinds. One part of their tactics consisted in their guarding and even garrisoning the big factories of the period: they held at one time, for instance, the whole of that place called Manchester which I spoke of just now. A sort of irregular war was carried on with varied success all over the country; and at last the Government, which at first pretended to ignore the struggle, or treat it as mere rioting, definitely declared for 'the Friends of Order,' and joined to their bands whatsoever of the regular army they could get together, and made a desperate effort to overwhelm 'the rebels,' as they were now once more called, and as indeed they called themselves.

"It was too late. All ideas of peace on a basis of compromise had disappeared on either side. The end, it was seen clearly, must be either absolute slavery for all but the privileged, or a system of life founded on equality and Communism. The sloth, the hopelessness, and if I may say so, the cowardice of the last century, had given place to the eager, restless heroism of a declared revolutionary period. I will not say that the people of that time foresaw the life we are leading now, but there was a general instinct amongst them towards the essential part of that life, and many men saw clearly beyond the desperate struggle of the day into the peace which it was to bring about. The men of that day who were on the side of freedom were not unhappy, I think, though they were harassed by hopes and fears, and sometimes torn by doubts, and the conflict of duties hard to reconcile."

"But how did the people, the revolutionists, carry on the war? What were the elements of success on their side?"

I put this question, because I wanted to bring the old man back to the definite history, and take him out of the musing mood so natural to an old man.

He answered: "Well, they did not lack organisers; for the very conflict itself, in days when, as I told you, men of any strength of mind cast away all consideration for the ordinary business of life, developed the necessary talent amongst them. Indeed, from all I have read and heard, I much doubt whether, without this seemingly dreadful civil war, the due talent for administration would have been developed amongst the working men. Anyhow, it was there, and they soon got leaders far more than equal to the best men amongst the reactionaries. For the rest, they had no difficulty about the material of their army; for that revolutionary instinct so acted on the ordinary soldier in the ranks that the greater part, certainly the best part, of the soldiers joined the side of the people. But the main element of their success was this, that wherever the working people were not coerced, they worked, not for the reactionists, but for 'the rebels.' The reactionists could get no work done for them outside the districts where they were all-powerful: and even in those districts they were harassed by continual risings; and in all cases and everywhere got nothing done without obstruction and black looks and sulkiness; so that not only were their armies quite worn out with the difficulties which they had to meet, but the non-combatants who were on their side were so worried and beset with hatred and a thousand little troubles and annoyances that life became almost unendurable to them on those terms. Not a few of them actually died of the worry; many committed suicide. Of course, a vast number of them joined actively in the cause of reaction, and found some solace to their misery in the eagerness of conflict. Lastly, many thousands gave way and submitted to 'the rebels'; and as the numbers of these latter increased, it at last became clear to all men that the cause which was once hopeless, was now triumphant, and that the hopeless cause was that of slavery and privilege."

18. THE BEGINNING OF THE NEW LIFE

"Well," said I, "so you got clear out of all your trouble. Were people satisfied with the new order of things when it came?"

"People?" he said. "Well, surely all must have been glad of peace when it came; especially when they found, as they must have found, that after all, they—even the once rich—were not living very badly. As to those who had been poor, all through the war, which lasted about two years, their condition had been bettering, in spite of the struggle; and when peace came at last, in a very short time they made great strides towards a decent life. The great difficulty was that the once-poor had such a feeble conception of the real pleasure of life: so to say, they did not ask enough, did not know how to ask enough, from the new state of things. It was perhaps rather a good than an evil thing that the necessity for restoring the wealth destroyed during the war forced them into working at first almost as hard as they had been used to before the Revolution. For all historians are agreed that there never was a war in which there was so much destruction of wares, and instruments for making them as in this civil war."

"I am rather surprised at that," said I.

"Are you? I don't see why," said Hammond.

"Why," I said, "because the party of order would surely look upon the wealth as their own property, no share of which, if they could help it, should go to their slaves, supposing they conquered. And on the other hand, it was just for the possession of that wealth that 'the rebels' were fighting, and I should have thought, especially when they saw that they were winning, that they would have been careful to destroy as little as possible of what was so soon to be their own."

"It was as I have told you, however," said he. "The party of order, when they recovered from their first cowardice of surprise—or, if you please, when they fairly saw that, whatever happened, they would be ruined, fought with great bitterness, and cared little what they did, so long as they injured the enemies who had destroyed the sweets of life for them. As to 'the rebels,' I have told you that the outbreak of actual war made them careless of trying to save the wretched scraps of wealth that they had. It was a common saying amongst them, Let the country be cleared of everything except valiant living men, rather than that we fall into slavery again!"

He sat silently thinking a little while, and then said:

"When the conflict was once really begun, it was seen how little of any value there was in the old world of slavery and inequality. Don't you see what it means? In the times which you are thinking of, and of which you seem to know so much, there was no hope; nothing but the dull jog of the mill-horse under compulsion of collar and whip; but in that fighting-time that followed, all was hope: 'the rebels' at least felt themselves strong enough to build up the world again from its dry bones,—and they did it, too!" said the old man, his eyes glittering under his beetling brows. He went on: "And their opponents at least and at last learned something about the reality of life, and its sorrows, which they—their class, I mean—had once known nothing of. In short, the two combatants, the workman and the gentleman, between them—"

"Between them," said I, quickly, "they destroyed commercialism!"

"Yes, yes, yes," said he; "that is it. Nor could it have been destroyed otherwise; except, perhaps, by the whole of society gradually falling into lower depths, till it should at last reach a condition as rude as barbarism, but lacking both the hope and the pleasures of barbarism. Surely the sharper, shorter remedy was the happiest."

"Most surely," said I.

"Yes," said the old man, "the world was being brought to its second birth; how could that take place without a tragedy? Moreover, think of it. The spirit of the new days, of our days, was to be delight in the life of the world; intense and overweening love of the very skin and surface of the earth on which man dwells, such as a lover has in the fair flesh of the woman he loves; this, I say, was to be the new spirit of the time. All other moods save this had been exhausted: the unceasing criticism, the boundless curiosity in the ways and thoughts of man, which was the mood of the ancient Greek, to whom these things were not so much a means, as an end, was gone past recovery; nor had there been really any shadow of it in the so-called science of the nineteenth century, which, as you must know, was in the main an appendage to the commercial system; nay, not seldom an appendage to the police of that system. In spite of appearances, it was limited and cowardly, because it did not really believe in itself. It was the outcome, as it was the sole relief, of the unhappiness of the period which made life so bitter even to the rich, and which, as you may see with your bodily eyes, the great change has swept away. More akin to our way of looking at life was the spirit of the Middle Ages, to whom heaven and the life of the next world was such a reality, that it became to them a part of the life upon the earth; which accordingly they loved and adorned, in spite of the ascetic doctrines of their formal creed, which bade them contemn it.

"But that also, with its assured belief in heaven and hell as two countries in which to live, has gone, and now we do, both in word and in deed, believe in the continuous life of the world of men, and as it were, add every day of that common life to the little stock of days which our own mere individual experience wins for us: and consequently we are happy. Do you wonder at it? In times past, indeed, men were told to love their kind, to believe in the religion of humanity, and so forth. But look you, just in the degree that a man had elevation of mind and refinement enough to be able to value this idea, was he repelled by the obvious aspect of the individuals composing the mass which he was to worship; and he could only evade that repulsion by making a conventional abstraction of mankind that had little actual or historical relation to the race; which to his eyes was divided into blind tyrants on the one hand and apathetic degraded slaves on the other. But now, where is the difficulty in accepting the religion of humanity, when the men and women who go to make up humanity are free, happy, and energetic at least, and most commonly beautiful of body also, and surrounded by beautiful things of their own fashioning, and a nature bettered and not worsened by contact with mankind? This is what this age of the world has reserved for us."

"It seems true," said I, "or ought to be, if what my eyes have seen is a token of the general life you lead. Can you now tell me anything of your progress after the years of the struggle?"

Said he: "I could easily tell you more than you have time to listen to; but I can at least hint at one of the chief difficulties which had to be met: and that was, that when men began to settle down after the war, and their labour had pretty much filled up the gap in wealth caused by the destruction of that war, a kind of disappointment seemed coming over us, and the prophecies of some of the reactionists of past times seemed as if they would come true, and a dull level of utilitarian comfort be the end for a while of our aspirations and success. The loss of the competitive spur to exertion had not, indeed, done anything to interfere with the necessary production of the community, but how if it should make men dull by giving them too much time for thought or idle musing? But, after all, this dull thunder-cloud only threatened us, and then passed over. Probably, from what I have told you before, you will have a guess at the remedy for such a disaster; remembering always that many of the things which used to be produced—slave-wares for the poor and mere wealth-wasting wares for the rich—ceased to be made. That remedy was, in short, the production of what used to be called art, but which has no name amongst us now, because it has become a necessary part of the labour of every man who produces."

Said I: "What! had men any time or opportunity for cultivating the fine arts amidst the desperate struggle for life and freedom that you have told me of?"

Said Hammond: "You must not suppose that the new form of art was founded chiefly on the memory of the art of the past; although, strange to say, the civil war was much less destructive of art than of other things, and though what of art existed under the old forms, revived in a wonderful way during the latter part of the struggle, especially as regards music and poetry. The art or work-pleasure, as one ought to call it, of which I am now speaking, sprung up almost spontaneously, it seems, from a kind of instinct amongst people, no longer driven desperately to painful and terrible over-work, to do the best they could with the work in hand—to make it excellent of its kind; and when that had gone on for a little, a craving for beauty seemed to awaken in men's minds, and they began rudely and awkwardly to ornament the wares which they made; and when they had once set to work at that, it soon began to grow. All this was much helped by the abolition of the squalor which our immediate ancestors put up with so coolly; and by the leisurely, but not stupid, country-life which now grew (as I told you before) to be common amongst us. Thus at last and by slow degrees we got pleasure into our work; then we became conscious of that pleasure, and cultivated it, and took care that we had our fill of it; and then all was gained, and we were happy. So may it be for ages and ages!"

The old man fell into a reverie, not altogether without melancholy I thought; but I would not break it. Suddenly he started, and said: "Well, dear guest, here are come Dick and Clara to fetch you away, and there is an end of my talk; which I daresay you will not be sorry for; the long day is coming to an end, and you will have a pleasant ride back to Hammersmith."

19. THE DRIVE BACK TO HAMMERSMITH

I said nothing, for I was not inclined for mere politeness to him after such very serious talk; but in fact I should liked to have gone on talking with the older man, who could understand something at least of my wonted ways of looking at life, whereas, with the younger people, in spite of all their kindness, I really was a being from another planet. However, I made the best of it, and smiled as amiably as I could on the young couple; and Dick returned the smile by saying, "Well, guest, I am glad to have you again, and to find that you and my kinsman have not quite talked yourselves into another world; I was half suspecting as I was listening to the Welshmen yonder that you would presently be vanishing away from us, and began to picture my kinsman sitting in the hall staring at nothing and finding that he had been talking a while past to nobody."

I felt rather uncomfortable at this speech, for suddenly the picture of the sordid squabble, the dirty and miserable tragedy of the life I had left for a while, came before my eyes; and I had, as it were, a vision of all my longings for rest and peace in the past, and I loathed the idea of going back to it again. But the old man chuckled and said:

"Don't be afraid, Dick. In any case, I have not been talking to thin air; nor, indeed to this new friend of ours only. Who knows but I may not have been talking to many people? For perhaps our guest may some day go back to the people he has come from, and may take a message from us which may bear fruit for them, and consequently for us."

Dick looked puzzled, and said: "Well, gaffer, I do not quite understand what you mean. All I can say is, that I hope he will not leave us: for don't you see, he is another kind of man to what we are used to, and somehow he makes us think of all kind of things; and already I feel as if I could understand Dickens the better for having talked with him."

"Yes," said Clara, "and I think in a few months we shall make him look younger; and I should like to see what he was like with the wrinkles smoothed out of his face. Don't you think he will look younger after a little time with us?"

The old man shook his head, and looked earnestly at me, but did not answer her, and for a moment or two we were all silent. Then Clara broke out:

"Kinsman, I don't like this: something or another troubles me, and I feel as if something untoward were going to happen. You have been talking of past miseries to the guest, and have been living in past unhappy times, and it is in the air all round us, and makes us feel as if we were longing for something that we cannot have."

The old man smiled on her kindly, and said: "Well, my child, if that be so, go and live in the present, and you will soon shake it off." Then he turned to me, and said: "Do you remember anything like that, guest, in the country from which you come?"

The lovers had turned aside now, and were talking together softly, and not heeding us; so I said, but in a low voice: "Yes, when I was a happy child on a sunny holiday, and had everything that I could think of."

"So it is," said he. "You remember just now you twitted me with living in the second childhood of the world. You will find it a happy world to live in; you will be happy there—for a while."

Again I did not like his scarcely veiled threat, and was beginning to trouble myself with trying to remember how I had got amongst this curious people, when the old man called out in a cheery voice: "Now, my children, take your guest away, and make much of him; for it is your business to make him sleek of skin and peaceful of mind: he has by no means been as lucky as you have. Farewell, guest!" and he grasped my hand warmly.

"Good-bye," said I, "and thank you very much for all that you have told me. I will come and see you as soon as I come back to London. May I?"

"Yes," he said, "come by all means—if you can."

"It won't be for some time yet," quoth Dick, in his cheery voice; "for when the hay is in up the river, I shall be for taking him a round through the country between hay and wheat harvest, to see how our friends live in the north country. Then in the wheat harvest we shall do a good stroke of work, I should hope,—in Wiltshire by preference; for he will be getting a little hard with all the open-air living, and I shall be as tough as nails."

"But you will take me along, won't you, Dick?" said Clara, laying her pretty hand on his shoulder.

"Will I not?" said Dick, somewhat boisterously. "And we will manage to send you to bed pretty tired every night; and you will look so beautiful with your neck all brown, and your hands too, and you under your gown as white as privet, that you will get some of those strange discontented whims out of your head, my dear. However, our week's haymaking will do all that for you."

The girl reddened very prettily, and not for shame but for pleasure; and the old man laughed, and said:

"Guest, I see that you will be as comfortable as need be; for you need not fear that those two will be too officious with you: they will be so busy with each other, that they will leave you a good deal to yourself, I am sure, and that is a real kindness to a guest, after all. O, you need not be afraid of being one too many, either: it is just what these birds in a nest like, to have a good convenient friend to turn to, so that they may relieve the ecstasies of love with the solid commonplace of friendship. Besides, Dick, and much more Clara, likes a little talking at times; and you know lovers do not talk unless they get into trouble, they only prattle. Good-bye, guest; may you be happy!"

Clara went up to old Hammond, threw her arms about his neck and kissed him heartily, and said:

"You are a dear old man, and may have your jest about me as much as you please; and it won't be long before we see you again; and you may be sure we shall make our guest happy; though, mind you, there is some truth in what you say."

Then I shook hands again, and we went out of the hall and into the cloisters, and so in the street found Greylocks in the shafts waiting for us. He was well looked after; for a little lad of about seven years old had his hand on the rein and was solemnly looking up into his face; on his back, withal, was a girl of fourteen, holding a three-year old sister on before her; while another girl, about a year older than the boy, hung on behind. The three were occupied partly with eating cherries, partly with patting and punching Greylocks, who took all their caresses in good part, but pricked up his ears when Dick made his appearance. The girls got off quietly, and going up to Clara, made much of her and snuggled up to her. And then we got into the carriage, Dick shook the reins, and we got under way at once, Greylocks trotting soberly between the lovely trees of the London streets, that were sending floods of fragrance into the cool evening air; for it was now getting toward sunset.

We could hardly go but fair and softly all the way, as there were a great many people abroad in that cool hour. Seeing so many people made me notice their looks the more; and I must say, my taste, cultivated in the sombre greyness, or rather brownness, of the nineteenth century, was rather apt to condemn the gaiety and brightness of the raiment; and I even ventured to say as much to Clara. She seemed rather surprised, and even slightly indignant, and said: "Well, well, what's the matter? They are not about any dirty work; they are only amusing themselves in the fine evening; there is nothing to foul their clothes. Come, doesn't it all look very pretty? It isn't gaudy, you know."

Indeed that was true; for many of the people were clad in colours that were sober enough, though beautiful, and the harmony of the colours was perfect and most delightful.

I said, "Yes, that is so; but how can everybody afford such costly garments? Look! there goes a middle-aged man in a sober grey dress; but I can see from here that it is made of very fine woollen stuff, and is covered with silk embroidery."

Said Clara: "He could wear shabby clothes if he pleased,—that is, if he didn't think he would hurt people's feelings by doing so."

"But please tell me," said I, "how can they afford it?"

As soon as I had spoken I perceived that I had got back to my old blunder; for I saw Dick's shoulders shaking with laughter; but he wouldn't say a word, but handed me over to the tender mercies of Clara, who said—

"Why, I don't know what you mean. Of course we can afford it, or else we shouldn't do it. It would be easy enough for us to say, we will only spend our labour on making our clothes comfortable: but we don't choose to stop there. Why do you find fault with us? Does it seem to you as if we starved ourselves of food in order to make ourselves fine clothes? Or do you think there is anything wrong in liking to see the coverings of our bodies beautiful like our bodies are?— just as a deer's or an otter's skin has been made beautiful from the first? Come, what is wrong with you?"

I bowed before the storm, and mumbled out some excuse or other. I must say, I might have known that people who were so fond of architecture generally, would not be backward in ornamenting themselves; all the more as the shape of their raiment, apart from its colour, was both beautiful and reasonable—veiling the form, without either muffling or caricaturing it.

Clara was soon mollified; and as we drove along toward the wood before mentioned, she said to Dick—

"I tell you what, Dick: now that kinsman Hammond the Elder has seen our guest in his queer clothes, I think we ought to find him something decent to put on for our journey to-morrow: especially since, if we do not, we shall have to answer all sorts of questions as to his clothes and where they came from. Besides," she said slily, "when he is clad in handsome garments he will not be so quick to blame us for our childishness in wasting our time in making ourselves look pleasant to each other."

"All right, Clara," said Dick; "he shall have everything that you—that he wants to have. I will look something out for him before he gets up to-morrow."

20. THE HAMMERSMITH GUEST-HOUSE AGAIN

Amidst such talk, driving quietly through the balmy evening, we came to Hammersmith, and were well received by our friends there. Boffin, in a fresh suit of clothes, welcomed me back with stately courtesy; the weaver wanted to buttonhole me and get out of me what old Hammond had said, but was very friendly and cheerful when Dick warned him off; Annie shook hands with me, and hoped I had had a pleasant day—so kindly, that I felt a slight pang as our hands parted; for to say the truth, I liked her better than Clara, who seemed to be always a little on the defensive, whereas Annie was as frank as could be, and seemed to get honest pleasure from everything and everybody about her without the least effort.

We had quite a little feast that evening, partly in my honour, and partly, I suspect, though nothing was said about it, in honour of Dick and Clara coming together again. The wine was of the best; the hall was redolent of rich summer flowers; and after supper we not only had music (Annie, to my mind, surpassing all the others for sweetness and clearness of voice, as well as for feeling and meaning), but at last we even got to telling stories, and sat there listening, with no other light but that of the summer moon streaming through the beautiful traceries of the windows, as if we had belonged to time long passed, when books were scarce and the art of reading somewhat rare. Indeed, I may say here, that, though, as you will have noted, my friends had mostly something to say about books, yet they were not great readers, considering the refinement of their manners and the great amount of leisure which they obviously had. In fact, when Dick, especially, mentioned a book, he did so with an air of a man who has accomplished an achievement; as much as to say, "There, you see, I have actually read that!"

The evening passed all too quickly for me; since that day, for the first time in my life, I was having my fill of the pleasure of the eyes without any of that sense of incongruity, that dread of approaching ruin, which had always beset me hitherto when I had been amongst the beautiful works of art of the past, mingled with the lovely nature of the present; both of them, in fact, the result of the long centuries of tradition, which had compelled men to produce the art, and compelled nature to run into the mould of the ages. Here I could enjoy everything without an afterthought of the injustice and miserable toil which made my leisure; the ignorance and dulness of life which went to make my keen appreciation of history; the tyranny and the struggle full of fear and mishap which went to make my romance. The only weight I had upon my heart was a vague fear as it drew toward bed-time concerning the place wherein I should wake on the morrow: but I choked that down, and went to bed happy, and in a very few moments was in a dreamless sleep.

21. GOING UP THE RIVER

When I did wake, to a beautiful sunny morning, I leapt out of bed with my overnight apprehension still clinging to me, which vanished delightfully however in a moment as I looked around my little sleeping chamber and saw the pale but pure-coloured figures painted on the plaster of the wall, with verses written underneath them which I knew somewhat over well. I dressed speedily, in a suit of blue laid ready for me, so handsome that I quite blushed when I had got into it, feeling as I did so that excited pleasure of anticipation of a holiday, which, well remembered as it was, I had not felt since I was a boy, new come home for the summer holidays.

It seemed quite early in the morning, and I expected to have the hall to myself when I came into it out of the corridor wherein was my sleeping chamber; but I met Annie at once, who let fall her broom and gave me a kiss, quite meaningless I fear, except as betokening friendship, though she reddened as she did it, not from shyness, but from friendly pleasure, and then stood and picked up her broom again, and went on with her sweeping, nodding to me as if to bid me stand out of the way and look on; which, to say the truth, I thought amusing enough, as there were five other girls helping her, and their graceful figures engaged in the leisurely work were worth going a long way to see, and their merry talk and laughing as they swept in quite a scientific manner was worth going a long way to hear. But Annie presently threw me back a word or two as she went on to the other end of the hall: "Guest," she said, "I am glad that you are up early, though we wouldn't disturb you; for our Thames is a lovely river at half-past six on a June morning: and as it would be a pity for you to lose it, I am told just to give you a cup of milk and a bit of bread outside there, and put you into the boat: for Dick and Clara are all ready now. Wait half a minute till I have swept down this row."

So presently she let her broom drop again, and came and took me by the hand and led me out on to the terrace above the river, to a little table under the boughs, where my bread and milk took the form of as dainty a breakfast as any one could desire, and then sat by me as I ate. And in a minute or two Dick and Clara came to me, the latter looking most fresh and beautiful in a light silk embroidered gown, which to my unused eyes was extravagantly gay and bright; while Dick was also handsomely dressed in white flannel prettily embroidered. Clara raised her gown in her hands as she gave me the morning greeting, and said laughingly: "Look, guest! you see we are at least as fine as any of the people you felt inclined to scold last night; you see we are not going to make the bright day and the flowers feel ashamed of themselves. Now scold me!"

Quoth I: "No, indeed; the pair of you seem as if you were born out of the summer day itself; and I will scold you when I scold it."

"Well, you know," said Dick, "this is a special day—all these days are, I mean. The hay-harvest is in some ways better than corn-harvest because of the beautiful weather; and really, unless you had worked in the hay-field in fine weather, you couldn't tell what pleasant work it is. The women look so pretty at it, too," he said, shyly; "so all things considered, I think we are right to adorn it in a simple manner."

"Do the women work at it in silk dresses?" said I, smiling.

Dick was going to answer me soberly; but Clara put her hand over his mouth, and said, "No, no, Dick; not too much information for him, or I shall think that you are your old kinsman again. Let him find out for himself: he will not have long to wait."

"Yes," quoth Annie, "don't make your description of the picture too fine, or else he will be disappointed when the curtain is drawn. I don't want him to be disappointed. But now it's time for you to be gone, if you are to have the best of the tide, and also of the sunny morning. Good-bye, guest."

She kissed me in her frank friendly way, and almost took away from me my desire for the expedition thereby; but I had to get over that, as it was clear that so delightful a woman would hardly be without a due lover of her own age. We went down the steps of the landing stage, and got into a pretty boat, not too light to hold us and our belongings comfortably, and handsomely ornamented; and just as we got in, down came Boffin and the weaver to see us off. The former had now veiled his splendour in a due suit of working clothes, crowned with a fantail hat, which he took off, however, to wave us farewell with his grave old-Spanish-like courtesy. Then Dick pushed off into the stream, and bent vigorously to his sculls, and Hammersmith, with its noble trees and beautiful water-side houses, began to slip away from us.

As we went, I could not help putting beside his promised picture of the hay-field as it was then the picture of it as I remembered it, and especially the images of the women engaged in the work rose up before me: the row of gaunt figures, lean, flat-breasted, ugly, without a grace of form or face about them; dressed in wretched skimpy print gowns, and hideous flapping sun-bonnets, moving their rakes in a listless mechanical way. How often had that marred the loveliness of the June day to me; how often had I longed to see the hay-fields peopled with men and women worthy of the sweet abundance of midsummer, of its endless wealth of beautiful sights, and delicious sounds and scents. And now, the world had grown old and wiser, and I was to see my hope realised at last!

22. HAMPTON COURT AND A PRAISER OF PAST TIMES

So on we went, Dick rowing in an easy tireless way, and Clara sitting by my side admiring his manly beauty and heartily good-natured face, and thinking, I fancy, of nothing else. As we went higher up the river, there was less difference between the Thames of that day and Thames as I remembered it; for setting aside the hideous vulgarity of the cockney villas of the well-to-do, stockbrokers and other such, which in older time marred the beauty of the bough-hung banks, even this beginning of the country Thames was always beautiful; and as we slipped between the lovely summer greenery, I almost felt my youth come back to me, and as if I were on one of those water excursions which I used to enjoy so much in days when I was too happy to think that there could be much amiss anywhere.

At last we came to a reach of the river where on the left hand a very pretty little village with some old houses in it came down to the edge of the water, over which was a ferry; and beyond these houses the elm-beset meadows ended in a fringe of tall willows, while on the right hand went the tow-path and a clear space before a row of trees, which rose up behind huge and ancient, the ornaments of a great park: but these drew back still further from the river at the end of the reach to make way for a little town of quaint and pretty houses, some new, some old, dominated by the long walls and sharp gables of a great red-brick pile of building, partly of the latest Gothic, partly of the court-style of Dutch William, but so blended together by the bright sun and beautiful surroundings, including the bright blue river, which it looked down upon, that even amidst the beautiful buildings of that new happy time it had a strange charm about it. A great wave of fragrance, amidst which the lime-tree blossom was clearly to be distinguished, came down to us from its unseen gardens, as Clara sat up in her place, and said:

"O Dick, dear, couldn't we stop at Hampton Court for to-day, and take the guest about the park a little, and show him those sweet old buildings? Somehow, I suppose because you have lived so near it, you have seldom taken me to Hampton Court."

Dick rested on his oars a little, and said: "Well, well, Clara, you are lazy to-day. I didn't feel like stopping short of Shepperton for the night; suppose we just go and have our dinner at the Court, and go on again about five o'clock?"

"Well," she said, "so be it; but I should like the guest to have spent an hour or two in the Park."

"The Park!" said Dick; "why, the whole Thames-side is a park this time of the year; and for my part, I had rather lie under an elm-tree on the borders of a wheat-field, with the bees humming about me and the corn-crake crying from furrow to furrow, than in any park in England. Besides——"

"Besides," said she, "you want to get on to your dearly-loved upper Thames, and show your prowess down the heavy swathes of the mowing grass."

She looked at him fondly, and I could tell that she was seeing him in her mind's eye showing his splendid form at its best amidst the rhymed strokes of the scythes; and she looked down at her own pretty feet with a half sigh, as though she were contrasting her slight woman's beauty with his man's beauty; as women will when they are really in love, and are not spoiled with conventional sentiment.

As for Dick, he looked at her admiringly a while, and then said at last: "Well, Clara, I do wish we were there! But, hilloa! we are getting back way." And he set to work sculling again, and in two minutes we were all standing on the gravelly strand below the bridge, which, as you may imagine, was no longer the old hideous iron abortion, but a handsome piece of very solid oak framing.

We went into the Court and straight into the great hall, so well remembered, where there were tables spread for dinner, and everything arranged much as in Hammersmith Guest-Hall. Dinner over, we sauntered through the ancient rooms, where the pictures and tapestry were still preserved, and nothing was much changed, except that the people whom we met there had an indefinable kind of look of being at home and at ease, which communicated itself to me, so that I felt that the beautiful old place was mine in the best sense of the word; and my pleasure of past days seemed to add itself to that of to-day, and filled my whole soul with content.

Dick (who, in spite of Clara's gibe, knew the place very well) told me that the beautiful old Tudor rooms, which I remembered had been the dwellings of the lesser fry of Court flunkies, were now much used by people coming and going; for, beautiful as architecture had now become, and although the whole face of the country had quite recovered its beauty, there was still a sort of tradition of pleasure and beauty which clung to that group of buildings, and people thought going to Hampton Court a necessary summer outing, as they did in the days when London was so grimy and miserable. We went into some of the rooms looking into the old garden, and were well received by the people in them, who got speedily into talk with us, and looked with politely half-concealed wonder at my strange face. Besides these birds of passage, and a few regular dwellers in the place, we saw out in the meadows near the garden, down "the Long Water," as it used to be called, many gay tents with men, women, and children round about them. As it seemed, this pleasure-loving people were fond of tent-life, with all its inconveniences, which, indeed, they turned into pleasure also.

We left this old friend by the time appointed, and I made some feeble show of taking the sculls; but Dick repulsed me, not much to my grief, I must say, as I found I had quite enough to do between the enjoyment of the beautiful time and my own lazily blended thoughts.

As to Dick, it was quite right to let him pull, for he was as strong as a horse, and had the greatest delight in bodily exercise, whatever it was. We really had some difficulty in getting him to stop when it was getting rather more than dusk, and the moon was brightening just as we were off Runnymede. We landed there, and were looking about for a place whereon to pitch our tents (for we had brought two with us), when an old man came up to us, bade us good evening, and asked if we were housed for that that night; and finding that we were not, bade us home to his house. Nothing loth, we went with him, and Clara took his hand in a coaxing way which I noticed she used with old men; and as we went on our way, made some commonplace remark about the beauty of the day. The old man stopped short, and looked at her and said: "You really like it then?"

"Yes," she said, looking very much astonished, "Don't you?"

"Well," said he, "perhaps I do. I did, at any rate, when I was younger; but now I think I should like it cooler."

She said nothing, and went on, the night growing about as dark as it would be; till just at the rise of the hill we came to a hedge with a gate in it, which the old man unlatched and led us into a garden, at the end of which we could see a little house, one of whose little windows was already yellow with candlelight. We could see even under the doubtful light of the moon and the last of the western glow that the garden was stuffed full of flowers; and the fragrance it gave out in the gathering coolness was so wonderfully sweet, that it seemed the very heart of the delight of the June dusk; so that we three stopped instinctively, and Clara gave forth a little sweet "O," like a bird beginning to sing.

"What's the matter?" said the old man, a little testily, and pulling at her hand. "There's no dog; or have you trodden on a thorn and hurt your foot?"

"No, no, neighbour," she said; "but how sweet, how sweet it is!"

"Of course it is," said he, "but do you care so much for that?"

She laughed out musically, and we followed suit in our gruffer voices; and then she said: "Of course I do, neighbour; don't you?"

"Well, I don't know," quoth the old fellow; then he added, as if somewhat ashamed of himself: "Besides, you know, when the waters are out and all Runnymede is flooded, it's none so pleasant."

"*I* should like it," quoth Dick. "What a jolly sail one would get about here on the floods on a bright frosty January morning!"

"*Would* you like it?" said our host. "Well, I won't argue with you, neighbour; it isn't worth while. Come in and have some supper."

We went up a paved path between the roses, and straight into a very pretty room, panelled and carved, and as clean as a new pin; but the chief ornament of which was a young woman, light-haired and grey-eyed, but with her face and hands and bare feet tanned quite brown with the sun. Though she was very lightly clad, that was clearly from choice, not from poverty, though these were the first cottage-dwellers I had come across; for her gown was of silk, and on her wrists were bracelets that seemed to me of great value. She was lying on a sheep-skin near the window, but jumped up as soon as we entered, and when she saw the guests behind the old man, she clapped her hands and cried out with pleasure, and when she got us into the middle of the room, fairly danced round us in delight of our company.

"What!" said the old man, "you are pleased, are you, Ellen?"

The girl danced up to him and threw her arms round him, and said: "Yes I am, and so ought you to be grandfather."

"Well, well, I am," said he, "as much as I can be pleased. Guests, please be seated."

This seemed rather strange to us; stranger, I suspect, to my friends than to me; but Dick took the opportunity of both the host and his grand-daughter being out of the room to say to me, softly: "A grumbler: there are a few of them still. Once upon a time, I am told, they were quite a nuisance."

The old man came in as he spoke and sat down beside us with a sigh, which, indeed, seemed fetched up as if he wanted us to take notice of it; but just then the girl came in with the victuals, and the carle missed his mark, what between our hunger generally and that I was pretty busy watching the grand-daughter moving about as beautiful as a picture.

Everything to eat and drink, though it was somewhat different to what we had had in London, was better than good, but the old man eyed rather sulkily the chief dish on the table, on which lay a leash of fine perch, and said:

"H'm, perch! I am sorry we can't do better for you, guests. The time was when we might have had a good piece of salmon up from London for you; but the times have grown mean and petty."

"Yes, but you might have had it now," said the girl, giggling, "if you had known that they were coming."

"It's our fault for not bringing it with us, neighbours," said Dick, good-humouredly. "But if the times have grown petty, at any rate the perch haven't; that fellow in the middle there must have weighed a good two pounds when he was showing his dark stripes and red fins to the minnows yonder. And as to the salmon, why, neighbour, my friend here, who comes from the outlands, was quite surprised yesterday morning when I told him we had plenty of salmon at Hammersmith. I am sure I have heard nothing of the times worsening."

He looked a little uncomfortable. And the old man, turning to me, said very courteously:

"Well, sir, I am happy to see a man from over the water; but I really must appeal to you to say whether on the whole you are not better off in your country; where I suppose, from what our guest says, you are brisker and more alive, because you have not wholly got rid of competition. You see, I have read not a few books of the past days, and certainly *they* are much more alive than those which are written now; and good sound unlimited competition was the condition under which they were written,—if we didn't know that from the record of history, we should know it from the books themselves. There is a spirit of adventure in them, and signs of a capacity to extract good out of evil which our literature quite lacks now; and I cannot help thinking that our moralists and historians exaggerate hugely the unhappiness of the past days, in which such splendid works of imagination and intellect were produced."

Clara listened to him with restless eyes, as if she were excited and pleased; Dick knitted his brow and looked still more uncomfortable, but said nothing. Indeed, the old man gradually, as he warmed to his subject, dropped his sneering manner, and both spoke and looked very seriously. But the girl broke out before I could deliver myself of the answer I was framing:

"Books, books! always books, grandfather! When will you understand that after all it is the world we live in which interests us; the world of which we are a part, and which we can never love too much? Look!" she said, throwing open the casement wider and showing us the white light sparkling between the black shadows of the moonlit garden, through which ran a little shiver of the summer night-wind, "look! these are our books in these days!—and these," she said, stepping lightly up to the two lovers and laying a hand on each of their shoulders; "and the guest there, with his over-sea knowledge and experience;—yes, and even you, grandfather" (a smile ran over her face as she spoke), "with all your grumbling and wishing yourself back again in the good old days,—in which, as far as I can make out, a harmless and lazy old man like you would either have pretty nearly starved, or have had to pay soldiers and people to take the folk's victuals and clothes and houses away from them by force. Yes, these are our books; and if we want more, can we not find work to do in the beautiful buildings that we raise up all over the country (and I know there was nothing like them in past times), wherein a man can put forth whatever is in him, and make his hands set forth his mind and his soul."

She paused a little, and I for my part could not help staring at her, and thinking that if she were a book, the pictures in it were most lovely. The colour mantled in her delicate sunburnt cheeks; her grey eyes, light amidst the tan of her face, kindly looked on us all as she spoke. She paused, and said again:

"As for your books, they were well enough for times when intelligent people had but little else in which they could take pleasure, and when they must needs supplement the sordid miseries of their own lives with imaginations of the lives of other people. But I say flatly that in spite of all their cleverness and vigour, and capacity for story-telling, there is something loathsome about them. Some of them, indeed, do here and there show some feeling for those whom the history-books call 'poor,' and of the misery of whose lives we have some inkling; but presently they give it up, and towards the end of the story we must be contented to see the hero and heroine living happily in an island of bliss on other people's troubles; and that after a long series of sham troubles (or mostly sham) of their own making, illustrated by dreary introspective nonsense about their feelings and aspirations, and all the rest of it; while the world must even then have gone on its way, and dug and sewed and baked and built and carpentered round about these useless—animals."

"There!" said the old man, reverting to his dry sulky manner again. "There's eloquence! I suppose you like it?"

"Yes," said I, very emphatically.

"Well," said he, "now the storm of eloquence has lulled for a little, suppose you answer my question?—that is, if you like, you know," quoth he, with a sudden access of courtesy.

"What question?" said I. For I must confess that Ellen's strange and almost wild beauty had put it out of my head.

Said he: "First of all (excuse my catechising), is there competition in life, after the old kind, in the country whence you come?"

"Yes," said I, "it is the rule there." And I wondered as I spoke what fresh complications I should get into as a result of this answer.

"Question two," said the carle: "Are you not on the whole much freer, more energetic—in a word, healthier and happier—for it?"

I smiled. "You wouldn't talk so if you had any idea of our life. To me you seem here as if you were living in heaven compared with us of the country from which I came."

"Heaven?" said he: "you like heaven, do you?"

"Yes," said I—snappishly, I am afraid; for I was beginning rather to resent his formula.

"Well, I am far from sure that I do," quoth he. "I think one may do more with one's life than sitting on a damp cloud and singing hymns."

I was rather nettled by this inconsequence, and said: "Well, neighbour, to be short, and without using metaphors, in the land whence I come, where the competition which produced those literary works which you admire so much is still the rule, most people are thoroughly unhappy; here, to me at least most people seem thoroughly happy."

"No offence, guest—no offence," said he; "but let me ask you; you like that, do you?"

His formula, put with such obstinate persistence, made us all laugh heartily; and even the old man joined in the laughter on the sly. However, he was by no means beaten, and said presently:

"From all I can hear, I should judge that a young woman so beautiful as my dear Ellen yonder would have been a lady, as they called it in the old time, and wouldn't have had to wear a few rags of silk as she does now, or to have browned herself in the sun as she has to do now. What do you say to that, eh?"

Here Clara, who had been pretty much silent hitherto, struck in, and said: "Well, really, I don't think that you would have mended matters, or that they want mending. Don't you see that she is dressed deliciously for this beautiful weather? And as for the sun-burning of your hay-fields, why, I hope to pick up some of that for myself when we get a little higher up the river. Look if I don't need a little sun on my pasty white skin!"

And she stripped up the sleeve from her arm and laid it beside Ellen's who was now sitting next her. To say the truth, it was rather amusing to me to see Clara putting herself forward as a town-bred fine lady, for she was as well-knit and clean-skinned a girl as might be met with anywhere at the best. Dick stroked the beautiful arm rather shyly, and pulled down the sleeve again, while she blushed at his touch; and the old man said laughingly: "Well, I suppose you *do* like that; don't you?"

Ellen kissed her new friend, and we all sat silent for a little, till she broke out into a sweet shrill song, and held us all entranced with the wonder of her clear voice; and the old grumbler sat looking at her lovingly. The other young people sang also in due time; and then Ellen showed us to our beds in small cottage chambers, fragrant and clean as the ideal of the old pastoral poets; and the pleasure of the evening quite extinguished my fear of the last night, that I should wake up in the old miserable world of worn-out pleasures, and hopes that were half fears.

23. AN EARLY MORNING BY RUNNYMEDE

Though there were no rough noises to wake me, I could not lie long abed the next morning, where the world seemed so well awake, and, despite the old grumbler, so happy; so I got up, and found that, early as it was, someone had been stirring, since all was trim and in its place in the little parlour, and the table laid for the morning meal. Nobody was afoot in the house as then, however, so I went out a-doors, and after a turn or two round the superabundant garden, I wandered down over the meadow to the river-side, where lay our boat, looking quite familiar and friendly to me. I walked up stream a little, watching the light mist curling up from the river till the sun gained power to draw it all away; saw the bleak speckling the water under the willow boughs, whence the tiny flies they fed on were falling in myriads; heard the great chub splashing here and there at some belated moth or other, and felt almost back again in my boyhood. Then I went back again to the boat, and loitered there a minute or two, and then walked slowly up the meadow towards the little house.
I noted now that there were four more houses of about the same size on the slope away from the river. The meadow in which I was going was not up for hay; but a row of flake-hurdles ran up the slope not far from me on each side, and in the field so parted off from ours on the left they were making hay busily by now, in the simple fashion of the days when I was a boy. My feet turned that way instinctively, as I wanted to see how haymakers looked in these new and better times, and also I rather expected to see Ellen there. I came to the hurdles and stood looking over into the hay-field, and was close to the end of the long line of haymakers who were spreading the low ridges to dry off the night dew. The majority of these were young women clad much like Ellen last night, though not mostly in silk, but in light woollen mostly gaily embroidered; the men being all clad in white flannel embroidered in bright colours. The meadow looked like a gigantic tulip-bed because of them. All hands were working deliberately but well and steadily, though they were as noisy with merry talk as a grove of autumn starlings. Half a dozen of them, men and women, came up to me and shook hands, gave me the sele of the morning, and asked a few questions as to whence and whither, and wishing me good luck, went back to their work. Ellen, to my disappointment, was not amongst them, but presently I saw a light figure come out of the hay-field higher up the slope, and make for our house; and that was Ellen, holding a basket in her hand. But before she had come to the garden gate, out came Dick and Clara, who, after a minute's pause, came down to meet me, leaving Ellen in the garden; then we three went down

to the boat, talking mere morning prattle. We stayed there a little, Dick arranging some of the matters in her, for we had only taken up to the house such things as we thought the dew might damage; and then we went toward the house again; but when we came near the garden, Dick stopped us by laying a hand on my arm and said,—

"Just look a moment."

I looked, and over the low hedge saw Ellen, shading her eyes against the sun as she looked toward the hay-field, a light wind stirring in her tawny hair, her eyes like light jewels amidst her sunburnt face, which looked as if the warmth of the sun were yet in it.

"Look, guest," said Dick; "doesn't it all look like one of those very stories out of Grimm that we were talking about up in Bloomsbury? Here are we two lovers wandering about the world, and we have come to a fairy garden, and there is the very fairy herself amidst of it: I wonder what she will do for us."

Said Clara demurely, but not stiffly: "Is she a good fairy, Dick?"

"O, yes," said he; "and according to the card, she would do better, if it were not for the gnome or wood-spirit, our grumbling friend of last night."

We laughed at this; and I said, "I hope you see that you have left me out of the tale."

"Well," said he, "that's true. You had better consider that you have got the cap of darkness, and are seeing everything, yourself invisible."

That touched me on my weak side of not feeling sure of my position in this beautiful new country; so in order not to make matters worse, I held my tongue, and we all went into the garden and up to the house together. I noticed by the way that Clara must really rather have felt the contrast between herself as a town madam and this piece of the summer country that we all admired so, for she had rather dressed after Ellen that morning as to thinness and scantiness, and went barefoot also, except for light sandals.

The old man greeted us kindly in the parlour, and said: "Well, guests, so you have been looking about to search into the nakedness of the land: I suppose your illusions of last night have given way a bit before the morning light? Do you still like, it, eh?"

"Very much," said I, doggedly; "it is one of the prettiest places on the lower Thames."

"Oho!" said he; "so you know the Thames, do you?"

I reddened, for I saw Dick and Clara looking at me, and scarcely knew what to say. However, since I had said in our early intercourse with my Hammersmith friends that I had known Epping Forest, I thought a hasty generalisation might be better in avoiding complications than a downright lie; so I said—

"I have been in this country before; and I have been on the Thames in those days."

"O," said the old man, eagerly, "so you have been in this country before.

Now really, don't you *find* it (apart from all theory, you know) much changed for the worse?"

"No, not at all," said I; "I find it much changed for the better."

"Ah," quoth he, "I fear that you have been prejudiced by some theory or another. However, of course the time when you were here before must have been so near our own days that the deterioration might not be very great: as then we were, of course, still living under the same customs as we are now. I was thinking of earlier days than that."

"In short," said Clara, "you have *theories* about the change which has taken place."

"I have facts as well," said he. "Look here! from this hill you can see just four little houses, including this one. Well, I know for certain that in old times, even in the summer, when the leaves were thickest, you could see from the same place six quite big and fine houses; and higher up the water, garden joined garden right up to Windsor; and there were big houses in all the gardens. Ah! England was an important place in those days."

I was getting nettled, and said: "What you mean is that you de-cockneyised the place, and sent the damned flunkies packing, and that everybody can live comfortably and happily, and not a few damned thieves only, who were centres of vulgarity and corruption wherever they were, and who, as to this lovely river, destroyed its beauty morally, and had almost destroyed it physically, when they were thrown out of it."

There was silence after this outburst, which for the life of me I could not help, remembering how I had suffered from cockneyism and its cause on those same waters of old time. But at last the old man said, quite coolly:

"My dear guest, I really don't know what you mean by either cockneys, or flunkies, or thieves, or damned; or how only a few people could live happily and comfortably in a wealthy country. All I can see is that you are angry, and I fear with me: so if you like we will change the subject."

I thought this kind and hospitable in him, considering his obstinacy about his theory; and hastened to say that I did not mean to be angry, only emphatic. He bowed gravely, and I thought the storm was over, when suddenly Ellen broke in:

"Grandfather, our guest is reticent from courtesy; but really what he has in his mind to say to you ought to be said; so as I know pretty well what it is, I will say it for him: for as you know, I have been taught these things by people who—"

"Yes," said the old man, "by the sage of Bloomsbury, and others."

"O," said Dick, "so you know my old kinsman Hammond?"

"Yes," said she, "and other people too, as my grandfather says, and they have taught me things: and this is the upshot of it. We live in a little house now, not because we have nothing grander to do than working in the fields, but because we please; for if we liked, we could go and live in a big house amongst pleasant companions."

Grumbled the old man: "Just so! As if I would live amongst those conceited fellows; all of them looking down upon me!"

She smiled on him kindly, but went on as if he had not spoken. "In the past times, when those big houses of which grandfather speaks were so plenty, we *must* have lived in a cottage whether we had liked it or not; and the said cottage, instead of having in it everything we want, would have been bare and empty. We should not have got enough to eat; our clothes would have been ugly to look at, dirty and frowsy. You, grandfather, have done no hard work for years now, but wander about and read your books and have nothing to worry you; and as for me, I work hard when I like it, because I like it, and think it does me good, and knits up my muscles, and makes me prettier to look at, and healthier and happier. But in those past days you, grandfather, would have had to work hard after you were old; and would have been always afraid of having to be shut up in a kind of prison along with other old men, half-starved and without amusement. And as for me, I am twenty years old. In those days my middle age would be beginning now, and in a few years I should be pinched, thin, and haggard, beset with troubles and miseries, so that no one could have guessed that I was once a beautiful girl."

"Is this what you have had in your mind, guest?" said she, the tears in her eyes at thought of the past miseries of people like herself.

"Yes," said I, much moved; "that and more. Often—in my country I have seen that wretched change you have spoken of, from the fresh handsome country lass to the poor draggle-tailed country woman."

The old man sat silent for a little, but presently recovered himself and took comfort in his old phrase of "Well, you like it so, do you?"

"Yes," said Ellen, "I love life better than death."

"O, you do, do you?" said he. "Well, for my part I like reading a good old book with plenty of fun in it, like Thackeray's 'Vanity Fair.' Why don't you write books like that now? Ask that question of your Bloomsbury sage."

Seeing Dick's cheeks reddening a little at this sally, and noting that silence followed, I thought I had better do something. So I said: "I am only the guest, friends; but I know you want to show me your river at its best, so don't you think we had better be moving presently, as it is certainly going to be a hot day?"

24. UP THE THAMES: THE SECOND DAY

They were not slow to take my hint; and indeed, as to the mere time of day, it was best for us to be off, as it was past seven o'clock, and the day promised to be very hot. So we got up and went down to our boat—Ellen thoughtful and abstracted; the old man very kind and courteous, as if to make up for his crabbedness of opinion. Clara was cheerful and natural, but a little subdued, I thought; and she at least was not sorry to be gone, and often looked shyly and timidly at Ellen and her strange wild beauty. So we got into the boat, Dick saying as he took his place, "Well, it *is* a fine day!" and the old man answering "What! you like that, do you?" once more; and presently Dick was sending the bows swiftly through the slow weed-checked stream. I turned round as we got into mid-stream, and waving my hand to our hosts, saw Ellen leaning on the old man's shoulder, and caressing his healthy apple-red cheek, and quite a keen pang smote me as I thought how I should never see the beautiful girl again. Presently I insisted on taking the sculls, and I rowed a good deal that day; which no doubt accounts for the fact that we got very late to the place which Dick had aimed at. Clara was particularly affectionate to Dick, as I noticed from the rowing thwart; but as for him, he was as frankly kind and merry as ever; and I was glad to see it, as a man of his temperament could not have taken her caresses cheerfully and without embarrassment if he had been at all entangled by the fairy of our last night's abode.

I need say little about the lovely reaches of the river here. I duly noted that absence of cockney villas which the old man had lamented; and I saw with pleasure that my old enemies the "Gothic" cast-iron bridges had been replaced by handsome oak and stone ones. Also the banks of the forest that we passed through had lost their courtly game-keeperish trimness, and were as wild and beautiful as need be, though the trees were clearly well seen to. I thought it best, in order to get the most direct information, to play the innocent about Eton and Windsor; but Dick volunteered his knowledge to me as we lay in Datchet lock about the first. Quoth he:

"Up yonder are some beautiful old buildings, which were built for a great college or teaching-place by one of the mediæval kings—Edward the Sixth, I think" (I smiled to myself at his rather natural blunder). "He meant poor people's sons to be taught there what knowledge was going in his days; but it was a matter of course that in the times of which you seem to know so much they spoilt whatever good there was in the founder's intentions. My old kinsman says that they treated them in a very simple way, and instead of teaching poor men's sons to know something, they taught rich men's sons to know nothing. It seems from what he says that it was a place for the 'aristocracy' (if you know what that word means; I have been told its meaning) to get rid of the company of their male children for a great part of the year. I daresay old Hammond would give you plenty of information in detail about it."

"What is it used for now?" said I.

"Well," said he, "the buildings were a good deal spoilt by the last few generations of aristocrats, who seem to have had a great hatred against beautiful old buildings, and indeed all records of past history; but it is still a delightful place. Of course, we cannot use it quite as the founder intended, since our ideas about teaching young people are so changed from the ideas of his time; so it is used now as a dwelling for people engaged in learning; and folk from round about come and get taught things that they want to learn; and there is a great library there of the best books. So that I don't think that the old dead king would be much hurt if he were to come to life and see what we are doing there."

"Well," said Clara, laughing, "I think he would miss the boys."

"Not always, my dear," said Dick, "for there are often plenty of boys there, who come to get taught; and also," said he, smiling, "to learn boating and swimming. I wish we could stop there: but perhaps we had better do that coming down the water."

The lock-gates opened as he spoke, and out we went, and on. And as for Windsor, he said nothing till I lay on my oars (for I was sculling then) in Clewer reach, and looking up, said, "What is all that building up there?"

Said he: "There, I thought I would wait till you asked, yourself. That is Windsor Castle: that also I thought I would keep for you till we come down the water. It looks fine from here, doesn't it? But a great deal of it has been built or skinned in the time of the Degradation, and we wouldn't pull the buildings down, since they were there; just as with the buildings of the Dung-Market. You know, of course, that it was the palace of our old mediæval kings, and was used later on for the same purpose by the parliamentary commercial sham-kings, as my old kinsman calls them."

"Yes," said I, "I know all that. What is it used for now?"

"A great many people live there," said he, "as, with all drawbacks, it is a pleasant place; there is also a well-arranged store of antiquities of various kinds that have seemed worth keeping—a museum, it would have been called in the times you understand so well."

I drew my sculls through the water at that last word, and pulled as if I were fleeing from those times which I understood so well; and we were soon going up the once sorely be-cockneyed reaches of the river about Maidenhead, which now looked as pleasant and enjoyable as the up-river reaches.

The morning was now getting on, the morning of a jewel of a summer day; one of those days which, if they were commoner in these islands, would make our climate the best of all climates, without dispute. A light wind blew from the west; the little clouds that had arisen at about our breakfast time had seemed to get higher and higher in the heavens; and in spite of the burning sun we no more longed for rain than we feared it. Burning as the sun was, there was a fresh feeling in the air that almost set us a-longing for the rest of the hot afternoon, and the stretch of blossoming wheat seen from the shadow of the boughs. No one unburdened with very heavy anxieties could have felt otherwise than happy that morning: and it must be said that whatever anxieties might lie beneath the surface of things, we didn't seem to come across any of them.

We passed by several fields where haymaking was going on, but Dick, and especially Clara, were so jealous of our up-river festival that they would not allow me to have much to say to them. I could only notice that the people in the fields looked strong and handsome, both men and women, and that so far from there being any appearance of sordidness about their attire, they seemed to be dressed specially for the occasion,—lightly, of course, but gaily and with plenty of adornment.

Both on this day as well as yesterday we had, as you may think, met and passed and been passed by many craft of one kind and another. The most part of these were being rowed like ourselves, or were sailing, in the sort of way that sailing is managed on the upper reaches of the river; but every now and then we came on barges, laden with hay or other country produce, or carrying bricks, lime, timber, and the like, and these were going on their way without any means of propulsion visible to me—just a man at the tiller, with often a friend or two laughing and talking with him. Dick, seeing on one occasion this day, that I was looking rather hard on one of these, said: "That is one of our force-barges; it is quite as easy to work vehicles by force by water as by land."

I understood pretty well that these "force vehicles" had taken the place of our old steam-power carrying; but I took good care not to ask any questions about them, as I knew well enough both that I should never be able to understand how they were worked, and that in attempting to do so I should betray myself, or get into some complication impossible to explain; so I merely said, "Yes, of course, I understand."

We went ashore at Bisham, where the remains of the old Abbey and the Elizabethan house that had been added to them yet remained, none the worse for many years of careful and appreciative habitation. The folk of the place, however, were mostly in the fields that day, both men and women; so we met only two old men there, and a younger one who had stayed at home to get on with some literary work, which I imagine we considerably interrupted. Yet I also think that the hard-working man who received us was not very sorry for the interruption. Anyhow, he kept on pressing us to stay over and over again, till at last we did not get away till the cool of the evening.

However, that mattered little to us; the nights were light, for the moon was shining in her third quarter, and it was all one to Dick whether he sculled or sat quiet in the boat: so we went away a great pace. The evening sun shone bright on the remains of the old buildings at Medmenham; close beside which arose an irregular pile of building which Dick told us was a very pleasant house; and there were plenty of houses visible on the wide meadows opposite, under the hill; for, as it seems that the beauty of Hurley had compelled people to build and live there a good deal. The sun very low down showed us Henley little altered in outward aspect from what I remembered it. Actual daylight failed us as we passed through the lovely reaches of Wargrave and Shiplake; but the moon rose behind us presently. I should like to have seen with my eyes what success the new order of things had had in getting rid of the sprawling mess with which commercialism had littered the banks of the wide stream about Reading and Caversham:

certainly everything smelt too deliciously in the early night for there to be any of the old careless sordidness of so-called manufacture; and in answer to my question as to what sort of a place Reading was, Dick answered:

"O, a nice town enough in its way; mostly rebuilt within the last hundred years; and there are a good many houses, as you can see by the lights just down under the hills yonder. In fact, it is one of the most populous places on the Thames round about here. Keep up your spirits, guest! we are close to our journey's end for the night. I ought to ask your pardon for not stopping at one of the houses here or higher up; but a friend, who is living in a very pleasant house in the Maple-Durham meads, particularly wanted me and Clara to come and see him on our way up the Thames; and I thought you wouldn't mind this bit of night travelling."

He need not have adjured me to keep up my spirits, which were as high as possible; though the strangeness and excitement of the happy and quiet life which I saw everywhere around me was, it is true, a little wearing off, yet a deep content, as different as possible from languid acquiescence, was taking its place, and I was, as it were, really new-born.

We landed presently just where I remembered the river making an elbow to the north towards the ancient house of the Blunts; with the wide meadows spreading on the right-hand side, and on the left the long line of beautiful old trees overhanging the water. As we got out of the boat, I said to Dick—

"Is it the old house we are going to?"

"No," he said, "though that is standing still in green old age, and is well inhabited. I see, by the way, that you know your Thames well. But my friend Walter Allen, who asked me to stop here, lives in a house, not very big, which has been built here lately, because these meadows are so much liked, especially in summer, that there was getting to be rather too much of tenting on the open field; so the parishes here about, who rather objected to that, built three houses between this and Caversham, and quite a large one at Basildon, a little higher up. Look, yonder are the lights of Walter Allen's house!"

So we walked over the grass of the meadows under a flood of moonlight, and soon came to the house, which was low and built round a quadrangle big enough to get plenty of sunshine in it. Walter Allen, Dick's friend, was leaning against the jamb of the doorway waiting for us, and took us into the hall without overplus of words. There were not many people in it, as some of the dwellers there were away at the haymaking in the neighbourhood, and some, as Walter told us, were wandering about the meadow enjoying the beautiful moonlit night. Dick's friend looked to be a man of about forty; tall, black-haired, very kind-looking and thoughtful; but rather to my surprise there was a shade of melancholy on his face, and he seemed a little abstracted and inattentive to our chat, in spite of obvious efforts to listen.

Dick looked on him from time to time, and seemed troubled; and at last he said: "I say, old fellow, if there is anything the matter which we didn't know of when you wrote to me, don't you think you had better tell us about it at once? Or else we shall think we have come here at an unlucky time, and are not quite wanted."

Walter turned red, and seemed to have some difficulty in restraining his tears, but said at last: "Of course everybody here is very glad to see you, Dick, and your friends; but it is true that we are not at our best, in spite of the fine weather and the glorious hay-crop. We have had a death here."

Said Dick: "Well, you should get over that, neighbour: such things must be."

"Yes," Walter said, "but this was a death by violence, and it seems likely to lead to at least one more; and somehow it makes us feel rather shy of one another; and to say the truth, that is one reason why there are so few of us present to-night."

"Tell us the story, Walter," said Dick; "perhaps telling it will help you to shake off your sadness."

Said Walter: "Well, I will; and I will make it short enough, though I daresay it might be spun out into a long one, as used to be done with such subjects in the old novels. There is a very charming girl here whom we all like, and whom some of us do more than like; and she very naturally liked one of us better than anybody else. And another of us (I won't name him) got fairly bitten with love-madness, and used to go about making himself as unpleasant as he could—not of malice prepense, of course; so that the girl, who liked him well enough at first, though she didn't love him, began fairly to dislike him. Of course, those of us who knew him best—myself amongst others—advised him to go away, as he was making matters worse and worse for himself every day. Well, he wouldn't take our advice (that also, I suppose, was a matter of course), so we had to tell him that he *must* go, or the inevitable sending to Coventry would follow; for his individual trouble had so overmastered him that we felt that *we* must go if he did not.

"He took that better than we expected, when something or other—an interview with the girl, I think, and some hot words with the successful lover following close upon it, threw him quite off his balance; and he got hold of an axe and fell upon his rival when there was no one by; and in the struggle that followed the man attacked, hit him an unlucky blow and killed him. And now the slayer in his turn is so upset that he is like to kill himself; and if he does, the girl will do as much, I fear. And all this we could no more help than the earthquake of the year before last."

"It is very unhappy," said Dick; "but since the man is dead, and cannot be brought to life again, and since the slayer had no malice in him, I cannot for the life of me see why he shouldn't get over it before long. Besides, it was the right man that was killed and not the wrong. Why should a man brood over a mere accident for ever? And the girl?"

"As to her," said Walter, "the whole thing seems to have inspired her with terror rather than grief. What you say about the man is true, or it should be; but then, you see, the excitement and jealousy that was the prelude to this tragedy had made an evil and feverish element round about him, from which he does not seem to be able to escape. However, we have advised him to go away—in fact, to cross the seas; but he is in such a state that I do not think he *can* go unless someone *takes* him, and I think it will fall to my lot to do so; which is scarcely a cheerful outlook for me."

"O, you will find a certain kind of interest in it," said Dick. "And of course he *must* soon look upon the affair from a reasonable point of view sooner or later."

"Well, at any rate," quoth Walter, "now that I have eased my mind by making you uncomfortable, let us have an end of the subject for the present. Are you going to take your guest to Oxford?"

"Why, of course we must pass through it," said Dick, smiling, "as we are going into the upper waters: but I thought that we wouldn't stop there, or we shall be belated as to the haymaking up our way. So Oxford and my learned lecture on it, all got at second-hand from my old kinsman, must wait till we come down the water a fortnight hence."

I listened to this story with much surprise, and could not help wondering at first that the man who had slain the other had not been put in custody till it could be proved that he killed his rival in self-defence only. However, the more I thought of it, the plainer it grew to me that no amount of examination of witnesses, who had witnessed nothing but the ill-blood between the two rivals, would have done anything to clear up the case. I could not help thinking, also, that the remorse of this homicide gave point to what old Hammond had said to me about the way in which this strange people dealt with what I had been used to hear called crimes. Truly, the remorse was exaggerated; but it was quite clear that the slayer took the whole consequences of the act upon himself, and did not expect society to whitewash him by punishing him. I had no fear any longer that "the sacredness of human life" was likely to suffer amongst my friends from the absence of gallows and prison.

25. THE THIRD DAY ON THE THAMES

As we went down to the boat next morning, Walter could not quite keep off the subject of last night, though he was more hopeful than he had been then, and seemed to think that if the unlucky homicide could not be got to go over-sea, he might at any rate go and live somewhere in the neighbourhood pretty much by himself; at any rate, that was what he himself had proposed. To Dick, and I must say to me also, this seemed a strange remedy; and Dick said as much. Quoth he:

"Friend Walter, don't set the man brooding on the tragedy by letting him live alone. That will only strengthen his idea that he has committed a crime, and you will have him killing himself in good earnest."

Said Clara: "I don't know. If I may say what I think of it, it is that he had better have his fill of gloom now, and, so to say, wake up presently to see how little need there has been for it; and then he will live happily afterwards. As for his killing himself, you need not be afraid of that; for, from all you tell me, he is really very much in love with the woman; and to speak plainly, until his love is satisfied, he will not only stick to life as tightly as he can, but will also make the most of every event of his life—will, so to say, hug himself up in it; and I think that this is the real explanation of his taking the whole matter with such an excess of tragedy."

Walter looked thoughtful, and said: "Well, you may be right; and perhaps we should have treated it all more lightly: but you see, guest" (turning to me), "such things happen so seldom, that when they do happen, we cannot help being much taken up with it. For the rest, we are all inclined, to excuse our poor friend for making us so unhappy, on the ground that he does it out of an exaggerated respect for human life and its happiness. Well, I will say no more about it; only this: will you give me a cast up stream, as I want to look after a lonely habitation for the poor fellow, since he will have it so, and I hear that there is one which would suit us very well on the downs beyond Streatley; so if you will put me ashore there I will walk up the hill and look to it."

"Is the house in question empty?" said I.

"No," said Walter, "but the man who lives there will go out of it, of course, when he hears that we want it. You see, we think that the fresh air of the downs and the very emptiness of the landscape will do our friend good."

"Yes," said Clara, smiling, "and he will not be so far from his beloved that they cannot easily meet if they have a mind to—as they certainly will."

This talk had brought us down to the boat, and we were presently afloat on the beautiful broad stream, Dick driving the prow swiftly through the windless water of the early summer morning, for it was not yet six o'clock. We were at the lock in a very little time; and as we lay rising and rising on the in-coming water, I could not help wondering that my old friend the pound-lock, and that of the very simplest and most rural kind, should hold its place there; so I said:

"I have been wondering, as we passed lock after lock, that you people, so prosperous as you are, and especially since you are so anxious for pleasant work to do, have not invented something which would get rid of this clumsy business of going up-stairs by means of these rude contrivances."

Dick laughed. "My dear friend," said he, "as long as water has the clumsy habit of running down hill, I fear we must humour it by going up-stairs when we have our faces turned from the sea. And really I don't see why you should fall foul of Maple-Durham lock, which I think a very pretty place."

There was no doubt about the latter assertion, I thought, as I looked up at the overhanging boughs of the great trees, with the sun coming glittering through the leaves, and listened to the song of the summer blackbirds as it mingled with the sound of the backwater near us. So not being able to say why I wanted the locks away—which, indeed, I didn't do at all—I held my peace. But Walter said—

"You see, guest, this is not an age of inventions. The last epoch did all that for us, and we are now content to use such of its inventions as we find handy, and leaving those alone which we don't want. I believe, as a matter of fact, that some time ago (I can't give you a date) some elaborate machinery was used for the locks, though people did not go so far as try to make the water run up hill. However, it was troublesome, I suppose, and the simple hatches, and the gates, with a big counterpoising beam, were found to answer every purpose, and were easily mended when wanted with material always to hand: so here they are, as you see."

"Besides," said Dick, "this kind of lock is pretty, as you can see; and I can't help thinking that your machine-lock, winding up like a watch, would have been ugly and would have spoiled the look of the river: and that is surely reason enough for keeping such locks as these. Good-bye, old fellow!" said he to the lock, as he pushed us out through the now open gates by a vigorous stroke of the boat-hook. "May you live long, and have your green old age renewed for ever!"

On we went; and the water had the familiar aspect to me of the days before Pangbourne had been thoroughly cocknified, as I have seen it. It (Pangbourne) was distinctly a village still—*i.e.*, a definite group of houses, and as pretty as might be. The beech-woods still covered the hill that rose above Basildon; but the flat fields beneath them were much more populous than I remembered them, as there were five large houses in sight, very carefully designed so as not to hurt the character of the country. Down on the green lip of the river, just where the water turns toward the Goring and Streatley reaches, were half a dozen girls playing about on the grass. They hailed us as we were about passing them, as they noted that we were travellers, and we stopped a minute to talk with them. They had been bathing, and were light clad and bare-footed, and were bound for the meadows on the Berkshire side, where the haymaking had begun, and were passing the time merrily enough till the Berkshire folk came in their punt to fetch them. At first nothing would content them but we must go with them into the hay-field, and breakfast with them; but Dick put forward his theory of beginning the hay-harvest higher up the water, and not spoiling my pleasure therein by giving me a taste of it elsewhere, and they gave way, though unwillingly. In revenge they asked me a great many questions about the country I came from and the manners of life there, which I found rather puzzling to answer; and doubtless what answers I did give were puzzling enough to them. I noticed both with these pretty girls and with everybody else we met, that in default of serious news, such as we had heard at Maple-Durham, they were eager to discuss all the little details of life: the weather, the hay-crop, the last new house, the plenty or lack of such and such birds, and so on; and they talked of these things not in a fatuous and conventional way, but as taking, I say, real interest in them. Moreover, I found that the women knew as much about all these things as the men: could name a flower, and knew its qualities; could tell you the habitat of such and such birds and fish, and the like.

It is almost strange what a difference this intelligence made in my estimate of the country life of that day; for it used to be said in past times, and on the whole truly, that outside their daily work country people knew little of the country, and at least could tell you nothing about it; while here were these people as eager about all the goings on in the fields and woods and downs as if they had been Cockneys newly escaped from the tyranny of bricks and mortar.

I may mention as a detail worth noticing that not only did there seem to be a great many more birds about of the non-predatory kinds, but their enemies the birds of prey were also commoner. A kite hung over our heads as we passed Medmenham yesterday; magpies were quite common in the hedgerows; I saw several sparrow-hawks, and I think a merlin; and now just as we were passing the pretty bridge which had taken the place of Basildon railway-bridge, a couple of ravens croaked above our boat, as they sailed off to the higher ground of the downs. I concluded from all this that the days of the gamekeeper were over, and did not even need to ask Dick a question about it.

26. THE OBSTINATE REFUSERS

Before we parted from these girls we saw two sturdy young men and a woman putting off from the Berkshire shore, and then Dick bethought him of a little banter of the girls, and asked them how it was that there was nobody of the male kind to go with them across the water, and where their boats were gone to. Said one, the youngest of the party: "O, they have got the big punt to lead stone from up the water."

"Who do you mean by 'they,' dear child?" said Dick.

Said an older girl, laughing: "You had better go and see them. Look there," and she pointed northwest, "don't you see building going on there?"

"Yes," said Dick, "and I am rather surprised at this time of the year; why are they not haymaking with you?"

The girls all laughed at this, and before their laugh was over, the Berkshire boat had run on to the grass and the girls stepped in lightly, still sniggering, while the new comers gave us the sele of the day. But before they were under way again, the tall girl said:

"Excuse us for laughing, dear neighbours, but we have had some friendly bickering with the builders up yonder, and as we have no time to tell you the story, you had better go and ask them: they will be glad to see you—if you don't hinder their work."

They all laughed again at that, and waved us a pretty farewell as the punters set them over toward the other shore, and left us standing on the bank beside our boat.

"Let us go and see them," said Clara; "that is, if you are not in a hurry to get to Streatley, Walter?"

"O no," said Walter, "I shall be glad of the excuse to have a little more of your company."

So we left the boat moored there, and went on up the slow slope of the hill; but I said to Dick on the way, being somewhat mystified: "What was all that laughing about? what was the joke!"

"I can guess pretty well," said Dick; "some of them up there have got a piece of work which interests them, and they won't go to the haymaking, which doesn't matter at all, because there are plenty of people to do such easy-hard work as that; only, since haymaking is a regular festival, the neighbours find it amusing to jeer good-humouredly at them."

"I see," said I, "much as if in Dickens's time some young people were so wrapped up in their work that they wouldn't keep Christmas."

"Just so," said Dick, "only these people need not be young either."

"But what did you mean by easy-hard work?" said I.

Quoth Dick: "Did I say that? I mean work that tries the muscles and hardens them and sends you pleasantly weary to bed, but which isn't trying in other ways: doesn't harass you in short. Such work is always pleasant if you don't overdo it. Only, mind you, good mowing requires some little skill. I'm a pretty good mower."

This talk brought us up to the house that was a-building, not a large one, which stood at the end of a beautiful orchard surrounded by an old stone wall. "O yes, I see," said Dick; "I remember, a beautiful place for a house: but a starveling of a nineteenth century house stood there: I am glad they are rebuilding: it's all stone, too, though it need not have been in this part of the country: my word, though, they are making a neat job of it: but I wouldn't have made it all ashlar."

Walter and Clara were already talking to a tall man clad in his mason's blouse, who looked about forty, but was I daresay older, who had his mallet and chisel in hand; there were at work in the shed and on the scaffold about half a dozen men and two women, blouse-clad like the carles, while a very pretty woman who was not in the work but was dressed in an elegant suit of blue linen came sauntering up to us with her knitting in her hand. She welcomed us and said, smiling: "So you are come up from the water to see the Obstinate Refusers: where are you going haymaking, neighbours?"

"O, right up above Oxford," said Dick; "it is rather a late country. But what share have you got with the Refusers, pretty neighbour?"

Said she, with a laugh: "O, I am the lucky one who doesn't want to work;

though sometimes I get it, for I serve as model to Mistress Philippa there when she wants one: she is our head carver; come and see her."

She led us up to the door of the unfinished house, where a rather little woman was working with mallet and chisel on the wall near by. She seemed very intent on what she was doing, and did not turn round when we came up; but a taller woman, quite a girl she seemed, who was at work near by, had already knocked off, and was standing looking from Clara to Dick with delighted eyes. None of the others paid much heed to us.

The blue-clad girl laid her hand on the carver's shoulder and said: "Now Philippa, if you gobble up your work like that, you will soon have none to do; and what will become of you then?"

The carver turned round hurriedly and showed us the face of a woman of forty (or so she seemed), and said rather pettishly, but in a sweet voice:

"Don't talk nonsense, Kate, and don't interrupt me if you can help it." She stopped short when she saw us, then went on with the kind smile of welcome which never failed us. "Thank you for coming to see us, neighbours; but I am sure that you won't think me unkind if I go on with my work, especially when I tell you that I was ill and unable to do anything all through April and May; and this open-air and the sun and the work together, and my feeling well again too, make a mere delight of every hour to me; and excuse me, I must go on."

She fell to work accordingly on a carving in low relief of flowers and figures, but talked on amidst her mallet strokes: "You see, we all think this the prettiest place for a house up and down these reaches; and the site has been so long encumbered with an unworthy one, that we masons were determined to pay off fate and destiny for once, and build the prettiest house we could compass here— and so—and so—"

Here she lapsed into mere carving, but the tall foreman came up and said: "Yes, neighbours, that is it: so it is going to be all ashlar because we want to carve a kind of a wreath of flowers and figures all round it; and we have been much hindered by one thing or other—Philippa's illness amongst others,—and though we could have managed our wreath without her—"

"Could you, though?" grumbled the last-named from the face of the wall.

"Well, at any rate, she is our best carver, and it would not have been kind to begin the carving without her. So you see," said he, looking at Dick and me, "we really couldn't go haymaking, could we, neighbours? But you see, we are getting on so fast now with this splendid weather, that I think we may well spare a week or ten days at wheat-harvest; and won't we go at that work then! Come down then to the acres that lie north and by west here at our backs and you shall see good harvesters, neighbours.

"Hurrah, for a good brag!" called a voice from the scaffold above us; "our foreman thinks that an easier job than putting one stone on another!"

There was a general laugh at this sally, in which the tall foreman joined; and with that we saw a lad bringing out a little table into the shadow of the stone-shed, which he set down there, and then going back, came out again with the inevitable big wickered flask and tall glasses, whereon the foreman led us up to due seats on blocks of stone, and said:

"Well, neighbours, drink to my brag coming true, or I shall think you don't believe me! Up there!" said he, hailing the scaffold, "are you coming down for a glass?" Three of the workmen came running down the ladder as men with good "building legs" will do; but the others didn't answer, except the joker (if he must so be called), who called out without turning round: "Excuse me, neighbours for not getting down. I must get on: my work is not superintending, like the gaffer's yonder; but, you fellows, send us up a glass to drink the haymakers' health." Of course, Philippa would not turn away from her beloved work; but the other woman carver came; she turned out to be Philippa's daughter, but was a tall strong girl, black-haired and gipsey-like of face and curiously solemn of manner. The rest gathered round us and clinked glasses, and the men on the scaffold turned about and drank to our healths; but the busy little woman by the door would have none of it all, but only shrugged her shoulders when her daughter came up to her and touched her.

So we shook hands and turned our backs on the Obstinate Refusers, went down the slope to our boat, and before we had gone many steps heard the full tune of tinkling trowels mingle with the humming of the bees and the singing of the larks above the little plain of Basildon.

27. THE UPPER WATERS

We set Walter ashore on the Berkshire side, amidst all the beauties of Streatley, and so went our ways into what once would have been the deeper country under the foot-hills of the White Horse; and though the contrast between half-cocknified and wholly unsophisticated country existed no longer, a feeling of exultation rose within me (as it used to do) at sight of the familiar and still unchanged hills of the Berkshire range.

We stopped at Wallingford for our mid-day meal; of course, all signs of squalor and poverty had disappeared from the streets of the ancient town, and many ugly houses had been taken down and many pretty new ones built, but I thought it curious, that the town still looked like the old place I remembered so well; for indeed it looked like that ought to have looked.

At dinner we fell in with an old, but very bright and intelligent man, who seemed in a country way to be another edition of old Hammond. He had an extraordinary detailed knowledge of the ancient history of the country-side from the time of Alfred to the days of the Parliamentary Wars, many events of which, as you may know, were enacted round about Wallingford. But, what was more interesting to us, he had detailed record of the period of the change to the present state of things, and told us a great deal about it, and especially of that exodus of the people from the town to the country, and the gradual recovery by the town-bred people on one side, and the country-bred people on the other, of those arts of life which they had each lost; which loss, as he told us, had at one time gone so far that not only was it impossible to find a carpenter or a smith in a village or small country town, but that people in such places had even forgotten how to bake bread, and that at Wallingford, for instance, the bread came down with the newspapers by an early train from London, worked in some way, the explanation of which I could not understand. He told us also that the townspeople who came into the country used to pick up the agricultural arts by carefully watching the way in which the machines worked, gathering an idea of handicraft from machinery; because at that time almost everything in and about the fields was done by elaborate machines used quite unintelligently by the labourers. On the other hand, the old men amongst the labourers managed to teach the younger ones gradually a little artizanship, such as the use of the saw and the plane, the work of the smithy, and so forth; for once more, by that time it was as much as—or rather, more than—a man could do to fix an ash pole to a rake by handiwork; so that it would take a machine worth a thousand pounds, a group of workmen, and half a day's travelling, to do five shillings' worth of work. He showed us, among other things, an account of a certain village council who were working hard at all this business; and the record of their intense earnestness in getting to the bottom of some matter which in time past would have been thought quite trivial, as, for example, the due proportions of alkali and oil for soap-making for the village wash, or the exact heat of the water into which a leg of mutton should be plunged for boiling—all this joined to the utter absence of anything like party feeling, which even in a village assembly would certainly have made its appearance in an earlier epoch, was very amusing, and at the same time instructive.

 This old man, whose name was Henry Morsom, took us, after our meal and a rest, into a biggish hall which contained a large collection of articles of manufacture and art from the last days of the machine period to that day; and he went over them with us, and explained them with great care. They also were very interesting, showing the transition from the makeshift work of the machines (which was at about its worst a little after the Civil War before told of) into the first years of the new handicraft period. Of course, there was much overlapping of the periods: and at first the new handwork came in very slowly.

 "You must remember," said the old antiquary, "that the handicraft was not the result of what used to be called material necessity: on the contrary, by that time the machines had been so much improved that almost all necessary work might have been done by them: and indeed many people at that time, and before it, used to think that machinery would entirely supersede handicraft; which certainly, on the face of it, seemed more than likely. But there was another opinion, far less logical, prevalent amongst the rich people before the days of freedom, which did not die out at once after that epoch had begun. This opinion, which from all I can learn seemed as natural then, as it seems absurd now, was, that while the ordinary daily work of the world would be done entirely by automatic machinery, the energies of the more intelligent part of mankind would be set free to follow the higher forms of the arts, as well as science and the study of history. It was strange, was it not, that they should thus ignore that aspiration after complete equality which we now recognise as the bond of all happy human society?"

I did not answer, but thought the more. Dick looked thoughtful, and said:

"Strange, neighbour? Well, I don't know. I have often heard my old kinsman say the one aim of all people before our time was to avoid work, or at least they thought it was; so of course the work which their daily life forced them to do, seemed more like work than that which they seemed to choose for themselves."

"True enough," said Morsom. "Anyhow, they soon began to find out their mistake, and that only slaves and slave-holders could live solely by setting machines going."

Clara broke in here, flushing a little as she spoke: "Was not their mistake once more bred of the life of slavery that they had been living?—a life which was always looking upon everything, except mankind, animate and inanimate—'nature,' as people used to call it—as one thing, and mankind as another, it was natural to people thinking in this way, that they should try to make 'nature' their slave, since they thought 'nature' was something outside them."

"Surely," said Morsom; "and they were puzzled as to what to do, till they found the feeling against a mechanical life, which had begun before the Great Change amongst people who had leisure to think of such things, was spreading insensibly; till at last under the guise of pleasure that was not supposed to be work, work that was pleasure began to push out the mechanical toil, which they had once hoped at the best to reduce to narrow limits indeed, but never to get rid of; and which, moreover, they found they could not limit as they had hoped to do."

"When did this new revolution gather head?" said I.

"In the half-century that followed the Great Change," said Morsom, "it began to be noteworthy; machine after machine was quietly dropped under the excuse that the machines could not produce works of art, and that works of art were more and more called for. Look here," he said, "here are some of the works of that time—rough and unskillful in handiwork, but solid and showing some sense of pleasure in the making."

"They are very curious," said I, taking up a piece of pottery from amongst the specimens which the antiquary was showing us; "not a bit like the work of either savages or barbarians, and yet with what would once have been called a hatred of civilisation impressed upon them."

"Yes," said Morsom, "you must not look for delicacy there: in that period you could only have got that from a man who was practically a slave. But now, you see," said he, leading me on a little, "we have learned the trick of handicraft, and have added the utmost refinement of workmanship to the freedom of fancy and imagination."

I looked, and wondered indeed at the deftness and abundance of beauty of the work of men who had at last learned to accept life itself as a pleasure, and the satisfaction of the common needs of mankind and the preparation for them, as work fit for the best of the race. I mused silently; but at last I said—

"What is to come after this?"

The old man laughed. "I don't know," said he; "we will meet it when it comes."

"Meanwhile," quoth Dick, "we have got to meet the rest of our day's journey; so out into the street and down to the strand! Will you come a turn with us, neighbour? Our friend is greedy of your stories."

"I will go as far as Oxford with you," said he; "I want a book or two out of the Bodleian Library. I suppose you will sleep in the old city?"

"No," said Dick, "we are going higher up; the hay is waiting us there, you know."

Morsom nodded, and we all went into the street together, and got into the boat a little above the town bridge. But just as Dick was getting the sculls into the rowlocks, the bows of another boat came thrusting through the low arch. Even at first sight it was a gay little craft indeed—bright green, and painted over with elegantly drawn flowers. As it cleared the arch, a figure as bright and gay-clad as the boat rose up in it; a slim girl dressed in light blue silk that fluttered in the draughty wind of the bridge. I thought I knew the figure, and sure enough, as she turned her head to us, and showed her beautiful face, I saw with joy that it was none other than the fairy godmother from the abundant garden on Runnymede—Ellen, to wit.

We all stopped to receive her. Dick rose in the boat and cried out a genial good morrow; I tried to be as genial as Dick, but failed; Clara waved a delicate hand to her; and Morsom nodded and looked on with interest. As to Ellen, the beautiful brown of her face was deepened by a flush, as she brought the gunwale of her boat alongside ours, and said:

"You see, neighbours, I had some doubt if you would all three come back past Runnymede, or if you did, whether you would stop there; and besides, I am not sure whether we—my father and I—shall not be away in a week or two, for he wants to see a brother of his in the north country, and I should not like him to go without me. So I thought I might never see you again, and that seemed uncomfortable to me, and—and so I came after you."

"Well," said Dick, "I am sure we are all very glad of that; although you may be sure that as for Clara and me, we should have made a point of coming to see you, and of coming the second time, if we had found you away the first. But, dear neighbour, there you are alone in the boat, and you have been sculling pretty hard I should think, and might find a little quiet sitting pleasant; so we had better part our company into two."

"Yes," said Ellen, "I thought you would do that, so I have brought a rudder for my boat: will you help me to ship it, please?"

And she went aft in her boat and pushed along our side till she had brought the stern close to Dick's hand. He knelt down in our boat and she in hers, and the usual fumbling took place over hanging the rudder on its hooks; for, as you may imagine, no change had taken place in the arrangement of such an unimportant matter as the rudder of a pleasure-boat. As the two beautiful young faces bent over the rudder, they seemed to me to be very close together, and though it only lasted a moment, a sort of pang shot through me as I looked on. Clara sat in her place and did not look round, but presently she said, with just the least stiffness in her tone:

"How shall we divide? Won't you go into Ellen's boat, Dick, since, without offence to our guest, you are the better sculler?"

Dick stood up and laid his hand on her shoulder, and said: "No, no; let Guest try what he can do—he ought to be getting into training now. Besides, we are in no hurry: we are not going far above Oxford; and even if we are benighted, we shall have the moon, which will give us nothing worse of a night than a greyer day."

"Besides," said I, "I may manage to do a little more with my sculling than merely keeping the boat from drifting down stream."

They all laughed at this, as if it had a been very good joke; and I thought that Ellen's laugh, even amongst the others, was one of the pleasantest sounds I had ever heard.

To be short, I got into the new-come boat, not a little elated, and taking the sculls, set to work to show off a little. For—must I say it?—I felt as if even that happy world were made the happier for my being so near this strange girl; although I must say that of all the persons I had seen in that world renewed, she was the most unfamiliar to me, the most unlike what I could have thought of. Clara, for instance, beautiful and bright as she was, was not unlike a *very* pleasant and unaffected young lady; and the other girls also seemed nothing more than specimens of very much improved types which I had known in other times. But this girl was not only beautiful with a beauty quite different from that of "a young lady," but was in all ways so strangely interesting; so that I kept wondering what she would say or do next to surprise and please me. Not, indeed, that there was anything startling in what she actually said or did; but it was all done in a new way, and always with that indefinable interest and pleasure of life, which I had noticed more or less in everybody, but which in her was more marked and more charming than in anyone else that I had seen.

We were soon under way and going at a fair pace through the beautiful reaches of the river, between Bensington and Dorchester. It was now about the middle of the afternoon, warm rather than hot, and quite windless; the clouds high up and light, pearly white, and gleaming, softened the sun's burning, but did not hide the pale blue in most places, though they seemed to give it height and consistency; the sky, in short, looked really like a vault, as poets have sometimes called it, and not like mere limitless air, but a vault so vast and full of light that it did not in any way oppress the spirits. It was the sort of afternoon that Tennyson must have been thinking about, when he said of the Lotos-Eaters' land that it was a land where it was always afternoon.

Ellen leaned back in the stern and seemed to enjoy herself thoroughly. I could see that she was really looking at things and let nothing escape her, and as I watched her, an uncomfortable feeling that she had been a little touched by love of the deft, ready, and handsome Dick, and that she had been constrained to follow us because of it, faded out of my mind; since if it had been so, she surely could not have been so excitedly pleased, even with the beautiful scenes we were passing through. For some time she did not say much, but at last, as we had passed under Shillingford Bridge (new built, but somewhat on its old lines), she bade me hold the boat while she had a good look at the landscape through the graceful arch. Then she turned about to me and said:

"I do not know whether to be sorry or glad that this is the first time that I have been in these reaches. It is true that it is a great pleasure to see all this for the first time; but if I had had a year or two of memory of it, how sweetly it would all have mingled with my life, waking or dreaming! I am so glad Dick has been pulling slowly, so as to linger out the time here. How do you feel about your first visit to these waters?"

I do not suppose she meant a trap for me, but anyhow I fell into it, and said: "My first visit! It is not my first visit by many a time. I know these reaches well; indeed, I may say that I know every yard of the Thames from Hammersmith to Cricklade."

I saw the complications that might follow, as her eyes fixed mine with a curious look in them, that I had seen before at Runnymede, when I had said something which made it difficult for others to understand my present position amongst these people. I reddened, and said, in order to cover my mistake: "I wonder you have never been up so high as this, since you live on the Thames, and moreover row so well that it would be no great labour to you. Let alone," quoth I, insinuatingly, "that anybody would be glad to row you."

She laughed, clearly not at my compliment (as I am sure she need not have done, since it was a very commonplace fact), but at something which was stirring in her mind; and she still looked at me kindly, but with the above-said keen look in her eyes, and then she said:

"Well, perhaps it is strange, though I have a good deal to do at home, what with looking after my father, and dealing with two or three young men who have taken a special liking to me, and all of whom I cannot please at once. But you, dear neighbour; it seems to me stranger that you should know the upper river, than that I should not know it; for, as I understand, you have only been in England a few days. But perhaps you mean that you have read about it in books, and seen pictures of it?—though that does not come to much, either."

"Truly," said I. "Besides, I have not read any books about the Thames: it was one of the minor stupidities of our time that no one thought fit to write a decent book about what may fairly be called our only English river."

The words were no sooner out of my mouth than I saw that I had made another mistake; and I felt really annoyed with myself, as I did not want to go into a long explanation just then, or begin another series of Odyssean lies. Somehow, Ellen seemed to see this, and she took no advantage of my slip; her piercing look changed into one of mere frank kindness, and she said:

"Well, anyhow I am glad that I am travelling these waters with you, since you know our river so well, and I know little of it past Pangbourne, for you can tell me all I want to know about it." She paused a minute, and then said: "Yet you must understand that the part I do know, I know as thoroughly as you do. I should be sorry for you to think that I am careless of a thing so beautiful and interesting as the Thames."

She said this quite earnestly, and with an air of affectionate appeal to me which pleased me very much; but I could see that she was only keeping her doubts about me for another time.

Presently we came to Day's Lock, where Dick and his two sitters had waited for us. He would have me go ashore, as if to show me something which I had never seen before; and nothing loth I followed him, Ellen by my side, to the well-remembered Dykes, and the long church beyond them, which was still used for various purposes by the good folk of Dorchester: where, by the way, the village guest-house still had the sign of the Fleur-de-luce which it used to bear in the days when hospitality had to be bought and sold. This time, however, I made no sign of all this being familiar to me: though as we sat for a while on the mound of the Dykes looking up at Sinodun and its clear-cut trench, and its sister *mamelon* of Whittenham, I felt somewhat uncomfortable under Ellen's serious attentive look, which almost drew from me the cry, "How little anything is changed here!"

We stopped again at Abingdon, which, like Wallingford, was in a way both old and new to me, since it had been lifted out of its nineteenth-century degradation, and otherwise was as little altered as might be.

Sunset was in the sky as we skirted Oxford by Oseney; we stopped a minute or two hard by the ancient castle to put Henry Morsom ashore. It was a matter of course that so far as they could be seen from the river, I missed none of the towers and spires of that once don-beridden city; but the meadows all round, which, when I had last passed through them, were getting daily more and more squalid, more and more impressed with the seal of the "stir and intellectual life of the nineteenth century," were no longer intellectual, but had once again become as beautiful as they should be, and the little hill of Hinksey, with two or three very pretty stone houses new-grown on it (I use the word advisedly; for they seemed to belong to it) looked down happily on the full streams and waving grass, grey now, but for the sunset, with its fast-ripening seeds.

The railway having disappeared, and therewith the various level bridges over the streams of Thames, we were soon through Medley Lock and in the wide water that washes Port Meadow, with its numerous population of geese nowise diminished; and I thought with interest how its name and use had survived from the older imperfect communal period, through the time of the confused struggle and tyranny of the rights of property, into the present rest and happiness of complete Communism.

I was taken ashore again at Godstow, to see the remains of the old nunnery, pretty nearly in the same condition as I had remembered them; and from the high bridge over the cut close by, I could see, even in the twilight, how beautiful the little village with its grey stone houses had become; for we had now come into the stone-country, in which every house must be either built, walls and roof, of grey stone or be a blot on the landscape.

We still rowed on after this, Ellen taking the sculls in my boat; we passed a weir a little higher up, and about three miles beyond it came by moonlight again to a little town, where we slept at a house thinly inhabited, as its folk were mostly tented in the hay-fields.

28. THE LITTLE RIVER

We started before six o'clock the next morning, as we were still twenty-five miles from our resting place, and Dick wanted to be there before dusk. The journey was pleasant, though to those who do not know the upper Thames, there is little to say about it. Ellen and I were once more together in her boat, though Dick, for fairness' sake, was for having me in his, and letting the two women scull the green toy. Ellen, however, would not allow this, but claimed me as the interesting person of the company. "After having come so far," said she, "I will not be put off with a companion who will be always thinking of somebody else than me: the guest is the only person who can amuse me properly. I mean that really," said she, turning to me, "and have not said it merely as a pretty saying."

Clara blushed and looked very happy at all this; for I think up to this time she had been rather frightened of Ellen. As for me I felt young again, and strange hopes of my youth were mingling with the pleasure of the present; almost destroying it, and quickening it into something like pain.

As we passed through the short and winding reaches of the now quickly lessening stream, Ellen said: "How pleasant this little river is to me, who am used to a great wide wash of water; it almost seems as if we shall have to stop at every reach-end. I expect before I get home this evening I shall have realised what a little country England is, since we can so soon get to the end of its biggest river."

"It is not big," said I, "but it is pretty."

"Yes," she said, "and don't you find it difficult to imagine the times when this little pretty country was treated by its folk as if it had been an ugly characterless waste, with no delicate beauty to be guarded, with no heed taken of the ever fresh pleasure of the recurring seasons, and changeful weather, and diverse quality of the soil, and so forth? How could people be so cruel to themselves?"

"And to each other," said I. Then a sudden resolution took hold of me, and I said: "Dear neighbour, I may as well tell you at once that I find it easier to imagine all that ugly past than you do, because I myself have been part of it. I see both that you have divined something of this in me; and also I think you will believe me when I tell you of it, so that I am going to hide nothing from you at all."

She was silent a little, and then she said: "My friend, you have guessed right about me; and to tell you the truth I have followed you up from Runnymede in order that I might ask you many questions, and because I saw that you were not one of us; and that interested and pleased me, and I wanted to make you as happy as you could be. To say the truth, there was a risk in it," said she, blushing —"I mean as to Dick and Clara; for I must tell you, since we are going to be such close friends, that even amongst us, where there are so many beautiful women, I have often troubled men's minds disastrously. That is one reason why I was living alone with my father in the cottage at Runnymede. But it did not answer on that score; for of course people came there, as the place is not a desert, and they seemed to find me all the more interesting for living alone like that, and fell to making stories of me to themselves—like I know you did, my friend. Well, let that pass. This evening, or to-morrow morning, I shall make a proposal to you to do something which would please me very much, and I think would not hurt you."

I broke in eagerly, saying that I would do anything in the world for her; for indeed, in spite of my years and the too obvious signs of them (though that feeling of renewed youth was not a mere passing sensation, I think)—in spite of my years, I say, I felt altogether too happy in the company of this delightful girl, and was prepared to take her confidences for more than they meant perhaps.

She laughed now, but looked very kindly on me. "Well," she said, "meantime for the present we will let it be; for I must look at this new country that we are passing through. See how the river has changed character again: it is broad now, and the reaches are long and very slow-running. And look, there is a ferry!"

I told her the name of it, as I slowed off to put the ferry-chain over our heads; and on we went passing by a bank clad with oak trees on our left hand, till the stream narrowed again and deepened, and we rowed on between walls of tall reeds, whose population of reed sparrows and warblers were delightfully restless, twittering and chuckling as the wash of the boats stirred the reeds from the water upwards in the still, hot morning.

She smiled with pleasure, and her lazy enjoyment of the new scene seemed to bring out her beauty doubly as she leaned back amidst the cushions, though she was far from languid; her idleness being the idleness of a person, strong and well-knit both in body and mind, deliberately resting.

"Look!" she said, springing up suddenly from her place without any obvious effort, and balancing herself with exquisite grace and ease; "look at the beautiful old bridge ahead!"

"I need scarcely look at that," said I, not turning my head away from her beauty. "I know what it is; though" (with a smile) "we used not to call it the Old Bridge time agone."

She looked down upon me kindly, and said, "How well we get on now you are no longer on your guard against me!"

And she stood looking thoughtfully at me still, till she had to sit down as we passed under the middle one of the row of little pointed arches of the oldest bridge across the Thames.

"O the beautiful fields!" she said; "I had no idea of the charm of a very small river like this. The smallness of the scale of everything, the short reaches, and the speedy change of the banks, give one a feeling of going somewhere, of coming to something strange, a feeling of adventure which I have not felt in bigger waters."

I looked up at her delightedly; for her voice, saying the very thing which I was thinking, was like a caress to me. She caught my eye and her cheeks reddened under their tan, and she said simply:

"I must tell you, my friend, that when my father leaves the Thames this summer he will take me away to a place near the Roman wall in Cumberland; so that this voyage of mine is farewell to the south; of course with my goodwill in a way; and yet I am sorry for it. I hadn't the heart to tell Dick yesterday that we were as good as gone from the Thames-side; but somehow to you I must needs tell it."

She stopped and seemed very thoughtful for awhile, and then said smiling:

"I must say that I don't like moving about from one home to another; one gets so pleasantly used to all the detail of the life about one; it fits so harmoniously and happily into one's own life, that beginning again, even in a small way, is a kind of pain. But I daresay in the country which you come from, you would think this petty and unadventurous, and would think the worse of me for it."

She smiled at me caressingly as she spoke, and I made haste to answer: "O, no, indeed; again you echo my very thoughts. But I hardly expected to hear you speak so. I gathered from all I have heard that there was a great deal of changing of abode amongst you in this country."

"Well," she said, "of course people are free to move about; but except for pleasure-parties, especially in harvest and hay-time, like this of ours, I don't think they do so much. I admit that I also have other moods than that of stay-at-home, as I hinted just now, and I should like to go with you all through the west country —thinking of nothing," concluded she smiling.

"I should have plenty to think of," said I.

29. A RESTING-PLACE ON THE UPPER THAMES

Presently at a place where the river flowed round a headland of the meadows, we stopped a while for rest and victuals, and settled ourselves on a beautiful bank which almost reached the dignity of a hill-side: the wide meadows spread before us, and already the scythe was busy amidst the hay. One change I noticed amidst the quiet beauty of the fields—to wit, that they were planted with trees here and there, often fruit-trees, and that there was none of the niggardly begrudging of space to a handsome tree which I remembered too well; and though the willows were often polled (or shrowded, as they call it in that country-side), this was done with some regard to beauty: I mean that there was no polling of rows on rows so as to destroy the pleasantness of half a mile of country, but a thoughtful sequence in the cutting, that prevented a sudden bareness anywhere. To be short, the fields were everywhere treated as a garden made for the pleasure as well as the livelihood of all, as old Hammond told me was the case.

On this bank or bent of the hill, then, we had our mid-day meal; somewhat early for dinner, if that mattered, but we had been stirring early: the slender stream of the Thames winding below us between the garden of a country I have been telling of; a furlong from us was a beautiful little islet begrown with graceful trees; on the slopes westward of us was a wood of varied growth overhanging the narrow meadow on the south side of the river; while to the north was a wide stretch of mead rising very gradually from the river's edge. A delicate spire of an ancient building rose up from out of the trees in the middle distance, with a few grey houses clustered about it; while nearer to us, in fact not half a furlong from the water, was a quite modern stone house—a wide quadrangle of one story, the buildings that made it being quite low. There was no garden between it and the river, nothing but a row of pear-trees still quite young and slender; and though there did not seem to be much ornament about it, it had a sort of natural elegance, like that of the trees themselves.

As we sat looking down on all this in the sweet June day, rather happy than merry, Ellen, who sat next me, her hand clasped about one knee, leaned sideways to me, and said in a low voice which Dick and Clara might have noted if they had not been busy in happy wordless love-making: "Friend, in your country were the houses of your field-labourers anything like that?"

I said: "Well, at any rate the houses of our rich men were not; they were mere blots upon the face of the land."

"I find that hard to understand," she said. "I can see why the workmen, who were so oppressed, should not have been able to live in beautiful houses; for it takes time and leisure, and minds not over-burdened with care, to make beautiful dwellings; and I quite understand that these poor people were not allowed to live in such a way as to have these (to us) necessary good things. But why the rich men, who had the time and the leisure and the materials for building, as it would be in this case, should not have housed themselves well, I do not understand as yet. I know what you are meaning to say to me," she said, looking me full in the eyes and blushing, "to wit that their houses and all belonging to them were generally ugly and base, unless they chanced to be ancient like yonder remnant of our forefathers' work" (pointing to the spire); "that they were—let me see; what is the word?"

"Vulgar," said I. "We used to say," said I, "that the ugliness and vulgarity of the rich men's dwellings was a necessary reflection from the sordidness and bareness of life which they forced upon the poor people."

She knit her brows as in thought; then turned a brightened face on me, as if she had caught the idea, and said: "Yes, friend, I see what you mean. We have sometimes—those of us who look into these things—talked this very matter over; because, to say the truth, we have plenty of record of the so-called arts of the time before Equality of Life; and there are not wanting people who say that the state of that society was not the cause of all that ugliness; that they were ugly in their life because they liked to be, and could have had beautiful things about them if they had chosen; just as a man or body of men now may, if they please, make things more or less beautiful—Stop! I know what you are going to say."

"Do you?" said I, smiling, yet with a beating heart.

"Yes," she said; "you are answering me, teaching me, in some way or another, although you have not spoken the words aloud. You were going to say that in times of inequality it was an essential condition of the life of these rich men that they should not themselves make what they wanted for the adornment of their lives, but should force those to make them whom they forced to live pinched and sordid lives; and that as a necessary consequence the sordidness and pinching, the ugly barrenness of those ruined lives, were worked up into the adornment of the lives of the rich, and art died out amongst men? Was that what you would say, my friend?"

"Yes, yes," I said, looking at her eagerly; for she had risen and was standing on the edge of the bent, the light wind stirring her dainty raiment, one hand laid on her bosom, the other arm stretched downward and clenched in her earnestness.

"It is true," she said, "it is true! We have proved it true!"

I think amidst my—something more than interest in her, and admiration for her, I was beginning to wonder how it would all end. I had a glimmering of fear of what might follow; of anxiety as to the remedy which this new age might offer for the missing of something one might set one's heart on. But now Dick rose to his feet and cried out in his hearty manner: "Neighbour Ellen, are you quarrelling with the guest, or are you worrying him to tell you things which he cannot properly explain to our ignorance?"

"Neither, dear neighbour," she said. "I was so far from quarrelling with him that I think I have been making him good friends both with himself and me. Is it so, dear guest?" she said, looking down at me with a delightful smile of confidence in being understood.

"Indeed it is," said I.

"Well, moreover," she said, "I must say for him that he has explained himself to me very well indeed, so that I quite understand him."

"All right," quoth Dick. "When I first set eyes on you at Runnymede I knew that there was something wonderful in your keenness of wits. I don't say that as a mere pretty speech to please you," said he quickly, "but because it is true; and it made me want to see more of you. But, come, we ought to be going; for we are not half way, and we ought to be in well before sunset."

And therewith he took Clara's hand, and led her down the bent. But Ellen stood thoughtfully looking down for a little, and as I took her hand to follow Dick, she turned round to me and said:

"You might tell me a great deal and make many things clear to me, if you would."

"Yes," said I, "I am pretty well fit for that,—and for nothing else—an old man like me."

She did not notice the bitterness which, whether I liked it or not, was in my voice as I spoke, but went on: "It is not so much for myself; I should be quite content to dream about past times, and if I could not idealise them, yet at least idealise some of the people who lived in them. But I think sometimes people are too careless of the history of the past—too apt to leave it in the hands of old learned men like Hammond. Who knows? Happy as we are, times may alter; we may be bitten with some impulse towards change, and many things may seem too wonderful for us to resist, too exciting not to catch at, if we do not know that they are but phases of what has been before; and withal ruinous, deceitful, and sordid."

As we went slowly down toward the boats she said again: "Not for myself alone, dear friend; I shall have children; perhaps before the end a good many;—I hope so. And though of course I cannot force any special kind of knowledge upon them, yet, my Friend, I cannot help thinking that just as they might be like me in body, so I might impress upon them some part of my ways of thinking; that is, indeed, some of the essential part of myself; that part which was not mere moods, created by the matters and events round about me. What do you think?"

Of one thing I was sure, that her beauty and kindness and eagerness combined, forced me to think as she did, when she was not earnestly laying herself open to receive my thoughts. I said, what at the time was true, that I thought it most important; and presently stood entranced by the wonder of her grace as she stepped into the light boat, and held out her hand to me. And so on we went up the Thames still—or whither?

30. THE JOURNEY'S END

On we went. In spite of my new-born excitement about Ellen, and my gathering fear of where it would land me, I could not help taking abundant interest in the condition of the river and its banks; all the more as she never seemed weary of the changing picture, but looked at every yard of flowery bank and gurgling eddy with the same kind of affectionate interest which I myself once had so fully, as I used to think, and perhaps had not altogether lost even in this strangely changed society with all its wonders. Ellen seemed delighted with my pleasure at this, that, or the other piece of carefulness in dealing with the river: the nursing of pretty corners; the ingenuity in dealing with difficulties of water-engineering, so that the most obviously useful works looked beautiful and natural also. All this, I say, pleased me hugely, and she was pleased at my pleasure—but rather puzzled too.

"You seem astonished," she said, just after we had passed a mill[2] which spanned all the stream save the water-way for traffic, but which was as beautiful in its way as a Gothic cathedral—"You seem astonished at this being so pleasant to look at."

"Yes," I said, "in a way I am; though I don't see why it should not be."

"Ah!" she said, looking at me admiringly, yet with a lurking smile in her face, "you know all about the history of the past. Were they not always careful about this little stream which now adds so much pleasantness to the country side? It would always be easy to manage this little river. Ah! I forgot, though," she said, as her eye caught mine, "in the days we are thinking of pleasure was wholly neglected in such matters. But how did they manage the river in the days that you—" Lived in she was going to say; but correcting herself, said—"in the days of which you have record?"

"They *mis*managed it," quoth I. "Up to the first half of the nineteenth century, when it was still more or less of a highway for the country people, some care was taken of the river and its banks; and though I don't suppose anyone troubled himself about its aspect, yet it was trim and beautiful. But when the railways—of which no doubt you have heard—came into power, they would not allow the people of the country to use either the natural or artificial waterways, of which latter there were a great many. I suppose when we get higher up we shall see one of these; a very important one, which one of these railways entirely closed to the public, so that they might force people to send their goods by their private road, and so tax them as heavily as they could."

Ellen laughed heartily. "Well," she said, "that is not stated clearly enough in our history-books, and it is worth knowing. But certainly the people of those days must have been a curiously lazy set. We are not either fidgety or quarrelsome now, but if any one tried such a piece of folly on us, we should use the said waterways, whoever gainsaid us: surely that would be simple enough. However, I remember other cases of this stupidity: when I was on the Rhine two years ago, I remember they showed us ruins of old castles, which, according to what we heard, must have been made for pretty much the same purpose as the railways were. But I am interrupting your history of the river: pray go on."

"It is both short and stupid enough," said I. "The river having lost its practical or commercial value—that is, being of no use to make money of—"

She nodded. "I understand what that queer phrase means," said she. "Go on!"

"Well, it was utterly neglected, till at last it became a nuisance—"

"Yes," quoth Ellen, "I understand: like the railways and the robber knights. Yes?"

"So then they turned the makeshift business on to it, and handed it over to a body up in London, who from time to time, in order to show that they had something to do, did some damage here and there,—cut down trees, destroying the banks thereby; dredged the river (where it was not needed always), and threw the dredgings on the fields so as to spoil them; and so forth. But for the most part they practised 'masterly inactivity,' as it was then called—that is, they drew their salaries, and let things alone."

"Drew their salaries," she said. "I know that means that they were allowed to take an extra lot of other people's goods for doing nothing. And if that had been all, it really might have been worth while to let them do so, if you couldn't find any other way of keeping them quiet; but it seems to me that being so paid, they could not help doing something, and that something was bound to be mischief,—because," said she, kindling with sudden anger, "the whole business was founded on lies and false pretensions. I don't mean only these river-guardians, but all these master-people I have read of."

"Yes," said I, "how happy you are to have got out of the parsimony of oppression!"

"Why do you sigh?" she said, kindly and somewhat anxiously. "You seem to think that it will not last?"

"It will last for you," quoth I.

"But why not for you?" said she. "Surely it is for all the world; and if your country is somewhat backward, it will come into line before long. Or," she said quickly, "are you thinking that you must soon go back again? I will make my proposal which I told you of at once, and so perhaps put an end to your anxiety. I was going to propose that you should live with us where we are going. I feel quite old friends with you, and should be sorry to lose you." Then she smiled on me, and said: "Do you know, I begin to suspect you of wanting to nurse a sham sorrow, like the ridiculous characters in some of those queer old novels that I have come across now and then."

I really had almost begun to suspect it myself, but I refused to admit so much; so I sighed no more, but fell to giving my delightful companion what little pieces of history I knew about the river and its borderlands; and the time passed pleasantly enough; and between the two of us (she was a better sculler than I was, and seemed quite tireless) we kept up fairly well with Dick, hot as the afternoon was, and swallowed up the way at a great rate. At last we passed under another ancient bridge; and through meadows bordered at first with huge elm-trees mingled with sweet chestnut of younger but very elegant growth; and the meadows widened out so much that it seemed as if the trees must now be on the bents only, or about the houses, except for the growth of willows on the immediate banks; so that the wide stretch of grass was little broken here. Dick got very much excited now, and often stood up in the boat to cry out to us that this was such and such a field, and so forth; and we caught fire at his enthusiasm for the hay-field and its harvest, and pulled our best.

At last as we were passing through a reach of the river where on the side of the towing-path was a highish bank with a thick whispering bed of reeds before it, and on the other side a higher bank, clothed with willows that dipped into the stream and crowned by ancient elm-trees, we saw bright figures coming along close to the bank, as if they were looking for something; as, indeed, they were, and we—that is, Dick and his company—were what they were looking for. Dick lay on his oars, and we followed his example. He gave a joyous shout to the people on the bank, which was echoed back from it in many voices, deep and sweetly shrill; for there were above a dozen persons, both men, women, and children. A tall handsome woman, with black wavy hair and deep-set grey eyes, came forward on the bank and waved her hand gracefully to us, and said:

"Dick, my friend, we have almost had to wait for you! What excuse have you to make for your slavish punctuality? Why didn't you take us by surprise, and come yesterday?"

"O," said Dick, with an almost imperceptible jerk of his head toward our boat, "we didn't want to come too quick up the water; there is so much to see for those who have not been up here before."

"True, true," said the stately lady, for stately is the word that must be used for her; "and we want them to get to know the wet way from the east thoroughly well, since they must often use it now. But come ashore at once, Dick, and you, dear neighbours; there is a break in the reeds and a good landing-place just round the corner. We can carry up your things, or send some of the lads after them."

"No, no," said Dick; "it is easier going by water, though it is but a step. Besides, I want to bring my friend here to the proper place. We will go on to the Ford; and you can talk to us from the bank as we paddle along."

He pulled his sculls through the water, and on we went, turning a sharp angle and going north a little. Presently we saw before us a bank of elm-trees, which told us of a house amidst them, though I looked in vain for the grey walls that I expected to see there. As we went, the folk on the bank talked indeed, mingling their kind voices with the cuckoo's song, the sweet strong whistle of the blackbirds, and the ceaseless note of the corn-crake as he crept through the long grass of the mowing-field; whence came waves of fragrance from the flowering clover amidst of the ripe grass.

In a few minutes we had passed through a deep eddying pool into the sharp stream that ran from the ford, and beached our craft on a tiny strand of limestone-gravel, and stepped ashore into the arms of our up-river friends, our journey done.

I disentangled myself from the merry throng, and mounting on the cart-road that ran along the river some feet above the water, I looked round about me. The river came down through a wide meadow on my left, which was grey now with the ripened seeding grasses; the gleaming water was lost presently by a turn of the bank, but over the meadow I could see the mingled gables of a building where I knew the lock must be, and which now seemed to combine a mill with it. A low wooded ridge bounded the river-plain to the south and south-east, whence we had come, and a few low houses lay about its feet and up its slope. I turned a little to my right, and through the hawthorn sprays and long shoots of the wild roses could see the flat country spreading out far away under the sun of the calm evening, till something that might be called hills with a look of sheep-pastures about them bounded it with a soft blue line. Before me, the elm-boughs still hid most of what houses there might be in this river-side dwelling of men; but to the right of the cart-road a few grey buildings of the simplest kind showed here and there.

There I stood in a dreamy mood, and rubbed my eyes as if I were not wholly awake, and half expected to see the gay-clad company of beautiful men and women change to two or three spindle-legged back-bowed men and haggard, hollow-eyed, ill-favoured women, who once wore down the soil of this land with their heavy hopeless feet, from day to day, and season to season, and year to year. But no change came as yet, and my heart swelled with joy as I thought of all the beautiful grey villages, from the river to the plain and the plain to the uplands, which I could picture to myself so well, all peopled now with this happy and lovely folk, who had cast away riches and attained to wealth.

31. AN OLD HOUSE AMONGST NEW FOLK

As I stood there Ellen detached herself from our happy friends who still stood on the little strand and came up to me. She took me by the hand, and said softly, "Take me on to the house at once; we need not wait for the others: I had rather not."

I had a mind to say that I did not know the way thither, and that the river-side dwellers should lead; but almost without my will my feet moved on along the road they knew. The raised way led us into a little field bounded by a backwater of the river on one side; on the right hand we could see a cluster of small houses and barns, new and old, and before us a grey stone barn and a wall partly overgrown with ivy, over which a few grey gables showed. The village road ended in the shallow of the aforesaid backwater. We crossed the road, and again almost without my will my hand raised the latch of a door in the wall, and we stood presently on a stone path which led up to the old house to which fate in the shape of Dick had so strangely brought me in this new world of men. My companion gave a sigh of pleased surprise and enjoyment; nor did I wonder, for the garden between the wall and the house was redolent of the June flowers, and the roses were rolling over one another with that delicious superabundance of small well-tended gardens which at first sight takes away all thought from the beholder save that of beauty. The blackbirds were singing their loudest, the doves were cooing on the roof-ridge, the rooks in the high elm-trees beyond were garrulous among the young leaves, and the swifts wheeled whining about the gables. And the house itself was a fit guardian for all the beauty of this heart of summer.

Once again Ellen echoed my thoughts as she said:

"Yes, friend, this is what I came out for to see; this many-gabled old house built by the simple country-folk of the long-past times, regardless of all the turmoil that was going on in cities and courts, is lovely still amidst all the beauty which these latter days have created; and I do not wonder at our friends tending it carefully and making much of it. It seems to me as if it had waited for these happy days, and held in it the gathered crumbs of happiness of the confused and turbulent past."

She led me up close to the house, and laid her shapely sun-browned hand and arm on the lichened wall as if to embrace it, and cried out, "O me! O me! How I love the earth, and the seasons, and weather, and all things that deal with it, and all that grows out of it,—as this has done!"

I could not answer her, or say a word. Her exultation and pleasure were so keen and exquisite, and her beauty, so delicate, yet so interfused with energy, expressed it so fully, that any added word would have been commonplace and futile. I dreaded lest the others should come in suddenly and break the spell she had cast about me; but we stood there a while by the corner of the big gable of the house, and no one came. I heard the merry voices some way off presently, and knew that they were going along the river to the great meadow on the other side of the house and garden.

We drew back a little, and looked up at the house: the door and the windows were open to the fragrant sun-cured air; from the upper window-sills hung festoons of flowers in honour of the festival, as if the others shared in the love for the old house.

"Come in," said Ellen. "I hope nothing will spoil it inside; but I don't think it will. Come! we must go back presently to the others. They have gone on to the tents; for surely they must have tents pitched for the haymakers—the house would not hold a tithe of the folk, I am sure."

She led me on to the door, murmuring little above her breath as she did so, "The earth and the growth of it and the life of it! If I could but say or show how I love it!"

We went in, and found no soul in any room as we wandered from room to room,—from the rose-covered porch to the strange and quaint garrets amongst the great timbers of the roof, where of old time the tillers and herdsmen of the manor slept, but which a-nights seemed now, by the small size of the beds, and the litter of useless and disregarded matters—bunches of dying flowers, feathers of birds, shells of starling's eggs, caddis worms in mugs, and the like—seemed to be inhabited for the time by children.

Everywhere there was but little furniture, and that only the most necessary, and of the simplest forms. The extravagant love of ornament which I had noted in this people elsewhere seemed here to have given place to the feeling that the house itself and its associations was the ornament of the country life amidst which it had been left stranded from old times, and that to re-ornament it would but take away its use as a piece of natural beauty.

We sat down at last in a room over the wall which Ellen had caressed, and which was still hung with old tapestry, originally of no artistic value, but now faded into pleasant grey tones which harmonised thoroughly well with the quiet of the place, and which would have been ill supplanted by brighter and more striking decoration.

I asked a few random questions of Ellen as we sat there, but scarcely listened to her answers, and presently became silent, and then scarce conscious of anything, but that I was there in that old room, the doves crooning from the roofs of the barn and dovecot beyond the window opposite to me.

My thought returned to me after what I think was but a minute or two, but which, as in a vivid dream, seemed as if it had lasted a long time, when I saw Ellen sitting, looking all the fuller of life and pleasure and desire from the contrast with the grey faded tapestry with its futile design, which was now only bearable because it had grown so faint and feeble.

She looked at me kindly, but as if she read me through and through. She said: "You have begun again your never-ending contrast between the past and this present. Is it not so?"

"True," said I. "I was thinking of what you, with your capacity and intelligence, joined to your love of pleasure, and your impatience of unreasonable restraint—of what you would have been in that past. And even now, when all is won and has been for a long time, my heart is sickened with thinking of all the waste of life that has gone on for so many years."

"So many centuries," she said, "so many ages!"

"True," I said; "too true," and sat silent again.

She rose up and said: "Come, I must not let you go off into a dream again so soon. If we must lose you, I want you to see all that you can see first before you go back again."

"Lose me?" I said—"go back again? Am I not to go up to the North with you? What do you mean?"

She smiled somewhat sadly, and said: "Not yet; we will not talk of that yet. Only, what were you thinking of just now?"

I said falteringly: "I was saying to myself, The past, the present? Should she not have said the contrast of the present with the future: of blind despair with hope?"

"I knew it," she said. Then she caught my hand and said excitedly, "Come, while there is yet time! Come!" And she led me out of the room; and as we were going downstairs and out of the house into the garden by a little side door which opened out of a curious lobby, she said in a calm voice, as if she wished me to forget her sudden nervousness: "Come! we ought to join the others before they come here looking for us. And let me tell you, my friend, that I can see you are too apt to fall into mere dreamy musing: no doubt because you are not yet used to our life of repose amidst of energy; of work which is pleasure and pleasure which is work."

She paused a little, and as we came out into the lovely garden again, she said: "My friend, you were saying that you wondered what I should have been if I had lived in those past days of turmoil and oppression. Well, I think I have studied the history of them to know pretty well. I should have been one of the poor, for my father when he was working was a mere tiller of the soil. Well, I could not have borne that; therefore my beauty and cleverness and brightness" (she spoke with no blush or simper of false shame) "would have been sold to rich men, and my life would have been wasted indeed; for I know enough of that to know that I should have had no choice, no power of will over my life; and that I should never have bought pleasure from the rich men, or even opportunity of action, whereby I might have won some true excitement. I should have wrecked and wasted in one way or another, either by penury or by luxury. Is it not so?"

"Indeed it is," said I.

She was going to say something else, when a little gate in the fence, which led into a small elm-shaded field, was opened, and Dick came with hasty cheerfulness up the garden path, and was presently standing between us, a hand laid on the shoulder of each. He said: "Well, neighbours, I thought you two would like to see the old house quietly without a crowd in it. Isn't it a jewel of a house after its kind? Well, come along, for it is getting towards dinner-time. Perhaps you, guest, would like a swim before we sit down to what I fancy will be a pretty long feast?"

"Yes," I said, "I should like that."

"Well, good-bye for the present, neighbour Ellen," said Dick. "Here comes Clara to take care of you, as I fancy she is more at home amongst our friends here."

Clara came out of the fields as he spoke; and with one look at Ellen I turned and went with Dick, doubting, if I must say the truth, whether I should see her again.

32. THE FEAST'S BEGINNING—THE END

Dick brought me at once into the little field which, as I had seen from the garden, was covered with gaily-coloured tents arranged in orderly lanes, about which were sitting and lying on the grass some fifty or sixty men, women, and children, all of them in the height of good temper and enjoyment—with their holiday mood on, so to say.

"You are thinking that we don't make a great show as to numbers," said Dick; "but you must remember that we shall have more to-morrow; because in this haymaking work there is room for a great many people who are not over-skilled in country matters: and there are many who lead sedentary lives, whom it would be unkind to deprive of their pleasure in the hay-field—scientific men and close students generally: so that the skilled workmen, outside those who are wanted as mowers, and foremen of the haymaking, stand aside, and take a little downright rest, which you know is good for them, whether they like it or not: or else they go to other countrysides, as I am doing here. You see, the scientific men and historians, and students generally, will not be wanted till we are fairly in the midst of the tedding, which of course will not be till the day after to-morrow." With that he brought me out of the little field on to a kind of causeway above the river-side meadow, and thence turning to the left on to a path through the mowing grass, which was thick and very tall, led on till we came to the river above the weir and its mill. There we had a delightful swim in the broad piece of water above the lock, where the river looked much bigger than its natural size from its being dammed up by the weir.

"Now we are in a fit mood for dinner," said Dick, when we had dressed and were going through the grass again; "and certainly of all the cheerful meals in the year, this one of haysel is the cheerfullest; not even excepting the corn-harvest feast; for then the year is beginning to fail, and one cannot help having a feeling behind all the gaiety, of the coming of the dark days, and the shorn fields and empty gardens; and the spring is almost too far off to look forward to. It is, then, in the autumn, when one almost believes in death."

"How strangely you talk," said I, "of such a constantly recurring and consequently commonplace matter as the sequence of the seasons." And indeed these people were like children about such things, and had what seemed to me a quite exaggerated interest in the weather, a fine day, a dark night, or a brilliant one, and the like.

"Strangely?" said he. "Is it strange to sympathise with the year and its gains and losses?"

"At any rate," said I, "if you look upon the course of the year as a beautiful and interesting drama, which is what I think you do, you should be as much pleased and interested with the winter and its trouble and pain as with this wonderful summer luxury."

"And am I not?" said Dick, rather warmly; "only I can't look upon it as if I were sitting in a theatre seeing the play going on before me, myself taking no part of it. It is difficult," said he, smiling good-humouredly, "for a non-literary man like me to explain myself properly, like that dear girl Ellen would; but I mean that I am part of it all, and feel the pain as well as the pleasure in my own person. It is not done for me by somebody else, merely that I may eat and drink and sleep; but I myself do my share of it."

In his way also, as Ellen in hers, I could see that Dick had that passionate love of the earth which was common to but few people at least, in the days I knew; in which the prevailing feeling amongst intellectual persons was a kind of sour distaste for the changing drama of the year, for the life of earth and its dealings with men. Indeed, in those days it was thought poetic and imaginative to look upon life as a thing to be borne, rather than enjoyed.

So I mused till Dick's laugh brought me back into the Oxfordshire hay-fields. "One thing seems strange to me," said he—"that I must needs trouble myself about the winter and its scantiness, in the midst of the summer abundance. If it hadn't happened to me before, I should have thought it was your doing, guest; that you had thrown a kind of evil charm over me. Now, you know," said he, suddenly, "that's only a joke, so you mustn't take it to heart."

"All right," said I; "I don't." Yet I did feel somewhat uneasy at his words, after all.

We crossed the causeway this time, and did not turn back to the house, but went along a path beside a field of wheat now almost ready to blossom. I said:

"We do not dine in the house or garden, then?—as indeed I did not expect to do. Where do we meet, then? For I can see that the houses are mostly very small."

"Yes," said Dick, "you are right, they are small in this country-side: there are so many good old houses left, that people dwell a good deal in such small detached houses. As to our dinner, we are going to have our feast in the church. I wish, for your sake, it were as big and handsome as that of the old Roman town to the west, or the forest town to the north;[3] but, however, it will hold us all; and though it is a little thing, it is beautiful in its way."

This was somewhat new to me, this dinner in a church, and I thought of the church-ales of the Middle Ages; but I said nothing, and presently we came out into the road which ran through the village. Dick looked up and down it, and seeing only two straggling groups before us, said: "It seems as if we must be somewhat late; they are all gone on; and they will be sure to make a point of waiting for you, as the guest of guests, since you come from so far."

He hastened as he spoke, and I kept up with him, and presently we came to a little avenue of lime-trees which led us straight to the church porch, from whose open door came the sound of cheerful voices and laughter, and varied merriment.

"Yes," said Dick, "it's the coolest place for one thing, this hot evening. Come along; they will be glad to see you."

Indeed, in spite of my bath, I felt the weather more sultry and oppressive than on any day of our journey yet.

We went into the church, which was a simple little building with one little aisle divided from the nave by three round arches, a chancel, and a rather roomy transept for so small a building, the windows mostly of the graceful Oxfordshire fourteenth century type. There was no modern architectural decoration in it; it looked, indeed, as if none had been attempted since the Puritans whitewashed the mediæval saints and histories on the wall. It was, however, gaily dressed up for this latter-day festival, with festoons of flowers from arch to arch, and great pitchers of flowers standing about on the floor; while under the west window hung two cross scythes, their blades polished white, and gleaming from out of the flowers that wreathed them. But its best ornament was the crowd of handsome, happy-looking men and women that were set down to table, and who, with their bright faces and rich hair over their gay holiday raiment, looked, as the Persian poet puts it, like a bed of tulips in the sun. Though the church was a small one, there was plenty of room; for a small church makes a biggish house; and on this evening there was no need to set cross tables along the transepts; though doubtless these would be wanted next day, when the learned men of whom Dick has been speaking should be come to take their more humble part in the haymaking.

I stood on the threshold with the expectant smile on my face of a man who is going to take part in a festivity which he is really prepared to enjoy. Dick, standing by me was looking round the company with an air of proprietorship in them, I thought. Opposite me sat Clara and Ellen, with Dick's place open between them: they were smiling, but their beautiful faces were each turned towards the neighbours on either side, who were talking to them, and they did not seem to see me. I turned to Dick, expecting him to lead me forward, and he turned his face to me; but strange to say, though it was as smiling and cheerful as ever, it made no response to my glance—nay, he seemed to take no heed at all of my presence, and I noticed that none of the company looked at me. A pang shot through me, as of some disaster long expected and suddenly realised. Dick moved on a little without a word to me. I was not three yards from the two women who, though they had been my companions for such a short time, had really, as I thought, become my friends. Clara's face was turned full upon me now, but she also did not seem to see me, though I know I was trying to catch her eye with an appealing look. I turned to Ellen, and she *did* seem to recognise me for an instant; but her bright face turned sad directly, and she shook her head with a mournful look, and the next moment all consciousness of my presence had faded from her face.

I felt lonely and sick at heart past the power of words to describe. I hung about a minute longer, and then turned and went out of the porch again and through the lime-avenue into the road, while the blackbirds sang their strongest from the bushes about me in the hot June evening.

Once more without any conscious effort of will I set my face toward the old house by the ford, but as I turned round the corner which led to the remains of the village cross, I came upon a figure strangely contrasting with the joyous, beautiful people I had left behind in the church. It was a man who looked old, but whom I knew from habit, now half forgotten, was really not much more than fifty. His face was rugged, and grimed rather than dirty; his eyes dull and bleared; his body bent, his calves thin and spindly, his feet dragging and limping. His clothing was a mixture of dirt and rags long over-familiar to me. As I passed him he touched his hat with some real goodwill and courtesy, and much servility.

Inexpressibly shocked, I hurried past him and hastened along the road that led to the river and the lower end of the village; but suddenly I saw as it were a black cloud rolling along to meet me, like a nightmare of my childish days; and for a while I was conscious of nothing else than being in the dark, and whether I was walking, or sitting, or lying down, I could not tell.

―――

I lay in my bed in my house at dingy Hammersmith thinking about it all; and trying to consider if I was overwhelmed with despair at finding I had been dreaming a dream; and strange to say, I found that I was not so despairing.

Or indeed *was* it a dream? If so, why was I so conscious all along that I was really seeing all that new life from the outside, still wrapped up in the prejudices, the anxieties, the distrust of this time of doubt and struggle?

All along, though those friends were so real to me, I had been feeling as if I had no business amongst them: as though the time would come when they would reject me, and say, as Ellen's last mournful look seemed to say, "No, it will not do; you cannot be of us; you belong so entirely to the unhappiness of the past that our happiness even would weary you. Go back again, now you have seen us, and your outward eyes have learned that in spite of all the infallible maxims of your day there is yet a time of rest in store for the world, when mastery has changed into fellowship—but not before. Go back again, then, and while you live you will see all round you people engaged in making others live lives which are not their own, while they themselves care nothing for their own real lives—men who hate life though they fear death. Go back and be the happier for having seen us, for having added a little hope to your struggle. Go on living while you may, striving, with whatsoever pain and labour needs must be, to build up little by little the new day of fellowship, and rest, and happiness."

Yes, surely! and if others can see it as I have seen it, then it may be called a vision rather than a dream.

---

1. "Elegant," I mean, as a Persian pattern is elegant; not like a rich "elegant" lady out for a morning call. I should rather call that genteel.
2. I should have said that all along the Thames there were abundance of mills used for various purposes; none of which were in any degree unsightly, and many strikingly beautiful; and the gardens about them marvels of loveliness.
3. Cirencester and Burford he must have meant.

A DREAM OF JOHN BALL

1. THE MEN OF KENT

Sometimes I am rewarded for fretting myself so much about present matters by a quite unasked-for pleasant dream. I mean when I am asleep. This dream is as it were a present of an architectural peep-show. I see some beautiful and noble building new made, as it were for the occasion, as clearly as if I were awake; not vaguely or absurdly, as often happens in dreams, but with all the detail clear and reasonable. Some Elizabethan house with its scrap of earlier fourteenth-century building, and its later degradations of Queen Anne and Silly Billy and Victoria, marring but not destroying it, in an old village once a clearing amid the sandy woodlands of Sussex. Or an old and unusually curious church, much churchwardened, and beside it a fragment of fifteenth-century domestic architecture amongst the not unpicturesque lath and plaster of an Essex farm, and looking natural enough among the sleepy elms and the meditative hens scratching about in the litter of the farmyard, whose trodden yellow straw comes up to the very jambs of the richly carved Norman doorway of the church. Or sometimes 'tis a splendid collegiate church, untouched by restoring parson and architect, standing amid an island of shapely trees and flower-beset cottages of thatched grey stone and cob, amidst the narrow stretch of bright green water-meadows that wind between the sweeping Wiltshire downs, so well beloved of William Cobbett. Or some new-seen and yet familiar cluster of houses in a grey village of the upper Thames overtopped by the delicate tracery of a fourteenth-century church; or even sometimes the very buildings of the past untouched by the degradation of the sordid utilitarianism that cares not and knows not of beauty and history: as once, when I was journeying (in a dream of the night) down the well-remembered reaches of the Thames betwixt Streatley and Wallingford, where the foothills of the White Horse fall back from the broad stream, I came upon a clear-seen mediaeval town standing up with roof and tower and spire within its walls, grey and ancient, but untouched from the days of its builders of old. All this I have seen in the dreams of the night clearer than I can force myself to see them in dreams of the day. So that it would have been nothing new to me the other night to fall into an architectural dream if that were all, and yet I have to tell of things strange and new that befell me after I had fallen asleep. I had begun my sojourn in the Land of Nod by a very confused attempt to conclude that it was all right for me to have an engagement to lecture at Manchester and Mitcham Fair Green at half-past eleven at night on one and the same Sunday, and that I could manage pretty well. And then I had gone on to try to make the best of addressing a large open-air audience in the costume I was really then wearing—to wit, my night-shirt, reinforced for the dream occasion by a pair of braceless trousers. The consciousness of this fact so bothered me, that the earnest faces of my audience—who would NOT notice it, but were clearly preparing terrible anti-Socialist posers for me—began to fade away and my dream grew thin, and I awoke (as I thought) to find myself lying on a strip of wayside waste by an oak copse just outside a country village.

 I got up and rubbed my eyes and looked about me, and the landscape seemed unfamiliar to me, though it was, as to the lie of the land, an ordinary English low-country, swelling into rising ground here and there. The road was narrow, and I was convinced that it was a piece of Roman road from its straightness. Copses were scattered over the country, and there were signs of two or three villages and hamlets in sight besides the one near me, between which and me there was some orchard-land, where the early apples were beginning to redden on the trees. Also, just on the other side of the road and the ditch which ran along it, was a small close of about a quarter of an acre, neatly hedged with quick, which was nearly full of white poppies, and, as far as I could see for the hedge, had also a good few rose-bushes of the bright-red nearly single kind, which I had heard are the ones from which rose-water used to be distilled. Otherwise the land was quite unhedged, but all under tillage of various kinds, mostly in small strips. From the other side of a copse not far off rose a tall spire white and brand-new, but at once bold in outline and unaffectedly graceful and also distinctly English in character. This, together with the unhedged tillage and a certain unwonted trimness and handiness about the enclosures of the garden and orchards, puzzled me for a minute or two, as I did not understand, new as the spire was, how it could have been designed by a modern architect; and I was of course used to the hedged tillage and tumbledown bankrupt-looking surroundings of our modern agriculture. So that the garden-like neatness and trimness of everything surprised me. But after a minute or two that surprise left me entirely; and if what I saw and heard afterwards seems strange to you, remember that it did not seem strange to me at the time, except where now and again I shall tell you of it. Also, once for all, if I were to give you the very words of those who spoke to me you would scarcely understand them, although their language was English too, and at the time I could understand them at once.

Well, as I stretched myself and turned my face toward the village, I heard horse-hoofs on the road, and presently a man and horse showed on the other end of the stretch of road and drew near at a swinging trot with plenty of clash of metal. The man soon came up to me, but paid me no more heed than throwing me a nod. He was clad in armour of mingled steel and leather, a sword girt to his side, and over his shoulder a long-handled bill-hook.

His armour was fantastic in form and well wrought; but by this time I was quite used to the strangeness of him, and merely muttered to myself, "He is coming to summon the squire to the leet;" so I turned toward the village in good earnest. Nor, again, was I surprised at my own garments, although I might well have been from their unwontedness. I was dressed in a black cloth gown reaching to my ankles, neatly embroidered about the collar and cuffs, with wide sleeves gathered in at the wrists; a hood with a sort of bag hanging down from it was on my head, a broad red leather girdle round my waist, on one side of which hung a pouch embroidered very prettily and a case made of hard leather chased with a hunting scene, which I knew to be a pen and ink case; on the other side a small sheath-knife, only an arm in case of dire necessity.

Well, I came into the village, where I did not see (nor by this time expected to see) a single modern building, although many of them were nearly new, notably the church, which was large, and quite ravished my heart with its extreme beauty, elegance, and fitness. The chancel of this was so new that the dust of the stone still lay white on the midsummer grass beneath the carvings of the windows. The houses were almost all built of oak frame-work filled with cob or plaster well whitewashed; though some had their lower stories of rubble-stone, with their windows and doors of well-moulded freestone. There was much curious and inventive carving about most of them; and though some were old and much worn, there was the same look of deftness and trimness, and even beauty, about every detail in them which I noticed before in the field-work. They were all roofed with oak shingles, mostly grown as grey as stone; but one was so newly built that its roof was yet pale and yellow. This was a corner house, and the corner post of it had a carved niche wherein stood a gaily painted figure holding an anchor—St. Clement to wit, as the dweller in the house was a blacksmith. Half a stone's throw from the east end of the churchyard wall was a tall cross of stone, new like the church, the head beautifully carved with a crucifix amidst leafage. It stood on a set of wide stone steps, octagonal in shape, where three roads from other villages met and formed a wide open space on which a thousand people or more could stand together with no great crowding.

All this I saw, and also that there was a goodish many people about, women and children, and a few old men at the doors, many of them somewhat gaily clad, and that men were coming into the village street by the other end to that by which I had entered, by twos and threes, most of them carrying what I could see were bows in cases of linen yellow with wax or oil; they had quivers at their backs, and most of them a short sword by their left side, and a pouch and knife on the right; they were mostly dressed in red or brightish green or blue cloth jerkins, with a hood on the head generally of another colour. As they came nearer I saw that the cloth of their garments was somewhat coarse, but stout and serviceable. I knew, somehow, that they had been shooting at the butts, and, indeed, I could still hear a noise of men thereabout, and even now and again when the wind set from that quarter the twang of the bowstring and the plump of the shaft in the target.

I leaned against the churchyard wall and watched these men, some of whom went straight into their houses and some loitered about still; they were rough-looking fellows, tall and stout, very black some of them, and some red-haired, but most had hair burnt by the sun into the colour of tow; and, indeed, they were all burned and tanned and freckled variously. Their arms and buckles and belts and the finishings and hems of their garments were all what we should now call beautiful, rough as the men were; nor in their speech was any of that drawling snarl or thick vulgarity which one is used to hear from labourers in civilisation; not that they talked like gentlemen either, but full and round and bold, and they were merry and good-tempered enough; I could see that, though I felt shy and timid amongst them.

One of them strode up to me across the road, a man some six feet high, with a short black beard and black eyes and berry-brown skin, with a huge bow in his hand bare of the case, a knife, a pouch, and a short hatchet, all clattering together at his girdle.

"Well, friend," said he, "thou lookest partly mazed; what tongue hast thou in thine head?"

"A tongue that can tell rhymes," said I.

"So I thought," said he. "Thirstest thou any?"

"Yea, and hunger," said I.

And therewith my hand went into my purse, and came out again with but a few small and thin silver coins with a cross stamped on each, and three pellets in each corner of the cross. The man grinned.

"Aha!" said he, "is it so? Never heed it, mate. It shall be a song for a supper this fair Sunday evening. But first, whose man art thou?"

"No one's man," said I, reddening angrily; "I am my own master."

He grinned again.

"Nay, that's not the custom of England, as one time belike it will be. Methinks thou comest from heaven down, and hast had a high place there too."

He seemed to hesitate a moment, and then leant forward and whispered in my ear: "John the Miller, that ground small, small, small," and stopped and winked at me, and from between my lips without my mind forming any meaning came the words, "The king's son of heaven shall pay for all."

He let his bow fall on to his shoulder, caught my right hand in his and gave it a great grip, while his left hand fell among the gear at his belt, and I could see that he half drew his knife.

"Well, brother," said he, "stand not here hungry in the highway when there is flesh and bread in the Rose yonder. Come on."

And with that he drew me along toward what was clearly a tavern door, outside which men were sitting on a couple of benches and drinking meditatively from curiously shaped earthen pots glazed green and yellow, some with quaint devices on them.

2. THE MAN FROM ESSEX

I entered the door and started at first with my old astonishment, with which I had woke up, so strange and beautiful did this interior seem to me, though it was but a pothouse parlour. A quaintly-carved side board held an array of bright pewter pots and dishes and wooden and earthen bowls; a stout oak table went up and down the room, and a carved oak chair stood by the chimney-corner, now filled by a very old man dim-eyed and white-bearded. That, except the rough stools and benches on which the company sat, was all the furniture. The walls were panelled roughly enough with oak boards to about six feet from the floor, and about three feet of plaster above that was wrought in a pattern of a rose stem running all round the room, freely and roughly done, but with (as it seemed to my unused eyes) wonderful skill and spirit. On the hood of the great chimney a huge rose was wrought in the plaster and brightly painted in its proper colours. There were a dozen or more of the men I had seen coming along the street sitting there, some eating and all drinking; their cased bows leaned against the wall, their quivers hung on pegs in the panelling, and in a corner of the room I saw half-a-dozen bill-hooks that looked made more for war than for hedge-shearing, with ashen handles some seven foot long. Three or four children were running about among the legs of the men, heeding them mighty little in their bold play, and the men seemed little troubled by it, although they were talking earnestly and seriously too. A well-made comely girl leaned up against the chimney close to the gaffer's chair, and seemed to be in waiting on the company: she was clad in a close-fitting gown of bright blue cloth, with a broad silver girdle daintily wrought, round her loins, a rose wreath was on her head and her hair hung down unbound; the gaffer grumbled a few words to her from time to time, so that I judged he was her grandfather.

The men all looked up as we came into the room, my mate leading me by the hand, and he called out in his rough, good-tempered voice, "Here, my masters, I bring you tidings and a tale; give it meat and drink that it may be strong and sweet."

"Whence are thy tidings, Will Green?" said one.

My mate grinned again with the pleasure of making his joke once more in a bigger company: "It seemeth from heaven, since this good old lad hath no master," said he.

"The more fool he to come here," said a thin man with a grizzled beard, amidst the laughter that followed, "unless he had the choice given him between hell and England."

"Nay," said I, "I come not from heaven, but from Essex."

As I said the word a great shout sprang from all mouths at once, as clear and sudden as a shot from a gun. For I must tell you that I knew somehow, but I know not how, that the men of Essex were gathering to rise against the poll-groat bailiffs and the lords that would turn them all into villeins again, as their grandfathers had been. And the people was weak and the lords were poor; for many a mother's son had fallen in the war in France in the old king's time, and the Black Death had slain a many; so that the lords had bethought them: "We are growing poorer, and these upland-bred villeins are growing richer, and the guilds of craft are waxing in the towns, and soon what will there be left for us who cannot weave and will not dig? Good it were if we fell on all who are not guildsmen or men of free land, if we fell on soccage tenants and others, and brought both the law and the strong hand on them, and made them all villeins in deed as they are now in name; for now these rascals make more than their bellies need of bread, and their backs of homespun, and the overplus they keep to themselves; and we are more worthy of it than they. So let us get the collar on their necks again, and make their day's work longer and their bever-time shorter, as the good statute of the old king bade. And good it were if the Holy Church were to look to it (and the Lollards might help herein) that all these naughty and wearisome holidays were done away with; or that it should be unlawful for any man below the degree of a squire to keep the holy days of the church, except in the heart and the spirit only, and let the body labour meanwhile; for does not the Apostle say, 'If a man work not, neither should he eat'? And if such things were done, and such an estate of noble rich men and worthy poor men upholden for ever, then would it be good times in England, and life were worth the living."

All this were the lords at work on, and such talk I knew was common not only among the lords themselves, but also among their sergeants and very servingmen. But the people would not abide it; therefore, as I said, in Essex they were on the point of rising, and word had gone how that at St. Albans they were wellnigh at blows with the Lord Abbot's soldiers; that north away at Norwich John Litster was wiping the woad from his arms, as who would have to stain them red again, but not with grain or madder; and that the valiant tiler of Dartford had smitten a poll-groat bailiff to death with his lath-rending axe for mishandling a young maid, his daughter; and that the men of Kent were on the move.

Now, knowing all this I was not astonished that they shouted at the thought of their fellows the men of Essex, but rather that they said little more about it; only Will Green saying quietly, "Well, the tidings shall be told when our fellowship is greater; fall-to now on the meat, brother, that we may the sooner have thy tale." As he spoke the blue-clad damsel bestirred herself and brought me a clean trencher—that is, a square piece of thin oak board scraped clean—and a pewter pot of liquor. So without more ado, and as one used to it, I drew my knife out of my girdle and cut myself what I would of the flesh and bread on the table. But Will Green mocked at me as I cut, and said, "Certes, brother, thou hast not been a lord's carver, though but for thy word thou mightest have been his reader. Hast thou seen Oxford, scholar?"

A vision of grey-roofed houses and a long winding street and the sound of many bells came over me at that word as I nodded "Yes" to him, my mouth full of salt pork and rye-bread; and then I lifted my pot and we made the clattering mugs kiss and I drank, and the fire of the good Kentish mead ran through my veins and deepened my dream of things past, present, and to come, as I said: "Now hearken a tale, since ye will have it so. For last autumn I was in Suffolk at the good town of Dunwich, and thither came the keels from Iceland, and on them were some men of Iceland, and many a tale they had on their tongues; and with these men I foregathered, for I am in sooth a gatherer of tales, and this that is now at my tongue's end is one of them."

So such a tale I told them, long familiar to me; but as I told it the words seemed to quicken and grow, so that I knew not the sound of my own voice, and they ran almost into rhyme and measure as I told it; and when I had done there was silence awhile, till one man spake, but not loudly:

"Yea, in that land was the summer short and the winter long; but men lived both summer and winter; and if the trees grew ill and the corn throve not, yet did the plant called man thrive and do well. God send us such men even here."

"Nay," said another, "such men have been and will be, and belike are not far from this same door even now."

"Yea," said a third, "hearken a stave of Robin Hood; maybe that shall hasten the coming of one I wot of." And he fell to singing in a clear voice, for he was a young man, and to a sweet wild melody, one of those ballads which in an incomplete and degraded form you have read perhaps. My heart rose high as I heard him, for it was concerning the struggle against tyranny for the freedom of life, how that the wildwood and the heath, despite of wind and weather, were better for a free man than the court and the cheaping-town; of the taking from the rich to give to the poor; of the life of a man doing his own will and not the will of another man commanding him for the commandment's sake. The men all listened eagerly, and at whiles took up as a refrain a couplet at the end of a stanza with their strong and rough, but not unmusical voices. As they sang, a picture of the wild-woods passed by me, as they were indeed, no park-like dainty glades and lawns, but rough and tangled thicket and bare waste and heath, solemn under the morning sun, and dreary with the rising of the evening wind and the drift of the night-long rain.

When he had done, another began in something of the same strain, but singing more of a song than a story ballad; and thus much I remember of it:

> The Sheriff is made a mighty lord,
> Of goodly gold he hath enow,
> And many a sergeant girt with sword;
> But forth will we and bend the bow.
> We shall bend the bow on the lily lea
> Betwixt the thorn and the oaken tree.
>
> With stone and lime is the burg wall built,
> And pit and prison are stark and strong,
> And many a true man there is spilt,
> And many a right man doomed by wrong.
>
> So forth shall we and bend the bow
> And the king's writ never the road shall know.
>
> Now yeomen walk ye warily,
> And heed ye the houses where ye go,
> For as fair and as fine as they may be,
> Lest behind your heels the door clap to.
> Fare forth with the bow to the lily lea
> Betwixt the thorn and the oaken tree.
>
> Now bills and bows! and out a-gate!
> And turn about on the lily lea!
> And though their company be great
> The grey-goose wing shall set us free.
> Now bent is the bow in the green abode
> And the king's writ knoweth not the road.
>
> So over the mead and over the hithe,
> And away to the wild-wood wend we forth;
> There dwell we yeomen bold and blithe
> Where the Sheriff's word is nought of worth.
> Bent is the bow on the lily lea

Betwixt the thorn and the oaken tree.

But here the song dropped suddenly, and one of the men held up his hand as who would say, Hist! Then through the open window came the sound of another song, gradually swelling as though sung by men on the march. This time the melody was a piece of the plain-song of the church, familiar enough to me to bring back to my mind the great arches of some cathedral in France and the canons singing in the choir.

All leapt up and hurried to take their bows from wall and corner; and some had bucklers withal, circles of leather, boiled and then moulded into shape and hardened: these were some two hand-breadths across, with iron or brass bosses in the centre. Will Green went to the corner where the bills leaned against the wall and handed them round to the first-comers as far as they would go, and out we all went gravely and quietly into the village street and the fair sunlight of the calm afternoon, now beginning to turn towards evening. None had said anything since we first heard the new-come singing, save that as we went out of the door the ballad-singer clapped me on the shoulder and said: "Was it not sooth that I said, brother, that Robin Hood should bring us John Ball?"

3. THEY MEET AT THE CROSS

The street was pretty full of men by then we were out in it, and all faces turned toward the cross. The song still grew nearer and louder, and even as we looked we saw it turning the corner through the hedges of the orchards and closes, a good clump of men, more armed, as it would seem, than our villagers, as the low sun flashed back from many points of bright iron and steel. The words of the song could now be heard, and amidst them I could pick out Will Green's late challenge to me and my answer; but as I was bending all my mind to disentangle more words from the music, suddenly from the new white tower behind us clashed out the church bells, harsh and hurried at first, but presently falling into measured chime; and at the first sound of them a great shout went up from us and was echoed by the new-comers, "John Ball hath rung our bell!" Then we pressed on, and presently we were all mingled together at the cross.

Will Green had good-naturedly thrust and pulled me forward, so that I found myself standing on the lowest step of the cross, his seventy-two inches of man on one side of me. He chuckled while I panted, and said:

"There's for thee a good hearing and seeing stead, old lad. Thou art tall across thy belly and not otherwise, and thy wind, belike, is none of the best, and but for me thou wouldst have been amidst the thickest of the throng, and have heard words muffled by Kentish bellies and seen little but swinky woollen elbows and greasy plates and jacks. Look no more on the ground, as though thou sawest a hare, but let thine eyes and thine ears be busy to gather tidings to bear back to Essex—or heaven!"

I grinned good-fellowship at him but said nothing, for in truth my eyes and ears were as busy as he would have them to be. A buzz of general talk went up from the throng amidst the regular cadence of the bells, which now seemed far away and as it were that they were not swayed by hands, but were living creatures making that noise of their own wills.

I looked around and saw that the newcomers mingled with us must have been a regular armed band; all had bucklers slung at their backs, few lacked a sword at the side. Some had bows, some "staves"—that is, bills, pole-axes, or pikes. Moreover, unlike our villagers, they had defensive arms. Most had steel-caps on their heads, and some had body armour, generally a "jack," or coat into which pieces of iron or horn were quilted; some had also steel or steel-and-leather arm or thigh pieces. There were a few mounted men among them, their horses being big-boned hammer-headed beasts, that looked as if they had been taken from plough or waggon, but their riders were well armed with steel armour on their heads, legs, and arms. Amongst the horsemen I noted the man that had ridden past me when I first awoke; but he seemed to be a prisoner, as he had a woollen hood on his head instead of his helmet, and carried neither bill, sword, nor dagger. He seemed by no means ill-at-ease, however, but was laughing and talking with the men who stood near him.

Above the heads of the crowd, and now slowly working towards the cross, was a banner on a high-raised cross-pole, a picture of a man and woman half-clad in skins of beasts seen against a background of green trees, the man holding a spade and the woman a distaff and spindle rudely done enough, but yet with a certain spirit and much meaning; and underneath this symbol of the early world and man's first contest with nature were the written words:

When Adam delved and Eve span
Who was then the gentleman?

The banner came on and through the crowd, which at last opened where we stood for its passage, and the banner-bearer turned and faced the throng and stood on the first step of the cross beside me.

A man followed him, clad in a long dark-brown gown of coarse woollen, girt with a cord, to which hung a "pair of beads" (or rosary, as we should call it today) and a book in a bag. The man was tall and big-boned, a ring of dark hair surrounded his priest's tonsure; his nose was big but clear cut and with wide nostrils; his shaven face showed a longish upper lip and a big but blunt chin; his mouth was big and the lips closed firmly; a face not very noteworthy but for his grey eyes well opened and wide apart, at whiles lighting up his whole face with a kindly smile, at whiles set and stern, at whiles resting in that look as if they were gazing at something a long way off, which is the wont of the eyes of the poet or enthusiast.

He went slowly up the steps of the cross and stood at the top with one hand laid on the shaft, and shout upon shout broke forth from the throng. When the shouting died away into a silence of the human voices, the bells were still quietly chiming with that far-away voice of theirs, and the long-winged dusky swifts, by no means scared by the concourse, swung round about the cross with their wild squeals; and the man stood still for a little, eyeing the throng, or rather looking first at one and then another man in it, as though he were trying to think what such an one was thinking of, or what he were fit for. Sometimes he caught the eye of one or other, and then that kindly smile spread over his face, but faded off it into the sternness and sadness of a man who has heavy and great thoughts hanging about him. But when John Ball first mounted the steps of the cross a lad at some one's bidding had run off to stop the ringers, and so presently the voice of the bells fell dead, leaving on men's minds that sense of blankness or even disappointment which is always caused by the sudden stopping of a sound one has got used to and found pleasant. But a great expectation had fallen by now on all that throng, and no word was spoken even in a whisper, and all men's hearts and eyes were fixed upon the dark figure standing straight up now by the tall white shaft of the cross, his hands stretched out before him, one palm laid upon the other.

And for me, as I made ready to hearken, I felt a joy in my soul that I had never yet felt.

4. THE VOICE OF JOHN BALL

SO now I heard John Ball; how he lifted up his voice and said:

"Ho, all ye good people! I am a priest of God, and in my day's work it cometh that I should tell you what ye should do, and what ye should forbear doing, and to that end I am come hither: yet first, if I myself have wronged any man here, let him say wherein my wrongdoing lieth, that I may ask his pardon and his pity."

A great hum of good-will ran through the crowd as he spoke; then he smiled as in a kind of pride, and again he spoke:

"Wherefore did ye take me out of the archbishop's prison but three days agone, when ye lighted the archbishop's house for the candle of Canterbury, but that I might speak to you and pray you: therefore I will not keep silence, whether I have done ill, or whether I have done well. And herein, good fellows and my very brethren, I would have you to follow me; and if there be such here, as I know full well there be some, and may be a good many, who have been robbers of their neighbours ('And who is my neighbour?' quoth the rich man), or lechers, or despiteful haters, or talebearers, or fawners on rich men for the hurt of the poor (and that is the worst of all)—Ah, my poor brethren who have gone astray, I say not to you, go home and repent lest you mar our great deeds, but rather come afield and there repent. Many a day have ye been fools, but hearken unto me and I shall make you wise above the wisdom of the earth; and if ye die in your wisdom, as God wot ye well may, since the fields ye wend to bear swords for daisies, and spears for bents, then shall ye be, though men call you dead, a part and parcel of the living wisdom of all things, very stones of the pillars that uphold the joyful earth.

"Forsooth, ye have heard it said that ye shall do well in this world that in the world to come ye may live happily for ever; do ye well then, and have your reward both on earth and in heaven; for I say to you that earth and heaven are not two but one; and this one is that which ye know, and are each one of you a part of, to wit, the Holy Church, and in each one of you dwelleth the life of the Church, unless ye slay it. Forsooth, brethren, will ye murder the Church any one of you, and go forth a wandering man and lonely, even as Cain did who slew his brother? Ah, my brothers, what an evil doom is this, to be an outcast from the Church, to have none to love you and to speak with you, to be without fellowship! Forsooth, brothers, fellowship is heaven, and lack of fellowship is hell: fellowship is life, and lack of fellowship is death: and the deeds that ye do upon the earth, it is for fellowship's sake that ye do them, and the life that is in it, that shall live on and on for ever, and each one of you part of it, while many a man's life upon the earth from the earth shall wane.

"Therefore, I bid you not dwell in hell but in heaven, or while ye must, upon earth, which is a part of heaven, and forsooth no foul part.

"Forsooth, he that waketh in hell and feeleth his heart fail him, shall have memory of the merry days of earth, and how that when his heart failed him there, he cried on his fellow, were it his wife or his son or his brother or his gossip or his brother sworn in arms, and how that his fellow heard him and came and they mourned together under the sun, till again they laughed together and were but half sorry between them. This shall he think on in hell, and cry on his fellow to help him, and shall find that therein is no help because there is no fellowship, but every man for himself. Therefore, I tell you that the proud, despiteous rich man, though he knoweth it not, is in hell already, because he hath no fellow; and he that hath so hardy a heart that in sorrow he thinketh of fellowship, his sorrow is soon but a story of sorrow—a little change in the life that knows not ill."

He left off for a little; and indeed for some time his voice had fallen, but it was so clear and the summer evening so soft and still, and the silence of the folk so complete, that every word told. His eyes fell down to the crowd as he stopped speaking, since for some little while they had been looking far away into the blue distance of summer; and the kind eyes of the man had a curious sight before him in that crowd, for amongst them were many who by this time were not dry-eyed, and some wept outright in spite of their black beards, while all had that look as if they were ashamed of themselves, and did not want others to see how deeply they were moved, after the fashion of their race when they are strongly stirred. I looked at Will Green beside me: his right hand clutched his bow so tight, that the knuckles whitened; he was staring straight before him, and the tears were running out of his eyes and down his big nose as though without his will, for his face was stolid and unmoved all the time till he caught my eye, and then he screwed up the strangest face, of scowling brow, weeping eyes, and smiling mouth, while he dealt me a sounding thump in the ribs with his left elbow, which, though it would have knocked me down but for the crowd, I took as an esquire does the accolade which makes a knight of him.

But while I pondered all these things, and how men fight and lose the battle, and the thing that they fought for comes about in spite of their defeat, and when it comes turns out not to be what they meant, and other men have to fight for what they meant under another name— while I pondered all this, John Ball began to speak again in the same soft and dear voice with which he had left off.

"Good fellows, it was your fellowship and your kindness that took me out of the archbishop's prison three days agone, though God wot ye had nought to gain by it save outlawry and the gallows; yet lacked I not your fellowship before ye drew near me in the body, and when between me and Canterbury street was yet a strong wall, and the turnkeys and sergeants and bailiffs.

"For hearken, my friends and helpers; many days ago, when April was yet young, I lay there, and the heart that I had strung up to bear all things because of the fellowship of men and the blessed saints and the angels and those that are, and those that are to be, this heart, that I had strung up like a strong bow, fell into feebleness, so that I lay there a-longing for the green fields and the white-thorn bushes and the lark singing over the corn, and the talk of good fellows round the ale-house bench, and the babble of the little children, and the team on the road and the beasts afield, and all the life of earth; and I alone all the while, near my foes and afar from my friends, mocked and flouted and starved with cold and hunger; and so weak was my heart that though I longed for all these things yet I saw them not, nor knew them but as names; and I longed so sore to be gone that I chided myself that I had once done well; and I said to myself:

"Forsooth, hadst thou kept thy tongue between thy teeth thou mightest have been something, if it had been but a parson of a town, and comfortable to many a poor man; and then mightest thou have clad here and there the naked back, and filled the empty belly, and holpen many, and men would have spoken well of thee, and of thyself thou hadst thought well; and all this hast thou lost for lack of a word here and there to some great man, and a little winking of the eyes amidst murder and wrong and unruth; and now thou art nought and helpless, and the hemp for thee is sown and grown and heckled and spun, and lo there, the rope for thy gallows-tree!—all for nought, for nought.

"Forsooth, my friends, thus I thought and sorrowed in my feebleness that I had not been a traitor to the Fellowship of the Church, for e'en so evil was my foolish imagination.

"Yet, forsooth, as I fell a-pondering over all the comfort and help that I might have been and that I might have had, if I had been but a little of a trembling cur to creep and crawl before abbot and bishop and baron and bailiff, came the thought over me of the evil of the world wherewith I, John Ball, the rascal hedge-priest, had fought and striven in the Fellowship of the saints in heaven and poor men upon earth.

"Yea, forsooth, once again I saw as of old, the great treading down the little, and the strong beating down the weak, and cruel men fearing not, and kind men daring not, and wise men caring not; and the saints in heaven forbearing and yet bidding me not to forbear; forsooth, I knew once more that he who doeth well in fellowship, and because of fellowship, shall not fail though he seem to fail to-day, but in days hereafter shall he and his work yet be alive, and men be holpen by them to strive again and yet again; and yet indeed even that was little, since, forsooth, to strive was my pleasure and my life.

"So I became a man once more, and I rose up to my feet and went up and down my prison what I could for my hopples, and into my mouth came words of good cheer, even such as we to-day have sung, and stoutly I sang them, even as we now have sung them; and then did I rest me, and once more thought of those pleasant fields where I would be, and all the life of man and beast about them, and I said to myself that I should see them once more before I died, if but once it were.

"Forsooth, this was strange, that whereas before I longed for them and yet saw them not, now that my longing was slaked my vision was cleared, and I saw them as though the prison walls opened to me and I was out of Canterbury street and amidst the green meadows of April; and therewithal along with me folk that I have known and who are dead, and folk that are living; yea, and all those of the Fellowship on earth and in heaven; yea, and all that are here this day. Overlong were the tale to tell of them, and of the time that is gone.

"So thenceforward I wore through the days with no such faint heart, until one day the prison opened verily and in the daylight, and there were ye, my fellows, in the door—your faces glad, your hearts light with hope, and your hands heavy with wrath; then I saw and understood what was to do. Now, therefore, do ye understand it!"

His voice was changed, and grew louder than loud now, as he cast his hands abroad towards that company with those last words of his; and I could feel that all shame and fear was falling from those men, and that mere fiery manhood was shining through their wonted English shamefast stubbornness, and that they were moved indeed and saw the road before them. Yet no man spoke, rather the silence of the men-folk deepened, as the sun's rays grew more level and more golden, and the swifts wheeled about shriller and louder than before.

Then again John Ball spoke and said, "In good sooth, I deem ye wot no worse than I do what is to do—and first that somewhat we shall do— since it is for him that is lonely or in prison to dream of fellowship, but for him that is of a fellowship to do and not to dream.

"And next, ye know who is the foeman, and that is the proud man, the oppressor, who scorneth fellowship, and himself is a world to himself and needeth no helper nor helpeth any, but, heeding no law, layeth law on other men because he is rich; and surely every one that is rich is such an one, nor may be other.

"Forsooth, in the belly of every rich man dwelleth a devil of hell, and when the man would give his goods to the poor, the devil within him gainsayeth it, and saith, 'Wilt thou then be of the poor, and suffer cold and hunger and mocking as they suffer, then give thou thy goods to them, and keep them not.' And when he would be compassionate, again saith the devil to him, 'If thou heed these losels and turn on them a face like to their faces, and deem of them as men, then shall they scorn thee, and evil shall come of it, and even one day they shall fall on thee to slay thee when they have learned that thou art but as they be.'

"Ah, woe worth the while! too oft he sayeth sooth, as the wont of the devil is, that lies may be born of the barren truth; and sooth it is that the poor deemeth the rich to be other than he, and meet to be his master, as though, forsooth, the poor were come of Adam, and the rich of him that made Adam, that is God; and thus the poor man oppresseth the poor man, because he feareth the oppressor. Nought such are ye, my brethren; or else why are ye gathered here in harness to bid all bear witness of you that ye are the sons of one man and one mother, begotten of the earth?"

As he said the words there came a stir among the weapons of the throng, and they pressed closer round the cross, yet with held the shout as yet which seemed gathering in their bosoms.

And again he said:

"Forsooth, too many rich men there are in this realm; and yet if there were but one, there would be one too many, for all should be his thralls. Hearken, then, ye men of Kent. For overlong belike have I held you with words; but the love of you constrained me, and the joy that a man hath to babble to his friends and his fellows whom he hath not seen for a long season.

"Now, hearken, I bid you: To the rich men that eat up a realm there cometh a time when they whom they eat up, that is the poor, seem poorer than of wont, and their complaint goeth up louder to the heavens; yet it is no riddle to say that oft at such times the fellowship of the poor is waxing stronger, else would no man have heard his cry. Also at such times is the rich man become fearful, and so waxeth in cruelty, and of that cruelty do people misdeem that it is power and might waxing. Forsooth, ye are stronger than your fathers, because ye are more grieved than they, and ye should have been less grieved than they had ye been horses and swine; and then, forsooth, would ye have been stronger to bear; but ye, ye are not strong to bear, but to do.

"And wot ye why we are come to you this fair eve of holiday? and wot ye why I have been telling of fellowship to you? Yea, forsooth, I deem ye wot well, that it is for this cause, that ye might bethink you of your fellowship with the men of Essex."

His last word let loose the shout that had been long on all men's lips, and great and fierce it was as it rang shattering through the quiet upland village. But John Ball held up his hand, and the shout was one and no more.

Then he spoke again:

"Men of Kent, I wot well that ye are not so hard bested as those of other shires, by the token of the day when behind the screen of leafy boughs ye met Duke William with bill and bow as he wended Londonward from that woeful field of Senlac; but I have told of fellowship, and ye have hearkened and understood what the Holy Church is, whereby ye know that ye are fellows of the saints in heaven and the poor men of Essex; and as one day the saints shall call you to the heavenly feast, so now do the poor men call you to the battle.

"Men of Kent, ye dwell fairly here, and your houses are framed of stout oak beams, and your own lands ye till; unless some accursed lawyer with his false lying sheepskin and forged custom of the Devil's Manor hath stolen it from you; but in Essex slaves they be and villeins, and worse they shall be, and the lords swear that ere a year be over ox and horse shall go free in Essex, and man and woman shall draw the team and the plough; and north away in the east countries dwell men in poor halls of wattled reeds and mud, and the north-east wind from off the fen whistles through them; and poor they be to the letter; and there him whom the lord spareth, the bailiff squeezeth, and him whom the bailiff forgetteth, the Easterling Chapman sheareth; yet be these stout men and valiant, and your very brethren.

"And yet if there be any man here so base as to think that a small matter, let him look to it that if these necks abide under the yoke, Kent shall sweat for it ere it be long; and ye shall lose acre and close and woodland, and be servants in your own houses, and your sons shall be the lords' lads, and your daughters their lemans, and ye shall buy a bold word with many stripes, and an honest deed with a leap from the gallows-tree.

"Bethink ye, too, that ye have no longer to deal with Duke William, who, if he were a thief and a cruel lord, was yet a prudent man and a wise warrior; but cruel are these, and headstrong, yea, thieves and fools in one—and ye shall lay their heads in the dust."

A shout would have arisen again, but his eager voice rising higher yet, restrained it as he said:

"And how shall it be then when these are gone? What else shall ye lack when ye lack masters? Ye shall not lack for the fields ye have tilled, nor the houses ye have built, nor the cloth ye have woven; all these shall be yours, and whatso ye will of all that the earth beareth; then shall no man mow the deep grass for another, while his own kine lack cow-meat; and he that soweth shall reap, and the reaper shall eat in fellowship the harvest that in fellowship he hath won; and he that buildeth a house shall dwell in it with those that he biddeth of his free will; and the tithe barn shall garner the wheat for all men to eat of when the seasons are untoward, and the rain-drift hideth the sheaves in August; and all shall be without money and without price. Faithfully and merrily then shall all men keep the holidays of the Church in peace of body and joy of heart. And man shall help man, and the saints in heaven shall be glad, because men no more fear each other; and the churl shall be ashamed, and shall hide his churlishness till it be gone, and he be no more a churl; and fellowship shall be established in heaven and on the earth."

5. THEY HEAR TIDINGS OF BATTLE AND MAKE THEM READY

He left off as one who had yet something else to say; and, indeed, I thought he would give us some word as to the trysting-place, and whither the army was to go from it; because it was now clear to me that this gathering was but a band of an army. But much happened before John Ball spoke again from the cross, and it was on this wise.

When there was silence after the last shout that the crowd had raised a while ago, I thought I heard a thin sharp noise far away, somewhat to the north of the cross, which I took rather for the sound of a trumpet or horn, than for the voice of a man or any beast. Will Green also seemed to have heard it, for he turned his head sharply and then back again, and looked keenly into the crowd as though seeking to catch some one's eye. There was a very tall man standing by the prisoner on the horse near the outskirts of the crowd, and holding his bridle. This man, who was well-armed, I saw look up and say something to the prisoner, who stooped down and seemed to whisper him in turn. The tall man nodded his head and the prisoner got off his horse, which was a cleaner-limbed, better-built beast than the others belonging to the band, and the tall man quietly led him a little way from the crowd, mounted him, and rode off northward at a smart pace.

Will Green looked on sharply at all this, and when the man rode off, smiled as one who is content, and deems that all is going well, and settled himself down again to listen to the priest.

But now when John Ball had ceased speaking, and after another shout, and a hum of excited pleasure and hope that followed it, there was silence again, and as the priest addressed himself to speaking once more, he paused and turned his head towards the wind, as if he heard something, which certainly I heard, and belike every one in the throng, though it was not over-loud, far as sounds carry in clear quiet evenings. It was the thump-a-thump of a horse drawing near at a hand-gallop along the grassy upland road; and I knew well it was the tall man coming back with tidings, the purport of which I could well guess.

I looked up at Will Green's face. He was smiling as one pleased, and said softly as he nodded to me, "Yea, shall we see the grey-goose fly this eve?"

But John Ball said in a great voice from the cross, "Hear ye the tidings on the way, fellows! Hold ye together and look to your gear; yet hurry not, for no great matter shall this be. I wot well there is little force between Canterbury and Kingston, for the lords are looking north of Thames toward Wat Tyler and his men. Yet well it is, well it is!"

The crowd opened and spread out a little, and the men moved about in it, some tightening a girdle, some getting their side arms more within reach of their right hands, and those who had bows stringing them.

Will Green set hand and foot to the great shapely piece of polished red yew, with its shining horn tips, which he carried, and bent it with no seeming effort; then he reached out his hand over his shoulder and drew out a long arrow, smooth, white, beautifully balanced, with a barbed iron head at one end, a horn nock and three strong goose feathers at the other. He held it loosely between the finger and thumb of his right hand, and there he stood with a thoughtful look on his face, and in his hands one of the most terrible weapons which a strong man has ever carried, the English long-bow and cloth-yard shaft.

But all this while the sound of the horse's hoofs was growing nearer, and presently from the corner of the road amidst the orchards broke out our long friend, his face red in the sun near sinking now. He waved his right hand as he came in sight of us, and sang out, "Bills and bows! bills and bows!" and the whole throng turned towards him and raised a great shout.

He reined up at the edge of the throng, and spoke in a loud voice, so that all might hear him:

"Fellows, these are the tidings; even while our priest was speaking we heard a horn blow far off; so I bade the sergeant we have taken, and who is now our fellow-in-arms, to tell me where away it was that there would be folk a-gathering, and what they were; and he did me to wit that mayhappen Sir John Newton was stirring from Rochester Castle; or, maybe, it was the sheriff and Rafe Hopton with him; so I rode off what I might towards Hartlip, and I rode warily, and that was well, for as I came through a little wood between Hartlip and Guildstead, I saw beyond it a gleam of steel, and lo in the field there a company, and a pennon of Rafe Hopton's arms, and that is blue and thereon three silver fish: and a pennon of the sheriff's arms, and that is a green tree; and withal another pennon of three red kine, and whose they be I know not."[1]

"There tied I my horse in the middle of the wood, and myself I crept along the dyke to see more and to hear somewhat; and no talk I heard to tell of save at whiles a big knight talking to five or six others, and saying somewhat, wherein came the words London and Nicholas Bramber, and King Richard; but I saw that of men-at-arms and sergeants there might be a hundred, and of bows not many, but of those outland arbalests maybe a fifty; and so, what with one and another of servants and tipstaves and lads, some three hundred, well armed, and the men-at-arms of the best. Forsooth, my masters, there had I been but a minute, ere the big knight broke off his talk, and cried out to the music to blow up, 'And let us go look on these villeins,' said he; and withal the men began to gather in a due and ordered company, and their faces turned hitherward; forsooth, I got to my horse, and led him out of the wood on the other side, and so to saddle and away along the green roads; neither was I seen or chased. So look ye to it, my masters, for these men will be coming to speak with us; nor is there need for haste, but rather for good speed; for in some twenty or thirty minutes will be more tidings to hand."

By this time one of our best-armed men had got through the throng and was standing on the cross beside John Ball. When the long man had done, there was confused noise of talk for a while, and the throng spread itself out more and more, but not in a disorderly manner; the bowmen drawing together toward the outside, and the billmen forming behind them. Will Green was still standing beside me and had hold of my arm, as though he knew both where he and I were to go.

"Fellows," quoth the captain from the cross, "belike this stour shall not live to be older than the day, if ye get not into a plump together for their arbalestiers to shoot bolts into, and their men-at-arms to thrust spears into. Get you to the edge of the crofts and spread out there six feet between man and man, and shoot, ye bowmen, from the hedges, and ye with the staves keep your heads below the level of the hedges, or else for all they be thick a bolt may win its way in."

He grinned as he said this, and there was laughter enough in the throng to have done honour to a better joke.

Then he sung out, "Hob Wright, Rafe Wood, John Pargetter, and thou Will Green, bestir ye and marshal the bowshot; and thou Nicholas Woodyer shall be under me Jack Straw in ordering of the staves. Gregory Tailor and John Clerk, fair and fine are ye clad in the arms of the Canterbury bailiffs; ye shall shine from afar; go ye with the banner into the highway, and the bows on either side shall ward you; yet jump, lads, and over the hedge with you when the bolts begin to fly your way! Take heed, good fellows all, that our business is to bestride the highway, and not let them get in on our flank the while; so half to the right, half to the left of the highway. Shoot straight and strong, and waste no breath with noise; let the loose of the bowstring cry for you! and look you! think it no loss of manhood to cover your bodies with tree and bush; for one of us who know is worth a hundred of those proud fools. To it, lads, and let them see what the grey goose bears between his wings! Abide us here, brother John Ball, and pray for us if thou wilt; but for me, if God will not do for Jack Straw what Jack Straw would do for God were he in like case, I can see no help for it."

"Yea, forsooth," said the priest, "here will I abide you my fellows if ye come back; or if ye come not back, here will I abide the foe. Depart, and the blessing of the Fellowship be with you."

Down then leapt Jack Straw from the cross, and the whole throng set off without noise or hurry, soberly and steadily in outward seeming. Will Green led me by the hand as if I were a boy, yet nothing he said, being forsooth intent on his charge. We were some four hundred men in all; but I said to myself that without some advantage of the ground we were lost men before the men-at-arms that long Gregory Tailor had told us of; for I had not seen as yet the yard-long shaft at its work.

We and somewhat more than half of our band turned into the orchards on the left of the road, through which the level rays of the low sun shone brightly. The others took up their position on the right side of it. We kept pretty near to the road till we had got through all the closes save the last, where we were brought up by a hedge and a dyke, beyond which lay a wide-open nearly treeless space, not of tillage, as at the other side of the place, but of pasture, the common grazing ground of the township. A little stream wound about through the ground, with a few willows here and there; there was only a thread of water in it in this hot summer tide, but its course could easily be traced by the deep blue-green of the rushes that grew plenteously in the bed. Geese were lazily wandering about and near this brook, and a herd of cows, accompanied by the town bull, were feeding on quietly, their heads all turned one way; while half a dozen calves marched close together side by side like a plump of soldiers, their tails swinging in a kind of measure to keep off the flies, of which there was great plenty. Three or four lads and girls were sauntering about, heeding or not heeding the cattle. They looked up toward us as we crowded into the last close, and slowly loitered off toward the village. Nothing looked like battle; yet battle sounded in the air; for now we heard the beat of the horse-hoofs of the men-at-arms coming on towards us like the rolling of distant thunder, and growing louder and louder every minute; we were none too soon in turning to face them. Jack Straw was on our side of the road, and with a few gestures and a word or two he got his men into their places. Six archers lined the hedge along the road where the banner of Adam and Eve, rising above the grey leaves of the apple-trees, challenged the new-comers; and of the billmen also he kept a good few ready to guard the road in case the enemy should try to rush it with the horsemen. The road, not being a Roman one, was, you must remember, little like the firm smooth country roads that you are used to; it was a mere track between the hedges and fields, partly grass-grown, and cut up by the deep-sunk ruts hardened by the drought of summer. There was a stack of fagot and small wood on the other side, and our men threw themselves upon it and set to work to stake the road across for a rough defence against the horsemen.

What befell more on the road itself I had not much time to note, for our bowmen spread themselves out along the hedge that looked into the pasture-field, leaving some six feet between man and man; the rest of the billmen went along with the bowmen, and halted in clumps of some half-dozen along their line, holding themselves ready to help the bowmen if the enemy should run up under their shafts, or to run on to lengthen the line in case they should try to break in on our flank. The hedge in front of us was of quick. It had been strongly plashed in the past February, and was stiff and stout. It stood on a low bank; moreover, the level of the orchard was some thirty inches higher than that of the field and the ditch some two foot deeper than the face of the field. The field went winding round to beyond the church, making a quarter of a circle about the village, and at the western end of it were the butts whence the folk were coming from shooting when I first came into the village street.

Altogether, to me who knew nothing of war the place seemed defensible enough. I have said that the road down which Long Gregory came with his tidings went north; and that was its general direction; but its first reach was nearly east, so that the low sun was not in the eyes of any of us, and where Will Green took his stand, and I with him, it was nearly at our backs.

6. THE BATTLE AT THE TOWNSHIP'S END

Our men had got into their places leisurely and coolly enough, and with no lack of jesting and laughter. As we went along the hedge by the road, the leaders tore off leafy twigs from the low oak bushes therein, and set them for a rallying sign in their hats and headpieces, and two or three of them had horns for blowing.

Will Green, when he got into his place, which was thirty yards from where Jack Straw and the billmen stood in the corner of the two hedges, the road hedge and the hedge between the close and field, looked to right and left of him a moment, then turned to the man on the left and said:

"Look you, mate, when you hear our horns blow ask no more questions, but shoot straight and strong at whatso cometh towards us, till ye hear more tidings from Jack Straw or from me. Pass that word onward."

Then he looked at me and said:

"Now, lad from Essex, thou hadst best sit down out of the way at once: forsooth I wot not why I brought thee hither. Wilt thou not back to the cross, for thou art little of a fighting-man?"

"Nay," said I, "I would see the play. What shall come of it?"

"Little," said he; "we shall slay a horse or twain maybe. I will tell thee, since thou hast not seen a fight belike, as I have seen some, that these men-at-arms cannot run fast either to the play or from it, if they be a-foot; and if they come on a-horseback, what shall hinder me to put a shaft into the poor beast? But down with thee on the daisies, for some shot there will be first."

As he spoke he was pulling off his belts and other gear, and his coat, which done, he laid his quiver on the ground, girt him again, did his axe and buckler on to his girdle, and hung up his other attire on the nearest tree behind us. Then he opened his quiver and took out of it some two dozen of arrows, which he stuck in the ground beside him ready to his hand. Most of the bowmen within sight were doing the like.

As I glanced toward the houses I saw three or four bright figures moving through the orchards, and presently noted that they were women, all clad more or less like the girl in the Rose, except that two of them wore white coifs on their heads. Their errand there was clear, for each carried a bundle of arrows under her arm.

One of them came straight up to Will Green, and I could see at once that she was his daughter. She was tall and strongly made, with black hair like her father, somewhat comely, though no great beauty; but as they met, her eyes smiled even more than her mouth, and made her face look very sweet and kind, and the smile was answered back in a way so quaintly like to her father's face, that I too smiled for goodwill and pleasure.

"Well, well, lass," said he, "dost thou think that here is Crecy field toward, that ye bring all this artillery? Turn back, my girl, and set the pot on the fire; for that shall we need when we come home, I and this ballad-maker here."

"Nay," she said, nodding kindly at me, "if this is to be no Crecy, then may I stop to see, as well as the ballad-maker, since he hath neither sword nor staff?"

"Sweetling," he said, "get thee home in haste. This play is but little, yet mightest thou be hurt in it; and trust me the time may come, sweetheart, when even thou and such as thou shalt hold a sword or a staff. Ere the moon throws a shadow we shall be back."

She turned away lingering, not without tears on her face, laid the sheaf of arrows at the foot of the tree, and hastened off through the orchard. I was going to say something, when Will Green held up his hand as who would bid us hearken. The noise of the horse-hoofs, after growing nearer and nearer, had ceased suddenly, and a confused murmur of voices had taken the place of it.

"Get thee down, and take cover, old lad," said Will Green; "the dance will soon begin, and ye shall hear the music presently."

Sure enough as I slipped down by the hedge close to which I had been standing, I heard the harsh twang of the bow-strings, one, two, three, almost together, from the road, and even the whew of the shafts, though that was drowned in a moment by a confused but loud and threatening shout from the other side, and again the bowstrings clanged, and this time a far-off clash of arms followed, and therewithal that cry of a strong man that comes without his will, and is so different from his wonted voice that one has a guess thereby of the change that death is. Then for a while was almost silence; nor did our horns blow up, though some half-dozen of the billmen had leapt into the road when the bows first shot.

But presently came a great blare of trumpets and horns from the other side, and therewith as it were a river of steel and bright coats poured into the field before us, and still their horns blew as they spread out toward the left of our line; the cattle in the pasture-field, heretofore feeding quietly, seemed frightened silly by the sudden noise, and ran about tail in air and lowing loudly; the old bull with his head a little lowered, and his stubborn legs planted firmly, growling threateningly; while the geese about the brook waddled away gobbling and squeaking; all which seemed so strange to us along with the threat of sudden death that rang out from the bright array over against us, that we laughed outright, the most of us, and Will Green put down his head in mockery of the bull and grunted like him, whereat we laughed yet more. He turned round to me as he nocked his arrow, and said:

"I would they were just fifty paces nigher, and they move not. Ho! Jack Straw, shall we shoot?"

For the latter-named was nigh us now; he shook his head and said nothing as he stood looking at the enemy's line.

"Fear not but they are the right folk, Jack," quoth Will Green.

"Yea, yea," said he, "but abide awhile; they could make nought of the highway, and two of their sergeants had a message from the grey-goose feather. Abide, for they have not crossed the road to our right hand, and belike have not seen our fellows on the other side, who are now for a bushment to them."

I looked hard at the man. He was a tall, wiry, and broad-shouldered fellow, clad in a handsome armour of bright steel that certainly had not been made for a yeoman, but over it he had a common linen smock-frock or gabardine, like our field workmen wear now or used to wear, and in his helmet he carried instead of a feather a wisp of wheaten straw. He bore a heavy axe in his hand besides the sword he was girt with, and round his neck hung a great horn for blowing. I should say that I knew that there were at least three "Jack Straws" among the fellowship of the discontented, one of whom was over in Essex.

As we waited there, every bowman with his shaft nocked on the string, there was a movement in the line opposite, and presently came from it a little knot of three men, the middle one on horseback, the other two armed with long-handled glaives; all three well muffled up in armour. As they came nearer I could see that the horseman had a tabard over his armour, gaily embroidered with a green tree on a gold ground, and in his hand a trumpet.

"They are come to summon us. Wilt thou that he speak, Jack?" said Will Green.

"Nay," said the other; "yet shall he have warning first. Shoot when my horn blows!"

And therewith he came up to the hedge, climbed over, slowly because of his armour, and stood some dozen yards out in the field. The man on horseback put his trumpet to his mouth and blew a long blast, and then took a scroll into his hand and made as if he were going to read; but Jack Straw lifted up his voice and cried out:

"Do it not, or thou art but dead! We will have no accursed lawyers and their sheep-skins here! Go back to those that sent thee——"

But the man broke in in a loud harsh voice:

"Ho! YE PEOPLE! what will ye gathering in arms?"

Then cried Jack Straw:

"Sir Fool, hold your peace till ye have heard me, or else we shoot at once. Go back to those that sent thee, and tell them that we free men of Kent are on the way to London to speak with King Richard, and to tell him that which he wots not; to wit, that there is a certain sort of fools and traitors to the realm who would put collars on our necks and make beasts of us, and that it is his right and his devoir to do as he swore when he was crowned and anointed at Westminster on the Stone of Doom, and gainsay these thieves and traitors; and if he be too weak, then shall we help him; and if he will not be king, then shall we have one who will be, and that is the King's Son of Heaven. Now, therefore, if any withstand us on our lawful errand as we go to speak with our own king and lord, let him look to it. Bear back this word to them that sent thee. But for thee, hearken, thou bastard of an inky sheep-skin! get thee gone and tarry not; three times shall I lift up my hand, and the third time look to thyself, for then shalt thou hear the loose of our bowstrings, and after that nought else till thou hearest the devil bidding thee welcome to hell!"

Our fellows shouted, but the summoner began again, yet in a quavering voice:

"Ho! YE PEOPLE! what will ye gathering in arms? Wot ye not that ye are doing or shall do great harm, loss, and hurt to the king's lieges——"

He stopped; Jack Straw's hand was lowered for the second time. He looked to his men right and left, and then turned rein and turned tail, and scuttled back to the main body at his swiftest. Huge laughter rattled out all along our line as Jack Straw climbed back into the orchard grinning also.

Then we noted more movement in the enemy's line. They were spreading the archers and arbalestiers to our left, and the men-at-arms and others also spread some, what under the three pennons of which Long Gregory had told us, and which were plain enough to us in the dear evening. Presently the moving line faced us, and the archers set off at a smart pace toward us, the men-at-arms holding back a little behind them. I knew now that they had been within bowshot all along, but our men were loth to shoot before their first shots would tell, like those half-dozen in the road when, as they told me afterwards, a plump of their men-at-arms had made a show of falling on.

But now as soon as those men began to move on us directly in face, Jack Straw put his horn to his lips and blew a loud rough blast that was echoed by five or six others along the orchard hedge. Every man had his shaft nocked on the string; I watched them, and Will Green specially; he and his bow and its string seemed all of a piece, so easily by seeming did he draw the nock of the arrow to his ear. A moment, as he took his aim, and then—O then did I understand the meaning of the awe with which the ancient poet speaks of the loose of the god Apollo's bow; for terrible indeed was the mingled sound of the twanging bowstring and the whirring shaft so close to me.

I was now on my knees right in front of Will and saw all clearly; the arbalestiers (for no long-bow men were over against our stead) had all of them bright headpieces, and stout body-armour of boiled leather with metal studs, and as they came towards us, I could see over their shoulders great wooden shields hanging at their backs. Further to our left their long-bow men had shot almost as soon as ours, and I heard or seemed to hear the rush of the arrows through the apple-boughs and a man's cry therewith; but with us the long-bow had been before the cross-bow; one of the arbalestiers fell outright, his great shield clattering down on him, and moved no more; while three others were hit and were crawling to the rear. The rest had shouldered their bows and were aiming, but I thought unsteadily; and before the triggers were drawn again Will Green had nocked and loosed, and not a few others of our folk; then came the wooden hail of the bolts rattling through the boughs, but all overhead and no one hit.

The next time Will Green nocked his arrow he drew with a great shout, which all our fellows took up; for the arbalestiers instead of turning about in their places covered by their great shields and winding up their cross-bows for a second shot, as is the custom of such soldiers, ran huddling together toward their men-at-arms, our arrows driving thump-thump into their shields as they ran: I saw four lying on the field dead or sore wounded.

But our archers shouted again, and kept on each plucking the arrows from the ground, and nocking and loosing swiftly but deliberately at the line before them; indeed now was the time for these terrible bowmen, for as Will Green told me afterwards they always reckoned to kill through cloth or leather at five hundred yards, and they had let the cross-bow men come nearly within three hundred, and these were now all mingled and muddled up with the men-at-arms at scant five hundred yards' distance; and belike, too, the latter were not treating them too well, but seemed to be belabouring them with their spear-staves in their anger at the poorness of the play; so that as Will Green said it was like shooting at hay-ricks.

All this you must understand lasted but a few minutes, and when our men had been shooting quite coolly, like good workmen at peaceful work, for a few minutes more, the enemy's line seemed to clear somewhat; the pennon with the three red kine showed in front and three men armed from head to foot in gleaming steel, except for their short coats bright with heraldry, were with it. One of them (and he bore the three kine on his coat) turned round and gave some word of command, and an angry shout went up from them, and they came on steadily towards us, the man with the red kine on his coat leading them, a great naked sword in his hand: you must note that they were all on foot; but as they drew nearer I saw their horses led by grooms and pages coming on slowly behind them.

Sooth said Will Green that the men-at-arms run not fast either to or fro the fray; they came on no faster than a hasty walk, their arms clashing about them and the twang of the bows and whistle of the arrows never failing all the while, but going on like the push of the westerly gale, as from time to time the men-at-arms shouted, "Ha! ha! out! out! Kentish thieves!"

But when they began to fall on, Jack Straw shouted out, "Bills to the field! bills to the field!"

Then all our billmen ran up and leapt over the hedge into the meadow and stood stoutly along the ditch under our bows, Jack Straw in the forefront handling his great axe. Then he cast it into his left hand, caught up his horn and winded it loudly. The men-at-arms drew near steadily, some fell under the arrow-storm, but not a many; for though the target was big, it was hard, since not even the cloth-yard shaft could pierce well-wrought armour of plate, and there was much armour among them. Withal the arbalestiers were shooting again, but high and at a venture, so they did us no hurt.

But as these soldiers made wise by the French war were now drawing near, and our bowmen were casting down their bows and drawing their short swords, or handling their axes, as did Will Green, muttering, "Now must Hob Wright's gear end this play"—while this was a-doing, lo, on a sudden a flight of arrows from our right on the flank of the sergeants' array, which stayed them somewhat; not because it slew many men, but because they began to bethink them that their foes were many and all around them; then the road-hedge on the right seemed alive with armed men, for whatever could hold sword or staff amongst us was there; every bowman also leapt our orchard-hedge sword or axe in hand, and with a great shout, billmen, archers, and all, ran in on them; half-armed, yea, and half-naked some of them; strong and stout and lithe and light withal, the wrath of battle and the hope of better times lifting up their hearts till nothing could withstand them. So was all mingled together, and for a minute or two was a confused clamour over which rose a clatter like the riveting of iron plates, or the noise of the street of coppersmiths at Florence; then the throng burst open and the steel-clad sergeants and squires and knights ran huddling and shuffling towards their horses; but some cast down their weapons and threw up their hands and cried for peace and ransom; and some stood and fought desperately, and slew some till they were hammered down by many strokes, and of these were the bailiffs and tipstaves, and the lawyers and their men, who could not run and hoped for no mercy.

I looked as on a picture and wondered, and my mind was at strain to remember something forgotten, which yet had left its mark on it. I heard the noise of the horse-hoofs of the fleeing men-at-arms (the archers and arbalestiers had scattered before the last minutes of the play), I heard the confused sound of laughter and rejoicing down in the meadow, and close by me the evening wind lifting the lighter twigs of the trees, and far away the many noises of the quiet country, till light and sound both began to fade from me and I saw and heard nothing.

I leapt up to my feet presently and there was Will Green before me as I had first seen him in the street with coat and hood and the gear at his girdle and his unstrung bow in his hand; his face smiling and kind again, but maybe a thought sad.

"Well," quoth I, "what is the tale for the ballad-maker?"

"As Jack Straw said it would be," said he, "'the end of the day and the end of the fray;'" and he pointed to the brave show of the sky over the sunken sun; "the knights fled and the sheriff dead: two of the lawyer kind slain afield, and one hanged: and cruel was he to make them cruel: and three bailiffs knocked on the head—stout men, and so witless, that none found their brains in their skulls; and five arbalestiers and one archer slain, and a score and a half of others, mostly men come back from the French wars, men of the Companions there, knowing no other craft than fighting for gold; and this is the end they are paid for. Well, brother, saving the lawyers who belike had no souls, but only parchment deeds and libels of the same, God rest their souls!"

He fell a-musing; but I said, "And of our Fellowship were any slain?"

"Two good men of the township," he said, "Hob Horner and Antony Webber, were slain outright, Hob with a shaft and Antony in the hand-play, and John Pargetter hurt very sore on the shoulder with a glaive; and five more men of the Fellowship slain in the hand-play, and some few hurt, but not sorely. And as to those slain, if God give their souls rest it is well; for little rest they had on the earth belike; but for me, I desire rest no more."

I looked at him and our eyes met with no little love; and I wondered to see how wrath and grief within him were contending with the kindness of the man, and how clear the tokens of it were in his face.

"Come now, old lad," said he, "for I deem that John Ball and Jack Straw have a word to say to us at the cross yet, since these men broke off the telling of the tale; there shall we know what we are to take in hand to-morrow. And afterwards thou shalt eat and drink in my house this once, if never again."

So we went through the orchard closes again; and others were about and anigh us, all turned towards the cross as we went over the dewy grass, whereon the moon was just beginning to throw shadows.

7. MORE WORDS AT THE CROSS

I got into my old place again on the steps of the cross, Will Green beside me, and above me John Ball and Jack Straw again. The moon was half-way up the heavens now, and the short summer night had begun, calm and fragrant, with just so much noise outside our quiet circle as made one feel the world alive and happy.

We waited silently until we had heard John Ball and the story of what was to do; and presently he began to speak.

"Good people, it is begun, but not ended. Which of you is hardy enough to wend the road to London to-morrow?"

"All! All!" they shouted.

"Yea," said he, "even so I deemed of you. Yet forsooth hearken! London is a great and grievous city; and mayhappen when ye come thither it shall seem to you overgreat to deal with, when ye remember the little townships and the cots ye came from.

"Moreover, when ye dwell here in Kent ye think forsooth of your brethren in Essex or Suffolk, and there belike an end. But from London ye may have an inkling of all the world, and over-burdensome maybe shall that seem to you, a few and a feeble people.

"Nevertheless I say to you, remember the Fellowship, in the hope of which ye have this day conquered; and when ye come to London be wise and wary; and that is as much as to say, be bold and hardy; for in these days are ye building a house which shall not be overthrown, and the world shall not be too great or too little to hold it: for indeed it shall be the world itself, set free from evil-doers for friends to dwell in."

He ceased awhile, but they hearkened still, as if something more was coming. Then he said:

"To-morrow we shall take the road for Rochester; and most like it were well to see what Sir John Newton in the castle may say to us: for the man is no ill man, and hath a tongue well-shapen for words; and it were well that we had him out of the castle and away with us, and that we put a word in his mouth to say to the King. And wot ye well, good fellows, that by then we come to Rochester we shall be a goodly company, and ere we come to Blackheath a very great company; and at London Bridge who shall stay our host?

"Therefore there is nought that can undo us except our own selves and our hearkening to soft words from those who would slay us. They shall bid us go home and abide peacefully with our wives and children while they, the lords and councillors and lawyers, imagine counsel and remedy for us; and even so shall our own folly bid us; and if we hearken thereto we are undone indeed; for they shall fall upon our peace with war, and our wives and children they shall take from us, and some of us they shall hang, and some they shall scourge, and the others shall be their yoke-beasts—yea, and worse, for they shall lack meat more.

"To fools hearken not, whether they be yourselves or your foemen, for either shall lead you astray.

"With the lords parley not, for ye know already what they would say to you, and that is, 'Churl, let me bridle thee and saddle thee, and eat thy livelihood that thou winnest, and call thee hard names because I eat thee up; and for thee, speak not and do not, save as I bid thee.'

"All that is the end of their parleying.

"Therefore be ye bold, and again bold, and thrice bold! Grip the bow, handle the staff, draw the sword, and set on in the name of the Fellowship!"

He ended amid loud shouts; but straight-way answering shouts were heard, and a great noise of the winding of horns, and I misdoubted a new onslaught; and some of those in the throng began to string their bows and handle their bills; but Will Green pulled me by the sleeve and said:

"Friends are these by the winding of their horns; thou art quit for this night, old lad." And then Jack Straw cried out from the cross: "Fair and softly, my masters! These be men of our Fellowship, and are for your guests this night; they are from the bents this side of Medway, and are with us here because of the pilgrimage road, and that is the best in these parts, and so the shortest to Rochester. And doubt ye nothing of our being taken unawares this night; for I have bidden and sent out watchers of the ways, and neither a man's son nor a mare's son may come in on us without espial. Now make we our friends welcome. Forsooth, I looked for them an hour later; and had they come an hour earlier yet, some heads would now lie on the cold grass which shall lie on a feather bed to-night. But let be, since all is well!

"Now get we home to our houses, and eat and drink and slumber this night, if never once again, amid the multitude of friends and fellows; and yet soberly and without riot, since so much work is to hand. Moreover the priest saith, bear ye the dead men, both friends and foes, into the chancel of the church, and there this night he will wake them: but after to-morrow let the dead abide to bury their dead!"

Therewith he leapt down from the cross, and Will and I bestirred ourselves and mingled with the new-comers. They were some three hundred strong, clad and armed in all ways like the people of our township, except some half-dozen whose armour shone cold like ice under the moonbeams. Will Green soon had a dozen of them by the sleeve to come home with him to board and bed, and then I lost him for some minutes, and turning about saw John Ball standing behind me, looking pensively on all the stir and merry humours of the joyous uplanders.

"Brother from Essex," said he, "shall I see thee again to-night? I were fain of speech with thee; for thou seemest like one that has seen more than most."

"Yea," said I, "if ye come to Will Green's house, for thither am I bidden."

"Thither shall I come," said he, smiling kindly, "or no man I know in field. Lo you, Will Green looking for something, and that is me. But in his house will be song and the talk of many friends; and forsooth I have words in me that crave to come out in a quiet place where they may have each one his own answer. If thou art not afraid of dead men who were alive and wicked this morning, come thou to the church when supper is done, and there we may talk all we will."

Will Green was standing beside us before he had done, with his hand laid on the priest's shoulder, waiting till he had spoken out; and as I nodded Yea to John Ball he said:

"Now, master priest, thou hast spoken enough this two or three hours, and this my new brother must tell and talk in my house; and there my maid will hear his wisdom which lay still under the hedge e'en now when the bolts were abroad. So come ye, and ye good fellows, come!"

So we turned away together into the little street. But while John Ball had been speaking to me I felt strangely, as though I had more things to say than the words I knew could make clear: as if I wanted to get from other people a new set of words. Moreover, as we passed up the street again I was once again smitten with the great beauty of the scene; the houses, the church with its new chancel and tower, snow-white in the moonbeams now; the dresses and arms of the people, men and women (for the latter were now mixed up with the men); their grave sonorous language, and the quaint and measured forms of speech, were again become a wonder to me and affected me almost to tears.

8. SUPPER AT WILL GREEN'S

I walked along with the others musing as if I did not belong to them, till we came to Will Green's house. He was one of the wealthier of the yeomen, and his house was one of those I told you of, the lower story of which was built of stone. It had not been built long, and was very trim and neat. The fit of wonder had worn off me again by then I reached it, or perhaps I should give you a closer description of it, for it was a handsome yeoman's dwelling of that day, which is as much as saying it was very beautiful. The house on the other side of it, the last house in the village, was old or even ancient; all built of stone, and except for a newer piece built on to it—a hall, it seemed—had round arches, some of them handsomely carved. I knew that this was the parson's house; but he was another sort of priest than John Ball, and what for fear, what for hatred, had gone back to his monastery with the two other chantrey priests who dwelt in that house; so that the men of the township, and more especially the women, were thinking gladly how John Ball should say mass in their new chancel on the morrow.

Will Green's daughter was waiting for him at the door and gave him a close and eager hug, and had a kiss to spare for each of us withal: a strong girl she was, as I have said, and sweet and wholesome also. She made merry with her father; yet it was easy to see that her heart was in her mouth all along. There was a younger girl some twelve summers old, and a lad of ten, who were easily to be known for his children; an old woman also, who had her livelihood there, and helped the household; and moreover three long young men, who came into the house after we had sat down, to whom Will nodded kindly. They were brisk lads and smart, but had been afield after the beasts that evening, and had not seen the fray.

The room we came into was indeed the house, for there was nothing but it on the ground floor, but a stair in the corner went up to the chamber or loft above. It was much like the room at the Rose, but bigger; the cupboard better wrought, and with more vessels on it, and handsomer. Also the walls, instead of being panelled, were hung with a coarse loosely-woven stuff of green worsted with birds and trees woven into it. There were flowers in plenty stuck about the room, mostly of the yellow blossoming flag or flower-de-luce, of which I had seen plenty in all the ditches, but in the window near the door was a pot full of those same white poppies I had seen when I first woke up; and the table was all set forth with meat and drink, a big salt-cellar of pewter in the middle, covered with a white cloth.

We sat down, the priest blessed the meat in the name of the Trinity, and we crossed ourselves and fell to. The victual was plentiful of broth and flesh-meat, and bread and cherries, so we ate and drank, and talked lightly together when we were full.

Yet was not the feast so gay as might have been. Will Green had me to sit next to him, and on the other side sat John Ball; but the priest had grown somewhat distraught, and sat as one thinking of somewhat that was like to escape his thought. Will Green looked at his daughter from time to time, and whiles his eyes glanced round the fair chamber as one who loved it, and his kind face grew sad, yet never sullen. When the herdsmen came into the hall they fell straightway to asking questions concerning those of the Fellowship who had been slain in the fray, and of their wives and children; so that for a while thereafter no man cared to jest, for they were a neighbourly and kind folk, and were sorry both for the dead, and also for the living that should suffer from that day's work.

So then we sat silent awhile. The unseen moon was bright over the roof of the house, so that outside all was gleaming bright save the black shadows, though the moon came not into the room, and the white wall of the tower was the whitest and the brightest thing we could see.

Wide open were the windows, and the scents of the fragrant night floated in upon us, and the sounds of the men at their meat or making merry about the township; and whiles we heard the gibber of an owl from the trees westward of the church, and the sharp cry of a blackbird made fearful by the prowling stoat, or the far-off lowing of a cow from the upland pastures; or the hoofs of a horse trotting on the pilgrimage road (and one of our watchers would that be).

Thus we sat awhile, and once again came that feeling over me of wonder and pleasure at the strange and beautiful sights, mingled with the sights and sounds and scents beautiful indeed, yet not strange, but rather long familiar to me.

But now Will Green started in his seat where he sat with his daughter hanging over his chair, her hand amidst his thick black curls, and she weeping softly, I thought; and his rough strong voice broke the silence.

"Why, lads and neighbours, what ails us? If the knights who fled from us this eve were to creep back hither and look in at the window, they would deem that they had slain us after all, and that we were but the ghosts of the men who fought them. Yet, forsooth, fair it is at whiles to sit with friends and let the summer night speak for us and tell us its tales. But now, sweetling, fetch the mazer and the wine."

"Forsooth," said John Ball, "if ye laugh not over-much now, ye shall laugh the more on the morrow of to-morrow, as ye draw nearer to the play of point and edge."

"That is sooth," said one of the upland guests. "So it was seen in France when we fought there; and the eve of fight was sober and the morn was merry."

"Yea," said another, "but there, forsooth, it was for nothing ye fought; and to-morrow it shall be for a fair reward."

"It was for life we fought," said the first.

"Yea," said the second, "for life; and leave to go home and find the lawyers at their fell game. Ho, Will Green, call a health over the cup!"

For now Will Green had a bowl of wine in his hand. He stood up and said: "Here, now, I call a health to the wrights of Kent who be turning our ploughshares into swords and our pruning-hooks into spears! Drink around, my masters!"

Then he drank, and his daughter filled the bowl brimming again and he passed it to me. As I took it I saw that it was of light polished wood curiously speckled, with a band of silver round it, on which was cut the legend, "In the name of the Trinity fill the cup and drink to me." And before I drank, it came upon me to say, "To-morrow, and the fair days afterwards!"

Then I drank a great draught of the strong red wine, and passed it on; and every man said something over it, as "The road to London Bridge!" "Hob Carter and his mate!" and so on, till last of all John Ball drank, saying:

"Ten years hence, and the freedom of the Fellowship!" Then he said to Will Green: "Now, Will, must I needs depart to go and wake the dead, both friend and foe in the church yonder; and whoso of you will be shriven let him come to me thither in the morn, nor spare for as little after sunrise as it may be. And this our friend and brother from over the water of Thames, he hath will to talk with me and I with him; so now will I take him by the hand: and so God keep you, fellows!"

I rose to meet him as he came round the head of the table, and took his hand. Will Green turned round to me and said:

"Thou wilt come back again timely, old lad; for betimes on the morrow must we rise if we shall dine at Rochester."

I stammered as I yea-said him; for John Ball was looking strangely at me with a half-smile, and my heart beat anxiously and fearfully: but we went quietly to the door and so out into the bright moonlight.

I lingered a little when we had passed the threshold, and looked back at the yellow-lighted window and the shapes of the men that I saw therein with a grief and longing that I could not give myself a reason for, since I was to come back so soon. John Ball did not press me to move forward, but held up his hand as if to bid me hearken. The folk and guests there had already shaken themselves down since our departure, and were gotten to be reasonably merry it seemed; for one of the guests, he who had spoken of France before, had fallen to singing a ballad of the war to a wild and melancholy tune. I remember the first rhymes of it, which I heard as I turned away my head and we moved on toward the church:

> "On a fair field of France
> We fought on a morning
> So lovely as it lieth
> Along by the water.
> There was many a lord there
> Mowed men in the medley,
> 'Midst the banners of the barons
> And bold men of the knighthood,
> And spearmen and sergeants
> And shooters of the shaft."

9. BETWIXT THE LIVING AND THE DEAD

We entered the church through the south porch under a round-arched door carved very richly, and with a sculpture over the doorway and under the arch, which, as far as I could see by the moonlight, figured St. Michael and the Dragon. As I came into the rich gloom of the nave I noticed for the first time that I had one of those white poppies in my hand; I must have taken it out of the pot by the window as I passed out of Will Green's house.

The nave was not very large, but it looked spacious too; it was somewhat old, but well-built and handsome; the roof of curved wooden rafters with great tie-beams going from wall to wall. There was no light in it but that of the moon streaming through the windows, which were by no means large, and were glazed with white fretwork, with here and there a little figure in very deep rich colours. Two larger windows near the east end of each aisle had just been made so that the church grew lighter toward the east, and I could see all the work on the great screen between the nave and chancel which glittered bright in new paint and gilding: a candle glimmered in the loft above it, before the huge rood that filled up the whole space between the loft and the chancel arch. There was an altar at the east end of each aisle, the one on the south side standing against the outside wall, the one on the north against a traceried gaily-painted screen, for that aisle ran on along the chancel. There were a few oak benches near this second altar, seemingly just made, and well carved and moulded; otherwise the floor of the nave, which was paved with a quaint pavement of glazed tiles like the crocks I had seen outside as to ware, was quite clear, and the shafts of the arches rose out of it white and beautiful under the moon as though out of a sea, dark but with gleams struck over it.

The priest let me linger and look round, when he had crossed himself and given me the holy water; and then I saw that the walls were figured all over with stories, a huge St. Christopher with his black beard looking like Will Green, being close to the porch by which we entered, and above the chancel arch the Doom of the last Day, in which the painter had not spared either kings or bishops, and in which a lawyer with his blue coif was one of the chief figures in the group which the Devil was hauling off to hell.

"Yea," said John Ball, "'tis a goodly church and fair as you may see 'twixt Canterbury and London as for its kind; and yet do I misdoubt me where those who are dead are housed, and where those shall house them after they are dead, who built this house for God to dwell in. God grant they be cleansed at last; forsooth one of them who is now alive is a foul swine and a cruel wolf. Art thou all so sure, scholar, that all such have souls? and if it be so, was it well done of God to make them? I speak to thee thus, for I think thou art no delator; and if thou be, why should I heed it, since I think not to come back from this journey."

I looked at him and, as it were, had some ado to answer him; but I said at last, "Friend, I never saw a soul, save in the body; I cannot tell."

He crossed himself and said, "Yet do I intend that ere many days are gone by my soul shall be in bliss among the fellowship of the saints, and merry shall it be, even before my body rises from the dead; for wisely I have wrought in the world, and I wot well of friends that are long ago gone from the world, as St. Martin, and St. Francis, and St. Thomas of Canterbury, who shall speak well of me to the heavenly Fellowship, and I shall in no wise lose my reward."

I looked shyly at him as he spoke; his face looked sweet and calm and happy, and I would have said no word to grieve him; and yet belike my eyes looked wonder on him: he seemed to note it and his face grew puzzled. "How deemest thou of these things?" said he: "why do men die else, if it be otherwise than this?"

I smiled: "Why then do they live?" said I.

Even in the white moonlight I saw his face flush, and he cried out in a great voice, "To do great deeds or to repent them that they ever were born." "Yea," said I, "they live to live because the world liveth." He stretched out his hand to me and grasped mine, but said no more; and went on till we came to the door in the rood-screen; then he turned to me with his hand on the ring-latch, and said, "Hast thou seen many dead men?"

"Nay, but few," said I.

"And I a many," said he; "but come now and look on these, our friends first and then our foes, so that ye may not look to see them while we sit and talk of the days that are to be on the earth before the Day of Doom cometh."

So he opened the door, and we went into the chancel; a light burned on the high altar before the host, and looked red and strange in the moonlight that came through the wide traceried windows unstained by the pictures and beflowerings of the glazing; there were new stalls for the priests and vicars where we entered, carved more abundantly and beautifully than any of the woodwork I had yet seen, and everywhere was rich and fair colour and delicate and dainty form. Our dead lay just before the high altar on low biers, their faces all covered with linen cloths, for some of them had been sore smitten and hacked in the fray. We went up to them and John Ball took the cloth from the face of one; he had been shot to the heart with a shaft and his face was calm and smooth. He had been a young man fair and comely, with hair flaxen almost to whiteness; he lay there in his clothes as he had fallen, the hands crossed over his breast and holding a rush cross. His bow lay on one side of him, his quiver of shafts and his sword on the other.

John Ball spake to me while he held the corner of the sheet: "What sayest thou, scholar? feelest thou sorrow of heart when thou lookest on this, either for the man himself, or for thyself and the time when thou shalt be as he is?"

I said, "Nay, I feel no sorrow for this; for the man is not here: this is an empty house, and the master has gone from it. Forsooth, this to me is but as a waxen image of a man; nay, not even that, for if it were an image, it would be an image of the man as he was when he was alive. But here is no life nor semblance of life, and I am not moved by it; nay, I am more moved by the man's clothes and war-gear—there is more life in them than in him."

"Thou sayest sooth," said he; "but sorrowest thou not for thine own death when thou lookest on him?"

I said, "And how can I sorrow for that which I cannot so much as think of? Bethink thee that while I am alive I cannot think that I shall die, or believe in death at all, although I know well that I shall die—I can but think of myself as living in some new way."

Again he looked on me as if puzzled; then his face cleared as he said, "Yea, forsooth, and that is what the Church meaneth by death, and even that I look for; and that hereafter I shall see all the deeds that I have done in the body, and what they really were, and what shall come of them; and ever shall I be a member of the Church, and that is the Fellowship; then, even as now."

I sighed as he spoke; then I said, "Yea, somewhat in this fashion have most of men thought, since no man that is can conceive of not being; and I mind me that in those stories of the old Danes, their common word for a man dying is to say, 'He changed his life.'"

"And so deemest thou?"

I shook my head and said nothing.

"What hast thou to say hereon?" said he, "for there seemeth something betwixt us twain as it were a wall that parteth us."

"This," said I, "that though I die and end, yet mankind yet liveth, therefore I end not, since I am a man; and even so thou deemest, good friend; or at the least even so thou doest, since now thou art ready to die in grief and torment rather than be unfaithful to the Fellowship, yea rather than fail to work thine utmost for it; whereas, as thou thyself saidst at the cross, with a few words spoken and a little huddling-up of the truth, with a few pennies paid, and a few masses sung, thou mightest have had a good place on this earth and in that heaven. And as thou doest, so now doth many a poor man unnamed and unknown, and shall do while the world lasteth: and they that do less than this, fail because of fear, and are ashamed of their cowardice, and make many tales to themselves to deceive themselves, lest they should grow too much ashamed to live. And trust me if this were not so, the world would not live, but would die, smothered by its own stink. Is the wall betwixt us gone, friend?"

He smiled as he looked at me, kindly, but sadly and shamefast, and shook his head.

Then in a while he said, "Now ye have seen the images of those who were our friends, come and see the images of those who were once our foes."

So he led the way through the side screen into the chancel aisle, and there on the pavement lay the bodies of the foemen, their weapons taken from them and they stripped of their armour, but not otherwise of their clothes, and their faces mostly, but not all, covered. At the east end of the aisle was another altar, covered with a rich cloth beautifully figured, and on the wall over it was a deal of tabernacle work, in the midmost niche of it an image painted and gilt of a gay knight on horseback, cutting his own cloak in two with his sword to give a cantle of it to a half-naked beggar. "Knowest thou any of these men?" said I.

He said, "Some I should know, could I see their faces; but let them be."

"Were they evil men?" said I.

"Yea," he said, "some two or three. But I will not tell thee of them; let St. Martin, whose house this is, tell their story if he will. As for the rest they were hapless fools, or else men who must earn their bread somehow, and were driven to this bad way of earning it; God rest their souls! I will be no tale-bearer, not even to God."

So we stood musing a little while, I gazing not on the dead men, but on the strange pictures on the wall, which were richer and deeper coloured than those in the nave; till at last John Ball turned to me and laid his hand on my shoulder. I started and said, "Yea, brother; now must I get me back to Will Green's house, as I promised to do so timely."

"Not yet, brother," said he; "I have still much to say to thee, and the night is yet young. Go we and sit in the stalls of the vicars, and let us ask and answer on matters concerning the fashion of this world of menfolk, and of this land wherein we dwell; for once more I deem of thee that thou hast seen things which I have not seen, and could not have seen." With that word he led me back into the chancel, and we sat down side by side in the stalls at the west end of it, facing the high altar and the great east window. By this time the chancel was getting dimmer as the moon wound round the heavens; but yet was there a twilight of the moon, so that I could still see the things about me for all the brightness of the window that faced us; and this moon twilight would last, I knew, until the short summer night should wane, and the twilight of the dawn begin to show us the colours of all things about us.

So we sat, and I gathered my thoughts to hear what he would say, and I myself was trying to think what I should ask of him; for I thought of him as he of me, that he had seen things which I could not have seen.

10. TWO TALK OF THE DAYS TO COME

"Brother," said John Ball, "how deemest thou of our adventure? I do not ask thee if thou thinkest we are right to play the play like men, but whether playing like men we shall fail like men."

"Why dost thou ask me?" said I; "how much further than beyond this church can I see?" "Far further," quoth he, "for I wot that thou art a scholar and hast read books; and withal, in some way that I cannot name, thou knowest more than we; as though with thee the world had lived longer than with us. Hide not, therefore, what thou hast in thine heart, for I think after this night I shall see thee no more, until we meet in the heavenly Fellowship."

"Friend," I said, "ask me what thou wilt; or rather ask thou the years to come to tell thee some little of their tale; and yet methinks thou thyself mayest have some deeming thereof."

He raised himself on the elbow of the stall and looked me full in the face, and said to me: "Is it so after all that thou art no man in the flesh, but art sent to me by the Master of the Fellowship, and the King's Son of Heaven, to tell me what shall be? If that be so tell me straight out, since I had some deeming hereof before; whereas thy speech is like ours and yet unlike, and thy face hath something in it which is not after the fashion of our day. And yet take heed, if thou art such an one, I fear thee not, nay, nor him that sent thee; nor for thy bidding, nor for his, will I turn back from London Bridge but will press on, for I do what is meet and right."

"Nay," said I, "did I not tell thee e'en now that I knew life but not death? I am not dead; and as to who hath sent me, I say not that I am come by my own will; for I know not; yet also I know not the will that hath sent me hither. And this I say to thee, moreover, that if I know more than thou, I do far less; therefore thou art my captain and I thy minstrel."

He sighed as one from whom a weight had been lifted, and said: "Well, then, since thou art alive on the earth and a man like myself, tell me how deemest thou of our adventure: shall we come to London, and how shall we fare there?"

Said I, "What shall hinder you to come to London, and to fare there as ye will? For be sure that the Fellowship in Essex shall not fail you; nor shall the Londoners who hate the king's uncles withstand you; nor hath the Court any great force to meet you in the field; ye shall cast fear and trembling into their hearts."

"Even so, I thought," said he; "but afterwards what shall betide?"

Said I, "It grieves my heart to say that which I think. Yet hearken; many a man's son shall die who is now alive and happy, and if the soldiers be slain, and of them most not on the field, but by the lawyers, how shall the captains escape? Surely thou goest to thy death."

He smiled very sweetly, yet proudly, as he said: "Yea, the road is long, but the end cometh at last. Friend, many a day have I been dying; for my sister, with whom I have played and been merry in the autumn tide about the edges of the stubble-fields; and we gathered the nuts and bramble-berries there, and started thence the missel-thrush, and wondered at his voice and thought him big; and the sparrow-hawk wheeled and turned over the hedges and the weasel ran across the path, and the sound of the sheep-bells came to us from the downs as we sat happy on the grass; and she is dead and gone from the earth, for she pined from famine after the years of the great sickness; and my brother was slain in the French wars, and none thanked him for dying save he that stripped him of his gear; and my unwedded wife with whom I dwelt in love after I had taken the tonsure, and all men said she was good and fair, and true she was and lovely; she also is dead and gone from the earth; and why should I abide save for the deeds of the flesh which must be done? Truly, friend, this is but an old tale that men must die; and I will tell thee another, to wit, that they live: and I live now and shall live. Tell me then what shall befall."

Somehow I could not heed him as a living man as much as I had done, and the voice that came from me seemed less of me as I answered:

"These men are strong and valiant as any that have been or shall be, and good fellows also and kindly; but they are simple, and see no great way before their own noses. The victory shall they have and shall not know what to do with it; they shall fight and overcome, because of their lack of knowledge, and because of their lack of knowledge shall they be cozened and betrayed when their captains are slain, and all shall come to nought by seeming; and the king's uncles shall prevail, that both they and the king may come to the shame that is appointed for them. And yet when the lords have vanquished, and all England lieth under them again, yet shall their victory be fruitless; for the free men that hold unfree lands shall they not bring under the collar again, and villeinage shall slip from their hands, till there be, and not long after ye are dead, but few unfree men in England; so that your lives and your deaths both shall bear fruit."

"Said I not," quoth John Ball, "that thou wert a sending from other times? Good is thy message, for the land shall be free. Tell on now."

He spoke eagerly, and I went on somewhat sadly: "The times shall better, though the king and lords shall worsen, the Gilds of Craft shall wax and become mightier; more recourse shall there be of foreign merchants. There shall be plenty in the land and not famine. Where a man now earneth two pennies he shall earn three."

"Yea," said he, "then shall those that labour become strong and stronger, and so soon shall it come about that all men shall work and none make to work, and so shall none be robbed, and at last shall all men labour and live and be happy, and have the goods of the earth without money and without price."

"Yea," said I, "that shall indeed come to pass, but not yet for a while, and belike a long while."

And I sat for long without speaking, and the church grew darker as the moon waned yet more.

Then I said: "Bethink thee that these men shall yet have masters over them, who have at hand many a law and custom for the behoof of masters, and being masters can make yet more laws in the same behoof; and they shall suffer poor people to thrive just so long as their thriving shall profit the mastership and no longer; and so shall it be in those days I tell of; for there shall be king and lords and knights and squires still, with servants to do their bidding, and make honest men afraid; and all these will make nothing and eat much as aforetime, and the more that is made in the land the more shall they crave."

"Yea," said he, "that wot I well, that these are of the kin of the daughters of the horse-leech; but how shall they slake their greed, seeing that as thou sayest villeinage shall be gone? Belike their men shall pay them quit-rents and do them service, as free men may, but all this according to law and not beyond it; so that though the workers shall be richer than they now be, the lords shall be no richer, and so all shall be on the road to being free and equal."

Said I, "Look you, friend; aforetime the lords, for the most part, held the land and all that was on it, and the men that were on it worked for them as their horses worked, and after they were fed and housed all was the lords'; but in the time to come the lords shall see their men thriving on the land and shall say once more, 'These men have more than they need, why have we not the surplus since we are their lords?' Moreover, in those days shall betide much chaffering for wares between man and man, and country and country; and the lords shall note that if there were less corn and less men on their lands there would be more sheep, that is to say more wool for chaffer, and that thereof they should have abundantly more than aforetime; since all the land they own, and it pays them quit-rent or service, save here and there a croft or a close of a yeoman; and all this might grow wool for them to sell to the Easterlings. Then shall England see a new thing, for whereas hitherto men have lived on the land and by it, the land shall no longer need them, but many sheep and a few shepherds shall make wool grow to be sold for money to the Easterlings, and that money shall the lords pouch: for, look you, they shall set the lawyers a-work and the strong hand moreover, and the land they shall take to themselves and their sheep; and except for these lords of land few shall be the free men that shall hold a rood of land whom the word of their lord may not turn adrift straightway."

"How mean you?" said John Ball: "shall all men be villeins again?"

"Nay," said I, "there shall be no villeins in England."

"Surely then," said he, "it shall be worse, and all men save a few shall be thralls to be bought and sold at the cross."

"Good friend," said I, "it shall not be so; all men shall be free even as ye would have it; yet, as I say, few indeed shall have so much land as they can stand upon save by buying such a grace of their masters."

"And now," said he, "I wot not what thou sayest. I know a thrall, and he is his master's every hour, and never his own; and a villein I know, and whiles he is his own and whiles his lord's; and I know a free man, and he is his own always; but how shall he be his own if he have nought whereby to make his livelihood? Or shall he be a thief and take from others? Then is he an outlaw. Wonderful is this thou tellest of a free man with nought whereby to live!"

"Yet so it shall be," said I, "and by such free men shall all wares be made."

"Nay, that cannot be; thou art talking riddles," said he; "for how shall a wood-wright make a chest without the wood and the tools?"

Said I, "He must needs buy leave to labour of them that own all things except himself and such as himself."

"Yea, but wherewith shall he buy it?" said John Ball. "What hath he except himself?"

"With himself then shall he buy it," quoth I, "with his body and the power of labour that lieth therein; with the price of his labour shall he buy leave to labour."

"Riddles again!" said he; "how can he sell his labour for aught else but his daily bread? He must win by his labour meat and drink and clothing and housing! Can he sell his labour twice over?"

"Not so," said I, "but this shall he do belike; he shall sell himself, that is the labour that is in him, to the master that suffers him to work, and that master shall give to him from out of the wares he maketh enough to keep him alive, and to beget children and nourish them till they be old enough to be sold like himself, and the residue shall the rich man keep to himself."

John Ball laughed aloud, and said: "Well, I perceive we are not yet out of the land of riddles. The man may well do what thou sayest and live, but he may not do it and live a free man."

"Thou sayest sooth," said I.

11. HARD IT IS FOR THE OLD WORLD TO SEE THE NEW

He held his peace awhile, and then he said: "But no man selleth himself and his children into thraldom uncompelled; nor is any fool so great a fool as willingly to take the name of freeman and the life of a thrall as payment for the very life of a freeman. Now would I ask thee somewhat else; and I am the readier to do so since I perceive that thou art a wondrous seer; for surely no man could of his own wit have imagined a tale of such follies as thou hast told me. Now well I wot that men having once shaken themselves clear of the burden of villeinage, as thou sayest we shall do (and I bless thee for the word), shall never bow down to this worser tyranny without sore strife in the world; and surely so sore shall it be, before our valiant sons give way, that maids and little lads shall take the sword and the spear, and in many a field men's blood and not water shall turn the gristmills of England. But when all this is over, and the tyranny is established, because there are but few men in the land after the great war, how shall it be with you then? Will there not be many soldiers and sergeants and few workers? Surely in every parish ye shall have the constables to see that the men work; and they shall be saying every day, 'Such an one, hast thou yet sold thyself for this day or this week or this year? Go to now, and get thy bargain done, or it shall be the worse for thee.' And wheresoever work is going on there shall be constables again, and those that labour shall labour under the whip like the Hebrews in the land of Egypt. And every man that may, will steal as a dog snatches at a bone; and there again shall ye need more soldiers and more constables till the land is eaten up by them; nor shall the lords and the masters even be able to bear the burden of it; nor will their gains be so great, since that which each man may do in a day is not right great when all is said."

"Friend," said I, "from thine own valiancy and high heart thou speakest, when thou sayest that they who fall under this tyranny shall fight to the death against it. Wars indeed there shall be in the world, great and grievous, and yet few on this score; rather shall men fight as they have been fighting in France at the bidding of some lord of the manor, or some king, or at last at the bidding of some usurer and forestaller of the market. Valiant men, forsooth, shall arise in the beginning of these evil times, but though they shall die as ye shall, yet shall not their deaths be fruitful as yours shall be; because ye, forsooth, are fighting against villeinage which is waning, but they shall fight against usury which is waxing. And, moreover, I have been telling thee how it shall be when the measure of the time is full; and we, looking at these things from afar, can see them as they are indeed; but they who live at the beginning of those times and amidst them, shall not know what is doing around them; they shall indeed feel the plague and yet not know the remedy; by little and by little they shall fall from their better livelihood, and weak and helpless shall they grow, and have no might to withstand the evil of this tyranny; and then again when the times mend somewhat and they have but a little more ease, then shall it be to them like the kingdom of heaven, and they shall have no will to withstand any tyranny, but shall think themselves happy that they be pinched somewhat less. Also whereas thou sayest that there shall be for ever constables and sergeants going to and fro to drive men to work, and that they will not work save under the lash, thou art wrong and it shall not be so; for there shall ever be more workers than the masters may set to work, so that men shall strive eagerly for leave to work; and when one says, I will sell my hours at such and such a price, then another will say, and I for so much less; so that never shall the lords lack slaves willing to work, but often the slaves shall lack lords to buy them."

"Thou tellest marvels indeed," said he; "but how then? if all the churls work not, shall there not be famine and lack of wares?"

"Famine enough," said I, "yet not from lack of wares; it shall be clean contrary. What wilt thou say when I tell thee that in the latter days there shall be such traffic and such speedy travel across the seas that most wares shall be good cheap, and bread of all things the cheapest?"

Quoth he: "I should say that then there would be better livelihood for men, for in times of plenty it is well; for then men eat that which their own hands have harvested, and need not to spend of their substance in buying of others. Truly, it is well for honest men, but not so well for forestallers and regraters;[2] but who heeds what befalls such foul swine, who filch the money from people's purses, and do not one hair's turn of work to help them?"

"Yea, friend," I said, "but in those latter days all power shall be in the hands of these foul swine, and they shall be the rulers of all; therefore, hearken, for I tell thee that times of plenty shall in those days be the times of famine, and all shall pray for the prices of wares to rise, so that the forestallers and regraters may thrive, and that some of their well-doing may overflow on to those on whom they live."

"I am weary of thy riddles," he said. "Yet at least I hope that there may be fewer and fewer folk in the land; as may well be, if life is then so foul and wretched."

"Alas, poor man!" I said; "nor mayst thou imagine how foul and wretched it may be for many of the folk; and yet I tell thee that men shall increase and multiply, till where there is one man in the land now, there shall be twenty in those days —yea, in some places ten times twenty."

"I have but little heart to ask thee more questions," said he; "and when thou answerest, thy words are plain, but the things they tell of I may scarce understand. But tell me this: in those days will men deem that so it must be for ever, as great men even now tell us of our ills, or will they think of some remedy?"

I looked about me. There was but a glimmer of light in the church now, but what there was, was no longer the strange light of the moon, but the first coming of the kindly day.

"Yea," said John Ball, "'tis the twilight of the dawn. God and St. Christopher send us a good day!"

"John Ball," said I, "I have told thee that thy death will bring about that which thy life has striven for: thinkest thou that the thing which thou strivest for is worth the labour? or dost thou believe in the tale I have told thee of the days to come?"

He said: "I tell thee once again that I trust thee for a seer; because no man could make up such a tale as thou; the things which thou tellest are too wonderful for a minstrel, the tale too grievous. And whereas thou askest as to whether I count my labour lost, I say nay; if so be that in those latter times (and worser than ours they will be) men shall yet seek a remedy: therefore again I ask thee, is it so that they shall?"

"Yea," said I, "and their remedy shall be the same as thine, although the days be different: for if the folk be enthralled, what remedy save that they be set free? and if they have tried many roads towards freedom, and found that they led nowhither, then shall they try yet another. Yet in the days to come they shall be slothful to try it, because their masters shall be so much mightier than thine, that they shall not need to show the high hand, and until the days get to their evilest, men shall be cozened into thinking that it is of their own free will that they must needs buy leave to labour by pawning their labour that is to be. Moreover, your lords and masters seem very mighty to you, each one of them, and so they are, but they are few; and the masters of the days to come shall not each one of them seem very mighty to the men of those days, but they shall be very many, and they shall be of one intent in these matters without knowing it; like as one sees the oars of a galley when the rowers are hidden, that rise and fall as it were with one will."

"And yet," he said, "shall it not be the same with those that these men devour? shall not they also have one will?"

"Friend," I said, "they shall have the will to live, as the wretchedest thing living has: therefore shall they sell themselves that they may live, as I told thee; and their hard need shall be their lord's easy livelihood, and because of it he shall sleep without fear, since their need compelleth them not to loiter by the way to lament with friend or brother that they are pinched in their servitude, or to devise means for ending it. And yet indeed thou sayest it: they also shall have one will if they but knew it: but for a long while they shall have but a glimmer of knowledge of it: yet doubt it not that in the end they shall come to know it clearly, and then shall they bring about the remedy; and in those days shall it be seen that thou hast not wrought for nothing, because thou hast seen beforehand what the remedy should be, even as those of later days have seen it."

We both sat silent a little while. The twilight was gaining on the night, though slowly. I looked at the poppy which I still held in my hand, and bethought me of Will Green, and said:

"Lo, how the light is spreading: now must I get me back to Will Green's house as I promised."

"Go, then," said he, "if thou wilt. Yet meseems before long he shall come to us; and then mayst thou sleep among the trees on the green grass till the sun is high, for the host shall not be on foot very early; and sweet it is to sleep in shadow by the sun in the full morning when one has been awake and troubled through the night-tide."

"Yet I will go now," said I; "I bid thee good-night, or rather good-morrow."

Therewith I half rose up; but as I did so the will to depart left me as though I had never had it, and I sat down again, and heard the voice of John Ball, at first as one speaking from far away, but little by little growing nearer and more familiar to me, and as if once more it were coming from the man himself whom I had got to know.

12. ILL WOULD CHANGE BE AT WHILES WERE IT NOT FOR THE CHANGE BEYOND THE CHANGE

He said: "Many strange things hast thou told me that I could not understand; yea, some my wit so failed to compass, that I cannot so much as ask thee questions concerning them; but of some matters would I ask thee, and I must hasten, for in very sooth the night is worn old and grey. Whereas thou sayest that in the days to come, when there shall be no labouring men who are not thralls after their new fashion, that their lords shall be many and very many, it seemeth to me that these same lords, if they be many, shall hardly be rich, or but very few of them, since they must verily feed and clothe and house their thralls, so that that which they take from them, since it will have to be dealt out amongst many, will not be enough to make many rich; since out of one man ye may get but one man's work; and pinch him never so sorely, still as aforesaid ye may not pinch him so sorely as not to feed him. Therefore, though the eyes of my mind may see a few lords and many slaves, yet can they not see many lords as well as many slaves; and if the slaves be many and the lords few, then some day shall the slaves make an end of that mastery by the force of their bodies. How then shall thy mastership of the latter days endure?"

"John Ball," said I, "mastership hath many shifts whereby it striveth to keep itself alive in the world. And now hear a marvel: whereas thou sayest these two times that out of one man ye may get but one man's work, in days to come one man shall do the work of a hundred men—yea, of a thousand or more: and this is the shift of mastership that shall make many masters and many rich men."

John Ball laughed. "Great is my harvest of riddles to-night," said he; "for even if a man sleep not, and eat and drink while he is a-working, ye shall but make two men, or three at the most, out of him."

Said I: "Sawest thou ever a weaver at his loom?"

"Yea," said he, "many a time."

He was silent a little, and then said: "Yet I marvelled not at it; but now I marvel, because I know what thou wouldst say. Time was when the shuttle was thrust in and out of all the thousand threads of the warp, and it was long to do; but now the spring-staves go up and down as the man's feet move, and this and that leaf of the warp cometh forward and the shuttle goeth in one shot through all the thousand warps. Yea, so it is that this multiplieth a man many times. But look you, he is so multiplied already; and so hath he been, meseemeth, for many hundred years."

"Yea," said I, "but what hitherto needed the masters to multiply him more? For many hundred years the workman was a thrall bought and sold at the cross; and for other hundreds of years he hath been a villein— that is, a working-beast and a part of the stock of the manor on which he liveth; but then thou and the like of thee shall free him, and then is mastership put to its shifts; for what should avail the mastery then, when the master no longer owneth the man by law as his chattel, nor any longer by law owneth him as stock of his land, if the master hath not that which he on whom he liveth may not lack and live withal, and cannot have without selling himself?"

He said nothing, but I saw his brow knitted and his lips pressed together as though in anger; and again I said:

"Thou hast seen the weaver at his loom: think how it should be if he sit no longer before the web and cast the shuttle and draw home the sley, but if the shed open of itself and the shuttle of itself speed through it as swift as the eye can follow, and the sley come home of itself; and the weaver standing by and whistling The Hunt's Up! the while, or looking to half-a-dozen looms and bidding them what to do. And as with the weaver so with the potter, and the smith, and every worker in metals, and all other crafts, that it shall be for them looking on and tending, as with the man that sitteth in the cart while the horse draws. Yea, at last so shall it be even with those who are mere husbandmen; and no longer shall the reaper fare afield in the morning with his hook over his shoulder, and smite and bind and smite again till the sun is down and the moon is up; but he shall draw a thing made by men into the field with one or two horses, and shall say the word and the horses shall go up and down, and the thing shall reap and gather and bind, and do the work of many men. Imagine all this in thy mind if thou canst, at least as ye may imagine a tale of enchantment told by a minstrel, and then tell me what shouldst thou deem that the life of men would be amidst all this, men such as these men of the township here, or the men of the Canterbury gilds."

"Yea," said he; "but before I tell thee my thoughts of thy tale of wonder, I would ask thee this: In those days when men work so easily, surely they shall make more wares than they can use in one countryside, or one good town, whereas in another, where things have not gone as well, they shall have less than they need; and even so it is with us now, and thereof cometh scarcity and famine; and if people may not come at each other's goods, it availeth the whole land little that one country-side hath more than enough while another hath less; for the goods shall abide there in the storehouses of the rich place till they perish. So if that be so in the days of wonder ye tell of (and I see not how it can be otherwise), then shall men be but little holpen by making all their wares so easily and with so little labour."

I smiled again and said: "Yea, but it shall not be so; not only shall men be multiplied a hundred and a thousand fold, but the distance of one place from another shall be as nothing; so that the wares which lie ready for market in Durham in the evening may be in London on the morrow morning; and the men of Wales may eat corn of Essex and the men of Essex wear wool of Wales; so that, so far as the flitting of goods to market goes, all the land shall be as one parish. Nay, what say I? Not as to this land only shall it be so, but even the Indies, and far countries of which thou knowest not, shall be, so to say, at every man's door, and wares which now ye account precious and dear-bought, shall then be common things bought and sold for little price at every huckster's stall. Say then, John, shall not those days be merry, and plentiful of ease and contentment for all men?"

"Brother," said he, "meseemeth some doleful mockery lieth under these joyful tidings of thine; since thou hast already partly told me to my sad bewilderment what the life of man shall be in those days. Yet will I now for a little set all that aside to consider thy strange tale as of a minstrel from over sea, even as thou biddest me. Therefore I say, that if men still abide men as I have known them, and unless these folk of England change as, the land changeth—and forsooth of the men, for good and for evil, I can think no other than I think now, or behold them other than I have known them and loved them—I say if the men be still men, what will happen except that there should be all plenty in the land, and not one poor man therein, unless of his own free will he choose to lack and be poor, as a man in religion or such like; for there would then be such abundance of all good things, that, as greedy as the lords might be, there would be enough to satisfy their greed and yet leave good living for all who laboured with their hands; so that these should labour far less than now, and they would have time to learn knowledge, so that there should be no learned or unlearned, for all should be learned; and they would have time also to learn how to order the matters of the parish and the hundred, and of the parliament of the realm, so that the king should take no more than his own; and to order the rule of the realm, so that all men, rich and unrich, should have part therein; and so by undoing of evil laws and making of good ones, that fashion would come to an end whereof thou speakest, that rich men make laws for their own behoof; for they should no longer be able to do thus when all had part in making the laws; whereby it would soon come about that there would be no men rich and tyrannous, but all should have enough and to spare of the increase of the earth and the work of their own hands. Yea surely, brother, if ever it cometh about that men shall be able to make things, and not men, work for their superfluities, and that the length of travel from one place to another be made of no account, and all the world be a market for all the world, then all shall live in health and wealth; and envy and grudging shall perish. For then shall we have conquered the earth and it shall be enough; and then shall the kingdom of heaven be come down to the earth in very deed. Why lookest thou so sad and sorry? what sayest thou?"

I said: "Hast thou forgotten already what I told thee, that in those latter days a man who hath nought save his own body (and such men shall be far the most of men) must needs pawn his labour for leave to labour? Can such a man be wealthy? Hast thou not called him a thrall?"

"Yea," he said; "but how could I deem that such things could be when those days should be come wherein men could make things work for them?"

"Poor man!" said I. "Learn that in those very days, when it shall be with the making of things as with the carter in the cart, that there he sitteth and shaketh the reins and the horse draweth and the cart goeth; in those days, I tell thee, many men shall be as poor and wretched always, year by year, as they are with thee when there is famine in the land; nor shall any have plenty and surety of livelihood save those that shall sit by and look on while others labour; and these, I tell thee, shall be a many, so that they shall see to the making of all laws, and in their hands shall be all power, and the labourers shall think that they cannot do without these men that live by robbing them, and shall praise them and wellnigh pray to them as ye pray to the saints, and the best worshipped man in the land shall be he who by forestalling and regrating hath gotten to him the most money."

"Yea," said he, "and shall they who see themselves robbed worship the robber? Then indeed shall men be changed from what they are now, and they shall be sluggards, dolts, and cowards beyond all the earth hath yet borne. Such are not the men I have known in my life-days, and that now I love in my death."

"Nay," I said, "but the robbery shall they not see; for have I not told thee that they shall hold themselves to be free men? And for why? I will tell thee: but first tell me how it fares with men now; may the labouring man become a lord?"

He said: "The thing hath been seen that churls have risen from the dortoir of the monastery to the abbot's chair and the bishop's throne; yet not often; and whiles hath a bold sergeant become a wise captain, and they have made him squire and knight; and yet but very seldom. And now I suppose thou wilt tell me that the Church will open her arms wider to this poor people, and that many through her shall rise into lordship. But what availeth that? Nought were it to me if the Abbot of St. Alban's with his golden mitre sitting guarded by his knights and sergeants, or the Prior of Merton with his hawks and his hounds, had once been poor men, if they were now tyrants of poor men; nor would it better the matter if there were ten times as many Houses of Religion in the land as now are, and each with a churl's son for abbot or prior over it."

I smiled and said: "Comfort thyself; for in those days shall there be neither abbey nor priory in the land, nor monks nor friars, nor any religious." (He started as I spoke.) "But thou hast told me that hardly in these days may a poor man rise to be a lord: now I tell thee that in the days to come poor men shall be able to become lords and masters and do-nothings; and oft will it be seen that they shall do so; and it shall be even for that cause that their eyes shall be blinded to the robbing of themselves by others, because they shall hope in their souls that they may each live to rob others: and this shall be the very safeguard of all rule and law in those days."

"Now am I sorrier than thou hast yet made me," said he; "for when once this is established, how then can it be changed? Strong shall be the tyranny of the latter days. And now meseems, if thou sayest sooth, this time of the conquest of the earth shall not bring heaven down to the earth, as erst I deemed it would, but rather that it shall bring hell up on to the earth. Woe's me, brother, for thy sad and weary foretelling! And yet saidst thou that the men of those days would seek a remedy. Canst thou yet tell me, brother, what that remedy shall be, lest the sun rise upon me made hopeless by thy tale of what is to be? And, lo you, soon shall she rise upon the earth."

In truth the dawn was widening now, and the colours coming into the pictures on wall and in window; and as well as I could see through the varied glazing of these last (and one window before me had as yet nothing but white glass in it), the ruddy glow, which had but so little a while quite died out in the west, was now beginning to gather in the east—the new day was beginning. I looked at the poppy that I still carried in my hand, and it seemed to me to have withered and dwindled. I felt anxious to speak to my companion and tell him much, and withal I felt that I must hasten, or for some reason or other I should be too late; so I spoke at last loud and hurriedly:

"John Ball, be of good cheer; for once more thou knowest, as I know, that the Fellowship of Men shall endure, however many tribulations it may have to wear through. Look you, a while ago was the light bright about us; but it was because of the moon, and the night was deep notwithstanding, and when the moonlight waned and died, and there was but a little glimmer in place of the bright light, yet was the world glad because all things knew that the glimmer was of day and not of night. Lo you, an image of the times to betide the hope of the Fellowship of Men. Yet forsooth, it may well be that this bright day of summer which is now dawning upon us is no image of the beginning of the day that shall be; but rather shall that day-dawn be cold and grey and surly; and yet by its light shall men see things as they verily are, and no longer enchanted by the gleam of the moon and the glamour of the dream-tide. By such grey light shall wise men and valiant souls see the remedy, and deal with it, a real thing that may be touched and handled, and no glory of the heavens to be worshipped from afar off. And what shall it be, as I told thee before, save that men shall be determined to be free; yea, free as thou wouldst have them, when thine hope rises the highest, and thou art thinking not of the king's uncles, and poll-groat bailiffs, and the villeinage of Essex, but of the end of all, when men shall have the fruits of the earth and the fruits of their toil thereon, without money and without price. The time shall come, John Ball, when that dream of thine that this shall one day be, shall be a thing that men shall talk of soberly, and as a thing soon to come about, as even with thee they talk of the villeins becoming tenants paying their lord quit-rent; therefore, hast thou done well to hope it; and, if thou heedest this also, as I suppose thou heedest it little, thy name shall abide by thy hope in those days to come, and thou shalt not be forgotten."

I heard his voice come out of the twilight, scarcely seeing him, though now the light was growing fast, as he said:

"Brother, thou givest me heart again; yet since now I wot well that thou art a sending from far-off times and far-off things: tell thou, if thou mayest, to a man who is going to his death how this shall come about."

"Only this may I tell thee" said I; "to thee, when thou didst try to conceive of them, the ways of the days to come seemed follies scarce to be thought of; yet shall they come to be familiar things, and an order by which every man liveth, ill as he liveth, so that men shall deem of them, that thus it hath been since the beginning of the world, and that thus it shall be while the world endureth; and in this wise so shall they be thought of a long while; and the complaint of the poor the rich man shall heed, even as much and no more as he who lieth in pleasure under the lime-trees in the summer heedeth the murmur of his toiling bees. Yet in time shall this also grow old, and doubt shall creep in, because men shall scarce be able to live by that order, and the complaint of the poor shall be hearkened, no longer as a tale not utterly grievous, but as a threat of ruin, and a fear. Then shall these things, which to thee seem follies, and to the men between thee and me mere wisdom and the bond of stability, seem follies once again; yet, whereas men have so long lived by them, they shall cling to them yet from blindness and from fear; and those that see, and that have thus much conquered fear that they are furthering the real time that cometh and not the dream that faileth, these men shall the blind and the fearful mock and missay, and torment and murder: and great and grievous shall be the strife in those days, and many the failures of the wise, and too oft sore shall be the despair of the valiant; and back-sliding, and doubt, and contest between friends and fellows lacking time in the hubbub to understand each other, shall grieve many hearts and hinder the Host of the Fellowship: yet shall all bring about the end, till thy deeming of folly and ours shall be one, and thy hope and our hope; and then—the Day will have come."

Once more I heard the voice of John Ball: "Now, brother, I say farewell; for now verily hath the Day of the Earth come, and thou and I are lonely of each other again; thou hast been a dream to me as I to thee, and sorry and glad have we made each other, as tales of old time and the longing of times to come shall ever make men to be. I go to life and to death, and leave thee; and scarce do I know whether to wish thee some dream of the days beyond thine to tell what shall be, as thou hast told me, for I know not if that shall help or hinder thee; but since we have been kind and very friends, I will not leave thee without a wish of good-will, so at least I wish thee what thou thyself wishest for thyself, and that is hopeful strife and blameless peace, which is to say in one word, life. Farewell, friend."

For some little time, although I had known that the daylight was growing and what was around me, I had scarce seen the things I had before noted so keenly; but now in a flash I saw all—the east crimson with sunrise through the white window on my right hand; the richly-carved stalls and gilded screen work, the pictures on the walls, the loveliness of the faultless colour of the mosaic window lights, the altar and the red light over it looking strange in the daylight, and the biers with the hidden dead men upon them that lay before the high altar. A great pain filled my heart at the sight of all that beauty, and withal I heard quick steps coming up the paved church-path to the porch, and the loud whistle of a sweet old tune therewith; then the footsteps stopped at the door; I heard the latch rattle, and knew that Will Green's hand was on the ring of it.

Then I strove to rise up, but fell back again; a white light, empty of all sights, broke upon me for a moment, and lo I behold, I was lying in my familiar bed, the south-westerly gale rattling the Venetian blinds and making their hold-fasts squeak.

I got up presently, and going to the window looked out on the winter morning; the river was before me broad between outer bank and bank, but it was nearly dead ebb, and there was a wide space of mud on each side of the hurrying stream, driven on the faster as it seemed by the push of the south-west wind. On the other side of the water the few willow-trees left us by the Thames Conservancy looked doubtfully alive against the bleak sky and the row of wretched-looking blue-slated houses, although, by the way, the latter were the backs of a sort of street of "villas" and not a slum; the road in front of the house was sooty and muddy at once, and in the air was that sense of dirty discomfort which one is never quit of in London. The morning was harsh, too, and though the wind was from the south-west it was as cold as a north wind; and yet amidst it all, I thought of the corner of the next bight of the river which I could not quite see from where I was, but over which one can see clear of houses and into Richmond Park, looking like the open country; and dirty as the river was, and harsh as was the January wind, they seemed to woo me toward the country-side, where away from the miseries of the "Great Wen" I might of my own will carry on a daydream of the friends I had made in the dream of the night and against my will.

But as I turned away shivering and downhearted, on a sudden came the frightful noise of the "hooters," one after the other, that call the workmen to the factories, this one the after-breakfast one, more by token. So I grinned surlily, and dressed and got ready for my day's "work" as I call it, but which many a man besides John Ruskin (though not many in his position) would call "play."

---

1. Probably one of the Calverlys, a Cheshire family, one of whom was a noted captain in the French wars.
2. Forestaller, one who buys up goods when they are cheap, and so raises the price for his own benefit; forestalls the due and real demand. Regrater, one who both buys and sells in the same market, or within five miles thereof; buys, say a ton of cheese at 10 A.M. and sells it at 5 P.M. a penny a pound dearer without moving from his chair. The word "monopolist" will cover both species of thief.

HOPES & FEARS FOR ART

FIVE LECTURES BY WILLIAM MORRIS

1. THE LESSER ARTS: DELIVERED BEFORE THE TRADES' GUILD OF LEARNING, DECEMBER 4, 1877.

Hereafter I hope in another lecture to have the pleasure of laying before you an historical survey of the lesser, or as they are called the Decorative Arts, and I must confess it would have been pleasanter to me to have begun my talk with you by entering at once upon the subject of the history of this great industry; but, as I have something to say in a third lecture about various matters connected with the practice of Decoration among ourselves in these days, I feel that I should be in a false position before you, and one that might lead to confusion, or overmuch explanation, if I did not let you know what I think on the nature and scope of these arts, on their condition at the present time, and their outlook in times to come. In doing this it is like enough that I shall say things with which you will very much disagree; I must ask you therefore from the outset to believe that whatever I may blame or whatever I may praise, I neither, when I think of what history has been, am inclined to lament the past, to despise the present, or despair of the future; that I believe all the change and stir about us is a sign of the world's life, and that it will lead—by ways, indeed, of which we have no guess—to the bettering of all mankind.

Now as to the scope and nature of these Arts I have to say, that though when I come more into the details of my subject I shall not meddle much with the great art of Architecture, and less still with the great arts commonly called Sculpture and Painting, yet I cannot in my own mind quite sever them from those lesser so-called Decorative Arts, which I have to speak about: it is only in latter times, and under the most intricate conditions of life, that they have fallen apart from one another; and I hold that, when they are so parted, it is ill for the Arts altogether: the lesser ones become trivial, mechanical, unintelligent, incapable of resisting the changes pressed upon them by fashion or dishonesty; while the greater, however they may be practised for a while by men of great minds and wonder-working hands, unhelped by the lesser, unhelped by each other, are sure to lose their dignity of popular arts, and become nothing but dull adjuncts to unmeaning pomp, or ingenious toys for a few rich and idle men.

However, I have not undertaken to talk to you of Architecture, Sculpture, and Painting, in the narrower sense of those words, since, most unhappily as I think, these master-arts, these arts more specially of the intellect, are at the present day divorced from decoration in its narrower sense. Our subject is that great body of art, by means of which men have at all times more or less striven to beautify the familiar matters of everyday life: a wide subject, a great industry; both a great part of the history of the world, and a most helpful instrument to the study of that history.

A very great industry indeed, comprising the crafts of house-building, painting, joinery and carpentry, smiths' work, pottery and glass-making, weaving, and many others: a body of art most important to the public in general, but still more so to us handicraftsmen; since there is scarce anything that they use, and that we fashion, but it has always been thought to be unfinished till it has had some touch or other of decoration about it. True it is that in many or most cases we have got so used to this ornament, that we look upon it as if it had grown of itself, and note it no more than the mosses on the dry sticks with which we light our fires. So much the worse! for there *is* the decoration, or some pretence of it, and it has, or ought to have, a use and a meaning. For, and this is at the root of the whole matter, everything made by man's hands has a form, which must be either beautiful or ugly; beautiful if it is in accord with Nature, and helps her; ugly if it is discordant with Nature, and thwarts her; it cannot be indifferent: we, for our parts, are busy or sluggish, eager or unhappy, and our eyes are apt to get dulled to this eventfulness of form in those things which we are always looking at. Now it is one of the chief uses of decoration, the chief part of its alliance with nature, that it has to sharpen our dulled senses in this matter: for this end are those wonders of intricate patterns interwoven, those strange forms invented, which men have so long delighted in: forms and intricacies that do not necessarily imitate nature, but in which the hand of the craftsman is guided to work in the way that she does, till the web, the cup, or the knife, look as natural, nay as lovely, as the green field, the river bank, or the mountain flint.

To give people pleasure in the things they must perforce *use*, that is one great office of decoration; to give people pleasure in the things they must perforce *make*, that is the other use of it.

Does not our subject look important enough now? I say that without these arts, our rest would be vacant and uninteresting, our labour mere endurance, mere wearing away of body and mind.

As for that last use of these arts, the giving us pleasure in our work, I scarcely know how to speak strongly enough of it; and yet if I did not know the value of repeating a truth again and again, I should have to excuse myself to you for saying any more about this, when I remember how a great man now living has spoken of it: I mean my friend Professor John Ruskin: if you read the chapter in the 2nd vol. of his *Stones of Venice* entitled, 'On the Nature of Gothic, and the Office of the Workman therein,' you will read at once the truest and the most eloquent words that can possibly be said on the subject. What I have to say upon it can scarcely be more than an echo of his words, yet I repeat there is some use in reiterating a truth, lest it be forgotten; so I will say this much further: we all know what people have said about the curse of labour, and what heavy and grievous nonsense are the more part of their words thereupon; whereas indeed the real curses of craftsmen have been the curse of stupidity, and the curse of injustice from within and from without: no, I cannot suppose there is anybody here who would think it either a good life, or an amusing one, to sit with one's hands before one doing nothing—to live like a gentleman, as fools call it.

Nevertheless there *is* dull work to be done, and a weary business it is setting men about such work, and seeing them through it, and I would rather do the work twice over with my own hands than have such a job: but now only let the arts which we are talking of beautify our labour, and be widely spread, intelligent, well understood both by the maker and the user, let them grow in one word *popular*, and there will be pretty much an end of dull work and its wearing slavery; and no man will any longer have an excuse for talking about the curse of labour, no man will any longer have an excuse for evading the blessing of labour. I believe there is nothing that will aid the world's progress so much as the attainment of this; I protest there is nothing in the world that I desire so much as this, wrapped up, as I am sure it is, with changes political and social, that in one way or another we all desire.

Now if the objection be made, that these arts have been the handmaids of luxury, of tyranny, and of superstition, I must needs say that it is true in a sense; they have been so used, as many other excellent things have been. But it is also true that, among some nations, their most vigorous and freest times have been the very blossoming times of art: while at the same time, I must allow that these decorative arts have flourished among oppressed peoples, who have seemed to have no hope of freedom: yet I do not think that we shall be wrong in thinking that at such times, among such peoples, art, at least, was free; when it has not been, when it has really been gripped by superstition, or by luxury, it has straightway begun to sicken under that grip. Nor must you forget that when men say popes, kings, and emperors built such and such buildings, it is a mere way of speaking. You look in your history-books to see who built Westminster Abbey, who built St.

Sophia at Constantinople, and they tell you Henry III., Justinian the Emperor. Did they? or, rather, men like you and me, handicraftsmen, who have left no names behind them, nothing but their work?

Now as these arts call people's attention and interest to the matters of everyday life in the present, so also, and that I think is no little matter, they call our attention at every step to that history, of which, I said before, they are so great a part; for no nation, no state of society, however rude, has been wholly without them: nay, there are peoples not a few, of whom we know scarce anything, save that they thought such and such forms beautiful. So strong is the bond between history and decoration, that in the practice of the latter we cannot, if we would, wholly shake off the influence of past times over what we do at present. I do not think it is too much to say that no man, however original he may be, can sit down to-day and draw the ornament of a cloth, or the form of an ordinary vessel or piece of furniture, that will be other than a development or a degradation of forms used hundreds of years ago; and these, too, very often, forms that once had a serious meaning, though they are now become little more than a habit of the hand; forms that were once perhaps the mysterious symbols of worships and beliefs now little remembered or wholly forgotten. Those who have diligently followed the delightful study of these arts are able as if through windows to look upon the life of the past:—the very first beginnings of thought among nations whom we cannot even name; the terrible empires of the ancient East; the free vigour and glory of Greece; the heavy weight, the firm grasp of Rome; the fall of her temporal Empire which spread so wide about the world all that good and evil which men can never forget, and never cease to feel; the clashing of East and West, South and North, about her rich and fruitful daughter Byzantium; the rise, the dissensions, and the waning of Islam; the wanderings of Scandinavia; the Crusades; the foundation of the States of modern Europe; the struggles of free thought with ancient dying system—with all these events and their meaning is the history of popular art interwoven; with all this, I say, the careful student of decoration as an historical industry must be familiar. When I think of this, and the usefulness of all this knowledge, at a time when history has become so earnest a study amongst us as to have given us, as it were, a new sense: at a time when we so long to know the reality of all that has happened, and are to be put off no longer with the dull records of the battles and intrigues of kings and scoundrels, —I say when I think of all this, I hardly know how to say that this interweaving of the Decorative Arts with the history of the past is of less importance than their dealings with the life of the present: for should not these memories also be a part of our daily life?

And now let me recapitulate a little before I go further, before we begin to look into the condition of the arts at the present day. These arts, I have said, are part of a great system invented for the expression of a man's delight in beauty: all peoples and times have used them; they have been the joy of free nations, and the solace of oppressed nations; religion has used and elevated them, has abused and degraded them; they are connected with all history, and are clear teachers of it; and, best of all, they are the sweeteners of human labour, both to the handicraftsman, whose life is spent in working in them, and to people in general who are influenced by the sight of them at every turn of the day's work: they make our toil happy, our rest fruitful.

And now if all I have said seems to you but mere open-mouthed praise of these arts, I must say that it is not for nothing that what I have hitherto put before you has taken that form.

It is because I must now ask you this question: All these good things—will you have them? will you cast them from you?

Are you surprised at my question—you, most of whom, like myself, are engaged in the actual practice of the arts that are, or ought to be, popular?

In explanation, I must somewhat repeat what I have already said. Time was when the mystery and wonder of handicrafts were well acknowledged by the world, when imagination and fancy mingled with all things made by man; and in those days all handicraftsmen were *artists*, as we should now call them. But the thought of man became more intricate, more difficult to express; art grew a heavier thing to deal with, and its labour was more divided among great men, lesser men, and little men; till that art, which was once scarce more than a rest of body and soul, as the hand cast the shuttle or swung the hammer, became to some men so serious labour, that their working lives have been one long tragedy of hope and fear, joy and trouble. This was the growth of art: like all growth, it was good and fruitful for awhile; like all fruitful growth, it grew into decay; like all decay of what was once fruitful, it will grow into something new.

Into decay; for as the arts sundered into the greater and the lesser, contempt on one side, carelessness on the other arose, both begotten of ignorance of that *philosophy* of the Decorative Arts, a hint of which I have tried just now to put before you. The artist came out from the handicraftsmen, and left them without hope of elevation, while he himself was left without the help of intelligent, industrious sympathy. Both have suffered; the artist no less than the workman. It is with art as it fares with a company of soldiers before a redoubt, when the captain runs forward full of hope and energy, but looks not behind him to see if his men are following, and they hang back, not knowing why they are brought there to die. The captain's life is spent for nothing, and his men are sullen prisoners in the redoubt of Unhappiness and Brutality.

I must in plain words say of the Decorative Arts, of all the arts, that it is not so much that we are inferior in them to all who have gone before us, but rather that they are in a state of anarchy and disorganisation, which makes a sweeping change necessary and certain.

So that again I ask my question, All that good fruit which the arts should bear, will you have it? will you cast it from you? Shall that sweeping change that must come, be the change of loss or of gain?

We who believe in the continuous life of the world, surely we are bound to hope that the change will bring us gain and not loss, and to strive to bring that gain about.

Yet how the world may answer my question, who can say? A man in his short life can see but a little way ahead, and even in mine wonderful and unexpected things have come to pass. I must needs say that therein lies my hope rather than in all I see going on round about us. Without disputing that if the imaginative arts perish, some new thing, at present unguessed of, *may* be put forward to supply their loss in men's lives, I cannot feel happy in that prospect, nor can I believe that mankind will endure such a loss for ever: but in the meantime the present state of the arts and their dealings with modern life and progress seem to me to point, in appearance at least, to this immediate future; that the world, which has for a long time busied itself about other matters than the arts, and has carelessly let them sink lower and lower, till many not uncultivated men, ignorant of what they once were, and hopeless of what they might yet be, look upon them with mere contempt; that the world, I say, thus busied and hurried, will one day wipe the slate, and be clean rid in her impatience of the whole matter with all its tangle and trouble.

And then—what then?

Even now amid the squalor of London it is hard to imagine what it will be. Architecture, Sculpture, Painting, with the crowd of lesser arts that belong to them, these, together with Music and Poetry, will be dead and forgotten, will no longer excite or amuse people in the least: for, once more, we must not deceive ourselves; the death of one art means the death of all; the only difference in their fate will be that the luckiest will be eaten the last—the luckiest, or the unluckiest: in all that has to do with beauty the invention and ingenuity of man will have come to a dead stop; and all the while Nature will go on with her eternal recurrence of lovely changes—spring, summer, autumn, and winter; sunshine, rain, and snow; storm and fair weather; dawn, noon, and sunset; day and night—ever bearing witness against man that he has deliberately chosen ugliness instead of beauty, and to live where he is strongest amidst squalor or blank emptiness.

You see, sirs, we cannot quite imagine it; any more, perhaps, than our forefathers of ancient London, living in the pretty, carefully whitened houses, with the famous church and its huge spire rising above them,—than they, passing about the fair gardens running down to the broad river, could have imagined a whole county or more covered over with hideous hovels, big, middle-sized, and little, which should one day be called London.

Sirs, I say that this dead blank of the arts that I more than dread is difficult even now to imagine; yet I fear that I must say that if it does not come about, it will be owing to some turn of events which we cannot at present foresee: but I hold that if it does happen, it will only last for a time, that it will be but a burning up of the gathered weeds, so that the field may bear more abundantly. I hold that men would wake up after a while, and look round and find the dullness unbearable, and begin once more inventing, imitating, and imagining, as in earlier days.

That faith comforts me, and I can say calmly if the blank space must happen, it must, and amidst its darkness the new seed must sprout. So it has been before: first comes birth, and hope scarcely conscious of itself; then the flower and fruit of mastery, with hope more than conscious enough, passing into insolence, as decay follows ripeness; and then—the new birth again.

Meantime it is the plain duty of all who look seriously on the arts to do their best to save the world from what at the best will be a loss, the result of ignorance and unwisdom; to prevent, in fact, that most discouraging of all changes, the supplying the place of an extinct brutality by a new one; nay, even if those who really care for the arts are so weak and few that they can do nothing else, it may be their business to keep alive some tradition, some memory of the past, so that the new life when it comes may not waste itself more than enough in fashioning wholly new forms for its new spirit.

To what side then shall those turn for help, who really understand the gain of a great art in the world, and the loss of peace and good life that must follow from the lack of it? I think that they must begin by acknowledging that the ancient art, the art of unconscious intelligence, as one should call it, which began without a date, at least so long ago as those strange and masterly scratchings on mammoth-bones and the like found but the other day in the drift—that this art of unconscious intelligence is all but dead; that what little of it is left lingers among half-civilised nations, and is growing coarser, feebler, less intelligent year by year; nay, it is mostly at the mercy of some commercial accident, such as the arrival of a few shiploads of European dye-stuffs or a few dozen orders from European merchants: this they must recognise, and must hope to see in time its place filled by a new art of conscious intelligence, the birth of wiser, simpler, freer ways of life than the world leads now, than the world has ever led.

I said, *to see* this in time; I do not mean to say that our own eyes will look upon it: it may be so far off, as indeed it seems to some, that many would scarcely think it worth while thinking of: but there are some of us who cannot turn our faces to the wall, or sit deedless because our hope seems somewhat dim; and, indeed, I think that while the signs of the last decay of the old art with all the evils that must follow in its train are only too obvious about us, so on the other hand there are not wanting signs of the new dawn beyond that possible night of the arts, of which I have before spoken; this sign chiefly, that there are some few at least who are heartily discontented with things as they are, and crave for something better, or at least some promise of it—this best of signs: for I suppose that if some half-dozen men at any time earnestly set their hearts on something coming about which is not discordant with nature, it will come to pass one day or other; because it is not by accident that an idea comes into the heads of a few; rather they are pushed on, and forced to speak or act by something stirring in the heart of the world which would otherwise be left without expression.

By what means then shall those work who long for reform in the arts, and who shall they seek to kindle into eager desire for possession of beauty, and better still, for the development of the faculty that creates beauty?

People say to me often enough: If you want to make your art succeed and flourish, you must make it the fashion: a phrase which I confess annoys me; for they mean by it that I should spend one day over my work to two days in trying to convince rich, and supposed influential people, that they care very much for what they really do not care in the least, so that it may happen according to the proverb: *Bell-wether took the leap, and we all went over*. Well, such advisers are right if they are content with the thing lasting but a little while; say till you can make a little money—if you don't get pinched by the door shutting too quickly: otherwise they are wrong: the people they are thinking of have too many strings to their bow, and can turn their backs too easily on a thing that fails, for it to be safe work trusting to their whims: it is not their fault, they cannot help it, but they have no chance of spending time enough over the arts to know anything practical of them, and they must of necessity be in the hands of those who spend their time in pushing fashion this way and that for their own advantage.

Sirs, there is no help to be got out of these latter, or those who let themselves be led by them: the only real help for the decorative arts must come from those who work in them; nor must they be led, they must lead.

You whose hands make those things that should be works of art, you must be all artists, and good artists too, before the public at large can take real interest in such things; and when you have become so, I promise you that you shall lead the fashion; fashion shall follow your hands obediently enough.

That is the only way in which we can get a supply of intelligent popular art: a few artists of the kind so-called now, what can they do working in the teeth of difficulties thrown in their way by what is called Commerce, but which should be called greed of money? working helplessly among the crowd of those who are ridiculously called manufacturers, *i.e.* handicraftsmen, though the more part of them never did a stroke of hand-work in their lives, and are nothing better than capitalists and salesmen. What can these grains of sand do, I say, amidst the enormous mass of work turned out every year which professes in some way to be decorative art, but the decoration of which no one heeds except the salesmen who have to do with it, and are hard put to it to supply the cravings of the public for something new, not for something pretty?

The remedy, I repeat, is plain if it can be applied; the handicraftsman, left behind by the artist when the arts sundered, must come up with him, must work side by side with him: apart from the difference between a great master and a scholar, apart from the differences of the natural bent of men's minds, which would make one man an imitative, and another an architectural or decorative artist, there should be no difference between those employed on strictly ornamental work; and the body of artists dealing with this should quicken with their art all makers of things into artists also, in proportion to the necessities and uses of the things they would make.

I know what stupendous difficulties, social and economical, there are in the way of this; yet I think that they seem to be greater than they are: and of one thing I am sure, that no real living decorative art is possible if this is impossible.

It is not impossible, on the contrary it is certain to come about, if you are at heart desirous to quicken the arts; if the world will, for the sake of beauty and decency, sacrifice some of the things it is so busy over (many of which I think are not very worthy of its trouble), art will begin to grow again; as for those difficulties above mentioned, some of them I know will in any case melt away before the steady change of the relative conditions of men; the rest, reason and resolute attention to the laws of nature, which are also the laws of art, will dispose of little by little: once more, the way will not be far to seek, if the will be with us.

Yet, granted the will, and though the way lies ready to us, we must not be discouraged if the journey seem barren enough at first, nay, not even if things seem to grow worse for a while: for it is natural enough that the very evil which has forced on the beginning of reform should look uglier, while on the one hand life and wisdom are building up the new, and on the other folly and deadness are hugging the old to them.

In this, as in all other matters, lapse of time will be needed before things seem to straighten, and the courage and patience that does not despise small things lying ready to be done; and care and watchfulness, lest we begin to build the wall ere the footings are well in; and always through all things much humility that is not easily cast down by failure, that seeks to be taught, and is ready to learn.

For your teachers, they must be Nature and History: as for the first, that you must learn of it is so obvious that I need not dwell upon that now: hereafter, when I have to speak more of matters of detail, I may have to speak of the manner in which you must learn of Nature. As to the second, I do not think that any man but one of the highest genius, could do anything in these days without much study of ancient art, and even he would be much hindered if he lacked it. If you think that this contradicts what I said about the death of that ancient art, and the necessity I implied for an art that should be characteristic of the present day, I can only say that, in these times of plenteous knowledge and meagre performance, if we do not study the ancient work directly and learn to understand it, we shall find ourselves influenced by the feeble work all round us, and shall be copying the better work through the copyists and *without* understanding it, which will by no means bring about intelligent art. Let us therefore study it wisely, be taught by it, kindled by it; all the while determining not to imitate or repeat it; to have either no art at all, or an art which we have made our own.

Yet I am almost brought to a stand-still when bidding you to study nature and the history of art, by remembering that this is London, and what it is like: how can I ask working-men passing up and down these hideous streets day by day to care about beauty? If it were politics, we must care about that; or science, you could wrap yourselves up in the study of facts, no doubt, without much caring what goes on about you—but beauty! do you not see what terrible difficulties beset art, owing to a long neglect of art—and neglect of reason, too, in this matter? It is such a heavy question by what effort, by what dead-lift, you can thrust this difficulty from you, that I must perforce set it aside for the present, and must at least hope that the study of history and its monuments will help you somewhat herein. If you can really fill your minds with memories of great works of art, and great times of art, you will, I think, be able to a certain extent to look through the aforesaid ugly surroundings, and will be moved to discontent of what is careless and brutal now, and will, I hope, at last be so much discontented with what is bad, that you will determine to bear no longer that short-sighted, reckless brutality of squalor that so disgraces our intricate civilisation.

Well, at any rate, London is good for this, that it is well off for museums,—which I heartily wish were to be got at seven days in the week instead of six, or at least on the only day on which an ordinarily busy man, one of the taxpayers who support them, can as a rule see them quietly,—and certainly any of us who may have any natural turn for art must get more help from frequenting them than one can well say. It is true, however, that people need some preliminary instruction before they can get all the good possible to be got from the prodigious treasures of art possessed by the country in that form: there also one sees things in a piece-meal way: nor can I deny that there is something melancholy about a museum, such a tale of violence, destruction, and carelessness, as its treasured scraps tell us.

But moreover you may sometimes have an opportunity of studying ancient art in a narrower but a more intimate, a more kindly form, the monuments of our own land. Sometimes only, since we live in the middle of this world of brick and mortar, and there is little else left us amidst it, except the ghost of the great church at Westminster, ruined as its exterior is by the stupidity of the restoring architect, and insulted as its glorious interior is by the pompous undertakers' lies, by the vainglory and ignorance of the last two centuries and a half—little besides that and the matchless Hall near it: but when we can get beyond that smoky world, there, out in the country we may still see the works of our fathers yet alive amidst the very nature they were wrought into, and of which they are so completely a part: for there indeed if anywhere, in the English country, in the days when people cared about such things, was there a full sympathy between the works of man, and the land they were made for:—the land is a little land; too much shut up within the narrow seas, as it seems, to have much space for swelling into hugeness: there are no great wastes overwhelming in their dreariness, no great solitudes of forests, no terrible untrodden mountain-walls: all is measured, mingled, varied, gliding easily one thing into another: little rivers, little plains; swelling, speedily-changing uplands, all beset with handsome orderly trees; little hills, little mountains, netted over with the walls of sheep-walks: all is little; yet not foolish and blank, but serious rather, and abundant of meaning for such as choose to seek it: it is neither prison nor palace, but a decent home.

All which I neither praise nor blame, but say that so it is: some people praise this homeliness overmuch, as if the land were the very axle-tree of the world; so do not I, nor any unblinded by pride in themselves and all that belongs to them: others there are who scorn it and the tameness of it: not I any the more: though it would indeed be hard if there were nothing else in the world, no wonders, no terrors, no unspeakable beauties: yet when we think what a small part of the world's history, past, present, and to come, is this land we live in, and how much smaller still in the history of the arts, and yet how our forefathers clung to it, and with what care and pains they adorned it, this unromantic, uneventful-looking land of England, surely by this too our hearts may be touched, and our hope quickened.

For as was the land, such was the art of it while folk yet troubled themselves about such things; it strove little to impress people either by pomp or ingenuity: not unseldom it fell into commonplace, rarely it rose into majesty; yet was it never oppressive, never a slave's nightmare nor an insolent boast: and at its best it had an inventiveness, an individuality that grander styles have never overpassed: its best too, and that was in its very heart, was given as freely to the yeoman's house, and the humble village church, as to the lord's palace or the mighty cathedral: never coarse, though often rude enough, sweet, natural and unaffected, an art of peasants rather than of merchant-princes or courtiers, it must be a hard heart, I think, that does not love it: whether a man has been born among it like ourselves, or has come wonderingly on its simplicity from all the grandeur over-seas. A peasant art, I say, and it clung fast to the life of the people, and still lived among the cottagers and yeomen in many parts of the country while the big houses were being built 'French and fine': still lived also in many a quaint pattern of loom and printing-block, and embroiderer's needle, while over-seas stupid pomp had extinguished all nature and freedom, and art was become, in France especially, the mere expression of that successful and exultant rascality, which in the flesh no long time afterwards went down into the pit for ever.

Such was the English art, whose history is in a sense at your doors, grown scarce indeed, and growing scarcer year by year, not only through greedy destruction, of which there is certainly less than there used to be, but also through the attacks of another foe, called nowadays 'restoration.'

I must not make a long story about this, but also I cannot quite pass it over, since I have pressed on you the study of these ancient monuments. Thus the matter stands: these old buildings have been altered and added to century after century, often beautifully, always historically; their very value, a great part of it, lay in that: they have suffered almost always from neglect also, often from violence (that latter a piece of history often far from uninteresting), but ordinary obvious mending would almost always have kept them standing, pieces of nature and of history.

But of late years a great uprising of ecclesiastical zeal, coinciding with a great increase of study, and consequently of knowledge of mediæval architecture, has driven people into spending their money on these buildings, not merely with the purpose of repairing them, of keeping them safe, clean, and wind and watertight, but also of 'restoring' them to some ideal state of perfection; sweeping away if possible all signs of what has befallen them at least since the Reformation, and often since dates much earlier: this has sometimes been done with much disregard of art and entirely from ecclesiastical zeal, but oftener it has been well meant enough as regards art: yet you will not have listened to what I have said to-night if you do not see that from my point of view this restoration must be as impossible to bring about, as the attempt at it is destructive to the buildings so dealt with: I scarcely like to think what a great part of them have been made nearly useless to students of art and history: unless you knew a great deal about architecture you perhaps would scarce understand what terrible damage has been done by that dangerous 'little knowledge' in this matter: but at least it is easy to be understood, that to deal recklessly with valuable (and national) monuments which, when once gone, can never be replaced by any splendour of modern art, is doing a very sorry service to the State.

You will see by all that I have said on this study of ancient art that I mean by education herein something much wider than the teaching of a definite art in schools of design, and that it must be something that we must do more or less for ourselves: I mean by it a systematic concentration of our thoughts on the matter, a studying of it in all ways, careful and laborious practice of it, and a determination to do nothing but what is known to be good in workmanship and design.

Of course, however, both as an instrument of that study we have been speaking of, as well as of the practice of the arts, all handicraftsmen should be taught to draw very carefully; as indeed all people should be taught drawing who are not physically incapable of learning it: but the art of drawing so taught would not be the art of designing, but only a means towards *this* end, *general capability in dealing with the arts*.

For I wish specially to impress this upon you, that *designing* cannot be taught at all in a school: continued practice will help a man who is naturally a designer, continual notice of nature and of art: no doubt those who have some faculty for designing are still numerous, and they want from a school certain technical teaching, just as they want tools: in these days also, when the best school, the school of successful practice going on around you, is at such a low ebb, they do undoubtedly want instruction in the history of the arts: these two things schools of design can give: but the royal road of a set of rules deduced from a sham science of design, that is itself not a science but another set of rules, will lead nowhere;—or, let us rather say, to beginning again.

As to the kind of drawing that should be taught to men engaged in ornamental work, there is only *one best* way of teaching drawing, and that is teaching the scholar to draw the human figure: both because the lines of a man's body are much more subtle than anything else, and because you can more surely be found out and set right if you go wrong. I do think that such teaching as this, given to all people who care for it, would help the revival of the arts very much: the habit of discriminating between right and wrong, the sense of pleasure in drawing a good line, would really, I think, be education in the due sense of the word for all such people as had the germs of invention in them; yet as aforesaid, in this age of the world it would be mere affectation to pretend to shut one's eyes to the art of past ages: that also we must study. If other circumstances, social and economical, do not stand in our way, that is to say, if the world is not too busy to allow us to have Decorative Arts at all, these two are the *direct* means by which we shall get them; that is, general cultivation of the powers of the mind, general cultivation of the powers of the eye and hand.

Perhaps that seems to you very commonplace advice and a very roundabout road; nevertheless 'tis a certain one, if by any road you desire to come to the new art, which is my subject to-night: if you do not, and if those germs of invention, which, as I said just now, are no doubt still common enough among men, are left neglected and undeveloped, the laws of Nature will assert themselves in this as in other matters, and the faculty of design itself will gradually fade from the race of man. Sirs, shall we approach nearer to perfection by casting away so large a part of that intelligence which makes us *men*?

And now before I make an end, I want to call your attention to certain things, that, owing to our neglect of the arts for other business, bar that good road to us and are such an hindrance, that, till they are dealt with, it is hard even to make a beginning of our endeavour. And if my talk should seem to grow too serious for our subject, as indeed I think it cannot do, I beg you to remember what I said earlier, of how the arts all hang together. Now there is one art of which the old architect of Edward the Third's time was thinking—he who founded New College at Oxford, I mean—when he took this for his motto: 'Manners maketh man:' he meant by manners the art of morals, the art of living worthily, and like a man. I must needs claim this art also as dealing with my subject.

There is a great deal of sham work in the world, hurtful to the buyer, more hurtful to the seller, if he only knew it, most hurtful to the maker: how good a foundation it would be towards getting good Decorative Art, that is ornamental workmanship, if we craftsmen were to resolve to turn out nothing but excellent workmanship in all things, instead of having, as we too often have now, a very low average standard of work, which we often fall below.

I do not blame either one class or another in this matter, I blame all: to set aside our own class of handicraftsmen, of whose shortcomings you and I know so much that we need talk no more about it, I know that the public in general are set on having things cheap, being so ignorant that they do not know when they get them nasty also; so ignorant that they neither know nor care whether they give a man his due: I know that the manufacturers (so called) are so set on carrying out competition to its utmost, competition of cheapness, not of excellence, that they meet the bargain-hunters half way, and cheerfully furnish them with nasty wares at the cheap rate they are asked for, by means of what can be called by no prettier name than fraud. England has of late been too much busied with the counting-house and not enough with the workshop: with the result that the counting-house at the present moment is rather barren of orders.

I say all classes are to blame in this matter, but also I say that the remedy lies with the handicraftsmen, who are not ignorant of these things like the public, and who have no call to be greedy and isolated like the manufacturers or middlemen; the duty and honour of educating the public lies with them, and they have in them the seeds of order and organisation which make that duty the easier.

When will they see to this and help to make men of us all by insisting on this most weighty piece of manners; so that we may adorn life with the pleasure of cheerfully *buying* goods at their due price; with the pleasure of *selling* goods that we could be proud of both for fair price and fair workmanship: with the pleasure of working soundly and without haste at *making* goods that we could be proud of?— much the greatest pleasure of the three is that last, such a pleasure as, I think, the world has none like it.

You must not say that this piece of manners lies out of my subject: it is essentially a part of it and most important: for I am bidding you learn to be artists, if art is not to come to an end amongst us: and what is an artist but a workman who is determined that, whatever else happens, his work shall be excellent? or, to put it in another way: the decoration of workmanship, what is it but the expression of man's pleasure in successful labour? But what pleasure can there be in *bad* work, in unsuccessful labour; why should we decorate *that*? and how can we bear to be always unsuccessful in our labour?

As greed of unfair gain, wanting to be paid for what we have not earned, cumbers our path with this tangle of bad work, of sham work, so the heaped-up money which this greed has brought us (for greed will have its way, like all other strong passions), this money, I say, gathered into heaps little and big, with all the false distinction which so unhappily it yet commands amongst us, has raised up against the arts a barrier of the love of luxury and show, which is of all obvious hindrances the worst to overpass: the highest and most cultivated classes are not free from the vulgarity of it, the lower are not free from its pretence. I beg you to remember both as a remedy against this, and as explaining exactly what I mean, that nothing can be a work of art which is not useful; that is to say, which does not minister to the body when well under command of the mind, or which does not amuse, soothe, or elevate the mind in a healthy state. What tons upon tons of unutterable rubbish pretending to be works of art in some degree would this maxim clear out of our London houses, if it were understood and acted upon! To my mind it is only here and there (out of the kitchen) that you can find in a well-to-do house things that are of any use at all: as a rule all the decoration (so called) that has got there is there for the sake of show, not because anybody likes it. I repeat, this stupidity goes through all classes of society: the silk curtains in my Lord's drawing-room are no more a matter of art to him than the powder in his footman's hair; the kitchen in a country farmhouse is most commonly a pleasant and homelike place, the parlour dreary and useless.

Simplicity of life, begetting simplicity of taste, that is, a love for sweet and lofty things, is of all matters most necessary for the birth of the new and better art we crave for; simplicity everywhere, in the palace as well as in the cottage.

Still more is this necessary, cleanliness and decency everywhere, in the cottage as well as in the palace: the lack of that is a serious piece of *manners* for us to correct: that lack and all the inequalities of life, and the heaped-up thoughtlessness and disorder of so many centuries that cause it: and as yet it is only a very few men who have begun to think about a remedy for it in its widest range: even in its narrower aspect, in the defacements of our big towns by all that commerce brings with it, who heeds it? who tries to control their squalor and hideousness? there is nothing but thoughtlessness and recklessness in the matter: the helplessness of people who don't live long enough to do a thing themselves, and have not manliness and foresight enough to begin the work, and pass it on to those that shall come after them.

Is money to be gathered? cut down the pleasant trees among the houses, pull down ancient and venerable buildings for the money that a few square yards of London dirt will fetch; blacken rivers, hide the sun and poison the air with smoke and worse, and it's nobody's business to see to it or mend it: that is all that modern commerce, the counting-house forgetful of the workshop, will do for us herein.

And Science—we have loved her well, and followed her diligently, what will she do? I fear she is so much in the pay of the counting-house, the counting-house and the drill-sergeant, that she is too busy, and will for the present do nothing. Yet there are matters which I should have thought easy for her; say for example teaching Manchester how to consume its own smoke, or Leeds how to get rid of its superfluous black dye without turning it into the river, which would be as much worth her attention as the production of the heaviest of heavy black silks, or the biggest of useless guns. Anyhow, however it be done, unless people care about carrying on their business without making the world hideous, how can they care about Art? I know it will cost much both of time and money to better these things even a little; but I do not see how these can be better spent than in making life cheerful and honourable for others and for ourselves; and the gain of good life to the country at large that would result from men seriously setting about the bettering of the decency of our big towns would be priceless, even if nothing specially good befell the arts in consequence: I do not know that it would; but I should begin to think matters hopeful if men turned their attention to such things, and I repeat that, unless they do so, we can scarcely even begin with any hope our endeavours for the bettering of the arts.

Unless something or other is done to give all men some pleasure for the eyes and rest for the mind in the aspect of their own and their neighbours' houses, until the contrast is less disgraceful between the fields where beasts live and the streets where men live, I suppose that the practice of the arts must be mainly kept in the hands of a few highly cultivated men, who can go often to beautiful places, whose education enables them, in the contemplation of the past glories of the world, to shut out from their view the everyday squalors that the most of men move in. Sirs, I believe that art has such sympathy with cheerful freedom, open-heartedness and reality, so much she sickens under selfishness and luxury, that she will not live thus isolated and exclusive. I will go further than this and say that on such terms I do not wish her to live. I protest that it would be a shame to an honest artist to enjoy what he had huddled up to himself of such art, as it would be for a rich man to sit and eat dainty food amongst starving soldiers in a beleaguered fort.

I do not want art for a few, any more than education for a few, or freedom for a few.

No, rather than art should live this poor thin life among a few exceptional men, despising those beneath them for an ignorance for which they themselves are responsible, for a brutality that they will not struggle with,—rather than this, I would that the world should indeed sweep away all art for awhile, as I said before I thought it possible she might do; rather than the wheat should rot in the miser's granary, I would that the earth had it, that it might yet have a chance to quicken in the dark.

I have a sort of faith, though, that this clearing way of all art will not happen, that men will get wiser, as well as more learned; that many of the intricacies of life, on which we now pride ourselves more than enough, partly because they are new, partly because they have come with the gain of better things, will be cast aside as having played their part, and being useful no longer. I hope that we shall have leisure from war,—war commercial, as well as war of the bullet and the bayonet; leisure from the knowledge that darkens counsel; leisure above all from the greed of money, and the craving for that overwhelming distinction that money now brings: I believe that as we have even now partly achieved LIBERTY, so we shall one day achieve EQUALITY, which, and which only, means FRATERNITY, and so have leisure from poverty and all its griping, sordid cares.

Then having leisure from all these things, amidst renewed simplicity of life we shall have leisure to think about our work, that faithful daily companion, which no man any longer will venture to call the Curse of labour: for surely then we shall be happy in it, each in his place, no man grudging at another; no one bidden to be any man's *servant*, every one scorning to be any man's *master*: men will then assuredly be happy in their work, and that happiness will assuredly bring forth decorative, noble, *popular* art.

That art will make our streets as beautiful as the woods, as elevating as the mountain-sides: it will be a pleasure and a rest, and not a weight upon the spirits to come from the open country into a town; every man's house will be fair and decent, soothing to his mind and helpful to his work: all the works of man that we live amongst and handle will be in harmony with nature, will be reasonable and beautiful: yet all will be simple and inspiriting, not childish nor enervating; for as nothing of beauty and splendour that man's mind and hand may compass shall be wanting from our public buildings, so in no private dwelling will there be any signs of waste, pomp, or insolence, and every man will have his share of the *best*.

It is a dream, you may say, of what has never been and never will be; true, it has never been, and therefore, since the world is alive and moving yet, my hope is the greater that it one day will be: true, it is a dream; but dreams have before now come about of things so good and necessary to us, that we scarcely think of them more than of the daylight, though once people had to live without them, without even the hope of them.

Anyhow, dream as it is, I pray you to pardon my setting it before you, for it lies at the bottom of all my work in the Decorative Arts, nor will it ever be out of my thoughts: and I am here with you to-night to ask you to help me in realising this dream, this *hope*.

2. THE ART OF THE PEOPLE: DELIVERED BEFORE THE BIRMINGHAM SOCIETY OF ARTS AND SCHOOL OF DESIGN, FEBRUARY 19, 1879.

> 'And the men of labour spent their strength in daily struggling for bread to maintain the vital strength they labour with: so living in a daily circulation of sorrow, living but to work, and working but to live, as if daily bread were the only end of a wearisome life, and a wearisome life the only occasion of daily bread.'
>
> — DANIEL DEFOE

I know that a large proportion of those here present are either already practising the Fine Arts, or are being specially educated to that end, and I feel that I may be expected to address myself specially to these. But since it is not to be doubted that we are *all* met together because of the interest we take in what concerns these arts, I would rather address myself to you *all* as representing the public in general. Indeed, those of you who are specially studying Art could learn little of me that would be useful to yourselves only. You are already learning under competent masters—most competent, I am glad to know—by means of a system which should teach you all you need, if you have been right in making the first step of devoting yourselves to Art; I mean if you are aiming at the right thing, and in some way or another understand what Art means, which you may well do without being able to express it, and if you are resolute to follow on the path which that inborn knowledge has shown to you; if it is otherwise with you than this, no system and no teachers will help you to produce real art of any kind, be it never so humble. Those of you who are real artists know well enough all the special advice I can give you, and in how few words it may be said—follow nature, study antiquity, make your own art, and do not steal it, grudge no expense of trouble, patience, or courage, in the striving to accomplish the hard thing you have set yourselves to do. You have had all that said to you twenty times, I doubt not; and twenty times twenty have said it to yourselves, and now I have said it again to you, and done neither you nor me good nor harm thereby. So true it all is, so well known, and so hard to follow.

But to me, and I hope to you, Art is a very serious thing, and cannot by any means be dissociated from the weighty matters that occupy the thoughts of men; and there are principles underlying the practice of it, on which all serious-minded men, may—nay, must—have their own thoughts. It is on some of these that I ask your leave to speak, and to address myself, not only to those who are consciously interested in the arts, but to all those also who have considered what the progress of civilisation promises and threatens to those who shall come after us: what there is to hope and fear for the future of the arts, which were born with the birth of civilisation and will only die with its death—what on this side of things, the present time of strife and doubt and change is preparing for the better time, when the change shall have come, the strife be lulled, and the doubt cleared: this is a question, I say, which is indeed weighty, and may well interest all thinking men.

Nay, so universally important is it, that I fear lest you should think I am taking too much upon myself to speak to you on so weighty a matter, nor should I have dared to do so, if I did not feel that I am to-night only the mouthpiece of better men than myself; whose hopes and fears I share; and that being so, I am the more emboldened to speak out, if I can, my full mind on the subject, because I am in a city where, if anywhere, men are not contented to live wholly for themselves and the present, but have fully accepted the duty of keeping their eyes open to whatever new is stirring, so that they may help and be helped by any truth that there may be in it. Nor can I forget, that, since you have done me the great honour of choosing me for the President of your Society of Arts for the past year, and of asking me to speak to you to-night, I should be doing less than my duty if I did not, according to my lights, speak out straightforwardly whatever seemed to me might be in a small degree useful to you. Indeed, I think I am among friends, who may forgive me if I speak rashly, but scarcely if I speak falsely.

The aim of your Society and School of Arts is, as I understand it, to further those arts by education widely spread. A very great object is that, and well worthy of the reputation of this great city; but since Birmingham has also, I rejoice to know, a great reputation for not allowing things to go about shamming life when the brains are knocked out of them, I think you should know and see clearly what it is you have undertaken to further by these institutions, and whether you really care about it, or only languidly aequiesce in it—whether, in short, you know it to the heart, and are indeed part and parcel of it, with your own will, or against it; or else have heard say that it is a good thing if any one care to meddle with it.

If you are surprised at my putting that question for your consideration, I will tell you why I do so. There are some of us who love Art most, and I may say most faithfully, who see for certain that such love is rare nowadays. We cannot help seeing, that besides a vast number of people, who (poor souls!) are sordid and brutal of mind and habits, and have had no chance or choice in the matter, there are many high-minded, thoughtful, and cultivated men who inwardly think the arts to be a foolish accident of civilisation—nay, worse perhaps, a nuisance, a disease, a hindrance to human progress. Some of these, doubtless, are very busy about other sides of thought. They are, as I should put it, so *artistically* engrossed by the study of science, politics, or what not, that they have necessarily narrowed their minds by their hard and praiseworthy labours. But since such men are few, this does not account for a prevalent habit of thought that looks upon Art as at best trifling.

What is wrong, then, with us or the arts, since what was once accounted so glorious, is now deemed paltry?

The question is no light one; for, to put the matter in its clearest light, I will say that the leaders of modern thought do for the most part sincerely and single-mindedly hate and despise the arts; and you know well that as the leaders are, so must the people be; and that means that we who are met together here for the furthering of Art by wide-spread education are either deceiving ourselves and wasting our time, since we shall one day be of the same opinion as the best men among us, or else we represent a small minority that is right, as minorities sometimes are, while those upright men aforesaid, and the great mass of civilised men, have been blinded by untoward circumstances.

That we are of this mind—the minority that is right—is, I hope, the case. I hope we know assuredly that the arts we have met together to further are necessary to the life of man, if the progress of civilisation is not to be as causeless as the turning of a wheel that makes nothing.

How, then, shall we, the minority, carry out the duty which our position thrusts upon us, of striving to grow into a majority?

If we could only explain to those thoughtful men, and the millions of whom they are the flower, what the thing is that we love, which is to us as the bread we eat, and the air we breathe, but about which they know nothing and feel nothing, save a vague instinct of repulsion, then the seed of victory might be sown. This is hard indeed to do; yet if we ponder upon a chapter of ancient or mediæval history, it seems to me some glimmer of a chance of doing so breaks in upon us. Take for example a century of the Byzantine Empire, weary yourselves with reading the names of the pedants, tyrants, and tax-gatherers to whom the terrible chain which long-dead Rome once forged, still gave the power of cheating people into thinking that they were necessary lords of the world. Turn then to the lands they governed, and read and forget a long string of the causeless murders of Northern and Saracen pirates and robbers. That is pretty much the sum of what so-called history has left us of the tale of those days—the stupid languor and the evil deeds of kings and scoundrels. Must we turn away then, and say that all was evil? How then did men live from day to day? How then did Europe grow into intelligence and freedom? It seems there were others than those of whom history (so called) has left us the names and the deeds. These, the raw material for the treasury and the slave-market, we now call 'the people,' and we know that they were working all that while. Yes, and that their work was not merely slaves' work, the meal-trough before them and the whip behind them; for though history (so called) has forgotten them, yet their work has not been forgotten, but has made another history—the history of Art. There is not an ancient city in the East or the West that does not bear some token of their grief, and joy, and hope. From Ispahan to Northumberland, there is no building built between the seventh and seventeenth centuries that does not show the influence of the labour of that oppressed and neglected herd of men. No one of them, indeed, rose high above his fellows. There was no Plato, or Shakespeare, or Michael Angelo amongst them. Yet scattered as it was among many men, how strong their thought was, how long it abided, how far it travelled!

And so it was ever through all those days when Art was so vigorous and progressive. Who can say how little we should know of many periods, but for their art? History (so called) has remembered the kings and warriors, because they destroyed; Art has remembered the people, because they created.

I think, then, that this knowledge we have of the life of past times gives us some token of the way we should take in meeting those honest and single-hearted men who above all things desire the world's progress, but whose minds are, as it were, sick on this point of the arts. Surely you may say to them: When all is gained that you (and we) so long for, what shall we do then? That great change which we are working for, each in his own way, will come like other changes, as a thief in the night, and will be with us before we know it; but let us imagine that its consummation has come suddenly and dramatically, acknowledged and hailed by all right-minded people; and what shall we do then, lest we begin once more to heap up fresh corruption for the woeful labour of ages once again? I say, as we turn away from the flagstaff where the new banner has been just run up; as we depart, our ears yet ringing with the blare of the heralds' trumpets that have proclaimed the new order of things, what shall we turn to then, what *must* we turn to then?

To what else, save to our work, our daily labour?

With what, then, shall we adorn it when we have become wholly free and reasonable? It is necessary toil, but shall it be toil only? Shall all we can do with it be to shorten the hours of that toil to the utmost, that the hours of leisure may be long beyond what men used to hope for? and what then shall we do with the leisure, if we say that all toil is irksome? Shall we sleep it all away?—Yes, and never wake up again, I should hope, in that case.

What shall we do then? what shall our necessary hours of labour bring forth?

That will be a question for all men in that day when many wrongs are righted, and when there will be no classes of degradation on whom the dirty work of the world can be shovelled; and if men's minds are still sick and loathe the arts, they will not be able to answer that question.

Once men sat under grinding tyrannies, amidst violence and fear so great, that nowadays we wonder how they lived through twenty-four hours of it, till we remember that then, as now, their daily labour was the main part of their lives, and that that daily labour was sweetened by the daily creation of Art; and shall we who are delivered from the evils they bore, live drearier days than they did? Shall men, who have come forth from so many tyrannies, bind themselves to yet another one, and become the slaves of nature, piling day upon day of hopeless, useless toil? Must this go on worsening till it comes to this at last—that the world shall have come into its inheritance, and with all foes conquered and nought to bind it, shall choose to sit down and labour for ever amidst grim ugliness? How, then, were all our hopes cheated, what a gulf of despair should we tumble into then?

In truth, it cannot be; yet if that sickness of repulsion to the arts were to go on hopelessly, nought else would be, and the extinction of the love of beauty and imagination would prove to be the extinction of civilisation. But that sickness the world will one day throw off, yet will, I believe, pass through many pains in so doing, some of which will look very like the death-throes of Art, and some, perhaps, will be grievous enough to the poor people of the world; since hard necessity, I doubt, works many of the world's changes, rather than the purblind striving to see, which we call the foresight of man.

Meanwhile, remember that I asked just now, what was amiss in Art or in ourselves that this sickness was upon us. Nothing is wrong or can be with Art in the abstract—that must always be good for mankind, or we are all wrong together: but with Art, as we of these latter days have known it, there is much wrong; nay, what are we here for to-night if that is not so? were not the schools of art founded all over the country some thirty years ago because we had found out that popular art was fading—or perhaps had faded out from amongst us?

As to the progress made since then in this country—and in this country only, if at all—it is hard for me to speak without being either ungracious or insincere, and yet speak I must. I say, then, that an apparent external progress in some ways is obvious, but I do not know how far that is hopeful, for time must try it, and prove whether it be a passing fashion or the first token of a real stir among the great mass of civilised men. To speak quite frankly, and as one friend to another, I must needs say that even as I say those words they seem too good to be true. And yet—who knows?—so wont are we to frame history for the future as well as for the past, so often are our eyes blind both when we look backward and when we look forward, because we have been gazing so intently at our own days, our own lines. May all be better than I think it!

At any rate let us count our gains, and set them against less hopeful signs of the times. In England, then—and as far as I know, in England only—painters of pictures have grown, I believe, more numerous, and certainly more conscientious in their work, and in some cases—and this more especially in England—have developed and expressed a sense of beauty which the world has not seen for the last three hundred years. This is certainly a very great gain, which is not easy to over-estimate, both for those who make the pictures and those who use them.

Furthermore, in England, and in England only, there has been a great improvement in architecture and the arts that attend it—arts which it was the special province of the afore-mentioned schools to revive and foster. This, also, is a considerable gain to the users of the works so made, but I fear a gain less important to most of those concerned in making them.

Against these gains we must, I am very sorry to say, set the fact not easy to be accounted for, that the rest of the civilised world (so called) seems to have done little more than stand still in these matters; and that among ourselves these improvements have concerned comparatively few people, the mass of our population not being in the least touched by them; so that the great bulk of our architecture—the art which most depends on the taste of the people at large—grows worse and worse every day. I must speak also of another piece of discouragement before I go further. I daresay many of you will remember how emphatically those who first had to do with the movement of which the foundation of our art-schools was a part, called the attention of our pattern-designers to the beautiful works of the East. This was surely most well judged of them, for they bade us look at an art at once beautiful, orderly, living in our own day, and above all, popular. Now, it is a grievous result of the sickness of civilisation that this art is fast disappearing before the advance of western conquest and commerce—fast, and every day faster. While we are met here in Birmingham to further the spread of education in art, Englishmen in India are, in their short-sightedness, actively destroying the very sources of that education—jewellery, metal-work, pottery, calico-printing, brocade-weaving, carpet-making—all the famous and historical arts of the great peninsula have been for long treated as matters of no importance, to be thrust aside for the advantage of any paltry scrap of so-called commerce; and matters are now speedily coming to an end there. I daresay some of you saw the presents which the native Princes gave to the Prince of Wales on the occasion of his progress through India. I did myself, I will not say with great disappointment, for I guessed what they would be like, but with great grief, since there was scarce here and there a piece of goods among these costly gifts, things given as great treasures, which faintly upheld the ancient fame of the cradle of the industrial arts. Nay, in some cases, it would have been laughable, if it had not been so sad, to see the piteous simplicity with which the conquered race had copied the blank vulgarity of their lords. And this deterioration we are now, as I have said, actively engaged in forwarding. I have read a little book,[1] a handbook to the Indian Court of last year's Paris Exhibition, which takes the occasion of noting the state of manufactures in India one by one. 'Art manufactures,' you would call them; but, indeed, all manufactures are, or were, 'art manufactures' in India. Dr. Birdwood, the author of this book, is of great experience in Indian life, a man of science, and a lover of the arts. His story, by no means a new one to me, or others interested in the East and its labour, is a sad one indeed. The conquered races in their hopelessness are everywhere giving up the genuine practice of their own arts, which we know ourselves, as we have indeed loudly proclaimed, are founded on the truest and most natural principles. The often-praised perfection of these arts is the blossom of many ages of labour and change, but the conquered races are casting it aside as a thing of no value, so that they may conform themselves to the inferior art, or rather the lack of art, of their conquerors. In some parts of the country the genuine arts are quite destroyed; in many others nearly so; in all they have more or less begun to sicken. So much so is this the case, that now for some time the Government has been furthering this deterioration. As for example, no doubt with the best intentions, and certainly in full sympathy with the general English public, both at home and in India, the Government is now manufacturing cheap Indian carpets in the Indian gaols. I do not say that it is a bad thing to turn out real work, or works of art, in gaols; on the contrary, I think it good if it be properly managed. But in this case, the Government, being, as I said, in full sympathy with the English public, has determined that it will make its wares cheap, whether it make them nasty or not. Cheap and nasty they are, I assure you; but, though they are the worst of their kind, they would not be made thus, if everything did not tend the same way. And it is the same everywhere and with all Indian manufactures, till it has come to this —that these poor people have all but lost the one distinction, the one glory that conquest had left them. Their famous wares, so praised by those who thirty years ago began to attempt the restoration of popular art amongst ourselves, are no longer to be bought at reasonable prices in the common market, but must be sought for and treasured as precious relics for the museums we have founded for our art education. In short, their art is dead, and the commerce of modern civilisation has slain it.

What is going on in India is also going on, more or less, all over the East; but I have spoken of India chiefly because I cannot help thinking that we ourselves are responsible for what is happening there. Chance-hap has made us the lords of many millions out there; surely, it behoves us to look to it, lest we give to the people whom we have made helpless scorpions for fish and stones for bread.

But since neither on this side, nor on any other, can art be amended, until the countries that lead civilisation are themselves in a healthy state about it, let us return to the consideration of its condition among ourselves. And again I say, that obvious as is that surface improvement of the arts within the last few years, I fear too much that there is something wrong about the root of the plant to exult over the bursting of its February buds.

I have just shown you for one thing that lovers of Indian and Eastern Art, including as they do the heads of our institutions for art education, and I am sure many among what are called the governing classes, are utterly powerless to stay its downward course. The general tendency of civilisation is against them, and is too strong for them.

Again, though many of us love architecture dearly, and believe that it helps the healthiness both of body and soul to live among beautiful things, we of the big towns are mostly compelled to live in houses which have become a byword of contempt for their ugliness and inconvenience. The stream of civilisation is against us, and we cannot battle against it.

Once more those devoted men who have upheld the standard of truth and beauty amongst us, and whose pictures, painted amidst difficulties that none but a painter can know, show qualities of mind unsurpassed in any age—these great men have but a narrow circle that can understand their works, and are utterly unknown to the great mass of the people: civilisation is so much against them, that they cannot move the people.

Therefore, looking at all this, I cannot think that all is well with the root of the tree we are cultivating. Indeed, I believe that if other things were but to stand still in the world, this improvement before mentioned would lead to a kind of art which, in that impossible case, would be in a way stable, would perhaps stand still also. This would be an art cultivated professedly by a few, and for a few, who would consider it necessary—a duty, if they could admit duties—to despise the common herd, to hold themselves aloof from all that the world has been struggling for from the first, to guard carefully every approach to their palace of art. It would be a pity to waste many words on the prospect of such a school of art as this, which does in a way, theoretically at least, exist at present, and has for its watchword a piece of slang that does not mean the harmless thing it seems to mean—art for art's sake. Its fore-doomed end must be, that art at last will seem too delicate a thing for even the hands of the initiated to touch; and the initiated must at last sit still and do nothing—to the grief of no one.

Well, certainly, if I thought you were come here to further such an art as this I could not have stood up and called you *friends*; though such a feeble folk as I have told you of one could scarce care to call foes.

Yet, as I say, such men exist, and I have troubled you with speaking of them, because I know that those honest and intelligent people, who are eager for human progress, and yet lack part of the human senses, and are anti-artistic, suppose that such men are artists, and that this is what art means, and what it does for people, and that such a narrow, cowardly life is what we, fellow-handicraftsmen, aim at. I see this taken for granted continually, even by many who, to say truth, ought to know better, and I long to put the slur from off us; to make people understand that we, least of all men, wish to widen the gulf between the classes, nay, worse still, to make new classes of elevation, and new classes of degradation—new lords and new slaves; that we, least of all men, want to cultivate the 'plant called man' in different ways—here stingily, there wastefully: I wish people to understand that the art we are striving for is a good thing which all can share, which will elevate all; in good sooth, if all people do not soon share it there will soon be none to share; if all are not elevated by it, mankind will lose the elevation it has gained. Nor is such an art as we long for a vain dream; such an art once was in times that were worse than these, when there was less courage, kindness, and truth in the world than there is now; such an art there will be hereafter, when there will be more courage, kindness, and truth than there is now in the world.

Let us look backward in history once more for a short while, and then steadily forward till my words are done: I began by saying that part of the common and necessary advice given to Art students was to study antiquity; and no doubt many of you, like me, have done so; have wandered, for instance, through the galleries of the admirable museum of South Kensington, and, like me, have been filled with wonder and gratitude at the beauty which has been born from the brain of man. Now, consider, I pray you, what these wonderful works are, and how they were made; and indeed, it is neither in extravagance nor without due meaning that I use the word 'wonderful' in speaking of them. Well, these things are just the common household goods of those past days, and that is one reason why they are so few and so carefully treasured. They were common things in their own day, used without fear of breaking or spoiling—no rarities then—and yet we have called them 'wonderful.'

And how were they made? Did a great artist draw the designs for them—a man of cultivation, highly paid, daintily fed, carefully housed, wrapped up in cotton wool, in short, when he was not at work? By no means. Wonderful as these works are, they were made by 'common fellows,' as the phrase goes, in the common course of their daily labour. Such were the men we honour in honouring those works. And their labour—do you think it was irksome to them?

Those of you who are artists know very well that it was not; that it could not be. Many a grin of pleasure, I'll be bound—and you will not contradict me—went to the carrying through of those mazes of mysterious beauty, to the invention of those strange beasts and birds and flowers that we ourselves have chuckled over at South Kensington. While they were at work, at least, these men were not unhappy, and I suppose they worked most days, and the most part of the day, as we do.

Or those treasures of architecture that we study so carefully nowadays—what are they? how were they made? There are great minsters among them, indeed, and palaces of kings and lords, but not many; and, noble and awe-inspiring as these may be, they differ only in size from the little grey church that still so often makes the commonplace English landscape beautiful, and the little grey house that still, in some parts of the country at least, makes an English village a thing apart, to be seen and pondered on by all who love romance and beauty. These form the mass of our architectural treasures, the houses that everyday people lived in, the unregarded churches in which they worshipped.

And, once more, who was it that designed and ornamented them? The great architect, carefully kept for the purpose, and guarded from the common troubles of common men? By no means. Sometimes, perhaps, it was the monk, the ploughman's brother; oftenest his other brother, the village carpenter, smith, mason, what not—'a common fellow,' whose common everyday labour fashioned works that are to-day the wonder and despair of many a hard-working 'cultivated' architect. And did he loathe his work? No, it is impossible. I have seen, as we most of us have, work done by such men in some out-of-the-way hamlet—where to-day even few strangers ever come, and whose people seldom go five miles from their own doors; in such places, I say, I have seen work so delicate, so careful, and so inventive, that nothing in its way could go further. And I will assert, without fear of contradiction, that no human ingenuity can produce work such as this without pleasure being a third party to the brain that conceived and the hand that fashioned it. Nor are such works rare. The throne of the great Plantagenet, or the great Valois, was no more daintily carved than the seat of the village mass-john, or the chest of the yeoman's good-wife.

So, you see, there was much going on to make life endurable in those times. Not every day, you may be sure, was a day of slaughter and tumult, though the histories read almost as if it were so; but every day the hammer chinked on the anvil, and the chisel played about the oak beam, and never without some beauty and invention being born of it, and consequently some human happiness.

That last word brings me to the very kernel and heart of what I have come here to say to you, and I pray you to think of it most seriously—not as to my words, but as to a thought which is stirring in the world, and will one day grow into something.

That thing which I understand by real art is the expression by man of his pleasure in labour. I do not believe he can be happy in his labour without expressing that happiness; and especially is this so when he is at work at anything in which he specially excels. A most kind gift is this of nature, since all men, nay, it seems all things too, must labour; so that not only does the dog take pleasure in hunting, and the horse in running, and the bird in flying, but so natural does the idea seem to us, that we imagine to ourselves that the earth and the very elements rejoice in doing their appointed work; and the poets have told us of the spring meadows smiling, of the exultation of the fire, of the countless laughter of the sea.

Nor until these latter days has man ever rejected this universal gift, but always, when he has not been too much perplexed, too much bound by disease or beaten down by trouble, has striven to make his work at least happy. Pain he has too often found in his pleasure, and weariness in his rest, to trust to these. What matter if his happiness lie with what must be always with him—his work?

And, once more, shall we, who have gained so much, forego this gain, the earliest, most natural gain of mankind? If we have to a great extent done so, as I verily fear we have, what strange fog-lights must have misled us; or rather let me say, how hard pressed we must have been in the battle with the evils we have overcome, to have forgotten the greatest of all evils. I cannot call it less than that. If a man has work to do which he despises, which does not satisfy his natural and rightful desire for pleasure, the greater part of his life must pass unhappily and without self-respect. Consider, I beg of you, what that means, and what ruin must come of it in the end.

If I could only persuade you of this, that the chief duty of the civilised world to-day is to set about making labour happy for all, to do its utmost to minimise the amount of unhappy labour—nay, if I could only persuade some two or three of you here present—I should have made a good night's work of it.

Do not, at any rate, shelter yourselves from any misgiving you may have behind the fallacy that the art-lacking labour of to-day is happy work: for the most of men it is not so. It would take long, perhaps, to show you, and make you fully understand that the would-be art which it produces is joyless. But there is another token of its being most unhappy work, which you cannot fail to understand at once—a grievous thing that token is—and I beg of you to believe that I feel the full shame of it, as I stand here speaking of it; but if we do not admit that we are sick, how can we be healed? This hapless token is, that the work done by the civilised world is mostly dishonest work. Look now: I admit that civilisation does make certain things well, things which it knows, consciously or unconsciously, are necessary to its present unhealthy condition. These things, to speak shortly, are chiefly machines for carrying on the competition in buying and selling, called falsely commerce; and machines for the violent destruction of life— that is to say, materials for two kinds of war; of which kinds the last is no doubt the worst, not so much in itself perhaps, but because on this point the conscience of the world is beginning to be somewhat pricked. But, on the other hand, matters for the carrying on of a dignified daily life, that life of mutual trust, forbearance, and help, which is the only real life of thinking men—these things the civilised world makes ill, and even increasingly worse and worse.

If I am wrong in saying this, you know well I am only saying what is widely thought, nay widely said too, for that matter. Let me give an instance, familiar enough, of that wide-spread opinion. There is a very clever book of pictures[2] now being sold at the railway bookstalls, called 'The British Working Man, by one who does not believe in him,'—a title and a book which make me both angry and ashamed, because the two express much injustice, and not a little truth in their quaint, and necessarily exaggerated way. It is quite true, and very sad to say, that if any one nowadays wants a piece of ordinary work done by gardener, carpenter, mason, dyer, weaver, smith, what you will, he will be a lucky rarity if he get it well done. He will, on the contrary, meet on every side with evasion of plain duties, and disregard of other men's rights; yet I cannot see how the 'British Working Man' is to be made to bear the whole burden of this blame, or indeed the chief part of it. I doubt if it be possible for a whole mass of men to do work to which they are driven, and in which there is no hope and no pleasure, without trying to shirk it—at any rate, shirked it has always been under such circumstances. On the other hand, I know that there are some men so right-minded, that they will, in despite of irksomeness and hopelessness, drive right through their work. Such men are the salt of the earth. But must there not be something wrong with a state of society which drives these into that bitter heroism, and the most part into shirking, into the depths often of half-conscious self-contempt and degradation? Be sure that there is, that the blindness and hurry of civilisation, as it now is, have to answer a heavy charge as to that enormous amount of pleasureless work—work that tries every muscle of the body and every atom of the brain, and which is done without pleasure and without aim—work which everybody who has to do with tries to shuffle off in the speediest way that dread of starvation or ruin will allow him.

I am as sure of one thing as that I am living and breathing, and it is this: that the dishonesty in the daily arts of life, complaints of which are in all men's mouths, and which I can answer for it does exist, is the natural and inevitable result of the world in the hurry of the war of the counting-house, and the war of the battlefield, having forgotten—of all men, I say, each for the other, having forgotten, that pleasure in our daily labour, which nature cries out for as its due.

Therefore, I say again, it is necessary to the further progress of civilisation that men should turn their thoughts to some means of limiting, and in the end of doing away with, degrading labour.

I do not think my words hitherto spoken have given you any occasion to think that I mean by this either hard or rough labour; I do not pity men much for their hardships, especially if they be accidental; not necessarily attached to one class or one condition, I mean. Nor do I think (I were crazy or dreaming else) that the work of the world can be carried on without rough labour; but I have seen enough of that to know that it need not be by any means degrading. To plough the earth, to cast the net, to fold the flock—these, and such as these, which are rough occupations enough, and which carry with them many hardships, are good enough for the best of us, certain conditions of leisure, freedom, and due wages being granted. As to the bricklayer, the mason, and the like—these would be artists, and doing not only necessary, but beautiful, and therefore happy work, if art were anything like what it should be. No, it is not such labour as this which we need to do away with, but the toil which makes the thousand and one things which nobody wants, which are used merely as the counters for the competitive buying and selling, falsely called commerce, which I have spoken of before—I know in my heart, and not merely by my reason, that this toil cries out to be done away with. But, besides that, the labour which now makes things good and necessary in themselves, merely as counters for the commercial war aforesaid, needs regulating and reforming. Nor can this reform be brought about save by art; and if we were only come to our right minds, and could see the necessity for making labour sweet to all men, as it is now to very few—the necessity, I repeat; lest discontent, unrest, and despair should at last swallow up all society—If we, then, with our eyes cleared, could but make some sacrifice of things which do us no good, since we unjustly and uneasily possess them, then indeed I believe we should sow the seeds of a happiness which the world has not yet known, of a rest and content which would make it what I cannot help thinking it was meant to be: and with that seed would be sown also the seed of real art, the expression of man's happiness in his labour,—an art made by the people, and for the people, as a happiness to the maker and the user.

That is the only real art there is, the only art which will be an instrument to the progress of the world, and not a hindrance. Nor can I seriously doubt that in your hearts you know that it is so, all of you, at any rate, who have in you an instinct for art. I believe that you agree with me in this, though you may differ from much else that I have said. I think assuredly that this is the art whose welfare we have met together to further, and the necessary instruction in which we have undertaken to spread as widely as may be.

Thus I have told you something of what I think is to be hoped and feared for the future of art; and if you ask me what I expect as a practical outcome of the admission of these opinions, I must say at once that I know, even if we were all of one mind, and that what I think the right mind on this subject, we should still have much work and many hindrances before us; we should still have need of all the prudence, foresight, and industry of the best among us; and, even so, our path would sometimes seem blind enough. And, to-day, when the opinions which we think right, and which one day will be generally thought so, have to struggle sorely to make themselves noticed at all, it is early days for us to try to see our exact and clearly mapped road. I suppose you will think it too commonplace of me to say that the general education that makes men think, will one day make them think rightly upon art. Commonplace as it is, I really believe it, and am indeed encouraged by it, when I remember how obviously this age is one of transition from the old to the new, and what a strange confusion, from out of which we shall one day come, our ignorance and half-ignorance is like to make of the exhausted rubbish of the old and the crude rubbish of the new, both of which lie so ready to our hands.

But, if I must say, furthermore, any words that seem like words of practical advice, I think my task is hard, and I fear I shall offend some of you whatever I say; for this is indeed an affair of morality, rather than of what people call art.

However, I cannot forget that, in my mind, it is not possible to dissociate art from morality, politics, and religion. Truth in these great matters of principle is of one, and it is only in formal treatises that it can be split up diversely. I must also ask you to remember how I have already said, that though my mouth alone speaks, it speaks, however feebly and disjointedly, the thoughts of many men better than myself. And further, though when things are tending to the best, we shall still, as aforesaid, need our best men to lead us quite right; yet even now surely, when it is far from that, the least of us can do some yeoman's service to the cause, and live and die not without honour.

So I will say that I believe there are two virtues much needed in modern life, if it is ever to become sweet; and I am quite sure that they are absolutely necessary in the sowing the seed of an *art which is to be made by the people and for the people, as a happiness to the maker and the user.* These virtues are honesty, and simplicity of life. To make my meaning clearer I will name the opposing vice of the second of these—luxury to wit. Also I mean by honesty, the careful and eager giving his due to every man, the determination not to gain by any man's loss, which in my experience is not a common virtue.

But note how the practice of either of these virtues will make the other easier to us. For if our wants are few, we shall have but little chance of being driven by our wants into injustice; and if we are fixed in the principle of giving every man his due, how can our self-respect bear that we should give too much to ourselves?

And in art, and in that preparation for it without which no art that is stable or worthy can be, the raising, namely, of those classes which have heretofore been degraded, the practice of these virtues would make a new world of it. For if you are rich, your simplicity of life will both go towards smoothing over the dreadful contrast between waste and want, which is the great horror of civilised countries, and will also give an example and standard of dignified life to those classes which you desire to raise, who, as it is indeed, being like enough to rich people, are given both to envy and to imitate the idleness and waste that the possession of much money produces.

Nay, and apart from the morality of the matter, which I am forced to speak to you of; let me tell you that though simplicity in art may be costly as well as uncostly, at least it is not wasteful, and nothing is more destructive to art than the want of it. I have never been in any rich man's house which would not have looked the better for having a bonfire made outside of it of nine-tenths of all that it held. Indeed, our sacrifice on the side of luxury will, it seems to me, be little or nothing: for, as far as I can make out, what people usually mean by it, is either a gathering of possessions which are sheer vexations to the owner, or a chain of pompous circumstance, which checks and annoys the rich man at every step. Yes, luxury cannot exist without slavery of some kind or other, and its abolition will be blessed, like the abolition of other slaveries, by the freeing both of the slaves and of their masters.

Lastly, if, besides attaining to simplicity of life, we attain also to the love of justice, then will all things be ready for the new springtime of the arts. For those of us that are employers of labour, how can we bear to give any man less money than he can decently live on, less leisure than his education and self-respect demand? or those of us who are workmen, how can we bear to fail in the contract we have undertaken, or to make it necessary for a foreman to go up and down spying out our mean tricks and evasions? or we the shopkeepers—can we endure to lie about our wares, that we may shuffle off our losses on to some one else's shoulders? or we the public—how can we bear to pay a price for a piece of goods which will help to trouble one man, to ruin another, and starve a third? Or, still more, I think, how can we bear to use, how can we enjoy something which has been a pain and a grief for the maker to make?

And now, I think, I have said what I came to say. I confess that there is nothing new in it, but you know the experience of the world is that a thing must be said over and over again before any great number of men can be got to listen to it. Let my words to-night, therefore, pass for one of the necessary times that the thought in them must be spoken out.

For the rest I believe that, however seriously these words may be gainsayed, I have been speaking to an audience in whom any words spoken from a sense of duty and in hearty goodwill, as mine have been, will quicken thought and sow some good seed. At any rate, it is good for a man who thinks seriously to face his fellows, and speak out whatever really burns in him, so that men may seem less strange to one another, and misunderstanding, the fruitful cause of aimless strife, may be avoided.

But if to any of you I have seemed to speak hopelessly, my words have been lacking in art; and you must remember that hopelessness would have locked my mouth, not opened it. I am, indeed, hopeful, but can I give a date to the accomplishment of my hope, and say that it will happen in my life or yours?

But I will say at least, Courage! for things wonderful, unhoped-for, glorious, have happened even in this short while I have been alive.

Yes, surely these times are wonderful and fruitful of change, which, as it wears and gathers new life even in its wearing, will one day bring better things for the toiling days of men, who, with freer hearts and clearer eyes, will once more gain the sense of outward beauty, and rejoice in it.

Meanwhile, if these hours be dark, as, indeed, in many ways they are, at least do not let us sit deedless, like fools and fine gentlemen, thinking the common toil not good enough for us, and beaten by the muddle; but rather let us work like good fellows trying by some dim candle-light to set our workshop ready against to-morrow's daylight—that to-morrow, when the civilised world, no longer greedy, strifeful, and destructive, shall have a new art, a glorious art, made by the people and for the people, as a happiness to the maker and the user.

3. THE BEAUTY OF LIFE: DELIVERED BEFORE THE BIRMINGHAM SOCIETY OF ARTS AND SCHOOL OF DESIGN, FEBRUARY 19, 1880.

'—propter vitam vivendi perdere causas.'

— JUVENAL

I stand before you this evening weighted with a disadvantage that I did not feel last year;—I have little fresh to tell you; I can somewhat enlarge on what I said then; here and there I may make bold to give you a practical suggestion, or I may put what I have to say in a way which will be clearer to some of you perhaps; but my message is really the same as it was when I first had the pleasure of meeting you.

It is true that if all were going smoothly with art, or at all events so smoothly that there were but a few malcontents in the world, you might listen with some pleasure, and perhaps advantage, to the talk of an old hand in the craft concerning ways of work, the snares that beset success, and the shortest road to it, to a tale of workshop receipts and the like: that would be a pleasant talk surely between friends and fellow-workmen; but it seems to me as if it were not for us as yet; nay, maybe we may live long and find no time fit for such restful talk as the cheerful histories of the hopes and fears of our workshops: anyhow to-night I cannot do it, but must once again call the faithful of art to a battle wider and more distracting than that kindly struggle with nature, to which all true craftsmen are born; which is both the building-up and the wearing-away of their lives.

As I look round on this assemblage, and think of all that it represents, I cannot choose but be moved to the soul by the troubles of the life of civilised man, and the hope that thrusts itself through them; I cannot refrain from giving you once again the message with which, as it seems, some chance-hap has charged me: that message is, in short, to call on you to face the latest danger which civilisation is threatened with, a danger of her own breeding: that men in struggling towards the complete attainment of all the luxuries of life for the strongest portion of their race should deprive their whole race of all the beauty of life: a danger that the strongest and wisest of mankind, in striving to attain to a complete mastery over nature, should destroy her simplest and widest-spread gifts, and thereby enslave simple people to them, and themselves to themselves, and so at last drag the world into a second barbarism more ignoble, and a thousandfold more hopeless, than the first.

Now of you who are listening to me, there are some, I feel sure, who have received this message, and taken it to heart, and are day by day fighting the battle that it calls on you to fight: to you I can say nothing but that if any word I speak discourage you, I shall heartily wish I had never spoken at all: but to be shown the enemy, and the castle we have got to storm, is not to be bidden to run from him; nor am I telling you to sit down deedless in the desert because between you and the promised land lies many a trouble, and death itself maybe: the hope before you you know, and nothing that I can say can take it away from you; but friend may with advantage cry out to friend in the battle that a stroke is coming from this side or that: take my hasty words in that sense, I beg of you.

But I think there will be others of you in whom vague discontent is stirring: who are oppressed by the life that surrounds you; confused and troubled by that oppression, and not knowing on which side to seek a remedy, though you are fain to do so: well, we, who have gone further into those troubles, believe that we can help you: true we cannot at once take your trouble from you; nay, we may at first rather add to it; but we can tell you what we think of the way out of it; and then amidst the many things you will have to do to set yourselves and others fairly on that way, you will many days, nay most days, forget your trouble in thinking of the good that lies beyond it, for which you are working.

But, again, there are others amongst you (and to speak plainly, I daresay they are the majority), who are not by any means troubled by doubt of the road the world is going, nor excited by any hope of its bettering that road: to them the cause of civilisation is simple and even commonplace: it wonder, hope, and fear no longer hang about it; has become to us like the rising and setting of the sun; it cannot err, and we have no call to meddle with it, either to complain of its course, or to try to direct it.

There is a ground of reason and wisdom in that way of looking at the matter: surely the world will go on its ways, thrust forward by impulses which we cannot understand or sway: but as it grows in strength for the journey, its necessary food is the life and aspirations of *all* of us: and we discontented strugglers with what at times seems the hurrying blindness of civilisation, no less than those who see nothing but smooth, unvarying progress in it, are bred of civilisation also, and shall be used up to further it in some way or other, I doubt not: and it may be of some service to those who think themselves the only loyal subjects of progress to hear of our existence, since their not hearing of it would not make an end of it: it may set them a-thinking not unprofitably to hear of burdens that they do not help to bear, but which are nevertheless real and weighty enough to some of their fellow-men, who are helping, even as they are, to form the civilisation that is to be.

The danger that the present course of civilisation will destroy the beauty of life—these are hard words, and I wish I could mend them, but I cannot, while I speak what I believe to be the truth.

That the beauty of life is a thing of no moment, I suppose few people would venture to assert, and yet most civilised people act as if it were of none, and in so doing are wronging both themselves and those that are to come after them; for that beauty, which is what is meant by *art*, using the word in its widest sense, is, I contend, no mere accident to human life, which people can take or leave as they choose, but a positive necessity of life, if we are to live as nature meant us to; that is, unless we are content to be less than men.

Now I ask you, as I have been asking myself this long while, what proportion of the population in civilised countries has any share at all in that necessity of life?

I say that the answer which must be made to that question justifies my fear that modern civilisation is on the road to trample out all the beauty of life, and to make us less than men.

Now if there should be any here who will say: It was always so; there always was a mass of rough ignorance that knew and cared nothing about art; I answer first, that if that be the case, then it was always wrong, and we, as soon as we have become conscious of that wrong, are bound to set it right if we can.

But moreover, strange to say, and in spite of all the suffering that the world has wantonly made for itself, and has in all ages so persistently clung to, as if it were a good and holy thing, this wrong of the mass of men being regardless of art was *not* always so.

So much is now known of the periods of art that have left abundant examples of their work behind them, that we can judge of the art of all periods by comparing these with the remains of times of which less has been left us; and we cannot fail to come to the conclusion that down to very recent days everything that the hand of man touched was more or less beautiful: so that in those days all people who made anything shared in art, as well as all people who used the things so made: that is, *all* people shared in art.

But some people may say: And was that to be wished for? would not this universal spreading of art stop progress in other matters, hinder the work of the world? Would it not make us unmanly? or if not that, would it not be intrusive, and push out other things necessary also for men to study?

Well, I have claimed a necessary place for art, a natural place, and it would be in the very essence of it, that it would apply its own rules of order and fitness to the general ways of life: it seems to me, therefore, that people who are over-anxious of the outward expression of beauty becoming too great a force among the other forces of life, would, if they had had the making of the external world, have been afraid of making an ear of wheat beautiful, lest it should not have been good to eat.

But indeed there seems no chance of art becoming universal, unless on the terms that it shall have little self-consciousness, and for the most part be done with little effort; so that the rough work of the world would be as little hindered by it, as the work of external nature is by the beauty of all her forms and moods: this was the case in the times that I have been speaking of: of art which was made by conscious effort, the result of the individual striving towards perfect expression of their thoughts by men very specially gifted, there was perhaps no more than there is now, except in very wonderful and short periods; though I believe that even for such men the struggle to produce beauty was not so bitter as it now is. But if there were not more great thinkers than there are now, there was a countless multitude of happy workers whose work did express, and could not choose but express, some original thought, and was consequently both interesting and beautiful: now there is certainly no chance of the more individual art becoming common, and either wearying us by its over-abundance, or by noisy self-assertion preventing highly cultivated men taking their due part in the other work of the world; it is too difficult to do: it will be always but the blossom of all the half-conscious work below it, the fulfilment of the shortcomings of less complete minds: but it will waste much of its power, and have much less influence on men's minds, unless it be surrounded by abundance of that commoner work, in which all men once shared, and which, I say, will, when art has really awakened, be done so easily and constantly, that it will stand in no man's way to hinder him from doing what he will, good or evil. And as, on the one hand, I believe that art made by the people and for the people as a joy both to the maker and the user would further progress in other matters rather than hinder it, so also I firmly believe that that higher art produced only by great brains and miraculously gifted hands cannot exist without it: I believe that the present state of things in which it does exist, while popular art is, let us say, asleep or sick, is a transitional state, which must end at last either in utter defeat or utter victory for the arts.

For whereas all works of craftsmanship were once beautiful, unwittingly or not, they are now divided into two kinds, works of art and non-works of art: now nothing made by man's hand can be indifferent: it must be either beautiful and elevating, or ugly and degrading; and those things that are without art are so aggressively; they wound it by their existence, and they are now so much in the majority that the works of art we are obliged to set ourselves to seek for, whereas the other things are the ordinary companions of our everyday life; so that if those who cultivate art intellectually were inclined never so much to wrap themselves in their special gifts and their high cultivation, and so live happily, apart from other men, and despising them, they could not do so: they are as it were living in an enemy's country; at every turn there is something lying in wait to offend and vex their nicer sense and educated eyes: they must share in the general discomfort—and I am glad of it.

So the matter stands: from the first dawn of history till quite modern times, art, which nature meant to solace all, fulfilled its purpose; all men shared in it; that was what made life romantic, as people call it, in those days; that and not robber-barons and inaccessible kings with their hierarchy of serving-nobles and other such rubbish: but art grew and grew, saw empires sicken and sickened with them; grew hale again, and haler, and grew so great at last, that she seemed in good truth to have conquered everything, and laid the material world under foot. Then came a change at a period of the greatest life and hope in many ways that Europe had known till then: a time of so much and such varied hope that people call it the time of the New Birth: as far as the arts are concerned I deny it that title; rather it seems to me that the great men who lived and glorified the practice of art in those days, were the fruit of the old, not the seed of the new order of things: but a stirring and hopeful time it was, and many things were newborn then which have since brought forth fruit enough: and it is strange and perplexing that from those days forward the lapse of time, which, through plenteous confusion and failure, has on the whole been steadily destroying privilege and exclusiveness in other matters, has delivered up art to be the exclusive privilege of a few, and has taken from the people their birthright; while both wronged and wrongers have been wholly unconscious of what they were doing.

Wholly unconscious—yes, but we are no longer so: there lies the sting of it, and there also the hope.

When the brightness of the so-called Renaissance faded, and it faded very suddenly, a deadly chill fell upon the arts: that New-birth mostly meant looking back to past times, wherein the men of those days thought they saw a perfection of art, which to their minds was different in kind, and not in degree only, from the ruder suggestive art of their own fathers: this perfection they were ambitious to imitate, this alone seemed to be art to them, the rest was childishness: so wonderful was their energy, their success so great, that no doubt to commonplace minds among them, though surely not to the great masters, that perfection seemed to be gained: and, perfection being gained, what are you to do?—you can go no further, you must aim at standing still—which you cannot do.

Art by no means stood still in those latter days of the Renaissance, but took the downward road with terrible swiftness, and tumbled down at the bottom of the hill, where as if bewitched it lay long in great content, believing itself to be the art of Michael Angelo, while it was the art of men whom nobody remembers but those who want to sell their pictures.

Thus it fared with the more individual forms of art. As to the art of the people; in countries and places where the greater art had flourished most, it went step by step on the downward path with that: in more out-of-the-way places,

England for instance, it still felt the influence of the life of its earlier and happy days, and in a way lived on a while; but its life was so feeble, and, so to say, illogical, that it could not resist any change in external circumstances, still less could it give birth to anything new; and before this century began, its last flicker had died out. Still, while it was living, in whatever dotage, it did imply something going on in those matters of daily use that we have been thinking of, and doubtless satisfied some cravings for beauty: and when it was dead, for a long time people did not know it, or what had taken its place, crept so to say into its dead body—that pretence of art, to wit, which is done with machines, though sometimes the machines are called men, and doubtless are so out of working hours: nevertheless long before it was quite dead it had fallen so low that the whole subject was usually treated with the utmost contempt by every one who had any pretence of being a sensible man, and in short the whole civilised world had forgotten that there had ever been an art *made by the people for the people as a joy for the maker and the user.*

But now it seems to me that the very suddenness of the change ought to comfort us, to make us look upon this break in the continuity of the golden chain as an accident only, that itself cannot last: for think how many thousand years it may be since that primeval man graved with a flint splinter on a bone the story of the mammoth he had seen, or told us of the slow uplifting of the heavily-horned heads of the reindeer that he stalked: think I say of the space of time from then till the dimming of the brightness of the Italian Renaissance! whereas from that time till popular art died unnoticed and despised among ourselves is just but two hundred years.

Strange too, that very death is contemporaneous with new-birth of something at all events; for out of all despair sprang a new time of hope lighted by the torch of the French Revolution: and things that have languished with the languishing of art, rose afresh and surely heralded its new birth: in good earnest poetry was born again, and the English Language, which under the hands of sycophantic verse-makers had been reduced to a miserable jargon, whose meaning, if it have a meaning, cannot be made out without translation, flowed clear, pure, and simple, along with the music of Blake and Coleridge: take those names, the earliest in date among ourselves, as a type of the change that has happened in literature since the time of George II.

With that literature in which romance, that is to say humanity, was re-born, there sprang up also a feeling for the romance of external nature, which is surely strong in us now, joined with a longing to know something real of the lives of those who have gone before us; of these feelings united you will find the broadest expression in the pages of Walter Scott: it is curious as showing how sometimes one art will lag behind another in a revival, that the man who wrote the exquisite and wholly unfettered naturalism of the Heart of Midlothian, for instance, thought himself continually bound to seem to feel ashamed of, and to excuse himself for, his love of Gothic Architecture: he felt that it was romantic, and he knew that it gave him pleasure, but somehow he had not found out that it was art, having been taught in many ways that nothing could be art that was not done by a named man under academical rules.

I need not perhaps dwell much on what of change has been since: you know well that one of the master-arts, the art of painting, has been revolutionised. I have a genuine difficulty in speaking to you of men who are my own personal friends, nay my masters: still, since I cannot quite say nothing of them I must say the plain truth, which is this; never in the whole history of art did any set of men come nearer to the feat of making something out of nothing than that little knot of painters who have raised English art from what it was, when as a boy I used to go to the Royal Academy Exhibition, to what it is now.

It would be ungracious indeed for me who have been so much taught by him, that I cannot help feeling continually as I speak that I am echoing his words, to leave out the name of John Ruskin from an account of what has happened since the tide, as we hope, began to turn in the direction of art. True it is, that his unequalled style of English and his wonderful eloquence would, whatever its subject-matter, have gained him some sort of a hearing in a time that has not lost its relish for literature; but surely the influence that he has exercised over cultivated people must be the result of that style and that eloquence expressing what was already stirring in men's minds; he could not have written what he has done unless people were in some sort ready for it; any more than those painters could have begun their crusade against the dulness and incompetency that was the rule in their art thirty years ago unless they had some hope that they would one day move people to understand them.

Well, we find that the gains since the turning-point of the tide are these: that there are some few artists who have, as it were, caught up the golden chain dropped two hundred years ago, and that there are a few highly cultivated people who can understand them; and that beyond these there is a vague feeling abroad among people of the same degree, of discontent at the ignoble ugliness that surrounds them.

That seems to me to mark the advance that we have made since the last of popular art came to an end amongst us, and I do not say, considering where we then were, that it is not a great advance, for it comes to this, that though the battle is still to win, there are those who are ready for the battle.

Indeed it would be a strange shame for this age if it were not so: for as every age of the world has its own troubles to confuse it, and its own follies to cumber it, so has each its own work to do, pointed out to it by unfailing signs of the times; and it is unmanly and stupid for the children of any age to say: We will not set our hands to the work; we did not make the troubles, we will not weary ourselves seeking a remedy for them: so heaping up for their sons a heavier load than they can lift without such struggles as will wound and cripple them sorely. Not thus our fathers served us, who, working late and early, left us at last that seething mass of people so terribly alive and energetic, that we call modern Europe; not thus those served us, who have made for us these present days, so fruitful of change and wondering expectation.

The century that is now beginning to draw to an end, if people were to take to nicknaming centuries, would be called the Century of Commerce; and I do not think I undervalue the work that it has done: it has broken down many a prejudice and taught many a lesson that the world has been hitherto slow to learn: it has made it possible for many a man to live free, who would in other times have been a slave, body or soul, or both: if it has not quite spread peace and justice through the world, as at the end of its first half we fondly hoped it would, it has at least stirred up in many fresh cravings for peace and justice: its work has been good and plenteous, but much of it was roughly done, as needs was; recklessness has commonly gone with its energy, blindness too often with its haste: so that perhaps it may be work enough for the next century to repair the blunders of that recklessness, to clear away the rubbish which that hurried work has piled up; nay even we in the second half of its last quarter may do something towards setting its house in order.

You, of this great and famous town, for instance, which has had so much to do with the Century of Commerce, your gains are obvious to all men, but the price you have paid for them is obvious to many—surely to yourselves most of all: I do not say that they are not worth the price; I know that England and the world could very ill afford to exchange the Birmingham of to-day for the Birmingham of the year 1700: but surely if what you have gained be more than a mockery, you cannot stop at those gains, or even go on always piling up similar ones. Nothing can make me believe that the present condition of your Black Country yonder is an unchangeable necessity of your life and position: such miseries as this were begun and carried on in pure thoughtlessness, and a hundredth part of the energy that was spent in creating them would get rid of them: I do think if we were not all of us too prone to acquiesce in the base byword 'after me the deluge,' it would soon be something more than an idle dream to hope that your pleasant midland hills and fields might begin to become pleasant again in some way or other, even without depopulating them; or that those once lovely valleys of Yorkshire in the 'heavy woollen district,' with their sweeping hill-sides and noble rivers, should not need the stroke of ruin to make them once more delightful abodes of men, instead of the dog-holes that the Century of Commerce has made them.

Well, people will not take the trouble or spend the money necessary to beginning this sort of reforms, because they do not feel the evils they live amongst, because they have degraded themselves into something less than men; they are unmanly because they have ceased to have their due share of art.

For again I say that therein rich people have defrauded themselves as well as the poor: you will see a refined and highly educated man nowadays, who has been to Italy and Egypt, and where not, who can talk learnedly enough (and fantastically enough sometimes) about art, and who has at his fingers' ends abundant lore concerning the art and literature of past days, sitting down without signs of discomfort in a house, that with all its surroundings is just brutally vulgar and hideous: all his education has not done more for him than that.

The truth is, that in art, and in other things besides, the laboured education of a few will not raise even those few above the reach of the evils that beset the ignorance of the great mass of the population: the brutality of which such a huge stock has been accumulated lower down, will often show without much peeling through the selfish refinement of those who have let it accumulate. The lack of art, or rather the murder of art, that curses our streets from the sordidness of the surroundings of the lower classes, has its exact counterpart in the dulness and vulgarity of those of the middle classes, and the double-distilled dulness, and scarcely less vulgarity of those of the upper classes.

I say this is as it should be; it is just and fair as far as it goes; and moreover the rich with their leisure are the more like to move if they feel the pinch themselves.

But how shall they and we, and all of us, move? What is the remedy?

What remedy can there be for the blunders of civilisation but further civilisation? You do not by any accident think that we have gone as far in that direction as it is possible to go, do you?—even in England, I mean?

When some changes have come to pass, that perhaps will be speedier than most people think, doubtless education will both grow in quality and in quantity; so that it may be, that as the nineteenth century is to be called the Century of Commerce, the twentieth may be called the Century of Education. But that education does not end when people leave school is now a mere commonplace; and how then can you really educate men who lead the life of machines, who only think for the few hours during which they are not at work, who in short spend almost their whole lives in doing work which is not proper for developing them body and mind in some worthy way? You cannot educate, you cannot civilise men, unless you can give them a share in art.

Yes, and it is hard indeed as things go to give most men that share; for they do not miss it, or ask for it, and it is impossible as things are that they should either miss or ask for it. Nevertheless everything has a beginning, and many great things have had very small ones; and since, as I have said, these ideas are already abroad in more than one form, we must not be too much discouraged at the seemingly boundless weight we have to lift.

After all, we are only bound to play our own parts, and do our own share of the lifting, and as in no case that share can be great, so also in all cases it is called for, it is necessary. Therefore let us work and faint not; remembering that though it be natural, and therefore excusable, amidst doubtful times to feel doubts of success oppress us at whiles, yet not to crush those doubts, and work as if we had them not, is simple cowardice, which is unforgivable. No man has any right to say that all has been done for nothing, that all the faithful unwearying strife of those that have gone before us shall lead us nowhither; that mankind will but go round and round in a circle for ever: no man has a right to say that, and then get up morning after morning to eat his victuals and sleep a-nights, all the while making other people toil to keep his worthless life a-going.

Be sure that some way or other will be found out of the tangle, even when things seem most tangled, and be no less sure that some use will then have come of our work, if it has been faithful, and therefore unsparingly careful and thoughtful.

So once more I say, if in any matters civilisation has gone astray, the remedy lies not in standing still, but in more complete civilisation.

Now whatever discussion there may be about that often used and often misused word, I believe all who hear me will agree with me in believing from their hearts, and not merely in saying in conventional phrase, that the civilisation which does not carry the whole people with it, is doomed to fall, and give place to one which at least aims at doing so.

We talk of the civilisation of the ancient peoples, of the classical times, well, civilised they were no doubt, some of their folk at least: an Athenian citizen for instance led a simple, dignified, almost perfect life; but there were drawbacks to happiness perhaps in the lives of his slaves: and the civilisation of the ancients was founded on slavery.

Indeed that ancient society did give a model to the world, and showed us for ever what blessings are freedom of life and thought, self-restraint and a generous education: all those blessings the ancient free peoples set forth to the world—and kept them to themselves.

Therefore no tyrant was too base, no pretext too hollow, for enslaving the grandsons of the men of Salamis and Thermopylæ: therefore did the descendants of those stern and self-restrained Romans, who were ready to give up everything, and life as the least of things, to the glory of their commonweal, produce monsters of license and reckless folly. Therefore did a little knot of Galilean peasants overthrow the Roman Empire.

Ancient civilisation was chained to slavery and exclusiveness, and it fell; the barbarism that took its place has delivered us from slavery and grown into modern civilisation; and that in its turn has before it the choice of never-ceasing growth, or destruction by that which has in it the seeds of higher growth.

There is an ugly word for a dreadful fact, which I must make bold to use—the residuum: that word since the time I first saw it used, has had a terrible significance to me, and I have felt from my heart that if this residuum were a necessary part of modern civilisation, as some people openly, and many more tacitly, assume that it is, then this civilisation carries with it the poison that shall one day destroy it, even as its elder sister did: if civilisation is to go no further than this, it had better not have gone so far: if it does not aim at getting rid of this misery and giving some share in the happiness and dignity of life to *all* the people that it has created, and which it spends such unwearying energy in creating, it is simply an organised injustice, a mere instrument for oppression, so much the worse than that which has gone before it, as its pretensions are higher, its slavery subtler, its mastery harder to overthrow, because supported by such a dense mass of commonplace well-being and comfort.

Surely this cannot be: surely there is a distinct feeling abroad of this injustice: so that if the residuum still clogs all the efforts of modern civilisation to rise above mere population-breeding and money-making, the difficulty of dealing with it is the legacy, first of the ages of violence and almost conscious brutal injustice, and next of the ages of thoughtlessness, of hurry and blindness; surely all those who think at all of the future of the world are at work in one way or other in striving to rid it of this shame.

That to my mind is the meaning of what we call National Education, which we have begun, and which is doubtless already bearing its fruits, and will bear greater, when all people are educated, not according to the money which they or their parents possess, but according to the capacity of their minds.

What effect that will have upon the future of the arts, I cannot say, but one would surely think a very great effect; for it will enable people to see clearly many things which are now as completely hidden from them as if they were blind in body and idiotic in mind: and this, I say, will act not only upon those who most directly feel the evils of ignorance, but also upon those who feel them indirectly, —upon us, the educated: the great wave of rising intelligence, rife with so many natural desires and aspirations, will carry all classes along with it, and force us all to see that many things which we have been used to look upon as necessary and eternal evils are merely the accidental and temporary growths of past stupidity, and can be escaped from by due effort, and the exercise of courage, goodwill, and forethought.

And among those evils, I do, and must always, believe will fall that one which last year I told you that I accounted the greatest of all evils, the heaviest of all slaveries; that evil of the greater part of the population being engaged for by far the most part of their lives in work, which at the best cannot interest them, or develop their best faculties, and at the worst (and that is the commonest, too) is mere unmitigated slavish toil, only to be wrung out of them by the sternest compulsion, a toil which they shirk all they can—small blame to them. And this toil degrades them into less than men: and they will some day come to know it, and cry out to be made men again, and art only can do it, and redeem them from this slavery; and I say once more that this is her highest and most glorious end and aim; and it is in her struggle to attain to it that she will most surely purify herself, and quicken her own aspirations towards perfection.

But we—in the meantime we must not sit waiting for obvious signs of these later and glorious days to show themselves on earth, and in the heavens, but rather turn to the commonplace, and maybe often dull work of fitting ourselves in detail to take part in them if we should live to see one of them; or in doing our best to make the path smooth for their coming, if we are to die before they are here.

What, therefore, can we do, to guard traditions of time past that we may not one day have to begin anew from the beginning with none to teach us? What are we to do, that we may take heed to, and spread the decencies of life, so that at the least we may have a field where it will be possible for art to grow when men begin to long for it: what finally can we do, each of us, to cherish some germ of art, so that it may meet with others, and spread and grow little by little into the thing that we need?

Now I cannot pretend to think that the first of these duties is a matter of indifference to you, after my experience of the enthusiastic meeting that I had the honour of addressing here last autumn on the subject of the (so called) restoration of St. Mark's at Venice; you thought, and most justly thought, it seems to me, that the subject was of such moment to art in general, that it was a simple and obvious thing for men who were anxious on the matter to address themselves to those who had the decision of it in their hands; even though the former were called Englishmen, and the latter Italians; for you felt that the name of lovers of art would cover those differences: if you had any misgivings, you remembered that there was but one such building in the world, and that it was worth while risking a breach of etiquette, if any words of ours could do anything towards saving it; well, the Italians were, some of them, very naturally, though surely unreasonably, irritated, for a time, and in some of their prints they bade us look at home; that was no argument in favour of the wisdom of wantonly rebuilding St. Mark's façade: but certainly those of us who have not yet looked at home in this matter had better do so speedily, late and over late though it be: for though we have no golden-pictured interiors like St. Mark's Church at home, we still have many buildings which are both works of ancient art and monuments of history: and just think what is happening to them, and note, since we profess to recognise their value, how helpless art is in the Century of Commerce!

In the first place, many and many a beautiful and ancient building is being destroyed all over civilised Europe as well as in England, because it is supposed to interfere with the convenience of the citizens, while a little forethought might save it without trenching on that convenience;[3] but even apart from that, I say that if we are not prepared to put up with a little inconvenience in our lifetimes for the sake of preserving a monument of art which will elevate and educate, not only ourselves, but our sons, and our sons' sons, it is vain and idle of us to talk about art—or education either. Brutality must be bred of such brutality.

The same thing may be said about enlarging, or otherwise altering for convenience' sake, old buildings still in use for something like their original purposes: in almost all such cases it is really nothing more than a question of a little money for a new site: and then a new building can be built exactly fitted for the uses it is needed for, with such art about it as our own days can furnish; while the old monument is left to tell its tale of change and progress, to hold out example and warning to us in the practice of the arts: and thus the convenience of the public, the progress of modern art, and the cause of education, are all furthered at once at the cost of a little money.

Surely if it be worth while troubling ourselves about the works of art of to-day, of which any amount almost can be done, since we are yet alive, it is worth while spending a little care, forethought, and money in preserving the art of bygone ages, of which (woe worth the while!) so little is left, and of which we can never have any more, whatever good-hap the world may attain to.

No man who consents to the destruction or the mutilation of an ancient building has any right to pretend that he cares about art; or has any excuse to plead in defence of his crime against civilisation and progress, save sheer brutal ignorance.

But before I leave this subject I must say a word or two about the curious invention of our own days called Restoration, a method of dealing with works of bygone days which, though not so degrading in its spirit as downright destruction, is nevertheless little better in its results on the condition of those works of art; it is obvious that I have no time to argue the question out to-night, so I will only make these assertions:

That ancient buildings, being both works of art and monuments of history, must obviously be treated with great care and delicacy: that the imitative art of to-day is not, and cannot be the same thing as ancient art, and cannot replace it; and that therefore if we superimpose this work on the old, we destroy it both as art and as a record of history: lastly, that the natural weathering of the surface of a building is beautiful, and its loss disastrous.

Now the restorers hold the exact contrary of all this: they think that any clever architect to-day can deal off-hand successfully with the ancient work; that while all things else have changed about us since (say) the thirteenth century, art has not changed, and that our workmen can turn out work identical with that of the thirteenth century; and, lastly, that the weather-beaten surface of an ancient building is worthless, and to be got rid of wherever possible.

You see the question is difficult to argue, because there seem to be no common grounds between the restorers and the anti-restorers: I appeal therefore to the public, and bid them note, that though our opinions may be wrong, the action we advise is not rash: let the question be shelved awhile: if, as we are always pressing on people, due care be taken of these monuments, so that they shall not fall into disrepair, they will be always there to 'restore' whenever people think proper and when we are proved wrong; but if it should turn out that we are right, how can the 'restored' buildings be restored? I beg of you therefore to let the question be shelved, till art has so advanced among us, that we can deal authoritatively with it, till there is no longer any doubt about the matter.

Surely these monuments of our art and history, which, whatever the lawyers may say, belong not to a coterie, or to a rich man here and there, but to the nation at large, are worth this delay: surely the last relics of the life of the 'famous men and our fathers that begat us' may justly claim of us the exercise of a little patience.

It will give us trouble no doubt, all this care of our possessions: but there is more trouble to come; for I must now speak of something else, of possessions which should be common to all of us, of the green grass, and the leaves, and the waters, of the very light and air of heaven, which the Century of Commerce has been too busy to pay any heed to. And first let me remind you that I am supposing every one here present professes to care about art.

Well, there are some rich men among us whom we oddly enough call manufacturers, by which we mean capitalists who pay other men to organise manufacturers; these gentlemen, many of whom buy pictures and profess to care about art, burn a deal of coal: there is an Act in existence which was passed to prevent them sometimes and in some places from pouring a dense cloud of smoke over the world, and, to my thinking, a very lame and partial Act it is: but nothing hinders these lovers of art from being a law to themselves, and making it a point of honour with them to minimise the smoke nuisance as far as their own works are concerned; and if they don't do so, when mere money, and even a very little of that, is what it will cost them, I say that their love of art is a mere pretence: how can you care about the image of a landscape when you show by your deeds that you don't care for the landscape itself? or what right have you to shut yourself up with beautiful form and colour when you make it impossible for other people to have any share in these things?

Well, and as to the smoke Act itself: I don't know what heed you pay to it in Birmingham,[4] but I have seen myself what heed is paid to it in other places; Bradford for instance: though close by them at Saltaire they have an example which I should have thought might have shamed them; for the huge chimney there which serves the acres of weaving and spinning sheds of Sir Titus Salt and his brothers is as guiltless of smoke as an ordinary kitchen chimney. Or Manchester: a gentleman of that city told me that the smoke Act was a mere dead letter there: well, they buy pictures in Manchester and profess to wish to further the arts: but you see it must be idle pretence as far as their rich people are concerned: they only want to talk about it, and have themselves talked of.

I don't know what you are doing about this matter here; but you must forgive my saying, that unless you are beginning to think of some way of dealing with it, you are not beginning yet to pave your way to success in the arts.

Well, I have spoken of a huge nuisance, which is a type of the worst nuisances of what an ill-tempered man might be excused for calling the Century of

Nuisances, rather than the Century of Commerce. I will now leave it to the consciences of the rich and influential among us, and speak of a minor nuisance which it is in the power of every one of us to abate, and which, small as it is, is so vexatious, that if I can prevail on a score of you to take heed to it by what I am saying, I shall think my evening's work a good one. Sandwich-papers I mean—of course you laugh: but come now, don't you, civilised as you are in Birmingham, leave them all about the Lickey hills and your public gardens and the like? If you don't I really scarcely know with what words to praise you. When we Londoners go to enjoy ourselves at Hampton Court, for instance, we take special good care to let everybody know that we have had something to eat: so that the park just outside the gates (and a beautiful place it is) looks as if it had been snowing dirty paper. I really think you might promise me one and all who are here present to have done with this sluttish habit, which is the type of many another in its way, just as the smoke nuisance is. I mean such things as scrawling one's name on monuments, tearing down tree boughs, and the like.

I suppose 'tis early days in the revival of the arts to express one's disgust at the daily increasing hideousness of the posters with which all our towns are daubed. Still we ought to be disgusted at such horrors, and I think make up our minds never to buy any of the articles so advertised. I can't believe they can be worth much if they need all that shouting to sell them.

Again, I must ask what do you do with the trees on a site that is going to be built over? do you try to save them, to adapt your houses at all to them? do you understand what treasures they are in a town or a suburb? or what a relief they will be to the hideous dog-holes which (forgive me!) you are probably going to build in their places? I ask this anxiously, and with grief in my soul, for in London and its suburbs we always[5] begin by clearing a site till it is as bare as the pavement: I really think that almost anybody would have been shocked, if I could have shown him some of the trees that have been wantonly murdered in the suburb in which I live (Hammersmith to wit), amongst them some of those magnificent cedars, for which we along the river used to be famous once.

But here again see how helpless those are who care about art or nature amidst the hurry of the Century of Commerce.

Pray do not forget, that any one who cuts down a tree wantonly or carelessly, especially in a great town or its suburbs, need make no pretence of caring about art.

What else can we do to help to educate ourselves and others in the path of art, to be on the road to attaining an *Art made by the people and for the people as a joy to the maker and the user?*

Why, having got to understand something of what art was, having got to look upon its ancient monuments as friends that can tell us something of times bygone, and whose faces we do not wish to alter, even though they be worn by time and grief: having got to spend money and trouble upon matters of decency, great and little; having made it clear that we really do care about nature even in the suburbs of a big town—having got so far, we shall begin to think of the houses in which we live.

For I must tell you that unless you are resolved to have good and rational architecture, it is, once again, useless your thinking about art at all.

I have spoken of the popular arts, but they might all be summed up in that one word Architecture; they are all parts of that great whole, and the art of house-building begins it all: if we did not know how to dye or to weave; if we had neither gold, nor silver, nor silk; and no pigments to paint with, but half-a-dozen ochres and umbers, we might yet frame a worthy art that would lead to everything, if we had but timber, stone, and lime, and a few cutting tools to make these common things not only shelter us from wind and weather, but also express the thoughts and aspirations that stir in us.

Architecture would lead us to all the arts, as it did with earlier men: but if we despise it and take no note of how we are housed, the other arts will have a hard time of it indeed.

Now I do not think the greatest of optimists would deny that, taking us one and all, we are at present housed in a perfectly shameful way, and since the greatest part of us have to live in houses already built for us, it must be admitted that it is rather hard to know what to do, beyond waiting till they tumble about our ears.

Only we must not lay the fault upon the builders, as some people seem inclined to do: they are our very humble servants, and will build what we ask for; remember, that rich men are not obliged to live in ugly houses, and yet you see they do; which the builders may be well excused for taking as a sign of what is wanted.

Well, the point is, we must do what we can, and make people understand what we want them to do for us, by letting them see what we do for ourselves.

Hitherto, judging us by that standard, the builders may well say, that we want the pretence of a thing rather than the thing itself; that we want a show of petty luxury if we are unrich, a show of insulting stupidity if we are rich: and they are quite clear that as a rule we want to get something that shall look as if it cost twice as much as it really did.

You cannot have Architecture on those terms: simplicity and solidity are the very first requisites of it: just think if it is not so: How we please ourselves with an old building by thinking of all the generations of men that have passed through it! do we not remember how it has received their joy, and borne their sorrow, and not even their folly has left sourness upon it? it still looks as kind to us as it did to them. And the converse of this we ought to feel when we look at a newly-built house if it were as it should be: we should feel a pleasure in thinking how he who had built it had left a piece of his soul behind him to greet the new-comers one after another long and long after he was gone:—but what sentiment can an ordinary modern house move in us, or what thought—save a hope that we may speedily forget its base ugliness?

But if you ask me how we are to pay for this solidity and extra expense, that seems to me a reasonable question; for you must dismiss at once as a delusion the hope that has been sometimes cherished, that you can have a building which is a work of art, and is therefore above all things properly built, at the same price as a building which only pretends to be this: never forget when people talk about cheap art in general, by the way, that all art costs time, trouble, and thought, and that money is only a counter to represent these things.

However, I must try to answer the question I have supposed put, how are we to pay for decent houses?

It seems to me that, by a great piece of good luck, the way to pay for them is by doing that which alone can produce popular art among us: living a simple life, I mean. Once more I say that the greatest foe to art is luxury, art cannot live in its atmosphere.

When you hear of the luxuries of the ancients, you must remember that they were not like our luxuries, they were rather indulgence in pieces of extravagant folly than what we to-day call luxury; which perhaps you would rather call comfort: well I accept the word, and say that a Greek or Roman of the luxurious time would stare astonished could he be brought back again, and shown the comforts of a well-to-do middle-class house.

But some, I know, think that the attainment of these very comforts is what makes the difference between civilisation and uncivilisation, that they are the essence of civilisation. Is it so indeed? Farewell my hope then!—I had thought that civilisation meant the attainment of peace and order and freedom, of good-will between man and man, of the love of truth and the hatred of injustice, and by consequence the attainment of the good life which these things breed, a life free from craven fear, but full of incident: that was what I thought it meant, not more stuffed chairs and more cushions, and more carpets and gas, and more dainty meat and drink—and therewithal more and sharper differences between class and class.

If that be what it is, I for my part wish I were well out of it, and living in a tent in the Persian desert, or a turf hut on the Iceland hill-side. But however it be, and I think my view is the true view, I tell you that art abhors that side of civilisation, she cannot breathe in the houses that lie under its stuffy slavery.

Believe me, if we want art to begin at home, as it must, we must clear our houses of troublesome superfluities that are for ever in our way: conventional comforts that are no real comforts, and do but make work for servants and doctors: if you want a golden rule that will fit everybody, this is it:

'*Have nothing in your houses that you do not know to be useful or believe to be beautiful.*'

And if we apply that rule strictly, we shall in the first place show the builders and such-like servants of the public what we really want, we shall create a demand for real art, as the phrase goes; and in the second place, we shall surely have more money to pay for decent houses.

Perhaps it will not try your patience too much if I lay before you my idea of the fittings necessary to the sitting-room of a healthy person: a room, I mean, in which he would not have to cook in much, or sleep in generally, or in which he would not have to do any very litter-making manual work.

First a book-case with a great many books in it: next a table that will keep steady when you write or work at it: then several chairs that you can move, and a bench that you can sit or lie upon: next a cupboard with drawers: next, unless either the book-case or the cupboard be very beautiful with painting or carving, you will want pictures or engravings, such as you can afford, only not stop-gaps, but real works of art on the wall; or else the wall itself must be ornamented with some beautiful and restful pattern: we shall also want a vase or two to put flowers in, which latter you must have sometimes, especially if you live in a town. Then there will be the fireplace of course, which in our climate is bound to be the chief object in the room.

That is all we shall want, especially if the floor be good; if it be not, as, by the way, in a modern house it is pretty certain not to be, I admit that a small carpet which can be bundled out of the room in two minutes will be useful, and we must also take care that it is beautiful, or it will annoy us terribly.

Now unless we are musical, and need a piano (in which case, as far as beauty is concerned, we are in a bad way), that is quite all we want: and we can add very little to these necessaries without troubling ourselves, and hindering our work, our thought, and our rest.

If these things were done at the least cost for which they could be done well and solidly, they ought not to cost much; and they are so few, that those that could afford to have them at all, could afford to spend some trouble to get them fitting and beautiful: and all those who care about art ought to take great trouble to do so, and to take care that there be no sham art amongst them, nothing that it has degraded a man to make or sell. And I feel sure, that if all who care about art were to take this pains, it would make a great impression upon the public.

This simplicity you may make as costly as you please or can, on the other hand: you may hang your walls with tapestry instead of whitewash or paper; or you may cover them with mosaic, or have them frescoed by a great painter: all this is not luxury, if it be done for beauty's sake, and not for show: it does not break our golden rule: *Have nothing in your houses which you do not know to be useful or believe to be beautiful.*

All art starts from this simplicity; and the higher the art rises, the greater the simplicity. I have been speaking of the fittings of a dwelling-house—a place in which we eat and drink, and pass familiar hours; but when you come to places which people want to make more specially beautiful because of the solemnity or dignity of their uses, they will be simpler still, and have little in them save the bare walls made as beautiful as may be. St. Mark's at Venice has very little furniture in it, much less than most Roman Catholic churches: its lovely and stately mother St. Sophia of Constantinople had less still, even when it was a Christian church: but we need not go either to Venice or Stamboul to take note of that: go into one of our own mighty Gothic naves (do any of you remember the first time you did so?) and note how the huge free space satisfies and elevates you, even now when window and wall are stripped of ornament: then think of the meaning of simplicity, and absence of encumbering gew-gaws.

Now after all, for us who are learning art, it is not far to seek what is the surest way to further it; that which most breeds art is art; every piece of work that we do which is well done, is so much help to the cause; every piece of pretence and half-heartedness is so much hurt to it. Most of you who take to the practice of art can find out in no very long time whether you have any gifts for it or not: if you have not, throw the thing up, or you will have a wretched time of it yourselves, and will be damaging the cause by laborious pretence: but if you have gifts of any kind, you are happy indeed beyond most men; for your pleasure is always with you, nor can you be intemperate in the enjoyment of it, and as you use it, it does not lessen, but grows: if you are by chance weary of it at night, you get up in the morning eager for it; or if perhaps in the morning it seems folly to you for a while, yet presently, when your hand has been moving a little in its wonted way, fresh hope has sprung up beneath it and you are happy again. While others are getting through the day like plants thrust into the earth, which cannot turn this way or that but as the wind blows them, you know what you want, and your will is on the alert to find it, and you, whatever happens, whether it be joy or grief, are at least alive.

Now when I spoke to you last year, after I had sat down I was half afraid that I had on some points said too much, that I had spoken too bitterly in my eagerness; that a rash word might have discouraged some of you; I was very far from meaning that: what I wanted to do, what I want to do to-night is to put definitely before you a cause for which to strive.

That cause is the Democracy of Art, the ennobling of daily and common work, which will one day put hope and pleasure in the place of fear and pain, as the forces which move men to labour and keep the world a-going.

If I have enlisted any one in that cause, rash as my words may have been, or feeble as they may have been, they have done more good than harm; nor do I believe that any words of mine can discourage any who have joined that cause or are ready to do so: their way is too clear before them for that, and every one of us can help the cause whether he be great or little.

I know indeed that men, wearied by the pettiness of the details of the strife, their patience tried by hope deferred, will at whiles, excusably enough, turn back in their hearts to other days, when if the issues were not clearer, the means of trying them were simpler; when, so stirring were the times, one might even have atoned for many a blunder and backsliding by visibly dying for the cause. To have breasted the Spanish pikes at Leyden, to have drawn sword with Oliver: that may well seem to us at times amidst the tangles of to-day a happy fate: for a man to be able to say, I have lived like a fool, but now I will cast away fooling for an hour, and die like a man—there is something in that certainly: and yet 'tis clear that few men can be so lucky as to die for a cause, without having first of all lived for it. And as this is the most that can be asked from the greatest man that follows a cause, so it is the least that can be taken from the smallest.

So to us who have a Cause at heart, our highest ambition and our simplest duty are one and the same thing: for the most part we shall be too busy doing the work that lies ready to our hands, to let impatience for visibly great progress vex us much; but surely since we are servants of a Cause, hope must be ever with us, and sometimes perhaps it will so quicken our vision that it will outrun the slow lapse of time, and show us the victorious days when millions of those who now sit in darkness will be enlightened by an *Art made by the people and for the people, a joy to the maker and the user.*

4. MAKING THE BEST OF IT: A PAPER READ BEFORE TILE TRADES' GUILD OF LEARNING AND THE BIRMINGHAM SOCIETY OF ARTISTS.

I have to-night to talk to you about certain things which my experience in my own craft has led me to notice, and which have bred in my mind something like a set of rules or maxims, which guide my practice. Every one who has followed a craft for long has such rules in his mind, and cannot help following them himself, and insisting on them practically in dealing with his pupils or workmen if he is in any degree a master; and when these rules, or if you will, impulses, are filling the minds and guiding the hands of many craftsmen at one time, they are busy forming a distinct school, and the art they represent is sure to be at least alive, however rude, timid, or lacking it may be; and the more imperious these rules are, the wider these impulses are spread, the more vigorously alive will be the art they produce; whereas in times when they are felt but lightly and rarely, when one man's maxims seem absurd or trivial to his brother craftsman, art is either sick or slumbering, or so thinly scattered amongst the great mass of men as to influence the general life of the world little or nothing.

For though this kind of rules of a craft may seem to some arbitrary, I think that it is because they are the result of such intricate combinations of circumstances, that only a great philosopher, if even he, could express in words the sources of them, and give us reasons for them all, and we who are craftsmen must be content to prove them in practice, believing that their roots are founded in human nature, even as we know that their first-fruits are to be found in that most wonderful of all histories, the history of the arts.

Will you, therefore, look upon me as a craftsman who shares certain impulses with many others, which impulses forbid him to question the rules they have forced on him? so looking on me you may afford perhaps to be more indulgent to me if I seem to dogmatise over much.

Yet I cannot claim to represent any one craft. The division of labour, which has played so great a part in furthering competitive commerce, till it has become a machine with powers both reproductive and destructive, which few dare to resist, and none can control or foresee the result of, has pressed specially hard on that part of the field of human culture in which I was born to labour. That field of the arts, whose harvest should be the chief part of human joy, hope, and consolation, has been, I say, dealt hardly with by the division of labour, once the servant, and now the master of competitive commerce, itself once the servant, and now the master of civilisation; nay, so searching has been this tyranny, that it has not passed by my own insignificant corner of labour, but as it has thwarted me in many ways, so chiefly perhaps in this, that it has so stood in the way of my getting the help from others which my art forces me to crave, that I have been compelled to learn many crafts, and belike, according to the proverb, forbidden to master any, so that I fear my lecture will seem to you both to run over too many things and not to go deep enough into any.

I cannot help it. That above-mentioned tyranny has turned some of us from being, as we should be, contented craftsmen, into being discontented agitators against it, so that our minds are not at rest, even when we have to talk over work-shop receipts and maxims; indeed I must confess that I should hold my peace on all matters connected with the arts, if I had not a lurking hope to stir up both others and myself to discontent with and rebellion against things as they are, clinging to the further hope that our discontent may be fruitful and our rebellion steadfast, at least to the end of our own lives, since we believe that we are rebels not against the laws of Nature, but the customs of folly.

Nevertheless, since even rebels desire to live, and since even they must sometimes crave for rest and peace—nay, since they must, as it were, make for themselves strongholds from whence to carry on the strife—we ought not to be accused of inconsistency, if to-night we consider how to make the best of it. By what forethought, pains, and patience, can we make endurable those strange dwellings—the basest, the ugliest, and the most inconvenient that men have ever built for themselves, and which our own haste, necessity, and stupidity, compel almost all of us to live in? That is our present question.

In dealing with this subject, I shall perforce be chiefly speaking of those middle-class dwellings of which I know most; but what I have to say will be as applicable to any other kind; for there is no dignity or unity of plan about any modern house, big or little. It has neither centre nor individuality, but is invariably a congeries of rooms tumbled together by chance hap. So that the unit I have to speak of is a room rather than a house.

Now there may be some here who have the good luck to dwell in those noble buildings which our forefathers built, out of their very souls, one may say; such good luck I call about the greatest that can befall a man in these days. But these happy people have little to do with our troubles of to-night, save as sympathetic onlookers. All we have to do with them is to remind them not to forget their duties to those places, which they doubtless love well; not to alter them or torment them to suit any passing whim or convenience, but to deal with them as if their builders, to whom they owe so much, could still be wounded by the griefs and rejoice in the well-doing of their ancient homes. Surely if they do this, they also will neither be forgotten nor unthanked in the time to come.

There may be others here who dwell in houses that can scarcely be called noble—nay, as compared with the last-named kind, may be almost called ignoble—but their builders still had some traditions left them of the times of art. They are built solidly and conscientiously at least, and if they have little or no beauty, yet have a certain common-sense and convenience about them; nor do they fail to represent the manners and feelings of their own time. The earliest of these, built about the reign of Queen Anne, stretch out a hand toward the Gothic times, and are not without picturesqueness, especially when their surroundings are beautiful. The latest built in the latter days of the Georges are certainly quite guiltless of picturesqueness, but are, as above said, solid, and not inconvenient. All these houses, both the so-called Queen Anne ones and the distinctively Georgian, are difficult enough to decorate, especially for those who have any leaning toward romance, because they have still some style left in them which one cannot ignore; at the same time that it is impossible for any one living out of the time in which they were built to sympathise with a style whose characteristics are mere whims, not founded on any principle. Still they are at the worst not aggressively ugly or base, and it is possible to live in them without serious disturbance to our work or thoughts; so that by the force of contrast they have become bright spots in the prevailing darkness of ugliness that has covered all modern life.

But we must not forget that that rebellion which we have met here, I hope, to further, has begun, and to-day shows visible tokens of its life; for of late there have been houses rising up among us here and there which have certainly not been planned either by the common cut-and-dried designers for builders, or by academical imitators of bygone styles. Though they may be called experimental, no one can say that they are not born of thought and principle, as well as of great capacity for design. It is nowise our business to-night to criticise them. I suspect their authors, who have gone through so many difficulties (not of their own breeding) in producing them, know their shortcomings much better than we can do, and are less elated by their successes than we are. At any rate, they are gifts to our country which will always be respected, whether the times better or worsen, and I call upon you to thank their designers most heartily for their forethought, labour, and hope.

Well, I have spoken of three qualifications to that degradation of our dwellings which characterises this period of history only.

First, there are the very few houses which have been left us from the times of art. Except that we may sometimes have the pleasure of seeing these, we most of us have little enough to do with them.

Secondly, there are those houses of the times when, though art was sick and all but dead, men had not quite given it up as a bad job, and at any rate had not learned systematic bad building; and when, moreover, they had what they wanted, and their lives were expressed by their architecture. Of these there are still left a good many all over the country, but they are lessening fast before the irresistible force of competition, and will soon be very rare indeed.

Thirdly, there are a few houses built and mostly inhabited by the ringleaders of the rebellion against sordid ugliness, which we are met here to further tonight. It is clear that as yet these are very few,—or you could never have thought it worth your while to come here to hear the simple words I have to say to you on this subject.

Now, these are the exceptions. The rest is what really amounts to the dwellings of all our people, which are built without any hope of beauty or care for it—without any thought that there can be any pleasure in the look of an ordinary dwelling-house, and also (in consequence of this neglect of manliness) with scarce any heed to real convenience. It will, I hope, one day be hard to believe that such houses were built for a people not lacking in honesty, in independence of life, in elevation of thought, and consideration for others; not a whit of all that do they express, but rather hypocrisy, flunkeyism, and careless selfishness. The fact is, they are no longer part of our lives. We have given it up as a bad job. We are heedless if our houses express nothing of us but the very worst side of our character both national and personal.

This unmanly heedlessness, so injurious to civilisation, so unjust to those that are to follow us, is the very thing we want to shake people out of. We want to make them think about their homes, to take the trouble to turn them into dwellings fit for people free in mind and body—much might come of that I think.

Now, to my mind, the first step towards this end is, to follow the fashion of our nation, so often, so *very* often, called practical, and leaving for a little an ideal scarce conceivable, to try to get people to bethink them of what we can best do with those makeshifts which we cannot get rid of all at once.

I know that those lesser arts, by which alone this can be done, are looked upon by many wise and witty people as not worth the notice of a sensible man; but, since I am addressing a society of artists, I believe I am speaking to people who have got beyond even that stage of wisdom and wit, and that you think all the arts of importance. Yet, indeed, I should think I had but little claim on your attention if I deemed the question involved nothing save the gain of a little more content and a little more pleasure for those who already have abundance of content and pleasure; let me say it, that either I have erred in the aim of my whole life, or that the welfare of these lesser arts involves the question of the content and self-respect of all craftsmen, whether you call them artists or artisans. So I say again, my hope is that those who begin to consider carefully how to make the best of the chambers in which they eat and sleep and study, and hold converse with their friends, will breed in their minds a wholesome and fruitful discontent with the sordidness that even when they have done their best will surround their island of comfort, and that as they try to appease this discontent they will find that there is no way out of it but by insisting that all men's work shall be fit for free men and not for machines: my extravagant hope is that people will some day learn something of art, and so long for more, and will find, as I have, that there is no getting it save by the general acknowledgment of the right of every man to have fit work to do in a beautiful home. Therein lies all that is indestructible of the pleasure of life; no man need ask for more than that, no man should be granted less; and if he falls short of it, it is through waste and injustice that he is kept out of his birthright.

And now I will try what I can do in my hints on this making the best of it, first asking your pardon for this, that I shall have to give a great deal of negative advice, and be always saying 'don't'—that, as you know, being much the lot of those who profess reform.

Before we go inside our house, nay, before we look at its outside, we may consider its garden, chiefly with reference to town gardening; which, indeed, I, in common, I suppose, with most others who have tried it, have found uphill work enough—all the more as in our part of the world few indeed have any mercy upon the one thing necessary for decent life in a town, its trees; till we have come to this, that one trembles at the very sound of an axe as one sits at one's work at home. However, uphill work or not, the town garden must not be neglected if we are to be in earnest in making the best of it.

Now I am bound to say town gardeners generally do rather the reverse of that: our suburban gardeners in London, for instance, oftenest wind about their little bit of gravel walk and grass plot in ridiculous imitation of an ugly big garden of the landscape-gardening style, and then with a strange perversity fill up the spaces with the most formal plants they can get; whereas the merest common sense should have taught them to lay out their morsel of ground in the simplest way, to fence it as orderly as might be, one part from the other (if it be big enough for that) and the whole from the road, and then to fill up the flower-growing space with things that are free and interesting in their growth, leaving nature to do the desired complexity, which she will certainly not fail to do if we do not desert her for the florist, who, I must say, has made it harder work than it should be to get the best of flowers.

It is scarcely a digression to note his way of dealing with flowers, which, moreover, gives us an apt illustration of that change without thought of beauty, change for the sake of change, which has played such a great part in the degradation of art in all times. So I ask you to note the way he has treated the rose, for instance: the rose has been grown double from I don't know when; the double rose was a gain to the world, a new beauty was given us by it, and nothing taken away, since the wild rose grows in every hedge. Yet even then one might be excused for thinking that the wild rose was scarce improved on, for nothing can be more beautiful in general growth or in detail than a wayside bush of it, nor can any scent be as sweet and pure as its scent. Nevertheless the garden rose had a new beauty of abundant form, while its leaves had not lost the wonderfully delicate texture of the wild one. The full colour it had gained, from the blush rose to the damask, was pure and true amidst all its added force, and though its scent had certainly lost some of the sweetness of the eglantine, it was fresh still, as well as so abundantly rich. Well, all that lasted till quite our own day, when the florists fell upon the rose—men who could never have enough—they strove for size and got it, a fine specimen of a florist's rose being about as big as a moderate Savoy cabbage. They tried for strong scent and got it—till a florist's rose has not unseldom a suspicion of the scent of the aforesaid cabbage—not at its best. They tried for strong colour and got it, strong and bad—like a conqueror. But all this while they missed the very essence of the rose's being; they thought there was nothing in it but redundance and luxury; they exaggerated these into coarseness, while they threw away the exquisite subtilty of form, delicacy of texture, and sweetness of colour, which, blent with the richness which the true garden rose shares with many other flowers, yet makes it the queen of them all—the flower of flowers. Indeed, the worst of this is that these sham roses are driving the real ones out of existence. If we do not look to it our descendants will know nothing of the cabbage rose, the loveliest in form of all, or the blush rose with its dark green stems and unequalled colour, or the yellow-centred rose of the East, which carries the richness of scent to the very furthest point it can go without losing freshness: they will know nothing of all these, and I fear they will reproach the poets of past time for having done according to their wont, and exaggerated grossly the beauties of the rose.

Well, as a Londoner perhaps I have said too much of roses, since we can scarcely grow them among suburban smoke, but what I have said of them applies to other flowers, of which I will say this much more. Be very shy of double flowers; choose the old columbine where the clustering doves are unmistakable and distinct, not the double one, where they run into mere tatters. Choose (if you can get it) the old china-aster with the yellow centre, that goes so well with the purple-brown stems and curiously coloured florets, instead of the lumps that look like cut paper, of which we are now so proud. Don't be swindled out of that wonder of beauty, a single snowdrop; there is no gain and plenty of loss in the double one. More loss still in the double sunflower, which is a coarse-coloured and dull plant, whereas the single one, though a late comer to our gardens, is by no means to be despised, since it will grow anywhere, and is both interesting and beautiful, with its sharply chiselled yellow florets relieved by the quaintly patterned sad-coloured centre clogged with honey and beset with bees and butterflies.

So much for over-artificiality in flowers. A word or two about the misplacing of them. Don't have ferns in your garden. The hart's tongue in the clefts of the rock, the queer things that grow within reach of the spray of the waterfall; these are right in their places. Still more the brake on the woodside, whether in late autumn, when its withered haulm helps out the well-remembered woodland scent, or in spring, when it is thrusting its volutes through last year's waste. But all this is nothing to a garden, and is not to be got out of it; and if you try it you will take away from it all possible romance, the romance of a garden.

The same thing may be said about many plants, which are curiosities only, which Nature meant to be grotesque, not beautiful, and which are generally the growth of hot countries, where things sprout over quick and rank. Take note that the strangest of these come from the jungle and the tropical waste, from places where man is not at home, but is an intruder, an enemy. Go to a botanical garden and look at them, and think of those strange places to your heart's content. But don't set them to starve in your smoke-drenched scrap of ground amongst the bricks, for they will be no ornament to it.

As to colour in gardens. Flowers in masses are mighty strong colour, and if not used with a great deal of caution are very destructive to pleasure in gardening. On the whole, I think the best and safest plan is to mix up your flowers, and rather eschew great masses of colour—in combination I mean. But there are some flowers (inventions of men, *i.e.* florists) which are bad colour altogether, and not to be used at all. Scarlet geraniums, for instance, or the yellow calceolaria, which indeed are not uncommonly grown together profusely, in order, I suppose, to show that even flowers can be thoroughly ugly.

Another thing also much too commonly seen is an aberration of the human mind, which otherwise I should have been ashamed to warn you of. It is technically called carpet-gardening. Need I explain it further? I had rather not, for when I think of it even when I am quite alone I blush with shame at the thought.

I am afraid it is specially necessary in these days when making the best of it is a hard job, and when the ordinary iron hurdles are so common and so destructive of any kind of beauty in a garden, to say when you fence anything in a garden use a live hedge, or stones set flatwise (as they do in some parts of the Cotswold country), or timber, or wattle, or, in short, anything but iron.[6]

And now to sum up as to a garden. Large or small, it should look both orderly and rich. It should be well fenced from the outside world. It should by no means imitate either the willfulness or the wildness of Nature, but should look like a thing never to be seen except near a house. It should, in fact, look like a part of the house. It follows from this that no private pleasure-garden should be very big, and a public garden should be divided and made to look like so many flower-closes in a meadow, or a wood, or amidst the pavement.

It will be a key to right thinking about gardens if you consider in what kind of places a garden is most desired. In a very beautiful country, especially if it be mountainous, we can do without it well enough; whereas in a flat and dull country we crave after it, and there it is often the very making of the homestead. While in great towns, gardens, both private and public, are positive necessities if the citizens are to live reasonable and healthy lives in body and mind.

So much for the garden, of which, since I have said that it ought to be part of the house, I hope I have not spoken too much.

Now, as to the outside of our makeshift house, I fear it is too ugly to keep us long. Let what painting you have to do about it be as simple as possible, and be chiefly white or whitish; for when a building is ugly in form it will bear no decoration, and to mark its parts by varying colour will be the way to bring out its ugliness. So I don't advise you to paint your houses blood-red and chocolate with white facings, as seems to be getting the fashion in some parts of London. You should, however, always paint your sash-bars and window-frames white to break up the dreary space of window somewhat. The only other thing I have to say, is to warn you against using at all a hot brownish-red, which some decorators are very fond of. Till some one invents a better name for it, let us call it cockroach colour, and have naught to do with it.

So we have got to the inside of our house, and are in the room we are to live in, call it by what name you will. As to its proportions, it will be great luck indeed in an ordinary modern house if they are tolerable; but let us hope for the best. If it is to be well proportioned, one of its parts, either its height, length, or breadth, ought to exceed the others, or be marked somehow. If it be square or so nearly as to seem so, it should not be high; if it be long and narrow, it might be high without any harm, but yet would be more interesting low; whereas if it be an obvious but moderate oblong on plan, great height will be decidedly good.

As to the parts of a room that we have to think of, they are wall, ceiling, floor, windows and doors, fireplace, and movables. Of these the wall is of so much the most importance to a decorator, and will lead us so far a-field that I will mostly clear off the other parts first, as to the mere arrangement of them, asking you meanwhile to understand that the greater part of what I shall be saying as to the design of the patterns for the wall, I consider more or less applicable to patterns everywhere.

As to the windows then; I fear we must grumble again. In most decent houses, or what are so called, the windows are much too big, and let in a flood of light in a haphazard and ill-considered way, which the indwellers are forced to obscure again by shutters, blinds, curtains, screens, heavy upholsteries, and such other nuisances. The windows, also, are almost always brought too low down, and often so low down as to have their sills on a level with our ankles, sending thereby a raking light across the room that destroys all pleasantness of tone. The windows, moreover, are either big rectangular holes in the wall, or, which is worse, have ill-proportioned round or segmental heads, while the common custom in 'good' houses is either to fill these openings with one huge sheet of plate-glass, or to divide them across the middle with a thin bar. If we insist on glazing them thus, we may make up our minds that we have done the worst we can for our windows, nor can a room look tolerable where it is so treated. You may see how people feel this by their admiration of the tracery of a Gothic window, or the lattice-work of a Cairo house. Our makeshift substitute for those beauties must be the filling of the window with moderate-sized panes of glass (plate-glass if you will) set in solid sash-bars; we shall then at all events feel as if we were indoors on a cold day—as if we had a roof over our heads.

As to the floor: a little time ago it was the universal custom for those who could afford it to cover it all up into its dustiest and crookedest corners with a carpet, good, bad, or indifferent. Now I daresay you have heard from others, whose subject is the health of houses rather than their art (if indeed the two subjects can be considered apart, as they cannot really be), you have heard from teachers like Dr. Richardson what a nasty and unwholesome custom this is, so I will only say that it looks nasty and unwholesome. Happily, however, it is now a custom so much broken into that we may consider it doomed; for in all houses that pretend to any taste of arrangement, the carpet is now a rug, large it may be, but at any rate not looking immovable, and not being a trap for dust in the corners. Still I would go further than this even and get rich people no longer to look upon a carpet as a necessity for a room at all, at least in the summer. This would have two advantages: 1st, It would compel us to have better floors (and less drafty), our present ones being one of the chief disgraces to modern building; and 2ndly, since we should have less carpet to provide, what we did have we could afford to have better. We could have a few real works of art at the same price for which we now have hundreds of yards of makeshift machine-woven goods. In any case it is a great comfort to see the actual floor; and the said floor may be, as you know, made very ornamental by either wood mosaic, or tile and marble mosaic; the latter especially is such an easy art as far as mere technicality goes, and so full of resources, that I think it is a great pity it is not used more. The contrast between its grey tones and the rich positive colour of Eastern carpet-work is so beautiful, that the two together make satisfactory decoration for a room with little addition.

When wood mosaic or parquet-work is used, owing to the necessary simplicity of the forms, I think it best not to vary the colour of the wood. The variation caused by the diverse lie of the grain and so forth, is enough. Most decorators will be willing, I believe, to accept it as an axiom, that when a pattern is made of very simple geometrical forms, strong contrast of colour is to be avoided.

So much for the floor. As for its fellow, the ceiling, that is, I must confess, a sore point with me in my attempts at making the best of it. The simplest and most natural way of decorating a ceiling is to show the underside of the joists and beams duly moulded, and if you will, painted in patterns. How far this is from being possible in our modern makeshift houses, I suppose I need not say. Then there is a natural and beautiful way of ornamenting a ceiling by working the plaster into delicate patterns, such as you see in our Elizabethan and Jacobean houses; which often enough, richly designed and skilfully wrought as they are, are by no means pedantically smooth in finish—nay, may sometimes be called rough as to workmanship. But, unhappily there are few of the lesser arts that have fallen so low as the plasterer's. The cast work one sees perpetually in pretentious rooms is a mere ghastly caricature of ornament, which no one is expected to look at if he can help it. It is simply meant to say, 'This house is built for a rich man.' The very material of it is all wrong, as, indeed, mostly happens with an art that has fallen sick. That richly designed, freely wrought plastering of our old houses was done with a slowly drying tough plaster, that encouraged the hand like modeller's clay, and could not have been done at all with the brittle plaster used in ceilings nowadays, whose excellence is supposed to consist in its smoothness only. To be good, according to our present false standard, it must shine like a sheet of hot-pressed paper, so that, for the present, and without the expenditure of abundant time and trouble, this kind of ceiling decoration is not to be hoped for.

It may be suggested that we should paper our ceilings like our walls, but I can't think that it will do. Theoretically, a paper-hanging is so much distemper colour applied to a surface by being printed on paper instead of being painted on plaster by the hand; but practically, we never forget that it is paper, and a room papered all over would be like a box to live in. Besides, the covering a room all over with cheap recurring patterns in an uninteresting material, is but a poor way out of our difficulty, and one which we should soon tire of.

There remains, then, nothing but to paint our ceilings cautiously and with as much refinement as we can, when we can afford it: though even that simple matter is complicated by the hideousness of the aforesaid plaster ornaments and cornices, which are so very bad that you must ignore them by leaving them unpainted, though even this neglect, while you paint the flat of the ceiling, makes them in a way part of the decoration, and so is apt to beat you out of every scheme of colour conceivable. Still, I see nothing for it but cautious painting, or leaving the blank white space alone, to be forgotten if possible. This painting, of course, assumes that you know better than to use gas in your rooms, which will indeed soon reduce all your decorations to a pretty general average.

So now we come to the walls of our room, the part which chiefly concerns us, since no one will admit the possibility of leaving them quite alone. And the first question is, how shall we space them out horizontally?

If the room be small and not high, or the wall be much broken by pictures and tall pieces of furniture, I would not divide it horizontally. One pattern of paper, or whatever it may be, or one tint may serve us, unless we have in hand an elaborate and architectural scheme of decoration, as in a makeshift house is not like to be the case; but if it be a good-sized room, and the wall be not much broken up, some horizontal division is good, even if the room be not very high.

How are we to divide it then? I need scarcely say not into two equal parts; no one out of the island of Laputa could do that. For the rest, unless again we have a very elaborate scheme of decoration, I think dividing it once, making it into two spaces is enough. Now there are practically two ways of doing that: you may either have a narrow frieze below the cornice, and hang the wall thence to the floor, or you may have a moderate dado, say 4 feet 6 inches high, and hang the wall from the cornice to the top of the dado. Either way is good according to circumstances; the first with the tall hanging and the narrow frieze is fittest if your wall is to be covered with stuffs, tapestry, or panelling, in which case making the frieze a piece of delicate painting is desirable in default of such plaster-work as I have spoken of above; or even if the proportions of the room very much cry out for it, you may, in default of hand-painting, use a strip of printed paper, though this, I must say, is a makeshift of makeshifts. The division into dado, and wall hung from thence to the cornice, is fittest for a wall which is to be covered with painted decoration, or its makeshift, paper-hangings. As to these, I would earnestly dissuade you from using more than one pattern in one room, unless one of them be but a breaking of the surface with a pattern so insignificant as scarce to be noticeable. I have seen a good deal of the practice of putting pattern over pattern in paper-hangings, and it seems to me a very unsatisfactory one, and I am, in short, convinced, as I hinted just now, that cheap recurring patterns in a material which has no play of light in it, and no special beauty of its own, should be employed rather sparingly, or they destroy all refinement of decoration and blunt our enjoyment of whatever beauty may lie in the designs of such things.

Before I leave this subject of the spacing out of the wall for decoration, I should say that in dealing with a very high room it is best to put nothing that attracts the eye above a level of about eight feet from the floor—to let everything above that be mere air and space, as it were. I think you will find that this will tend to take off that look of dreariness that often besets tall rooms.

So much then for the spacing out of our wall. We have now to consider what the covering of it is to be, which subject, before we have done with it, will take us over a great deal of ground and lead us into the consideration of designing for flat spaces in general with work other than picture work.

To clear the way, I have a word or two to say about the treatment of the wood-work in our room. If I could I would have no wood-work in it that needed flat painting, meaning by that word a mere paying it over with four coats of tinted lead-pigment ground in oils or varnish, but unless one can have a noble wood, such as oak, I don't see what else is to be done. I have never seen deal stained transparently with success, and its natural colour is poor, and will not enter into any scheme of decoration, while polishing it makes it worse. In short, it is such a poor material that it must be hidden unless it be used on a big scale as mere timber. Even then, in a church roof or what not, colouring it with distemper will not hurt it, and in a room I should certainly do this to the wood-work of roof and ceiling, while I painted such wood-work as came within touch of hand. As to the colour of this, it should, as a rule, be of the same general tone as the walls, but a shade or two darker in tint. Very dark wood-work makes a room dreary and disagreeable, while unless the decoration be in a very bright key of colour, it does not do to have the wood-work lighter than the walls. For the rest, if you are lucky enough to be able to use oak, and plenty of it, found your decoration on that, leaving it just as it comes from the plane.

Now, as you are not bound to use anything for the decoration of your walls but simple tints, I will here say a few words on the main colours, before I go on to what is more properly decoration, only in speaking of them one can scarce think only of such tints as are fit to colour a wall with, of which, to say truth, there are not many.

Though we may each have our special preferences among the main colours, which we shall do quite right to indulge, it is a sign of disease in an artist to have a prejudice against any particular colour, though such prejudices are common and violent enough among people imperfectly educated in art, or with naturally dull perceptions of it. Still, colours have their ways in decoration, so to say, both positively in themselves, and relatively to each man's way of using them. So I may be excused for setting down some things I seem to have noticed about these ways.

Yellow is not a colour that can be used in masses unless it be much broken or mingled with other colours, and even then it wants some material to help it out, which has great play of light and shade in it. You know people are always calling yellow things golden, even when they are not at all the colour of gold, which, even unalloyed, is not a bright yellow. That shows that delightful yellows are not very positive, and that, as aforesaid, they need gleaming materials to help them. The light bright yellows, like jonquil and primrose, are scarcely usable in art, save in silk, whose gleam takes colour from and adds light to the local tint, just as sunlight does to the yellow blossoms which are so common in Nature. In dead materials, such as distemper colour, a positive yellow can only be used sparingly in combination with other tints.

Red is also a difficult colour to use, unless it be helped by some beauty of material, for, whether it tend toward yellow and be called scarlet, or towards blue and be crimson, there is but little pleasure in it, unless it be deep and full. If the scarlet pass a certain degree of impurity it falls into the hot brown-red, very disagreeable in large masses. If the crimson be much reduced it tends towards a cold colour called in these latter days magenta, impossible for an artist to use either by itself or in combination. The finest tint of red is a central one between crimson and scarlet, and is a very powerful colour indeed, but scarce to be got in a flat tint. A crimson broken by greyish-brown, and tending towards russet, is also a very useful colour, but, like all the finest reds, is rather a dyer's colour than a house-painter's; the world being very rich in soluble reds, which of course are not the most enduring of pigments, though very fast as soluble colours.

Pink, though one of the most beautiful colours in combination, is not easy to use as a flat tint even over moderate spaces; the more orangy shades of it are the most useful, a cold pink being a colour much to be avoided.

As to purple, no one in his senses would think of using it bright in masses. In combination it may be used somewhat bright, if it be warm and tend towards red; but the best and most characteristic shade of purple is nowise bright, but tends towards russet. Egyptian porphyry, especially when contrasted with orange, as in the pavement of St. Mark's at Venice, will represent the colour for you. At the British Museum, and one or two other famous libraries, are still left specimens of this tint, as Byzantine art in its palmy days understood it. These are books written with gold and silver on vellum stained purple, probably with the now lost murex or fish-dye of the ancients, the tint of which dye-stuff Pliny describes minutely and accurately in his 'Natural History.' I need scarcely say that no ordinary flat tint could reproduce this most splendid of colours.

Though green (at all events in England) is the colour widest used by Nature, yet there is not so much bright green used by her as many people seem to think; the most of it being used for a week or two in spring, when the leafage is small, and blended with the greys and other negative colours of the twigs; when 'leaves grow large and long,' as the ballad has it, they also grow grey. I believe it has been noted by Mr. Ruskin, and it certainly seems true, that the pleasure we take in the young spring foliage comes largely from its tenderness of tone rather than its brightness of hue. Anyhow, you may be sure that if we try to outdo Nature's green tints on our walls we shall fail, and make ourselves uncomfortable to boot. We must, in short, be very careful of bright greens, and seldom, if ever, use them at once bright and strong.

On the other hand, do not fall into the trap of a dingy bilious-looking yellow-green, a colour to which I have a special and personal hatred, because (if you will excuse my mentioning personal matters) I have been supposed to have somewhat brought it into vogue. I assure you I am not really responsible for it.

The truth is, that to get a green that is at once pure and neither cold nor rank, and not too bright to live with, is of simple things as difficult as anything a decorator has to do; but it can be done,—and without the help of special material; and when done such a green is so useful, and so restful to the eyes, that in this matter also we are bound to follow Nature and make large use of that work-a-day colour green.

But if green be called a work-a-day colour, surely blue must be called the holiday one, and those who long most for bright colours may please themselves most with it; for if you duly guard against getting it cold if it tend towards red, or rank if it tend towards green, you need not be much afraid of its brightness. Now, as red is above all a dyer's colour, so blue is especially a pigment and an enamel colour; the world is rich in insoluble blues, many of which are practically indestructible.

I have said that there are not many tints fit to colour a wall with: this is my list of them as far as I know; a solid red, not very deep, but rather describable as a full pink, and toned both with yellow and blue, a very fine colour if you can hit it; a light orangy pink, to be used rather sparingly. A pale golden tint, *i.e.*, a yellowish-brown; a very difficult colour to hit. A colour between these two last; call it pale copper colour. All these three you must be careful over, for if you get them muddy or dirty you are lost.

Tints of green from pure and pale to deepish and grey: always remembering that the purer the paler, and the deeper the greyer.

Tints of pure pale blue from a greenish one, the colour of a starling's egg, to a grey ultramarine colour, hard to use because so full of colour, but incomparable when right. In these you must carefully avoid the point at which the green overcomes the blue and turns it rank, or that at which the red overcomes the blue and produces those woeful hues of pale lavender and starch blue which have not seldom been favourites with decorators of elegant drawing-rooms and respectable dining-rooms.

You will understand that I am here speaking of distemper tinting, and in that material these are all the tints I can think of; if you use bolder, deeper or stronger colours I think you will find yourself beaten out of monochrome in order to get your colour harmonious.

One last word as to distemper which is not monochrome, and its makeshift, paper-hanging. I think it is always best not to force the colour, but to be content with getting it either quite light or quite grey in these materials, and in no case very dark, trusting for richness to stuffs, or to painting which allows of gilding being introduced.

I must finish these crude notes about general colour by reminding you that you must be moderate with your colour on the walls of an ordinary dwelling-room; according to the material you are using, you may go along the scale from light and bright to deep and rich, but some soberness of tone is absolutely necessary if you would not weary people till they cry out against all decoration. But I suppose this is a caution which only very young decorators are likely to need. It is the right-hand defection; the left-hand falling away is to get your colour dingy and muddy, a worse fault than the other because less likely to be curable. All right-minded craftsmen who work in colour will strive to make their work as bright as possible, as full of colour as the nature of the work will allow it to be. The meaning they may be bound to express, the nature of its material, or the use it may be put to may limit this fulness; but in whatever key of colour they are working, if they do not succeed in getting the colour pure and clear, they have not learned their craft, and if they do not see their fault when it is present in their work, they are not likely to learn it.

Now, hitherto we have not got further into the matter of decoration than to talk of its arrangement. Before I speak of some general matters connected with our subject, I must say a little on the design of the patterns which will form the chief part of your decoration. The subject is a wide and difficult one, and my time much too short to do it any justice, but here and there, perhaps, a hint may crop up, and I may put it in a way somewhat new.

On the whole, in speaking of these patterns I shall be thinking of those that necessarily recur; designs which have to be carried out by more or less mechanical appliances, such as the printing block or the loom.

Since we have been considering colour lately, we had better take that side first, though I know it will be difficult to separate the consideration of it from that of the other necessary qualifications of design.

The first step away from monochrome is breaking the ground by putting a pattern on it of the same colour, but of a lighter or darker shade, the first being the best and most natural way. I need say but little on this as a matter of colour, though many very important designs are so treated. One thing I have noticed about these damasks, as I should call them; that of the three chief colours, red is the one where the two shades must be the nearest to one another, or you get the effect poor and weak; while in blue you may have a great deal of difference without losing colour, and green holds a middle place between the two.

Next, if you make these two shades different in tint as well as, or instead of, in depth, you have fairly got out of monochrome, and will find plenty of difficulties in getting your two tints to go well together. The putting, for instance, of a light greenish blue on a deep reddish one, turquoise on sapphire, will try all your skill. The Persians practise this feat, but not often without adding a third colour, and so getting into the next stage. In fact, this plan of relieving the pattern by shifting its tint as well as its depth, is chiefly of use in dealing with quite low-toned colours—golden browns or greys, for instance. In dealing with the more forcible ones, you will find it in general necessary to add a third colour at least, and so get into the next stage.

This is the relieving a pattern of more than one colour, but all the colours light, upon a dark ground. This is above all useful in cases where your palette is somewhat limited; say, for instance, in a figured cloth which has to be woven mechanically, and where you have but three or four colours in a line, including the ground.

You will not find this a difficult way of relieving your pattern, if you only are not too ambitious of getting the diverse superimposed colours too forcible on the one hand, so that they fly out from one another, or on the other hand too delicate, so that they run together into confusion. The excellence of this sort of work lies in a clear but soft relief of the form, in colours each beautiful in itself, and harmonious one with the other on ground whose colour is also beautiful, though unobtrusive. Hardness ruins the work, confusion of form caused by timidity of colour annoys the eye, and makes it restless, and lack of colour is felt as destroying the *raison d'être* of it. So you see it taxes the designer heavily enough after all. Nevertheless I still call it the easiest way of complete pattern-designing.

I have spoken of it as the placing of a light pattern on dark ground. I should mention that in the fully developed form of the design I am thinking of there is often an impression given, of there being more than one plane in the pattern. Where the pattern is strictly on one plane, we have not reached the full development of this manner of designing, the full development of colour and form used together, but form predominant.

We are not left without examples of this kind of design at its best. The looms of Corinth, Palermo, and Lucca, in the twelfth, thirteenth, and fourteenth centuries, turned out figured silk cloths, which were so widely sought for, that you may see specimens of their work figured on fifteenth-century screens in East Anglian churches, or the background of pictures by the Van Eycks, while one of the most important collections of the actual goods is preserved in the treasury of the Mary Church at Dantzig; the South Kensington Museum has also a very fine collection of these, which I can't help thinking are not quite as visible to the public as they should be. They are, however, discoverable by the help of Dr. Rock's excellent catalogue published by the department, and I hope will, as the Museum gains space, be more easy to see.

Now to sum up: This method of pattern-designing must be considered the Western and civilised method; that used by craftsmen who were always seeing pictures, and whose minds were full of definite ideas of form. Colour was essential to their work, and they loved it, and understood it, but always subordinated it to form.

There is next the method of relief by placing a dark figure on a light ground. Sometimes this method is but the converse of the last, and is not so useful, because it is capable of less variety and play of colour and tone. Sometimes it must be looked on as a transition from the last-mentioned method to the next of colour laid by colour. Thus used there is something incomplete about it. One finds oneself longing for more colours than one's shuttles or blocks allow one. There is a need felt for the speciality of the next method, where the dividing line is used, and it gradually gets drawn into that method. Which, indeed, is the last I have to speak to you of, and in which colour is laid by colour.

In this method it is necessary that the diverse colours should be separated each by a line of another colour, and that not merely to mark the form, but to complete the colour itself; which outlining, while it serves the purpose of gradation, which in more naturalistic work is got by shading, makes the design quite flat, and takes from it any idea of there being more than one plane in it.

This way of treating pattern design is so much more difficult than the others, as to be almost an art by itself, and to demand a study apart. As the method of relief by laying light upon dark may be called the Western way of treatment and the civilised, so this is the Eastern, and, to a certain extent, the uncivilised.

But it has a wide range, from works where the form is of little importance and only exists to make boundaries for colour, to those in which the form is so studied, so elaborate, and so lovely, that it is hardly true to say that the form is subordinate to the colour; while, on the other hand, so much delight is taken in the colour, it is so inventive and so unerringly harmonious, that it is scarcely possible to think of the form without it—the two interpenetrate.

Such things as these, which, as far as I know, are only found in Persian art at its best, do carry the art of mere pattern-designing to its utmost perfection, and it seems somewhat hard to call such an art uncivilised. But, you see, its whole soul was given up to producing matters of subsidiary art, as people call it; its carpets were of more importance than its pictures; nay, properly speaking, they were its pictures. And it may be that such an art never has a future of change before it, save the change of death, which has now certainly come over that Eastern art; while the more impatient, more aspiring, less sensuous art which belongs to Western civilisation may bear many a change and not die utterly; nay, may feed on its intellect alone for a season, and enduring the martyrdom of a grim time of ugliness, may live on, rebuking at once the narrow-minded pedant of science, and the luxurious tyrant of plutocracy, till change bring back the spring again, and it blossoms once more into pleasure. May it be so.

Meanwhile, we may say for certain that colour for colour's sake only will never take real hold on the art of our civilisation, not even in its subsidiary art. Imitation and affectation may deceive people into thinking that such an instinct is quickening amongst us, but the deception will not last. To have a meaning and to make others feel and understand it, must ever be the aim and end of our Western art.

Before I leave this subject of the colouring of patterns, I must warn you against the abuse of the dotting, hatching, and lining of backgrounds, and other mechanical contrivances for breaking them; such practices are too often the resource to which want of invention is driven, and unless used with great caution they vulgarise a pattern completely. Compare, for instance, those Sicilian and other silk cloths I have mentioned with the brocades (common everywhere) turned out from the looms of Lyons, Venice, and Genoa, at the end of the seventeenth and beginning of the eighteenth centuries. The first perfectly simple in manufacture, trusting wholly to beauty of design, and the play of light on the naturally woven surface, while the latter eke out their gaudy feebleness with spots and ribs and long floats, and all kinds of meaningless tormenting of the web, till there is nothing to be learned from them save a warning.

So much for the colour of pattern-designing. Now, for a space, let us consider some other things that are necessary to it, and which I am driven to call its moral qualities, and which are finally reducible to two—order and meaning.

Without order your work cannot even exist; without meaning, it were better not to exist.

Now order imposes on us certain limitations, which partly spring from the nature of the art itself, and partly from the materials in which we have to work; and it is a sign of mere incompetence in either a school or an individual to refuse to accept such limitations, or even not to accept them joyfully and turn them to special account, much as if a poet should complain of having to write in measure and rhyme.

Now, in our craft the chief of the limitations that spring from the essence of the art is that the decorator's art cannot be imitative even to the limited extent that the picture-painter's art is.

This you have been told hundreds of times, and in theory it is accepted everywhere, so I need not say much about it—chiefly this, that it does not excuse want of observation of nature, or laziness of drawing, as some people seem to think. On the contrary, unless you know plenty about the natural form that you are conventionalising, you will not only find it impossible to give people a satisfactory impression of what is in your own mind about it, but you will also be so hampered by your ignorance, that you will not be able to make your conventionalised form ornamental. It will not fill a space properly, or look crisp and sharp, or fulfil any purpose you may strive to put it to.

It follows from this that your convention must be your own, and not borrowed from other times and peoples; or, at the least, that you must make it your own by thoroughly understanding both the nature and the art you are dealing with. If you do not heed this, I do not know but what you may not as well turn to and draw laborious portraits of natural forms of flower and bird and beast, and stick them on your walls anyhow. It is true you will not get ornament so, but you may learn something for your trouble; whereas, using an obviously true principle as a stalking-horse for laziness of purpose and lack of invention, will but injure art all round, and blind people to the truth of that very principle.

Limitations also, both as to imitation and exuberance, are imposed on us by the office our pattern has to fulfil. A small and often-recurring pattern of a subordinate kind will bear much less naturalism than one in a freer space and more important position, and the more obvious the geometrical structure of a pattern is, the less its parts should tend toward naturalism. This has been well understood from the earliest days of art to the very latest times during which pattern-designing has clung to any wholesome tradition, but is pretty generally unheeded at present.

As to the limitations that arise from the material we may be working in, we must remember that all material offers certain difficulties to be overcome, and certain facilities to be made the most of. Up to a certain point you must be the master of your material, but you must never be so much the master as to turn it surly, so to say. You must not make it your slave, or presently you will be a slave also. You must master it so far as to make it express a meaning, and to serve your aim at beauty. You may go beyond that necessary point for your own pleasure and amusement, and still be in the right way; but if you go on after that merely to make people stare at your dexterity in dealing with a difficult thing, you have forgotten art along with the rights of your material, and you will make not a work of art, but a mere toy; you are no longer an artist, but a juggler. The history of the arts gives us abundant examples and warnings in this matter. First clear steady principle, then playing with the danger, and lastly falling into the snare, mark with the utmost distinctness the times of the health, the decline, and the last sickness of art.

Allow me to give you one example in the noble art of mosaic. The difficulty in it necessary to be overcome was the making of a pure and true flexible line, not over thick, with little bits of glass or marble nearly rectangular. Its glory lay in its durability, the lovely colour to be got in it, the play of light on its faceted and gleaming surface, and the clearness mingled with softness, with which forms were relieved on the lustrous gold which was so freely used in its best days. Moreover, however bright were the colours used, they were toned delightfully by the greyness which the innumerable joints between the tesseræ spread over the whole surface.

Now the difficulty of the art was overcome in its earliest and best days, and no care or pains were spared in making the most of its special qualities, while for long and long no force was put upon the material to make it imitate the qualities of brush-painting, either in power of colour, in delicacy of gradation, or intricacy of treating a subject; and, moreover, easy as it would have been to minimise the jointing of the tesseræ, no attempt was made at it.

But as time went on, men began to tire of the solemn simplicity of the art, and began to aim at making it keep pace with the growing complexity of picture painting, and, though still beautiful, it lost colour without gaining form. From that point (say about 1460), it went on from bad to worse, till at last men were set to work in it merely because it was an intractable material in which to imitate oil-painting, and by this time it was fallen from being a master art, the crowning beauty of the most solemn buildings, to being a mere tax on the craftsmen's patience, and a toy for people who no longer cared for art. And just such a history may be told of every art that deals with special material.

Under this head of order should be included something about the structure of patterns, but time for dealing with such an intricate question obviously fails me; so I will but note that, whereas it has been said that a recurring pattern should be constructed on a geometrical basis, it is clear that it cannot be constructed otherwise; only the structure may be more or less masked, and some designers take a great deal of pains to do so.

I cannot say that I think this always necessary. It may be so when the pattern is on a very small scale, and meant to attract but little attention. But it is sometimes the reverse of desirable in large and important patterns, and, to my mind, all noble patterns should at least *look* large. Some of the finest and pleasantest of these show their geometrical structure clearly enough; and if the lines of them grow strongly and flow gracefully, I think they are decidedly helped by their structure not being elaborately concealed.

At the same time in all patterns which are meant to fill the eye and satisfy the mind, there should be a certain mystery. We should not be able to read the whole thing at once, nor desire to do so, nor be impelled by that desire to go on tracing line after line to find out how the pattern is made, and I think that the obvious presence of a geometrical order, if it be, as it should be, beautiful, tends towards this end, and prevents our feeling restless over a pattern.

That every line in a pattern should have its due growth, and be traceable to its beginning, this, which you have doubtless heard before, is undoubtedly essential to the finest pattern work; equally so is it that no stem should be so far from its parent stock as to look weak or wavering. Mutual support and unceasing progress distinguish real and natural order from its mockery, pedantic tyranny.

Every one who has practised the designing of patterns knows the necessity for covering the ground equably and richly. This is really to a great extent the secret of obtaining the look of satisfying mystery aforesaid, and it is the very test of capacity in a designer.

Finally, no amount of delicacy is too great in drawing the curves of a pattern, no amount of care in getting the leading lines right from the first, can be thrown away, for beauty of detail cannot afterwards cure any shortcoming in this. Remember that a pattern is either right or wrong. It cannot be forgiven for blundering, as a picture may be which has otherwise great qualities in it. It is with a pattern as with a fortress, it is no stronger than its weakest point. A failure for ever recurring torments the eye too much to allow the mind to take any pleasure in suggestion and intention.

As to the second moral quality of design, meaning, I include in that the invention and imagination which forms the soul of this art, as of all others, and which, when submitted to the bonds of order, has a body and a visible existence.

Now you may well think that there is less to be said of this than the other quality; for form may be taught, but the spirit that breathes through it cannot be. So I will content myself with saying this on these qualities, that though a designer may put all manner of strangeness and surprise into his patterns, he must not do so at the expense of beauty. You will never find a case in this kind of work where ugliness and violence are not the result of barrenness, and not of fertility of invention. The fertile man, he of resource, has not to worry himself about invention. He need but think of beauty and simplicity of expression; his work will grow on and on, one thing leading to another, as it fares with a beautiful tree.

Whereas the laborious paste-and-scissors man goes hunting up and down for oddities, sticks one in here and another there, and tries to connect them with commonplace; and when it is all done, the oddities are not more inventive than the commonplace, nor the commonplace more graceful than the oddities.

No pattern should be without some sort of meaning. True it is that that meaning may have come down to us traditionally, and not be our own invention, yet we must at heart understand it, or we can neither receive it, nor hand it down to our successors. It is no longer tradition if it is servilely copied, without change, the token of life. You may be sure that the softest and loveliest of patterns will weary the steadiest admirers of their school as soon as they see that there is no hope of growth in them. For you know all art is compact of effort, of failure and of hope, and we cannot but think that somewhere perfection lies ahead, as we look anxiously for the better thing that is to come from the good.

Furthermore, you must not only mean something in your patterns, but must also be able to make others understand that meaning. They say that the difference between a genius and a madman is that the genius can get one or two people to believe in him, whereas the madman, poor fellow, has himself only for his audience. Now the only way in our craft of design for compelling people to understand you is to follow hard on Nature; for what else can you refer people to, or what else is there which everybody can understand?—everybody that it is worth addressing yourself to, which includes all people who can feel and think.

Now let us end the talk about those qualities of invention and imagination with a word of memory and of thanks to the designers of time past. Surely he who runs may read them abundantly set forth in those lesser arts they practised. Surely it had been pity indeed, if so much of this had been lost as would have been if it had been crushed out by the pride of intellect, that will not stoop to look at beauty, unless its own kings and great men have had a hand in it. Belike the thoughts of the men who wrought this kind of art could not have been expressed in grander ways or more definitely, or, at least, would not have been; therefore I believe I am not thinking only of my own pleasure, but of the pleasure of many people, when I praise the usefulness of the lives of these men, whose names are long forgotten, but whose works we still wonder at. In their own way they meant to tell us how the flowers grew in the gardens of Damascus, or how the hunt was up on the plains of Kirman, or how the tulips shone among the grass in the Mid-Persian valley, and how their souls delighted in it all, and what joy they had in life; nor did they fail to make their meaning clear to some of us.

But, indeed, they and other matters have led us afar from our makeshift house, and the room we have to decorate therein. And there is still left the fireplace to consider.

Now I think there is nothing about a house in which a contrast is greater between old and new than this piece of architecture. The old, either delightful in its comfortable simplicity, or decorated with the noblest and most meaning art in the place; the modern, mean, miserable, uncomfortable, and showy, plastered about with wretched sham ornament, trumpery of cast-iron, and brass and polished steel, and what not—offensive to look at, and a nuisance to clean—and the whole thing huddled up with rubbish of ash-pan, and fender, and rug, till surely the hearths which we have been bidden so often to defend (whether there was a chance of their being attacked or not) have now become a mere figure of speech the meaning of which in a short time it will be impossible for learned philologists to find out.

    I do most seriously advise you to get rid of all this, or as much of it as you can without absolute ruin to your prospects in life; and even if you do not know how to decorate it, at least have a hole in the wall of a convenient shape, faced with such bricks or tiles as will at once bear fire and clean; then some sort of iron basket in it, and out from that a real hearth of cleanable brick or tile, which will not make you blush when you look at it, and as little in the way of guard and fender as you think will be safe; that will do to begin with. For the rest, if you have wooden work about the fireplace, which is often good to have, don't mix up the wood and the tiles together; let the wood-work look like part of the wall-covering, and the tiles like part of the chimney.

    As for movable furniture, even if time did not fail us, 'tis a large subject—or a very small one—so I will but say, don't have too much of it; have none for mere finery's sake, or to satisfy the claims of custom—these are flat truisms, are they not? But really it seems as if some people had never thought of them, for 'tis almost the universal custom to stuff up some rooms so that you can scarcely move in them, and to leave others deadly bare; whereas all rooms ought to look as if they were lived in, and to have, so to say, a friendly welcome ready for the incomer.

    A dining-room ought not to look as if one went into it as one goes into a dentist's parlour—for an operation, and came out of it when the operation was over—the tooth out, or the dinner in. A drawing-room ought to look as if some kind of work could be done in it less toilsome than being bored. A library certainly ought to have books in it, not boots only, as in Thackeray's country snob's house, but so ought each and every room in the house more or less; also, though all rooms should look tidy, and even very tidy, they ought not to look too tidy.

    Furthermore, no room of the richest man should look grand enough to make a simple man shrink in it, or luxurious enough to make a thoughtful man feel ashamed in it; it will not do so if Art be at home there, for she has no foes so deadly as insolence and waste. Indeed, I fear that at present the decoration of rich men's houses is mostly wrought out at the bidding of grandeur and luxury, and that art has been mostly cowed or shamed out of them; nor when I come to think of it will I lament it overmuch. Art was not born in the palace; rather she fell sick there, and it will take more bracing air than that of rich men's houses to heal her again. If she is ever to be strong enough to help mankind once more, she must gather strength in simple places; the refuge from wind and weather to which the goodman comes home from field or hill-side; the well-tidied space into which the craftsman draws from the litter of loom, and smithy, and bench; the scholar's island in the sea of books; the artist's clearing in the canvas-grove; it is from these places that Art must come if she is ever again to be enthroned in that other kind of building, which I think, under some name or other, whether you call it church or hall of reason, or what not, will always be needed; the building in which people meet to forget their own transient personal and family troubles in aspirations for their fellows and the days to come, and which to a certain extent make up to town-dwellers for their loss of field, and river, and mountain.

Well, it seems to me that these two kinds of buildings are all we have really to think of, together with whatsoever outhouses, workshops, and the like may be necessary. Surely the rest may quietly drop to pieces for aught we care—unless it should be thought good in the interest of history to keep one standing in each big town to show posterity what strange, ugly, uncomfortable houses rich men dwelt in once upon a time.

Meantime now, when rich men won't have art, and poor men can't, there is, nevertheless, some unthinking craving for it, some restless feeling in men's minds of something lacking somewhere, which has made many benevolent people seek for the possibility of cheap art.

What do they mean by that? One art for the rich and another for the poor? No, it won't do. Art is not so accommodating as the justice or religion of society, and she won't have it.

What then? there has been cheap art at some times certainly, at the expense of the starvation of the craftsmen. But people can't mean that; and if they did, would, happily, no longer have the same chance of getting it that they once had. Still they think art can be got round some way or other—jockeyed, so to say. I rather think in this fashion: that a highly gifted and carefully educated man shall, like Mr. Pecksniff, squint at a sheet of paper, and that the results of that squint shall set a vast number of well-fed, contented operatives (they are ashamed to call them workmen) turning crank handles for ten hours a-day, bidding them keep what gifts and education they may have been born with for their—I was going to say leisure hours, but I don't know how to, for if I were to work ten hours a-day at work I despised and hated, I should spend my leisure I hope in political agitation, but I fear—in drinking. So let us say that the aforesaid operatives will have to keep their inborn gifts and education for their dreams. Well, from this system are to come threefold blessings—food and clothing, poorish lodgings and a little leisure to the operatives, enormous riches to the capitalists that rent them, together with moderate riches to the squinter on the paper; and lastly, very decidedly lastly, abundance of cheap art for the operatives or crank turners to buy—in their dreams.

Well, there have been many other benevolent and economical schemes for keeping your cake after you have eaten it, for skinning a flint, and boiling a flea down for its tallow and glue, and this one of cheap art may just go its way with the others.

Yet to my mind real art is cheap, even at the price that must be paid for it. That price is, in short, the providing of a handicraftsman who shall put his own individual intelligence and enthusiasm into the goods he fashions. So far from his labour being 'divided,' which is the technical phrase for his always doing one minute piece of work, and never being allowed to think of any other; so far from that, he must know all about the ware he is making and its relation to similar wares; he must have a natural aptitude for his work so strong, that no education can force him away from his special bent. He must be allowed to think of what he is doing, and to vary his work as the circumstances of it vary, and his own moods. He must be for ever striving to make the piece he is at work at better than the last. He must refuse at anybody's bidding to turn out, I won't say a bad, but even an indifferent piece of work, whatever the public want, or think they want. He must have a voice, and a voice worth listening to in the whole affair.

Such a man I should call, not an operative, but a workman. You may call him an artist if you will, for I have been describing the qualities of artists as I know them; but a capitalist will be apt to call him a 'troublesome fellow,' a radical of radicals, and, in fact, he will be troublesome—mere grit and friction in the wheels of the money-grinding machine.

Yes, such a man will stop the machine perhaps; but it is only through him that you can have art, *i.e.* civilisation unmaimed, if you really want it; so consider, if you do want it, and will pay the price and give the workman his due.

What is his due? that is, what can he take from you, and be the man that you want? Money enough to keep him from fear of want or degradation for him and his; leisure enough from bread-earning work (even though it be pleasant to him) to give him time to read and think, and connect his own life with the life of the great world; work enough of the kind aforesaid, and praise of it, and encouragement enough to make him feel good friends with his fellows; and lastly (not least, for 'tis verily part of the bargain), his own due share of art, the chief part of which will be a dwelling that does not lack the beauty which Nature would freely allow it, if our own perversity did not turn Nature out of doors.

That is the bargain to be struck, such work and such wages; and I believe that if the world wants the work and is willing to pay the wages, the workmen will not long be wanting.

On the other hand, if it be certain that the world—that is, modern civilised society—will nevermore ask for such workmen, then I am as sure as that I stand here breathing, that art is dying: that the spark still smouldering is not to be quickened into life, but damped into death. And indeed, often, in my fear of that, I think, 'Would that I could see what is to take the place of art!' For, whether modern civilised society *can* make that bargain aforesaid, who shall say? I know well—who could fail to know it?—that the difficulties are great.

Too apt has the world ever been, 'for the sake of life to cast away the reasons for living,' and perhaps is more and more apt to it as the conditions of life get more intricate, as the race to avoid ruin, which seems always imminent and overwhelming, gets swifter and more terrible. Yet how would it be if we were to lay aside fear and turn in the face of all that, and stand by our claim to have, one and all of us, reasons for living. Mayhap the heavens would not fall on us if we did.

Anyhow, let us make up our minds which we want, art, or the absence of art, and be prepared if we want art, to give up many things, and in many ways to change the conditions of life. Perhaps there are those who will understand me when I say that that necessary change may make life poorer for the rich, rougher for the refined, and, it may be, duller for the gifted—for a while; that it may even take such forms that not the best or wisest of us shall always be able to know it for a friend, but may at whiles fight against it as a foe. Yet, when the day comes that gives us visible token of art rising like the sun from below—when it is no longer a justly despised whim of the rich, or a lazy habit of the so-called educated, but a thing that labour begins to crave as a necessity, even as labour is a necessity for all men—in that day how shall all trouble be forgotten, all folly forgiven—even our own!

Little by little it must come, I know. Patience and prudence must not be lacking to us, but courage still less. Let us be a Gideon's band. 'Whosoever is fearful and afraid, let him return, and depart early from Mount Gilead.' And among that band let there be no delusions; let the last encouraging lie have been told, the last after-dinner humbug spoken, for surely, though the days seem dark, we may remember that men longed for freedom while yet they were slaves; that it was in times when swords were reddened every day that men began to think of peace and order, and to strive to win them.

We who think, and can enjoy the feast that Nature has spread for us, is it not both our right and our duty to rebel against that slavery of the waste of life's joys, which people thoughtless and joyless, by no fault of their own, have wrapped the world in? From our own selves we can tell that there is hope of victory in our rebellion, since we have art enough in our lives, not to content us, but to make us long for more, and that longing drives us into trying to spread art and the longing for art; and as it is with us so it will be with those that we win over: little by little, we may well hope, will do its work, till at last a great many men will have enough of art to see how little they have, and how much they might better their lives, if every man had his due share of art—that is, just so much as he could use if a fair chance were given him.

Is that, indeed, too extravagant a hope? Have you not heard how it has gone with many a cause before now? First few men heed it; next most men contemn it; lastly, all men accept it—and the cause is won.

5. THE PROSPECTS OF ARCHITECTURE IN CIVILISATION: DELIVERED AT THE LONDON INSTITUTION, MARCH 10, 1880.

> '—the horrible doctrine that this universe is a Cockney Nightmare—which no creature ought for a moment to believe or listen to.'
>
> — THOMAS CARLYLE

The word Architecture has, I suppose, to most of you the meaning of the art of building nobly and ornamentally. Now I believe the practice of this art to be one of the most important things which man can turn his hand to, and the consideration of it to be worth the attention of serious people, not for an hour only, but for a good part of their lives, even though they may not have to do with it professionally.

But, noble as that art is by itself, and though it is specially the art of civilisation, it neither ever has existed nor never can exist alive and progressive by itself, but must cherish and be cherished by all the crafts whereby men make the things which they intend shall be beautiful, and shall last somewhat beyond the passing day.

It is this union of the arts, mutually helpful and harmoniously subordinated one to another, which I have learned to think of as Architecture, and when I use the word to-night, that is what I shall mean by it and nothing narrower.

A great subject truly, for it embraces the consideration of the whole external surroundings of the life of man; we cannot escape from it if we would so long as we are part of civilisation, for it means the moulding and altering to human needs of the very face of the earth itself, except in the outermost desert.

Neither can we hand over our interests in it to a little band of learned men, and bid them seek and discover, and fashion, that we may at last stand by and wonder at the work, and learn a little of how 'twas all done: 'tis we ourselves, each one of us, who must keep watch and ward over the fairness of the earth, and each with his own soul and hand do his due share therein, lest we deliver to our sons a lesser treasure than our fathers left to us. Nor, again, is there time enough and to spare that we may leave this matter alone till our latter days or let our sons deal with it: for so busy and eager is mankind, that the desire of to-day makes us utterly forget the desire of yesterday and the gain it brought; and whensoever in any object of pursuit we cease to long for perfection, corruption sure and speedy leads from life to death and all is soon over and forgotten: time enough there may be for many things: for peopling the desert; for breaking down the walls between nation and nation; for learning the innermost secrets of the fashion of our souls and bodies, the air we breathe, and the earth we tread on: time enough for subduing all the forces of nature to our material wants: but no time to spare before we turn our eyes and our longing to the fairness of the earth; lest the wave of human need sweep over it and make it not a hopeful desert as it once was, but a hopeless prison; lest man should find at last that he has toiled and striven, and conquered, and set all things on the earth under his feet, that he might live thereon himself unhappy.

Most true it is that when any spot of earth's surface has been marred by the haste or carelessness of civilisation, it is heavy work to seek a remedy, nay a work scarce conceivable; for the desire to live on any terms which nature has implanted in us, and the terrible swift multiplication of the race which is the result of it, thrusts out of men's minds all thought of other hopes, and bars the way before us as with a wall of iron: no force but a force equal to that which marred can ever mend, or give back those ruined places to hope and civilisation.

Therefore I entreat you to turn your minds to thinking of what is to come of Architecture, that is to say, the fairness of the earth amidst the habitations of men: for the hope and the fear of it will follow us though we try to escape it; it concerns us all, and needs the help of all; and what we do herein must be done at once, since every day of our neglect adds to the heap of troubles a blind force is making for us; till it may come to this if we do not look to it, that we shall one day have to call, not on peace and prosperity, but on violence and ruin to rid us of them.

In making this appeal to you, I will not suppose that I am speaking to any who refuse to admit that we who are part of civilisation are responsible to posterity for what may befall the fairness of the earth in our own days, for what we have done, in other words, towards the progress of Architecture;—if any such exists among cultivated people, I need not trouble myself about them; for they would not listen to me, nor should I know what to say to them.

On the other hand, there may be some here who have a knowledge of their responsibility in this matter, but to whom the duty that it involves seems an easy one, since they are fairly satisfied with the state of Architecture as it now is: I do not suppose that they fail to note the strange contrast which exists between the beauty that still clings to some habitations of men and the ugliness which is the rule in others, but it seems to them natural and inevitable, and therefore does not trouble them: and they fulfil their duties to civilisation and the arts by sometimes going to see the beautiful places, and gathering together a few matters to remind them of these for the adornment of the ugly dwellings in which their homes are enshrined: for the rest they have no doubt that it is natural and not wrong that while all ancient towns, I mean towns whose houses are largely ancient, should be beautiful and romantic, all modern ones should be ugly and commonplace: it does not seem to them that this contrast is of any import to civilisation, or that it expresses anything save that one town *is* ancient as to its buildings and the other modern. If their thoughts carry them into looking any farther into the contrasts between ancient art and modern, they are not dissatisfied with the result: they may see things to reform here and there, but they suppose, or, let me say, take for granted, that art is alive and healthy, is on the right road, and that following that road, it will go on living for ever, much as it is now.

It is not unfair to say that this languid complacency is the general attitude of cultivated people towards the arts: of course if they were ever to think seriously of them, they would be startled into discomfort by the thought that civilisation as it now is brings inevitable ugliness with it: surely if they thought this, they would begin to think that this was not natural and right; they would see that this was not what civilisation aimed at in its struggling days: but they do not think seriously of the arts because they have been hitherto defended by a law of nature which forbids men to see evils which they are not ready to redress.

Hitherto: but there are not wanting signs that that defence may fail them one day, and it has become the duty of all true artists, and all men who love life though it be troublous better than death though it be peaceful, to strive to pierce that defence and sting the world, cultivated and uncultivated, into discontent and struggle.

Therefore I will say that the contrast between past art and present, the universal beauty of men's habitations as they *were* fashioned, and the universal ugliness of them as they *are* fashioned, is of the utmost import to civilisation, and that it expresses much; it expresses no less than a blind brutality which will destroy art at least, whatever else it may leave alive: art is not healthy, it even scarcely lives; it is on the wrong road, and if it follow that road will speedily meet its death on it.

Now perhaps you will say that by asserting that the general attitude of cultivated people towards the arts is a languid complacency with this unhealthy state of things, I am admitting that cultivated people generally do not care about the arts, and that therefore this threatened death of them will not frighten people much, even if the threat be founded on truth: so that those are but beating the air who strive to rouse people into discontent and struggle.

Well, I will run the risk of offending you by speaking plainly, and saying, that to me it seems over true that cultivated people in general do *not* care about the arts: nevertheless I will answer any possible challenge as to the usefulness of trying to rouse them to thought about the matter, by saying that they do not care about the arts because they do not know what they mean, or what they lose in lacking them: cultivated, that is rich, as they are, they are also under that harrow of hard necessity which is driven onward so remorselessly by the competitive commerce of the latter days; a system which is drawing near now I hope to its perfection, and therefore to its death and change: the many millions of civilisation, as labour is now organised, can scarce think seriously of anything but the means of earning their daily bread; they do not know of art, it does not touch their lives at all: the few thousands of cultivated people whom Fate, not always as kind to them as she looks, has placed above the material necessity for this hard struggle, are nevertheless bound by it in spirit: the reflex of the grinding trouble of those who toil to live that they may live to toil weighs upon them also, and forbids them to look upon art as a matter of importance: they know it but as a toy, not as a serious help to life: as they know it, it can no more lift the burden from the conscience of the rich, than it can from the weariness of the poor. They do not know what art means: as I have said, they think that as labour is now organised art can go indefinitely as it is now organised, practised by a few for a few, adding a little interest, a little refinement to the lives of those who have come to look upon intellectual interest and spiritual refinement as their birthright.

No, no, it can never be: believe me, if it were otherwise possible that it should be an enduring condition of humanity that there must be one class utterly refined and another utterly brutal, art would bar the way and forbid the monstrosity to exist:—such refinement would have to do as well as it might without the aid of Art: it may be she will die, but it cannot be that she will live the slave of the rich, and the token of the enduring slavery of the poor. If the life of the world is to be brutalised by her death, the rich must share that brutalisation with the poor.

I know that there are people of good-will now, as there have been in all ages, who have conceived of art as going hand in hand with luxury, nay, as being much the same thing; but it is an idea false from the root up, and most hurtful to art, as I could demonstrate to you by many examples if I had time, lacking which I will only meet it with one, which I hope will be enough.

We are here in the richest city of the richest country of the richest age of the world: no luxury of time past can compare with our luxury; and yet if you could clear your eyes from habitual blindness you would have to confess that there is no crime against art, no ugliness, no vulgarity which is not shared with perfect fairness and equality between the modern hovels of Bethnal Green and the modern palaces of the West End: and then if you looked at the matter deeply and seriously you would not regret it, but rejoice at it, and as you went past some notable example of the aforesaid palaces you would exult indeed as you said, 'So that is all that luxury and money can do for refinement.'

For the rest, if of late there has been any change for the better in the prospects of the arts; if there has been a struggle both to throw off the chains of dead and powerless tradition, and to understand the thoughts and aspirations of those among whom those traditions were once alive powerful and beneficent; if there has been abroad any spirit of resistance to the flood of sordid ugliness that modern civilisation has created to make modern civilisation miserable: in a word, if any of us have had the courage to be discontented that art seems dying, and to hope for her new birth, it is because others have been discontented and hopeful in other matters than the arts; I believe most sincerely that the steady progress of those whom the stupidity of language forces me to call the lower classes in material, political, and social condition, has been our real help in all that we have been able to do or to hope, although both the helpers and the helped have been mostly unconscious of it.

It is indeed in this belief, the belief in the beneficent progress of civilisation, that I venture to face you and to entreat you to strive to enter into the real meaning of the arts, which are surely the expression of reverence for nature, and the crown of nature, the life of man upon the earth.

With this intent in view I may, I think, hope to move you, I do not say to agree to all I urge upon you, yet at least to think the matter worth thinking about; and if you once do that, I believe I shall have won you. Maybe indeed that many things which I think beautiful you will deem of small account; nay, that even some things I think base and ugly will not vex your eyes or your minds: but one thing I know you will none of you like to plead guilty to; blindness to the natural beauty of the earth; and of that beauty art is the only possible guardian.

No one of you can fail to know what neglect of art has done to this great treasure of mankind: the earth which was beautiful before man lived on it, which for many ages grew in beauty as men grew in numbers and power, is now growing uglier day by day, and there the swiftest where civilisation is the mightiest: this is quite certain; no one can deny it: are you contented that it should be so?

Surely there must be few of us to whom this degrading change has not been brought home personally. I think you will most of you understand me but too well when I ask you to remember the pang of dismay that comes on us when we revisit some spot of country which has been specially sympathetic to us in times past; which has refreshed us after toil, or soothed us after trouble; but where now as we turn the corner of the road or crown the hill's brow we can see first the inevitable blue slate roof, and then the blotched mud-coloured stucco, or ill-built wall of ill-made bricks of the new buildings; then as we come nearer and see the arid and pretentious little gardens, and cast-iron horrors of railings, and miseries of squalid out-houses breaking through the sweet meadows and abundant hedgerows of our old quiet hamlet, do not our hearts sink within us, and are we not troubled with a perplexity not altogether selfish, when we think what a little bit of carelessness it takes to destroy a world of pleasure and delight, which now whatever happens can never be recovered?

Well may we feel the perplexity and sickness of heart, which some day the whole world shall feel to find its hopes disappointed, if we do not look to it; for this is not what civilisation looked for: a new house added to the old village, where is the harm of that? Should it not have been a gain and not a loss; a sign of growth and prosperity which should have rejoiced the eye of an old friend? a new family come in health and hope to share the modest pleasures and labours of the place we loved; that should have been no grief, but a fresh pleasure to us.

Yes, and time was that it would have been so; the new house indeed would have taken away a little piece of the flowery green sward, a few yards of the teeming hedge-row; but a new order, a new beauty would have taken the place of the old: the very flowers of the field would have but given place to flowers fashioned by man's hand and mind: the hedge-row oak would have blossomed into fresh beauty in roof-tree and lintel and door-post: and though the new house would have looked young and trim beside the older houses and the ancient church; ancient even in those days; yet it would have a piece of history for the time to come, and its dear and dainty cream-white walls would have been a genuine link among the numberless links of that long chain, whose beginnings we know not of, but on whose mighty length even the many-pillared garth of Pallas, and the stately dome of the Eternal Wisdom, are but single links, wondrous and resplendent though they be.

Such I say can a new house be, such it has been: for 'tis no ideal house I am thinking of: no rare marvel of art, of which but few can ever be vouchsafed to the best times and countries; no palace either, not even a manor-house, but a yeoman's steading at grandest, or even his shepherd's cottage: there they stand at this day, dozens of them yet, in some parts of England: such an one, and of the smallest, is before my eyes as I speak to you, standing by the roadside on one of the western slopes of the Cotswolds: the tops of the great trees near it can see a long way off the mountains of the Welsh border, and between a great county of hill, and waving woodland, and meadow and plain where lies hidden many a famous battlefield of our stout forefathers: there to the right a wavering patch of blue is the smoke of Worcester town, but Evesham smoke, though near, is unseen, so small it is: then a long line of haze just traceable shows where the Avon wends its way thence towards Severn, till Bredon Hill hides the sight both of it and Tewkesbury smoke: just below on either side the Broadway lie the grey houses of the village street ending with a lovely house of the fourteenth century; above the road winds serpentine up the steep hill-side, whose crest looking westward sees the glorious map I have been telling of spread before it, but eastward strains to look on Oxfordshire, and thence all waters run towards Thames: all about lie the sunny slopes, lovely of outline, flowery and sweetly grassed, dotted with the best-grown and most graceful of trees: 'tis a beautiful countryside indeed, not undignified, not unromantic, but most familiar.

And there stands the little house that was new once, a labourer's cottage built of the Cotswold limestone, and grown now, walls and roof, a lovely warm grey, though it was creamy white in its earliest day; no line of it could ever have marred the Cotswold beauty; everything about it is solid and well wrought: it is skilfully planned and well proportioned: there is a little sharp and delicate carving about its arched doorway, and every part of it is well cared for: 'tis in fact beautiful, a work of art and a piece of nature—no less: there is no man who could have done it better considering its use and its place.

Who built it then? No strange race of men, but just the mason of Broadway village: even such a man as is now running up down yonder three or four cottages of the wretched type we know too well: nor did he get an architect from London, or even Worcester, to design it: I believe 'tis but two hundred years old, and at that time, though beauty still lingered among the peasants' houses, your learned architects were building houses for the high gentry that were ugly enough, though solid and well built; nor are its materials far-fetched; from the neighbouring field came its walling stones; and at the top of the hill they are quarrying now as good freestone as ever.

No, there was no effort or wonder about it when it was built, though its beauty makes it strange now.

And are you contented that we should lose all this; this simple, harmless beauty that was no hindrance or trouble to any man, and that added to the natural beauty of the earth instead of marring it?

You cannot be contented with it; all you can do is to try to forget it, and to say that such things are the necessary and inevitable consequences of civilisation. Is it so indeed? The loss of suchlike beauty is an undoubted evil: but civilisation cannot mean at heart to produce evils for mankind: such losses therefore must be accidents of civilisation, produced by its carelessness, not its malice; and we, if we be men and not machines, must try to amend them: or civilisation itself will be undone.

But, now let us leave the sunny slopes of the Cotswolds, and their little grey houses, lest we fall a-dreaming over past time, and let us think about the suburbs of London, neither dull nor unpleasant once, where surely we ought to have some power to do something: let me remind you how it fares with the beauty of the earth when some big house near our dwelling-place, which has passed through many vicissitudes of rich merchant's dwelling, school, hospital, or what not, is at last to be turned into ready money, and is sold to A, who lets it to B, who is going to build houses on it which he will sell to C, who will let them to D, and the other letters of the alphabet: well, the old house comes down; that was to be looked for, and perhaps you don't much mind it; it was never a work of art, was stupid and unimaginative enough, though creditably built, and without pretence; but even while it is being pulled down, you hear the axe falling on the trees of its generous garden, which it was such a pleasure even to pass by, and where man and nature together have worked so long and patiently for the blessing of the neighbours: so you see the boys dragging about the streets great boughs of the flowering may-trees covered with blossom, and you know what is going to happen. Next morning when you get up you look towards that great plane-tree which has been such a friend to you so long through sun and rain and wind, which was a world in itself of incident and beauty: but now there is a gap and no plane-tree; next morning 'tis the turn of the great sweeping layers of darkness that the ancient cedars thrust out from them, very treasures of loveliness and romance; they are gone too: you may have a faint hope left that the thick bank of lilac next your house may be spared, since the newcomers may like lilac; but 'tis gone in the afternoon, and the next day when you look in with a sore heart, you see that once fair great garden turned into a petty miserable clay-trampled yard, and everything is ready for the latest development of Victorian architecture—which in due time (two months) arises from the wreck.

Do you like it? You I mean, who have not studied art and do not think you care about it?

Look at the houses (there are plenty to choose from)! I will not say, are they beautiful, for you say you don't care whether they are or not: but just look at the wretched pennyworths of material, of accommodation, of ornament doled out to you! if there were one touch of generosity, of honest pride, of wish to please about them, I would forgive them in the lump. But there is none—not one.

It is for this that you have sacrificed your cedars and planes and may-trees, which I do believe you really liked—are you satisfied?

Indeed you cannot be: all you can do is to go to your business, converse with your family, eat, drink, and sleep, and try to forget it, but whenever you think of it, you will admit that a loss without compensation has befallen you and your neighbours.

Once more neglect of art has done it; for though it is conceivable that the loss of your neighbouring open space might in any case have been a loss to you, still the building of a new quarter of a town ought not to be an unmixed calamity to the neighbours: nor would it have been once: for first, the builder doesn't now murder the trees (at any rate not all of them) for the trifling sum of money their corpses will bring him, but because it will take him too much trouble to fit them into the planning of his houses: so to begin with you would have saved the more part of your trees; and I say your trees, advisedly, for they were at least as much your trees, who loved them and would have saved them, as they were the trees of the man who neglected and murdered them. And next, for any space you would have lost, and for any unavoidable destruction of natural growth, you would in the times of art have been compensated by orderly beauty, by visible signs of the ingenuity of man and his delight both in the works of nature and the works of his own hands.

Yes indeed, if we had lived in Venice in early days, as islet after islet was built upon, we should have grudged it but little, I think, though we had been merchants and rich men, that the Greek shafted work, and the carving of the Lombards was drawn nearer and nearer to us and blocked us out a little from the sight of the blue Euganean hills or the Northern mountains. Nay, to come nearer home, much as I know I should have loved the willowy meadows between the network of the streams of Thames and Cherwell; yet I should not have been ill content as Oxford crept northward from its early home of Oseney, and Rewley, and the Castle, as townsman's house, and scholar's hall, and the great College and the noble church hid year by year more and more of the grass and flowers of Oxfordshire.[7]

That was the natural course of things then; men could do no otherwise when they built than give some gift of beauty to the world: but all is turned inside out now, and when men build they cannot but take away some gift of beauty, which nature or their own forefathers have given to the world.

Wonderful it is indeed, and perplexing, that the course of civilisation towards perfection should have brought this about: so perplexing, that to some it seems as if civilisation were eating her own children, and the arts first of all.

I will not say that; time is big with so many a change; surely there must be some remedy, and whether there be or no, at least it is better to die seeking one, than to leave it alone and do nothing.

I have said, are you satisfied? and assumed that you are not, though to many you may seem to be at least helpless: yet indeed it is something or even a great deal that I can reasonably assume that you are discontented: fifty years ago, thirty years ago, nay perhaps twenty years ago, it would have been useless to have asked such a question, it could only have been answered in one way: We are perfectly satisfied: whereas now we may at least hope that discontent will grow till some remedy will be sought for.

And if sought for, should it not, in England at least, be as good as found already, and acted upon? At first sight it seems so truly; for I may say without fear of contradiction that we of the English middle classes are the most powerful body of men that the world has yet seen, and that anything we have set our heart upon we will have: and yet when we come to look the matter in the face, we cannot fail to see that even for us with all our strength it will be a hard matter to bring about that birth of the new art: for between us and that which is to be, if art is not to perish utterly, there is something alive and devouring; something as it were a river of fire that will put all that tries to swim across to a hard proof indeed, and scare from the plunge every soul that is not made fearless by desire of truth and insight of the happy days to come beyond.

That fire is the hurry of life bred by the gradual perfection of competitive commerce which we, the English middle classes, when we had won our political liberty, set ourselves to further with an energy, an eagerness, a single-heartedness that has no parallel in history; we would suffer none to bar the way to us, we called on none to help us, we thought of that one thing and forgot all else, and so attained to our desire, and fashioned a terrible thing indeed from the very hearts of the strongest of mankind.

Indeed I don't suppose that the feeble discontent with our own creation that I have noted before can deal with such a force as this—not yet—not till it swells to very strong discontent: nevertheless as we were blind to its destructive power, and have not even yet learned all about that, so we may well be blind to what it has of constructive force in it, and that one day may give us a chance to deal with it again and turn it toward accomplishing our new and worthier desire: in that day at least when we have at last learned what we want, let us work no less strenuously and fearlessly, I will not say to quench it, but to force it to burn itself out, as we once did to quicken and sustain it.

Meantime if we could but get ourselves ready by casting off certain old prejudices and delusions in this matter of the arts, we should the sooner reach the pitch of discontent which would drive us into action: such a one I mean as the aforesaid idea that luxury fosters art, and especially the Architectural arts; or its companion one, that the arts flourish best in a rich country, *i.e.* a country where the contrast between rich and poor is greatest; or this, the worst because the most plausible, the assertion of the hierarchy of intellect in the arts: an old foe with a new face indeed: born out of the times that gave the death-blow to the political and social hierarchies, and waxing as they waned, it proclaimed from a new side the divinity of the few and the subjugation of the many, and cries out, like they did, that it is expedient, not that one man should die for the people, but that the people should die for one man.

Now perhaps these three things, though they have different forms, are in fact but one thing; tyranny to wit: but however that may be, they are to be met by one answer, and there is no other: if art which is now sick is to live and not die, it must in the future be of the people for the people, and by the people; it must understand all and be understood by all: equality must be the answer to tyranny: if that be not attained, art will die.

The past art of what has grown to be civilised Europe from the time of the decline of the ancient classical peoples, was the outcome of instinct working on an unbroken chain of tradition: it was fed not by knowledge but by hope, and though many a strange and wild illusion mingled with that hope, yet was it human and fruitful ever: many a man it solaced, many a slave in body it freed in soul; boundless pleasure it gave to those who wrought it and those who used it: long and long it lived, passing that torch of hope from hand to hand, while it kept but little record of its best and noblest; for least of all things could it abide to make for itself kings and tyrants: every man's hand and soul it used, the lowest as the highest, and in its bosom at least were all men free: it did its work, not creating an art more perfect than itself, but rather other things than art, freedom of thought and speech, and the longing for light and knowledge and the coming days that should slay it: and so at last it died in the hour of its highest hope, almost before the greatest men that came of it had passed away from the world. It is dead now; no longing will bring it back to us; no echo of it is left among the peoples whom it once made happy.

Of the art that is to come who may prophesy? But this at least seems to follow from comparing that past with the confusion in which we are now struggling and the light which glimmers through it; that that art will no longer be an art of instinct, of ignorance which is hopeful to learn and strives to see; since ignorance is now no longer hopeful. In this and in many other ways it may differ from the past art, but in one thing it must needs be like it; it will not be an esoteric mystery shared by a little band of superior beings; it will be no more hierarchical than the art of past time was, but like it will be a gift of the people to the people, a thing which everybody can understand, and every one surround with love; it will be a part of every life, and a hindrance to none.

For this is the essence of art, and the thing that is eternal to it, whatever else may be passing and accidental.

Here it is, you see, wherein the art of to-day is so far astray, would that I could say wherein it *has been* astray; it has been sick because of this packing and peeling with tyranny, and now with what of life it has it must struggle back towards equality.

There is the hard business for us! to get all simple people to care about art, to get them to insist on making it part of their lives, whatever becomes of systems of commerce and labour held perfect by some of us.

This is henceforward for a long time to come the real business of art: and—yes I will say it since I think it—of civilisation too for that matter: but how shall we set to work about it? How shall we give people without traditions of art eyes with which to see the works we do to move them? How shall we give them leisure from toil, and truce with anxiety, so that they may have time to brood over the longing for beauty which men are born with, as 'tis said, even in London streets? And chiefly, for this will breed the others swiftly and certainly, how shall we give them hope and pleasure in their daily work?

How shall we give them this soul of art without which men are worse than savages? If they would but drive us to it! But what and where are the forces that shall drive them to drive us? Where is the lever and the standpoint?

Hard questions indeed! but unless we are prepared to seek an answer for them, our art is a mere toy, which may amuse us for a little, but which will not sustain us at our need: the cultivated classes, as they are called, will feel it slipping away from under them: till some of them will but mock it as a worthless thing; and some will stand by and look at it as a curious exercise of the intellect, useless when done, though amusing to watch a-doing. How long will art live on those terms? Yet such were even now the state of art were it not for that hope which I am here to set forth to you, the hope of an art that shall express the soul of the people.

Therefore, I say, that in these days we men of civilisation have to choose if we will cast art aside or not; if we choose to do so I have no more to say, save that we *may* find something to take its place for the solace and joy of mankind, but I scarce think we shall: but if we refuse to cast art aside, then must we seek an answer for those hard questions aforesaid, of which this is the first.

How shall we set about giving people without traditions of art eyes with which to see works of art? It will doubtless take many years of striving and success, before we can think of answering that question fully: and if we strive to do our duty herein, long before it is answered fully there will be some kind of a popular art abiding among us: but meantime, and setting aside the answer which every artist must make to his own share of the question, there is one duty obvious to us all; it is that we should set ourselves, each one of us, to doing our best to guard the natural beauty of the earth: we ought to look upon it as a crime, an injury to our fellows, only excusable because of ignorance, to mar the natural beauty, which is the property of all men; and scarce less than a crime to look on and do nothing while others are marring it, if we can no longer plead this ignorance.

Now this duty, as it is the most obvious to us, and the first and readiest way of giving people back their eyes, so happily it is the easiest to set about; up to a certain point you will have all people of good will to the public good on your side: nay, small as the beginning is, something has actually been begun in this direction, and we may well say, considering how hopeless things looked twenty years ago, that it is marvelous in our eyes! Yet if we ever get out of the troubles that we are now wallowing in, it will seem perhaps more marvelous still to those that come after us that the dwellers in the richest city in the world were at one time rather proud that the members of a small, humble, and rather obscure, though I will say it, a beneficent society, should have felt it their duty to shut their eyes to the apparent hopelessness of attacking with their feeble means the stupendous evils they had become alive to, so that they might be able to make some small beginnings towards awakening the general public to a due sense of those evils.

I say, that though I ask your earnest support for such associations as the Kyrle and the Commons Preservation Societies, and though I feel sure that they have begun at the right end, since neither gods nor governments will help those who don't help themselves; though we are bound to wait for nobody's help than our own in dealing with the devouring hideousness and squalor of our great towns, and especially of London, for which the whole country is responsible; yet it would be idle not to acknowledge that the difficulties in our way are far too huge and wide-spreading to be grappled by private or semi-private efforts only.

All we can do in this way we must look on not as palliatives of an unendurable state of things, but as tokens of what we desire; which is in short the giving back to our country of the natural beauty of the earth, which we are so ashamed of having taken away from it: and our chief duty herein will be to quicken this shame and the pain that comes from it in the hearts of our fellows: this I say is one of the chief duties of all those who have any right to the title of cultivated men: and I believe that if we are faithful to it, we may help to further a great impulse towards beauty among us, which will be so irresistible that it will fashion for itself a national machinery which will sweep away all difficulties between us and a decent life, though they may have increased a thousand-fold meantime, as is only too like to be the case.

Surely that light will arise, though neither we nor our children's children see it, though civilisation may have to go down into dark places enough meantime:

surely one day making will be thought more honourable, more worthy the majesty of a great nation than destruction.

It is strange indeed, it is woeful, it is scarcely comprehensible, if we come to think of it as men, and not as machines, that, after all the progress of civilisation, it should be so easy for a little official talk, a few lines on a sheet of paper, to set a terrible engine to work, which without any trouble on our part will slay us ten thousand men, and ruin who can say how many thousand of families; and it lies light enough on the conscience of *all* of us; while, if it is a question of striking a blow at grievous and crushing evils which lie at our own doors, evils which every thoughtful man feels and laments, and for which we alone are responsible, not only is there no national machinery for dealing with them, though they grow ranker and ranker every year, but any hint that such a thing may be possible is received with laughter or with terror, or with severe and heavy blame. The rights of property, the necessities of morality, the interests of religion—these are the sacramental words of cowardice that silence us!

Sirs, I have spoken of thoughtful men who feel these evils: but think of all the millions of men whom our civilisation has bred, who are not thoughtful, and have had no chance of being so; how can you fail then to acknowledge the duty of defending the fairness of the Earth? and what is the use of our cultivation if it is to cultivate us into cowards? Let us answer those feeble counsels of despair and say, We also have a property which your tyranny of squalor cheats us of; we also have a morality which its baseness crushes; we also have a religion which its injustice makes a mock of.

Well, whatever lesser helps there may be to our endeavour of giving people back the eyes we have robbed them of, we may pass them by at present, for they are chiefly of use to people who are beginning to get their eyesight again; to people who, though they have no traditions of art, can study those mighty impulses that once led nations and races: it is to such that museums and art education are of service; but it is clear they cannot get at the great mass of people, who will at present stare at them in unintelligent wonder.

Until our streets are decent and orderly, and our town gardens break the bricks and mortar every here and there, and are open to all people; until our meadows even near our towns become fair and sweet, and are unspoiled by patches of hideousness: until we have clear sky above our heads and green grass beneath our feet; until the great drama of the seasons can touch our workmen with other feelings than the misery of winter and the weariness of summer; till all this happens our museums and art schools will be but amusements of the rich; and they will soon cease to be of any use to them also, unless they make up their minds that they will do their best to give us back the fairness of the Earth.

In what I have been saying on this last point I have been thinking of our own special duties as cultivated people; but in our endeavours towards this end, as in all others, cultivated people cannot stand alone; nor can we do much to open people's eyes till they cry out to us to have them opened. Now I cannot doubt that the longing to attack and overcome the sordidness of the city life of to-day still dwells in the minds of workmen, as well as in ours, but it can scarcely be otherwise than vague and lacking guidance with men who have so little leisure, and are so hemmed in with hideousness as they are. So this brings us to our second question. How shall people in general get leisure enough from toil, and truce enough with anxiety to give scope to their inborn longing for beauty?

Now the part of this question that is not involved in the next one, How shall they get proper work to do? is I think in a fair way to be answered.

The mighty change which the success of competitive commerce has wrought in the world, whatever it may have destroyed, has at least unwittingly made one thing,—from out of it has been born the increasing power of the working-class. The determination which this power has bred in it to raise their class as a class will I doubt not make way and prosper with our goodwill, or even in spite of it; but it seems to me that both to the working-class and especially to ourselves it is important that it should have our abundant goodwill, and also what help we may be able otherwise to give it, by our determination to deal fairly with workmen, even when that justice may seem to involve our own loss. The time of unreasonable and blind outcry against the Trades Unions is, I am happy to think, gone by; and has given place to the hope of a time when these great Associations, well organised, well served, and earnestly supported, as I *know* them to be, will find other work before them than the temporary support of their members and the adjustment of due wages for their crafts: when that hope begins to be realised, and they find they can make use of the help of us scattered units of the cultivated classes, I feel sure that the claims of art, as we and they will then understand the word, will by no means be disregarded by them.

Meantime with us who are called artists, since most unhappily that word means at present another thing than artisan: with us who either practise the arts with our own hands, or who love them so wholly that we can enter into the inmost feelings of those who do,—with us it lies to deal with our last question, to stir up others to think of answering this: How shall we give people in general hope and pleasure in their daily work in such a way that in those days to come the word art *shall* be rightly understood?

Of all that I have to say to you this seems to me the most important, that our daily and necessary work, which we could not escape if we would, which we would not forego if we could, should be human, serious, and pleasurable, not machine-like, trivial, or grievous. I call this not only the very foundation of Architecture in all senses of the word, but of happiness also in all conditions of life.

Let me say before I go further, that though I am nowise ashamed of repeating the words of men who have been before me in both senses, of time and insight, I mean, I should be ashamed of letting you think that I forget their labours on which mine are founded. I know that the pith of what I am saying on this subject was set forth years ago, and for the first time by Mr. Ruskin in that chapter of the Stones of Venice, which is entitled, 'On the Nature of Gothic,' in words more clear and eloquent than any man else now living could use. So important do they seem to me, that to my mind they should have been posted up in every school of art throughout the country; nay, in every association of English-speaking people which professes in any way to further the culture of mankind. But I am sorry to have to say it, my excuse for doing little more now than repeating those words is that they have been less heeded than most things which Mr. Ruskin has said: I suppose because people have been afraid of them, lest they should find the truth they express sticking so fast in their minds that it would either compel them to act on it or confess themselves slothful and cowardly.

Nor can I pretend to wonder at that: for if people were once to accept it as true, that it is nothing but just and fair that every man's work should have some hope and pleasure always present in it, they must try to bring the change about that would make it so: and all history tells of no greater change in man's life than that would be.

Nevertheless, great as the change may be, Architecture has no prospects in civilisation unless the change be brought about: and 'tis my business to-day, I will not say to convince you of this, but to send some of you away uneasy lest perhaps it may be true; if I can manage that I shall have spoken to some purpose.

Let us see however in what light cultivated people, men not without serious thoughts about life, look to this matter, lest perchance we may seem to be beating the air only: when I have given you an example of this way of thinking, I will answer it to the best of my power in the hopes of making some of you uneasy, discontented, and revolutionary.

Some few months ago I read in a paper the report of a speech made to the assembled work-people of a famous firm of manufacturers (as they are called). The speech was a very humane and thoughtful one, spoken by one of the leaders of modern thought: the firm to whose people it was addressed was and is famous not only for successful commerce, but also for the consideration and goodwill with which it treats its work-people, men and women. No wonder, therefore, that the speech was pleasant reading; for the tone of it was that of a man speaking to his friends who could well understand him and from whom he need hide nothing; but towards the end of it I came across a sentence, which set me a-thinking so hard, that I forgot all that had gone before. It was to this effect, and I think nearly in these very words, 'Since no man would work if it were not that he hoped by working to earn leisure:' and the context showed that this was assumed as a self-evident truth.

Well, for many years I have had my mind fixed on what I in my turn regarded as an axiom which may be worded thus: No work which cannot be done without pleasure in the doing is worth doing; so you may think I was much disturbed at a grave and learned man taking such a completely different view of it with such calmness of certainty. What a little way, I thought, has all Ruskin's fire and eloquence made in driving into people so great a truth, a truth so fertile of consequences!

Then I turned the intrusive sentence over again in my mind: 'No man would work unless he hoped by working to earn leisure:' and I saw that this was another way of putting it: first, all the work of the world is done against the grain: second, what a man does in his 'leisure' is not work.

A poor bribe the hope of such leisure to supplement the other inducement to toil, which I take to be the fear of death by starvation: a poor bribe; for the most of men, like those Yorkshire weavers and spinners (and the more part far worse than they), work for such a very small share of leisure that, one must needs say that if all their hope be in that, they are pretty much beguiled of their hope!

So I thought, and this next, that if it were indeed true and beyond remedy, that no man would work unless he hoped by working to earn leisure, the hell of theologians was but little needed; for a thickly populated civilised country, where, you know, after all people must work at something, would serve their turn well enough. Yet again I knew that this theory of the general and necessary hatefulness of work was indeed the common one, and that all sorts of people held it, who without being monsters of insensibility grew fat and jolly nevertheless.

So to explain this puzzle, I fell to thinking of the one life of which I knew something—my own to wit—and out tumbled the bottom of the theory.

For I tried to think what would happen to me if I were forbidden my ordinary daily work; and I knew that I should die of despair and weariness, unless I could straightway take to something else which I could make my daily work: and it was clear to me that I worked not in the least in the world for the sake of earning leisure by it, but partly driven by the fear of starvation or disgrace, and partly, and even a very great deal, because I love the work itself: and as for my leisure: well I had to confess that part of it I do indeed spend as a dog does—in contemplation, let us say; and like it well enough: but part of it also I spend in work: which work gives me just as much pleasure as my bread-earning work—neither more nor less; and therefore could be no bribe or hope for my work-a-day hours.

Then next I turned my thought to my friends: mere artists, and therefore, you know, lazy people by prescriptive right: I found that the one thing they enjoyed was their work, and that their only idea of happy leisure was other work, just as valuable to the world as their work-a-day work: they only differed from me in liking the dog-like leisure less and the man-like labour more than I do.

I got no further when I turned from mere artists, to important men—public men: I could see no signs of their working merely to earn leisure: they all worked for the work and the deeds' sake. Do rich gentlemen sit up all night in the House of Commons for the sake of earning leisure? if so, 'tis a sad waste of labour. Or Mr. Gladstone? he doesn't seem to have succeeded in winning much leisure by tolerably strenuous work; what he does get he might have got on much easier terms, I am sure.

Does it then come to this, that there are men, say a class of men, whose daily work, though maybe they cannot escape from doing it, is chiefly pleasure to them; and other classes of men whose daily work is wholly irksome to them, and only endurable because they hope while they are about it to earn thereby a little leisure at the day's end?

If that were wholly true the contrast between the two kinds of lives would be greater than the contrast between the utmost delicacy of life and the utmost hardship could show, or between the utmost calm and utmost trouble. The difference would be literally immeasurable.

But I dare not, if I would, in so serious a matter overstate the evils I call on you to attack: it is not wholly true that such immeasurable difference exists between the lives of divers classes of men, or the world would scarce have got through to past the middle of this century: misery, grudging, and tyranny would have destroyed us all.

The inequality even at the worst is not really so great as that: any employment in which a thing can be done better or worse has some pleasure in it, for all men more or less like doing what they can do well: even mechanical labour is pleasant to some people (to me amongst others) if it be not too mechanical.

Nevertheless though it be not wholly true that the daily work of some men is merely pleasant and of others merely grievous; yet it is over true both that things are not very far short of this, and also that if people do not open their eyes in time they will speedily worsen. Some work, nay, almost all the work done by artisans *is* too mechanical; and those that work at it must either abstract their thoughts from it altogether, in which case they are but machines while they are at work; or else they must suffer such dreadful weariness in getting through it, as one can scarcely bear to think of. Nature desires that we shall at least live, but seldom, I suppose, allows this latter misery to happen; and the workmen who do purely mechanical work do as a rule become mere machines as far as their work is concerned. Now as I am quite sure that no art, not even the feeblest, rudest, or least intelligent, can come of such work, so also I am sure that such work makes the workman less than a man and degrades him grievously and unjustly, and that nothing can compensate him or us for such degradation: and I want you specially to note that this was instinctively felt in the very earliest days of what are called the industrial arts.

When a man turned the wheel, or threw the shuttle, or hammered the iron, he was expected to make something more than a water-pot, a cloth, or a knife: he was expected to make a work of art also: he could scarcely altogether fail in this, he might attain to making a work of the greatest beauty: this was felt to be positively necessary to the peace of mind both of the maker and the user; and this is it which I have called Architecture: the turning of necessary articles of daily use into works of art.

Certainly, when we come to think of it thus, there does seem to be little less than that immeasurable contrast above mentioned between such work and mechanical work: and most assuredly do I believe that the crafts which fashion our familiar wares need this enlightenment of happiness no less now than they did in the days of the early Pharaohs: but we have forgotten this necessity, and in consequence have reduced handicraft to such degradation, that a learned, thoughtful, and humane man can set forth as an axiom that no man will work except to earn leisure thereby.

But now let us forget any conventional ways of looking at the labour which produces the matters of our daily life, which ways come partly from the wretched state of the arts in modern times, and partly I suppose from that repulsion to handicraft which seems to have beset some minds in all ages: let us forget this, and try to think how it really fares with the divers ways of work in handicrafts.

I think one may divide the work with which Architecture is conversant into three classes: first there is the purely mechanical: those who do this are machines only, and the less they think of what they are doing the better for the purpose, supposing they are properly drilled: the purpose of this work, to speak plainly, is not the making of wares of any kind, but what on the one hand is called employment, on the other what is called money-making: that is to say, in other words, the multiplication of the species of the mechanical workman, and the increase of the riches of the man who sets him to work, called in our modern jargon by a strange perversion of language, a manufacturer:[8] Let us call this kind of work Mechanical Toil.

The second kind is more or less mechanical as the case may be; but it can always be done better or worse: if it is to be well done, it claims attention from the workman, and he must leave on it signs of his individuality: there will be more or less of art in it, over which the workman has at least some control; and he will work on it partly to earn his bread in not too toilsome or disgusting a way, but in a way which makes even his work-hours pass pleasantly to him, and partly to make wares, which when made will be a distinct gain to the world; things that will be praised and delighted in. This work I would call Intelligent Work.

The third kind of work has but little if anything mechanical about it; it is altogether individual; that is to say, that what any man does by means of it could never have been done by any other man. Properly speaking, this work is all pleasure: true, there are pains and perplexities and weariness in it, but they are like the troubles of a beautiful life; the dark places that make the bright ones brighter: they are the romance of the work and do but elevate the workman, not depress him: I would call this Imaginative Work.

Now I can fancy that at first sight it may seem to you as if there were more difference between this last and Intelligent Work, than between Intelligent Work and Mechanical Toil: but 'tis not so. The difference between these two is the difference between light and darkness, between Ormuzd and Ahriman: whereas the difference between Intelligent work and what for want of a better word I am calling Imaginative work, is a matter of degree only; and in times when art is abundant and noble there is no break in the chain from the humblest of the lower to the greatest of the higher class; from the poor weaver's who chuckles as the bright colour comes round again, to the great painter anxious and doubtful if he can give to the world the whole of his thought or only nine-tenths of it, they are all artists—that is men; while the mechanical workman, who does not note the difference between bright and dull in his colours, but only knows them by numbers, is, while he is at his work, no man, but a machine. Indeed when Intelligent work coexists with Imaginative, there is no hard and fast line between them; in the very best and happiest times of art, there is scarce any Intelligent work which is not Imaginative also; and there is but little of effort or doubt, or sign of unexpressed desires even in the highest of the Imaginative work: the blessing of Equality elevates the lesser, and calms the greater, art.

Now further, Mechanical Toil is bred of that hurry and thoughtfulness of civilisation of which, as aforesaid, the middle classes of this country have been such powerful furtherers: on the face of it it is hostile to civilisation, a curse that civilisation has made for itself and can no longer think of abolishing or controlling: such it seems, I say; but since it bears with it change and tremendous change, it may well be that there is something more than mere loss in it: it will full surely destroy art as we know art, unless art newborn destroy it: yet belike at the worst it will destroy other things beside which are the poison of art, and in the long run itself also, and thus make way for the new art, of whose form we know nothing.

Intelligent work is the child of struggling, hopeful, progressive civilisation: and its office is to add fresh interest to simple and uneventful lives, to soothe discontent with innocent pleasure fertile of deeds gainful to mankind; to bless the many toiling millions with hope daily recurring, and which it will by no means disappoint.

Imaginative work is the very blossom of civilisation triumphant and hopeful; it would fain lead men to aspire towards perfection: each hope that it fulfils gives birth to yet another hope: it bears in its bosom the worth and the meaning of life and the counsel to strive to understand everything; to fear nothing and to hate nothing: in a word, 'tis the symbol and sacrament of the Courage of the World.

Now thus it stands to-day with these three kinds of work; Mechanical Toil has swallowed Intelligent Work and all the lower part of Imaginative Work, and the enormous mass of the very worst now confronts the slender but still bright array of the very best: what is left of art is rallied to its citadel of the highest intellectual art, and stands at bay there.

At first sight its hope of victory is slender indeed: yet to us now living it seems as if man had not yet lost all that part of his soul which longs for beauty: nay we cannot but hope that it is not yet dying. If we are not deceived in that hope, if the art of to-day has really come alive out of the slough of despond which we call the eighteenth century, it will surely grow and gather strength and draw to it other forms of intellect and hope that now scarcely know it; and then, whatever changes it may go through, it will at the last be victorious, and bring abundant content to mankind. On the other hand, if, as some think, it be but the reflection and feeble ghost of that glorious autumn which ended the good days of the mighty art of the Middle Ages, it will take but little killing: Mechanical Toil will sweep over all the handiwork of man, and art will be gone.

I myself am too busy a man to trouble myself much as to what may happen after that: I can only say that if you do not like the thought of that dull blank, even if you know or care little for art, do not cast the thought of it aside, but think of it again and again, and cherish the trouble it breeds till such a future seems unendurable to you; and then make up your minds that you will not bear it; and even if you distrust the artists that now are, set yourself to clear the way for the artists that are to come. We shall not count you among our enemies then, however hardly you deal with us.

I have spoken of one most important part of that task; I have prayed you to set yourselves earnestly to protecting what is left, and recovering what is lost of the Natural Fairness of the Earth: no less I pray you to do what you may to raise up some firm ground amid the great flood of mechanical toil, to make an effort to win human and hopeful work for yourselves and your fellows.

But if our first task of guarding the beauty of the Earth was hard, this is far harder, nor can I pretend to think that we can attack our enemy directly; yet indirectly surely something may be done, or at least the foundations laid for something.

For Art breeds Art, and every worthy work done and delighted in by maker and user begets a longing for more: and since art cannot be fashioned by mechanical toil, the demand for real art will mean a demand for intelligent work, which if persisted in will in time create its due supply—at least I hope so.

I believe that what I am now saying will be well understood by those who really care about art, but to speak plainly I know that these are rarely to be found even among the cultivated classes: it must be confessed that the middle classes of our civilisation have embraced luxury instead of art, and that we are even so blindly base as to hug ourselves on it, and to insult the memory of valiant people of past times and to mock at them because they were not encumbered with the nuisances that foolish habit has made us look on as necessaries. Be sure that we are not beginning to prepare for the art that is to be, till we have swept all that out of our minds, and are setting to work to rid ourselves of all the useless luxuries (by some called comforts) that make our stuffy art-stifling houses more truly savage than a Zulu's kraal or an East Greenlander's snow hut.

I feel sure that many a man is longing to set his hand to this if he only durst; I believe that there are simple people who think that they are dull to art, and who are really only perplexed and wearied by finery and rubbish: if not from these, 'tis at least from the children of these that we may look for the beginnings of the building up of the art that is to be.

Meanwhile, I say, till the beginning of new construction is obvious, let us be at least destructive of the sham art: it is full surely one of the curses of modern life, that if people have not time and eyes to discern or money to buy the real object of their desire, they must needs have its mechanical substitute. On this lazy and cowardly habit feeds and grows and flourishes mechanical toil and all the slavery of mind and body it brings with it: from this stupidity are born the itch of the public to over-reach the tradesmen they deal with, the determination (usually successful) of the tradesmen to over-reach them, and all the mockery and flouting that has been cast of late (not without reason) on the British tradesman and the British workman,—men just as honest as ourselves, if we would not compel them to cheat us, and reward them for doing it.

Now if the public knew anything of art, that is excellence in things made by man, they would not abide the shams of it; and if the real thing were not to be had, they would learn to do without, nor think their gentility injured by the forbearance.

Simplicity of life, even the barest, is not a misery, but the very foundation of refinement: a sanded floor and whitewashed walls, and the green trees, and flowery meads, and living waters outside; or a grimy palace amid the smoke with a regiment of housemaids always working to smear the dirt together so that it may be unnoticed; which, think you, is the most refined, the most fit for a gentleman of those two dwellings?

So I say, if you cannot learn to love real art, at least learn to hate sham art and reject it. It is not so much because the wretched thing is so ugly and silly and useless that I ask you to cast it from you; it is much more because these are but the outward symbols of the poison that lies within them: look through them and see all that has gone to their fashioning, and you will see how vain labour, and sorrow, and disgrace have been their companions from the first,—and all this for trifles that no man really needs!

Learn to do without; there is virtue in those words; a force that rightly used would choke both demand and supply of Mechanical Toil: would make it stick to its last: the making of machines.

And then from simplicity of life would rise up the longing for beauty, which cannot yet be dead in men's souls, and we know that nothing can satisfy that demand but Intelligent work rising gradually into Imaginative work; which will turn all 'operatives' into workmen, into artists, into men.

Now, I have been trying to show you how the hurry of modern Civilisation, accompanied by the tyrannous Organisation of labour which was a necessity to the full development of Competitive Commerce, has taken from the people at large, gentle and simple, the eyes to discern and the hands to fashion that popular art which was once the chief solace and joy of the world: I have asked you to think of that as no light matter, but a grievous mishap: I have prayed you to strive to remedy this evil: first by guarding jealously what is left, and by trying earnestly to win back what is lost of the Fairness of the Earth; and next by rejecting luxury, that you may embrace art, if you can, or if indeed you in your short lives cannot learn what art means, that you may at least live a simple life fit for men.

And in all I have been saying, what I have been really urging on you is this—Reverence for the life of Man upon the Earth: let the past be past, every whit of it that is not still living in us: let the dead bury their dead, but let us turn to the living, and with boundless courage and what hope we may, refuse to let the Earth be joyless in the days to come.

What lies before us of hope or fear for this? Well, let us remember that those past days whose art was so worthy, did nevertheless forget much of what was due to the Life of Man upon the Earth; and so belike it was to revenge this neglect that art was delivered to our hands for maiming: to us, who were blinded by our eager chase of those things which our forefathers had neglected, and by the chase of other things which seemed revealed to us on our hurried way, not seldom, it may be for our beguiling.

And of that to which we were blinded, not all was unworthy: nay the most of it was deep-rooted in men's souls, and was a necessary part of their Life upon the Earth, and claims our reverence still: let us add this knowledge to our other knowledge: and there will still be a future for the arts. Let us remember this, and amid simplicity of life turn our eyes to real beauty that can be shared by all: and then though the days worsen, and no rag of the elder art be left for our teaching, yet the new art may yet arise among us, and even if it have the hands of a child together with the heart of a troubled man, still it may bear on for us to better times the tokens of our reverence for the Life of Man upon the Earth. For we indeed freed from the bondage of foolish habit and dulling luxury might at last have eyes wherewith to see: and should have to babble to one another many things of our joy in the life around us: the faces of people in the streets bearing the tokens of mirth and sorrow and hope, and all the tale of their lives: the scraps of nature the busiest of us would come across; birds and beasts and the little worlds they live in; and even in the very town the sky above us and the drift of the clouds across it; the wind's hand on the slim trees, and its voice amid their branches, and all the ever-recurring deeds of nature; nor would the road or the river winding past our homes fail to tell us stories of the country-side, and men's doings in field and fell. And whiles we should fall to muse on the times when all the ways of nature were mere wonders to men, yet so well beloved of them that they called them by men's names and gave them deeds of men to do; and many a time there would come before us memories of the deed of past times, and of the aspirations of those mighty peoples whose deaths have made our lives, and their sorrows our joys.

How could we keep silence of all this? and what voice could tell it but the voice of art: and what audience for such a tale would content us but all men living on the Earth?

This is what Architecture hopes to be: it will have this life, or else death; and it is for us now living between the past and the future to say whether it shall live or die.

---

1. Now incorporated in the *Handbook of Indian Art*, by Dr. (now Sir George) Birdwood, published by the Science and Art Department.
2. These were originally published in *Fun*.
3. As I corrected these sheets for the press, the case of two such pieces of destruction is forced upon me: first, the remains of the Refectory of Westminster Abbey, with the adjacent Ashburnham House, a beautiful work, probably by Inigo Jones; and second, Magdalen Bridge at Oxford. Certainly this seems to mock my hope of the influence of education on the Beauty of Life; since the first scheme of destruction is eagerly pressed forward by the authorities of Westminster School, the second scarcely opposed by the resident members of the University of Oxford.
4. Since perhaps some people may read these words who are not of Birmingham, I ought to say that it was authoritatively explained at the meeting to which I addressed these words, that in Birmingham the law is strictly enforced.
5. Not *quite* always: in the little colony at Bedford Park, Chiswick, as many trees have been left as possible, to the boundless advantage of its quaint and pretty architecture.
6. I know that well-designed hammered iron trellises and gates have been used happily enough, though chiefly in rather grandiose gardens, and so they might be again—one of these days—but I fear not yet awhile.
7. Indeed it is a new world now, when the new Cowley dog-holes must needs slay Magdalen Bridge!—Nov. 1881.
8. Or, to put it plainer still, the unlimited breeding of mechanical workmen as *mechanical workmen*, not as *men*.

Printed in Great Britain
by Amazon